DAREDEVIL

THE MAN WITHOUT FEAR!

W9-DIL-885

THE DEVIL, INSIDE AND OUT

VOLUME ONE

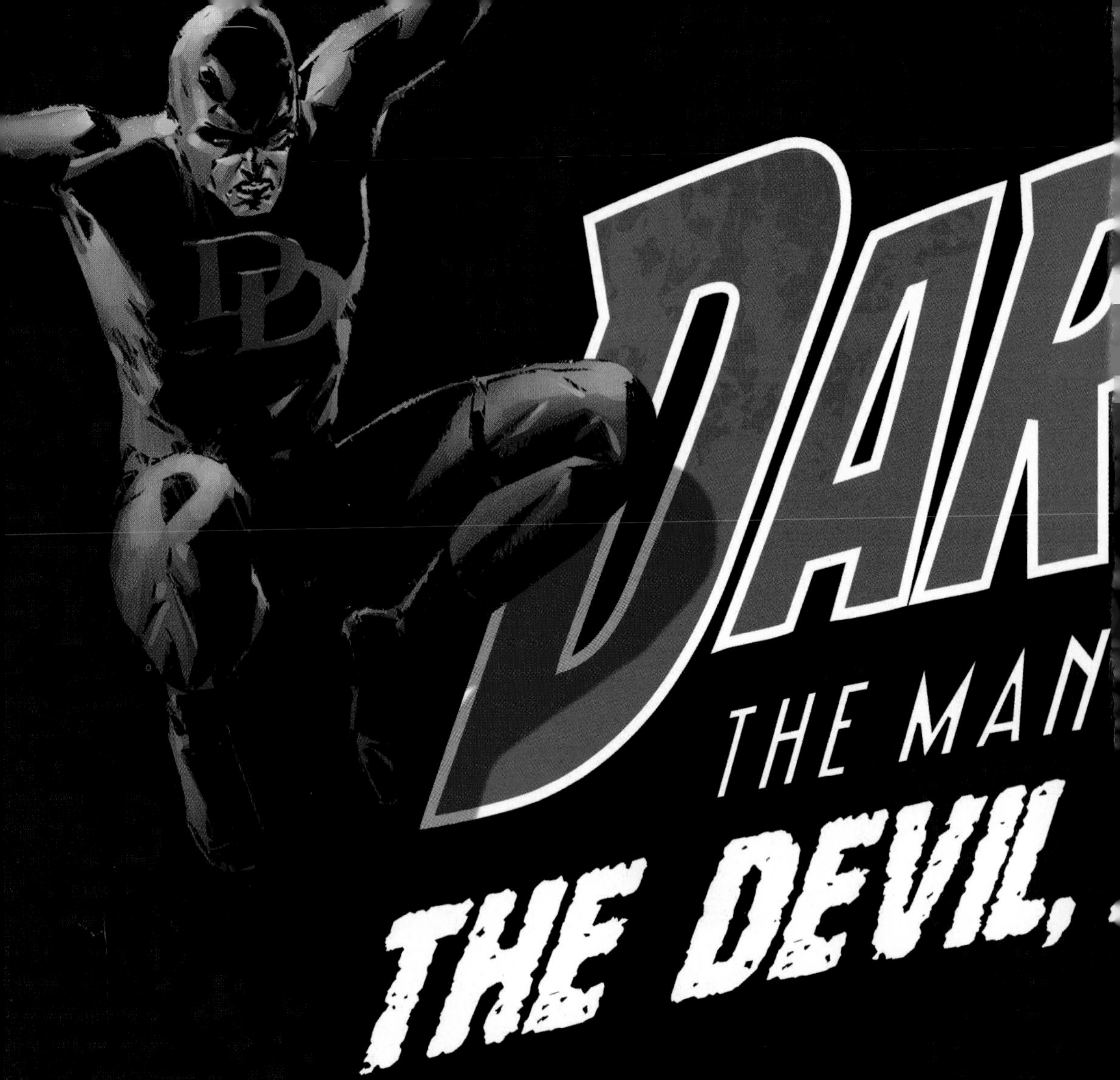
DAR
THE MAN
THE DEVIL,

Writer: **Ed Brubaker**

Artists: **Michael Lark & Stefano Gaudiano**

Colorist: **Frank D'Armata**

Letterer: **Virtual Calligraphy's Cory Petit**

Cover Art: **Tommy Lee Edwards, David Finch & Michael Lark**

Consulting Editor: **Axel Alonso**

Editor: **Warren Simons**

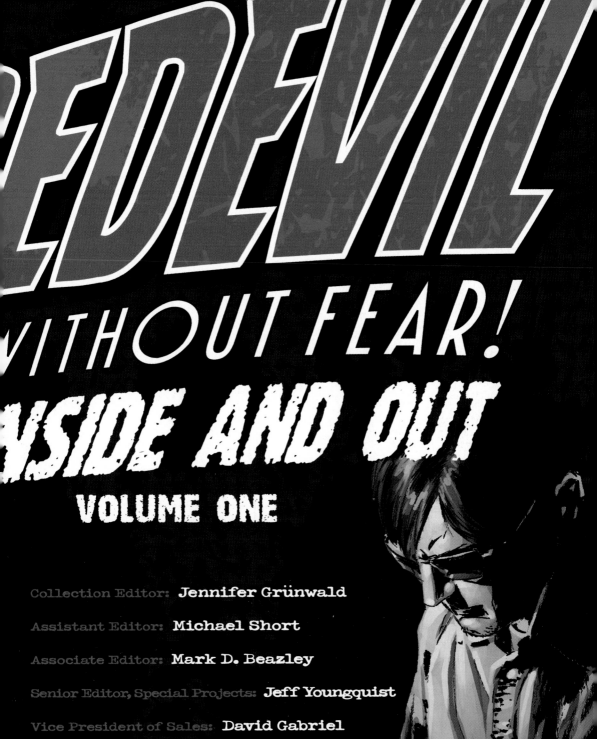

EDEVIL
WITHOUT FEAR!

NSIDE AND OUT

VOLUME ONE

Collection Editor: **Jennifer Grünwald**

Assistant Editor: **Michael Short**

Associate Editor: **Mark D. Beazley**

Senior Editor, Special Projects: **Jeff Youngquist**

Vice President of Sales: **David Gabriel**

Production: **Jerry Kalinowski**

Book Designer: **Adam Cichowski**

Vice President of Creative: **Tom Marvelli**

Editor in Chief: **Joe Quesada**

Publisher: **Dan Buckley**

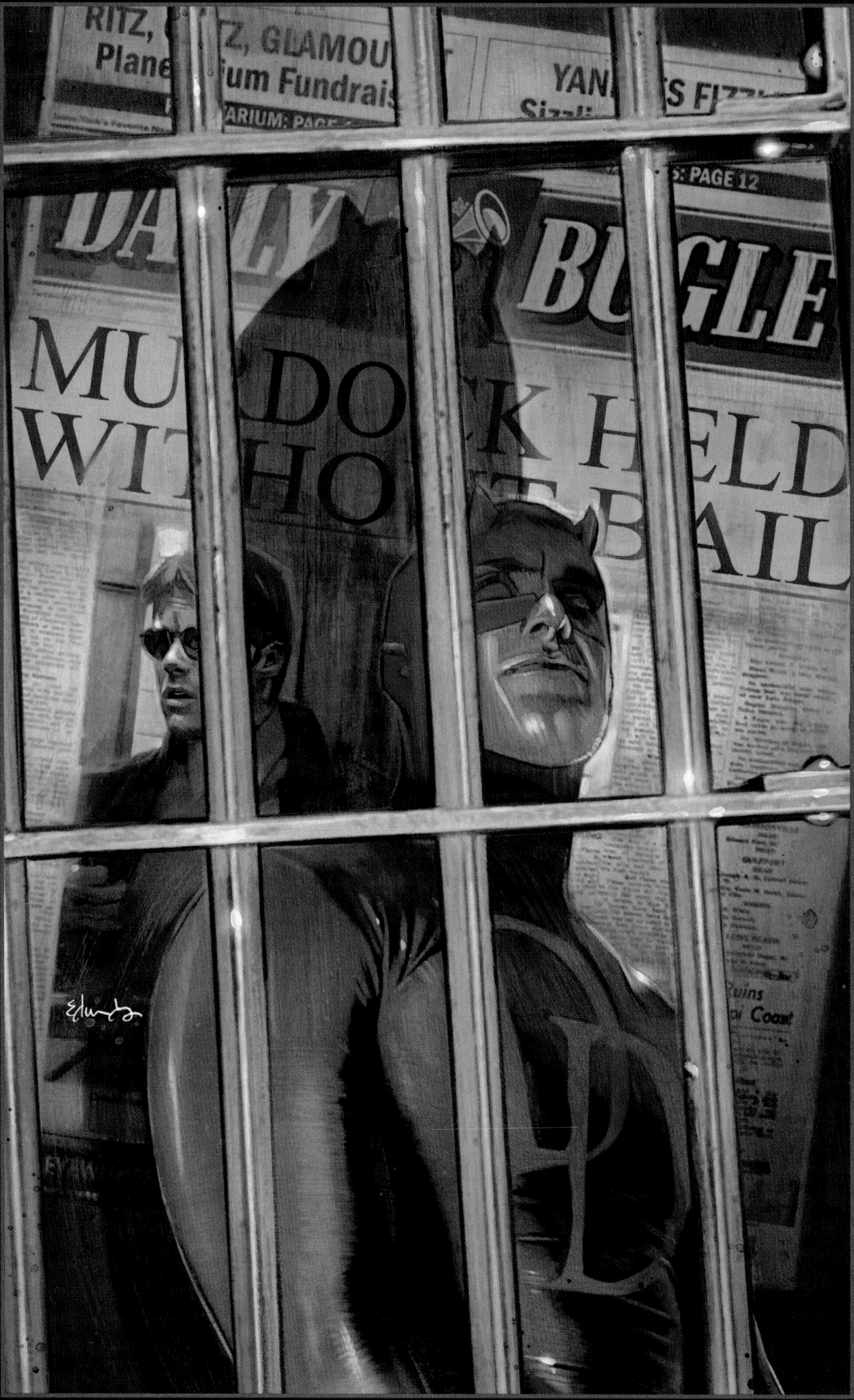
RITZ,
Z, GLAMOU
ium Fundrais
ARIUM: PAGE
S: PAGE 12
BUGLE
Coast

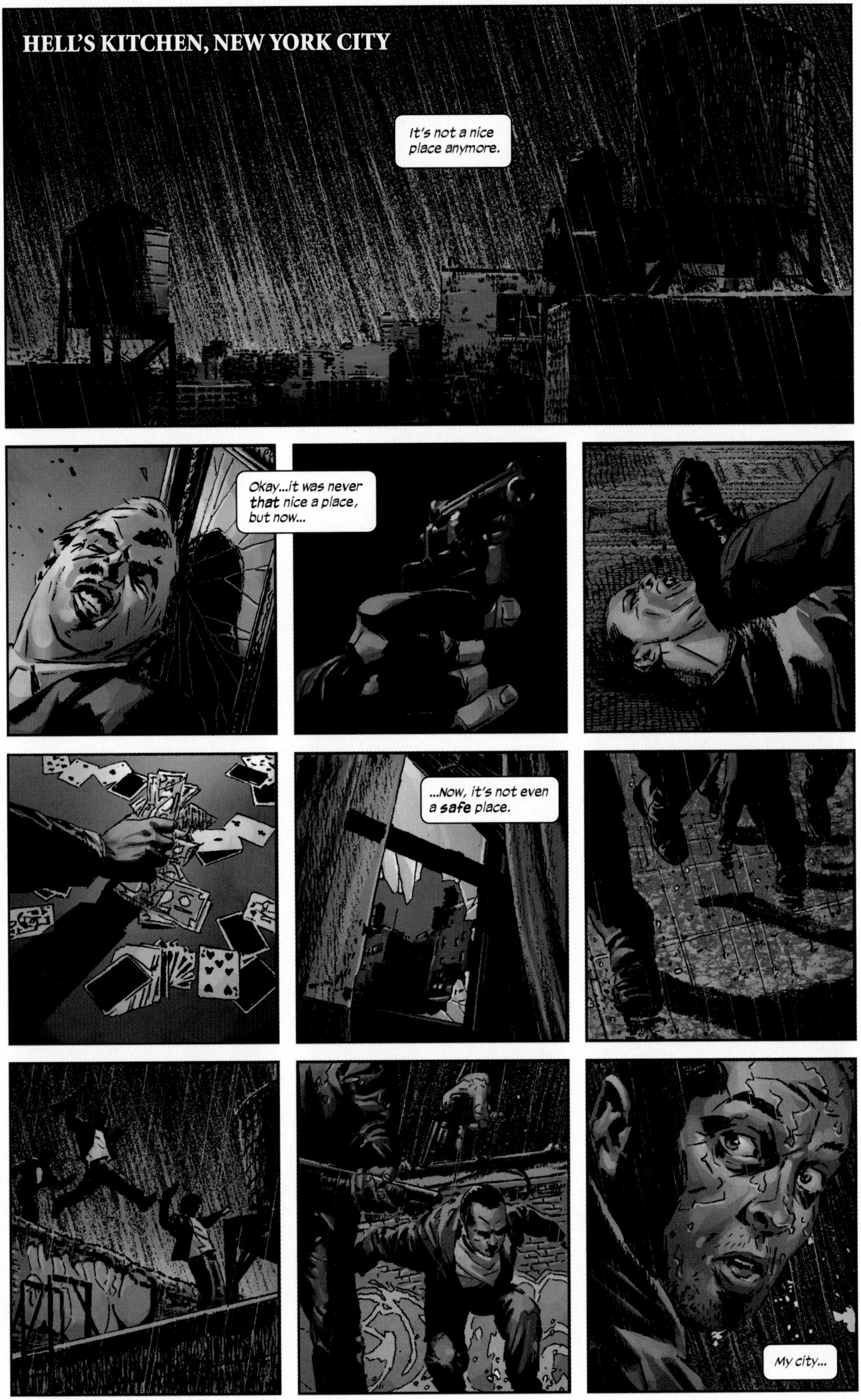
HELL'S KITCHEN, NEW YORK CITY
It's not a nice place anymore.
Okay...it was never that nice a place, but now...
...Now, it's not even a safe place.
My city...

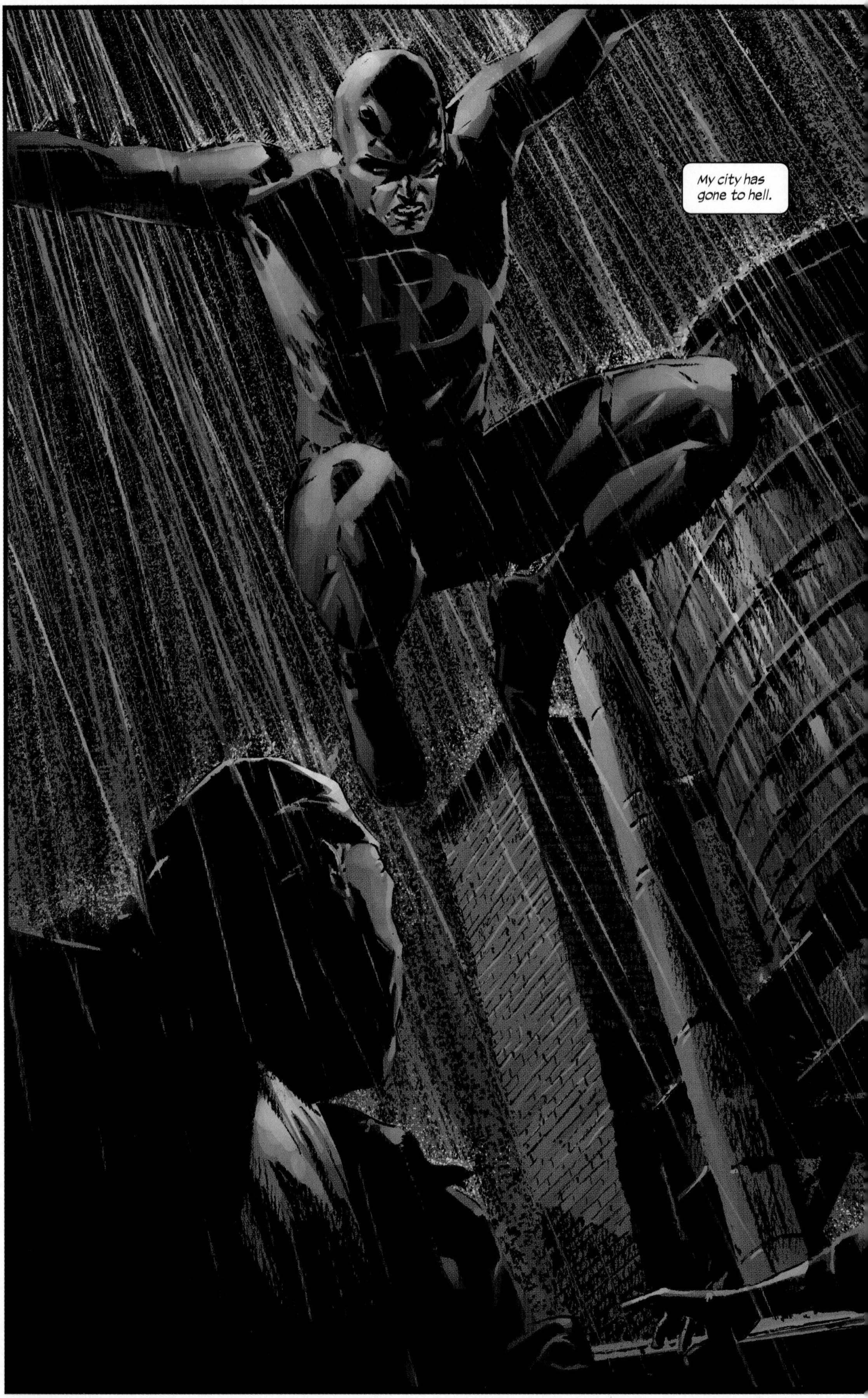
My city has
gone to hell.

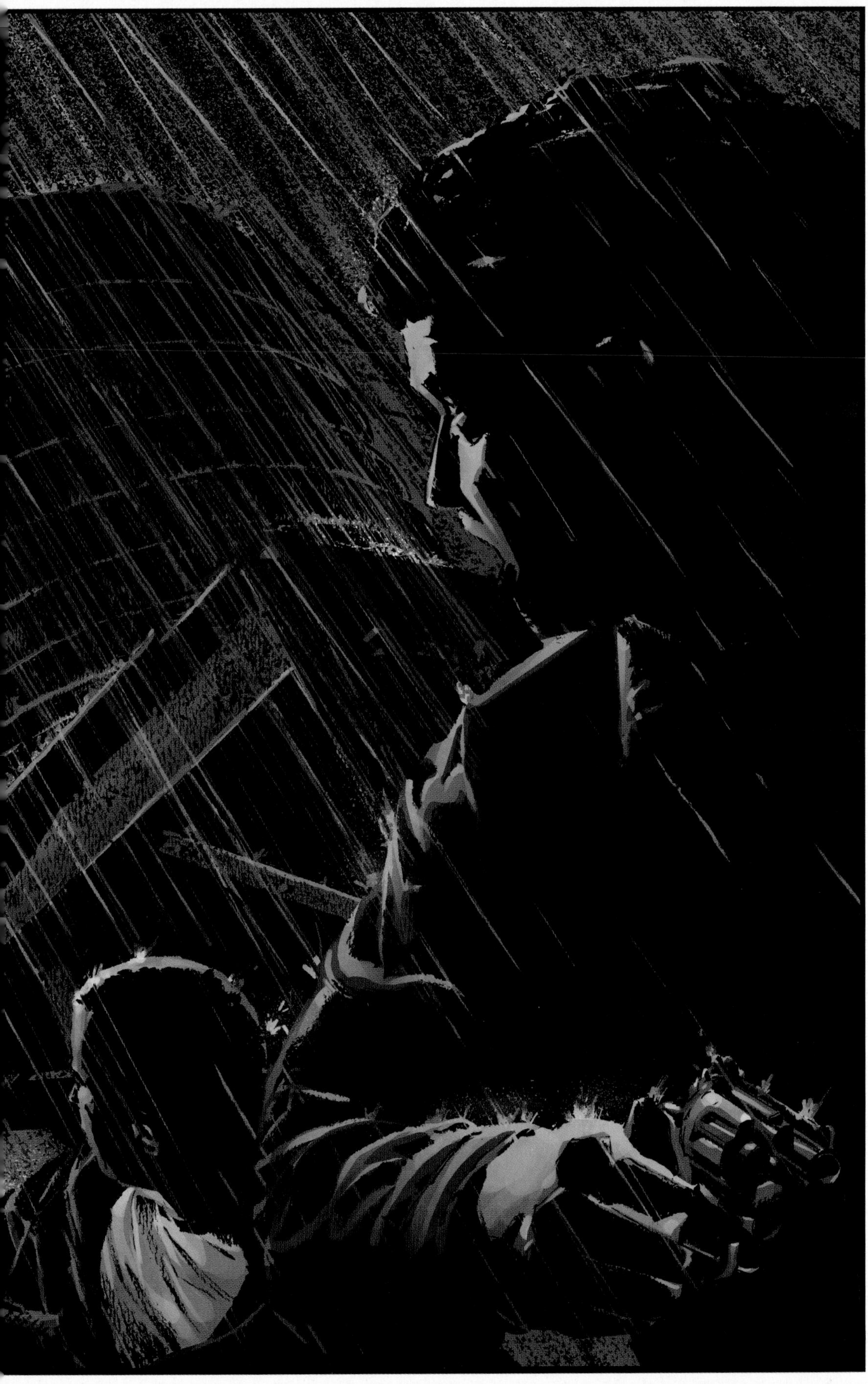

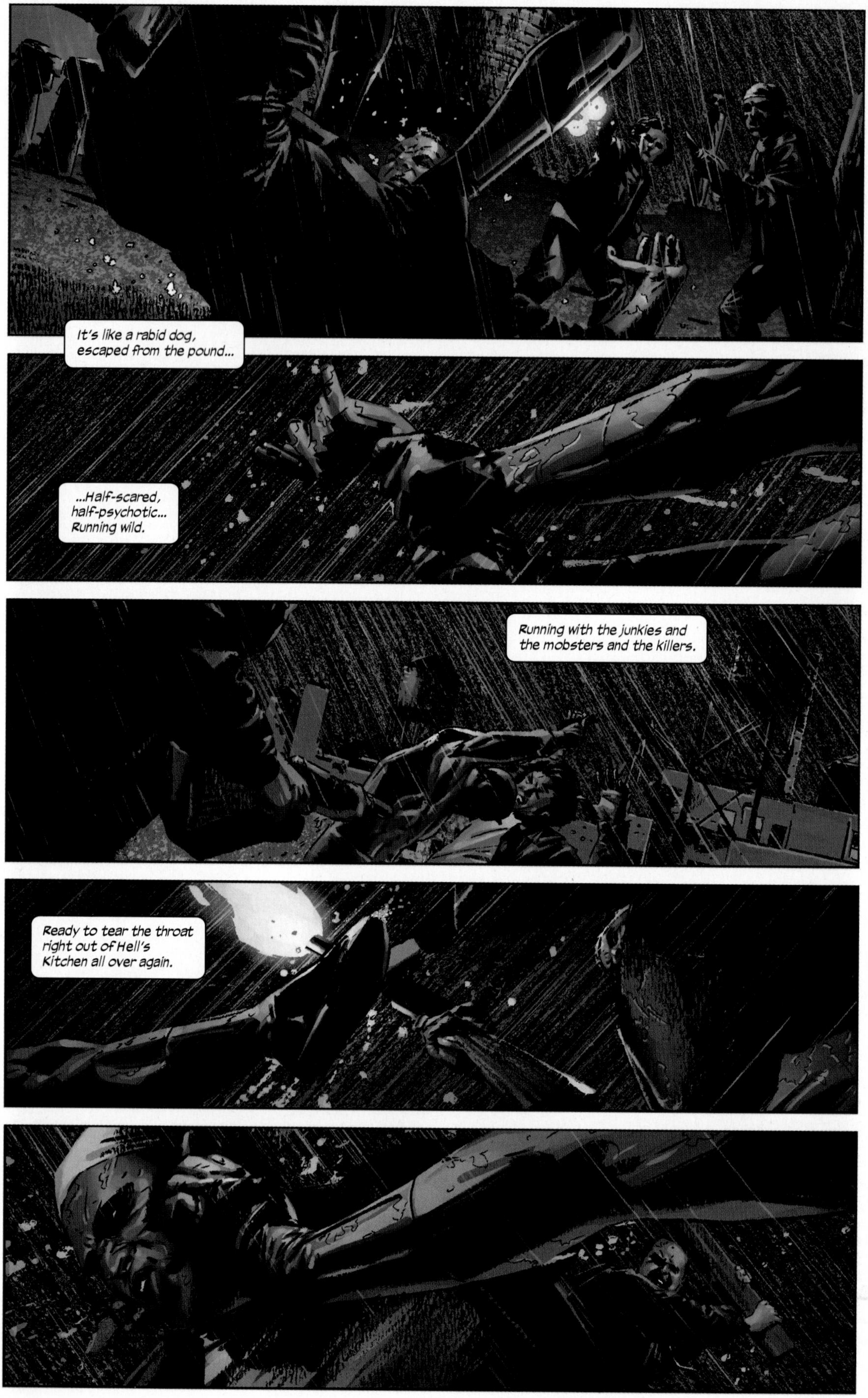
It's like a rabid dog, escaped from the pound...
...Half-scared, half-psychotic... Running wild.
Running with the junkies and the mobsters and the killers.
Ready to tear the throat right out of Hell's Kitchen all over again.

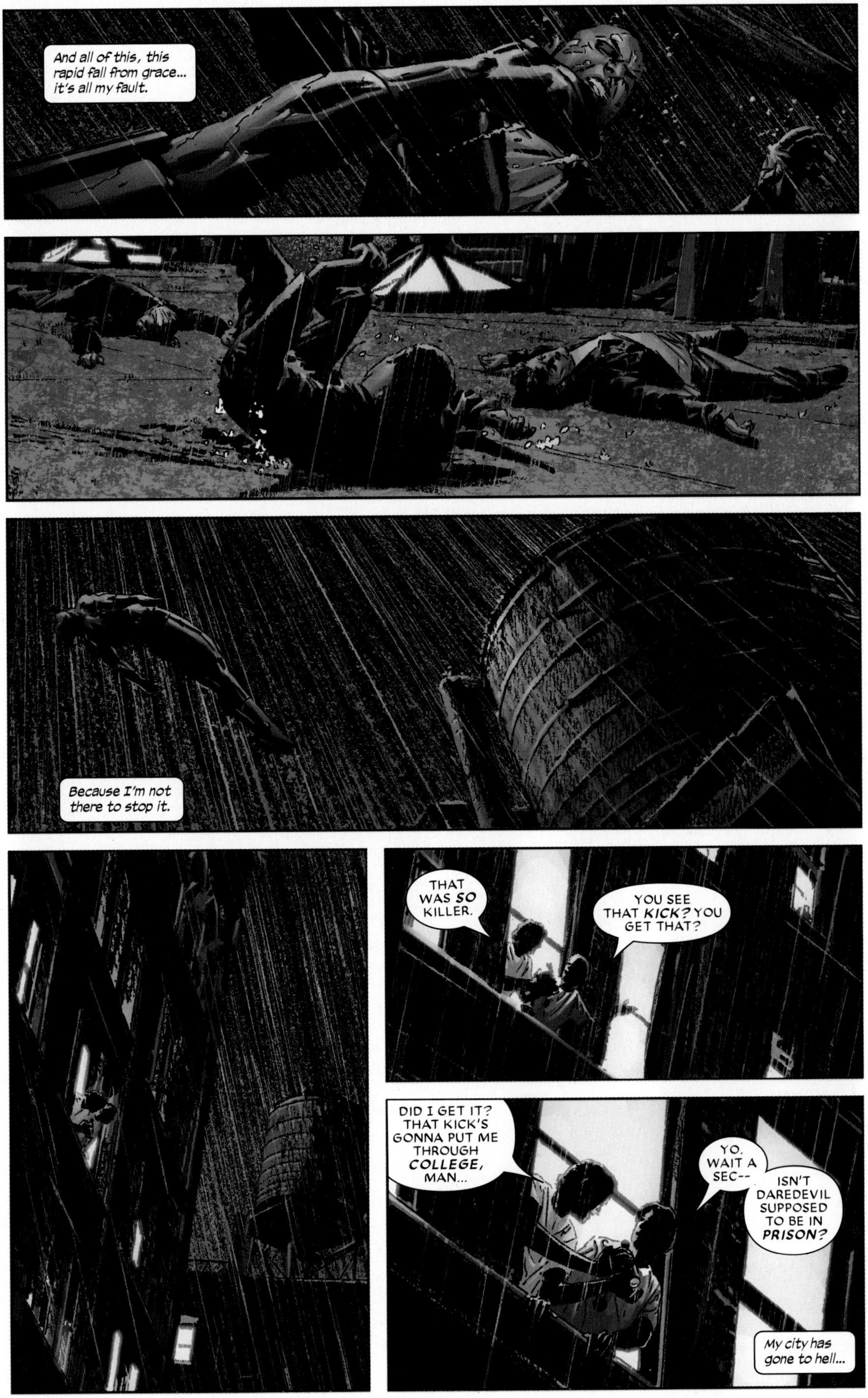

And all of this, this rapid fall from grace... it's all my fault.
Because I'm not there to stop it.
THAT WAS SO KILLER.
YOU SEE THAT KICK? YOU GET THAT?
DID I GET IT? THAT KICK'S GONNA PUT ME THROUGH COLLEGE, MAN...
YO. WAIT A SEC--
ISN'T DAREDEVIL SUPPOSED TO BE IN PRISON?
My city has gone to hell...

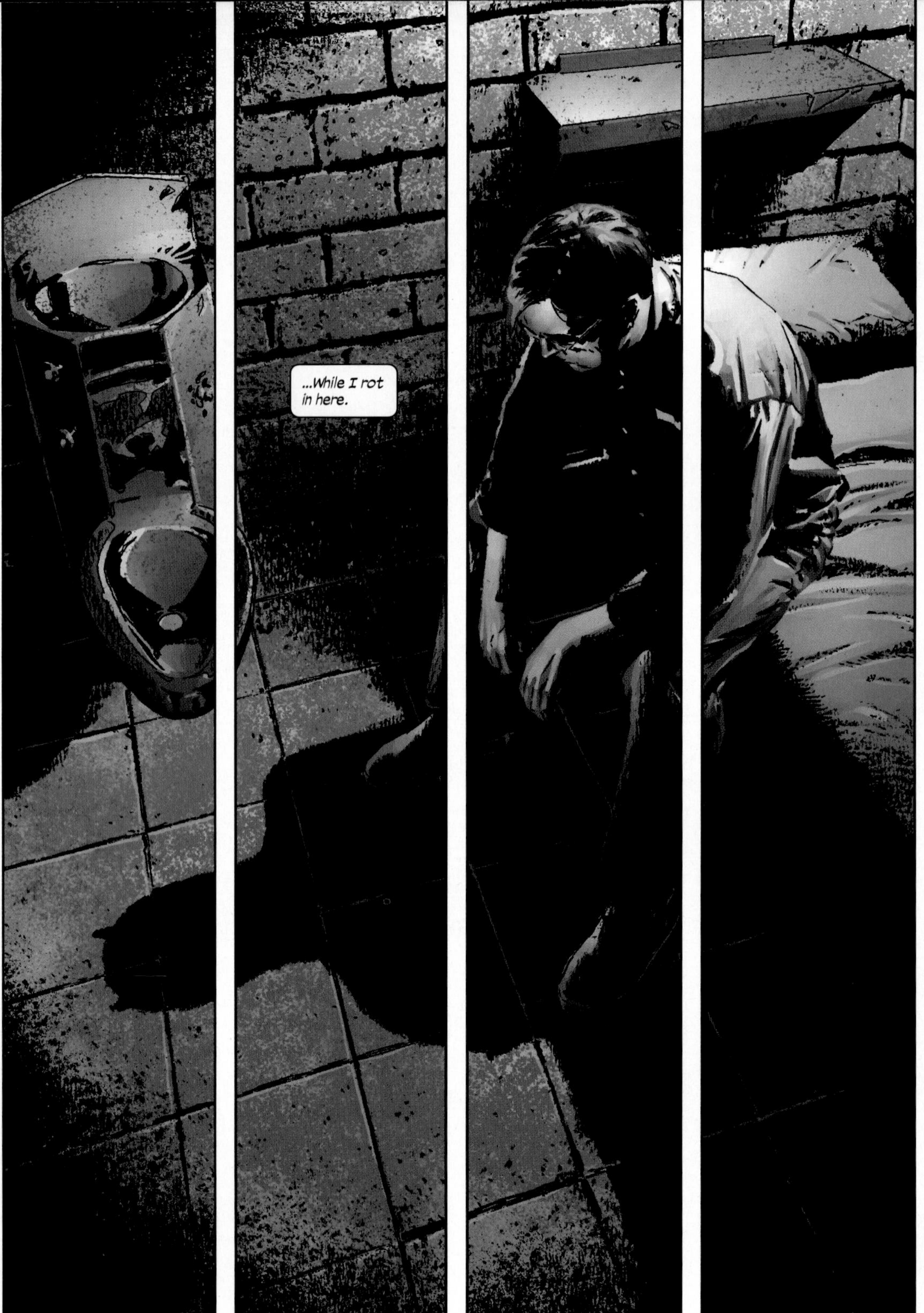
...While I rot in here.

ATTORNEY MATT MURDOCK WAS BLINDED AS A CHILD, BUT HIS OTHER FOUR SENSES FUNCTION WITH SUPERHUMAN SHARPNESS AND FORM A RADAR SENSE. WITH AMAZING FIGHTING SKILLS, HE STALKS THE STREETS AT NIGHT, IN RELENTLESS PURSUIT OF JUSTICE AS **DAREDEVIL, THE MAN WITHOUT FEAR!**

THE DEVIL IN CELL-BLOCK D

PART ONE

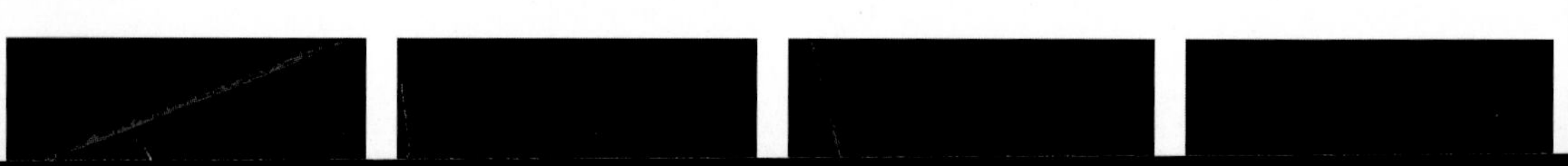

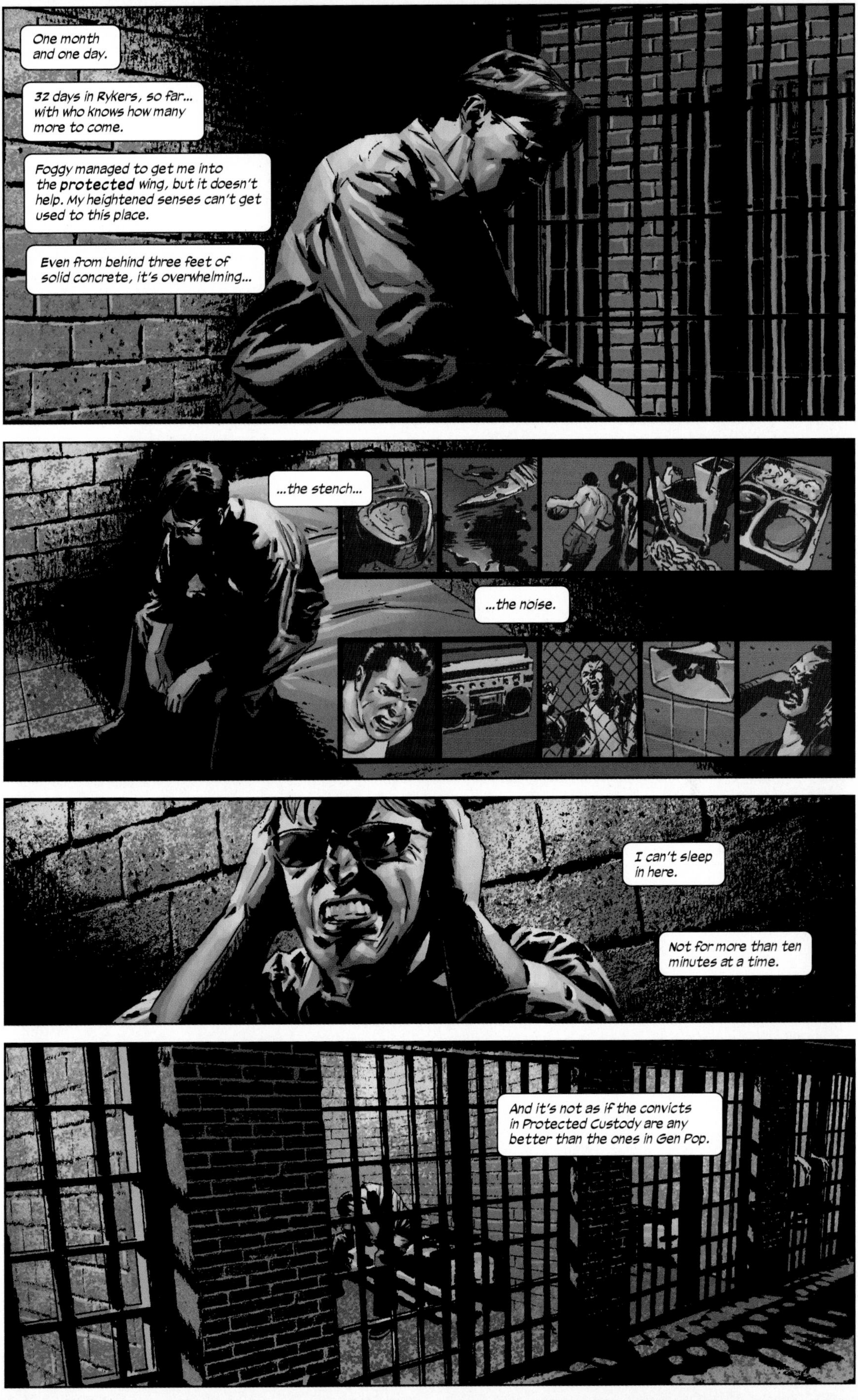

One month and one day.
32 days in Rykers, so far... with who knows how many more to come.
Foggy managed to get me into the **protected** wing, but it doesn't help. My heightened senses can't get used to this place.
Even from behind three feet of solid concrete, it's overwhelming...
...the stench...
...the noise.
I can't sleep in here.
Not for more than ten minutes at a time.
And it's not as if the convicts in Protected Custody are any better than the ones in Gen Pop.

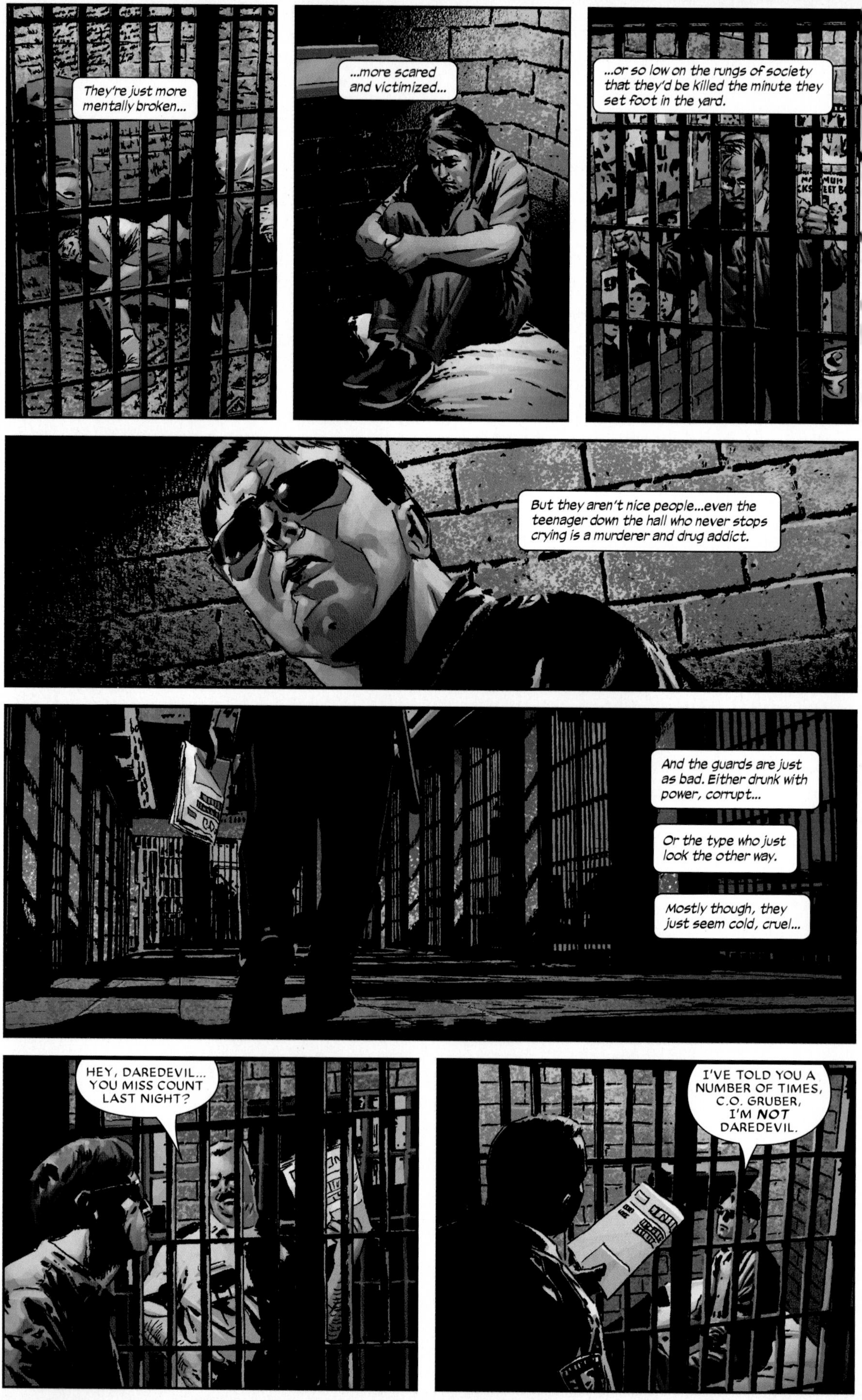

They're just more mentally broken...
...more scared and victimized...
...or so low on the rungs of society that they'd be killed the minute they set foot in the yard.
But they aren't nice people...even the teenager down the hall who never stops crying is a murderer and drug addict.
And the guards are just as bad. Either drunk with power, corrupt...
Or the type who just look the other way.
Mostly though, they just seem cold, cruel...
HEY, DAREDEVIL... YOU MISS COUNT LAST NIGHT?
I'VE TOLD YOU A NUMBER OF TIMES, C.O. GRUBER, I'M NOT DAREDEVIL.

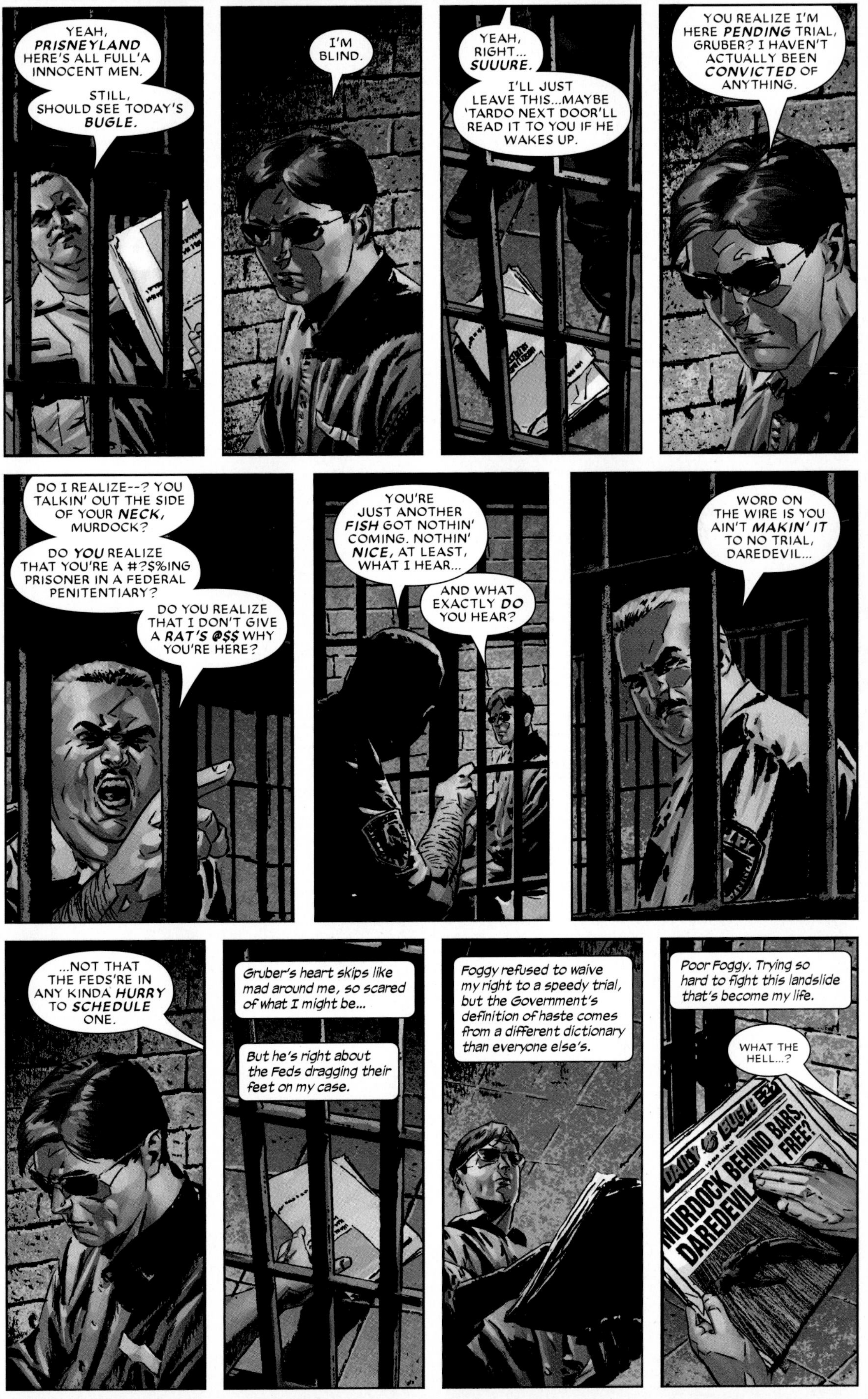
YEAH, PRISNEYLAND HERE'S ALL FULL'A INNOCENT MEN.
STILL, SHOULD SEE TODAY'S BUGLE.
I'M BLIND.
YEAH, RIGHT... SUUURE.
I'LL JUST LEAVE THIS...MAYBE 'TARDO NEXT DOOR'LL READ IT TO YOU IF HE WAKES UP.
YOU REALIZE I'M HERE PENDING TRIAL, GRUBER? I HAVEN'T ACTUALLY BEEN CONVICTED OF ANYTHING.
DO I REALIZE--? YOU TALKIN' OUT THE SIDE OF YOUR NECK, MURDOCK?
DO YOU REALIZE THAT YOU'RE A #?$%ING PRISONER IN A FEDERAL PENITENTIARY?
DO YOU REALIZE THAT I DON'T GIVE A RAT'S @$$ WHY YOU'RE HERE?
YOU'RE JUST ANOTHER FISH GOT NOTHIN' COMING. NOTHIN' NICE, AT LEAST, WHAT I HEAR...
AND WHAT EXACTLY DO YOU HEAR?
WORD ON THE WIRE IS YOU AIN'T MAKIN' IT TO NO TRIAL, DAREDEVIL...
...NOT THAT THE FEDS'RE IN ANY KINDA HURRY TO SCHEDULE ONE.
Gruber's heart skips like mad around me, so scared of what I might be...
But he's right about the Feds dragging their feet on my case.
Foggy refused to waive my right to a speedy trial, but the Government's definition of haste comes from a different dictionary than everyone else's.
Poor Foggy. Trying so hard to fight this landslide that's become my life.
WHAT THE HELL...?
DAILY BUGLE
MURDOCK BEHIND BARS. DAREDEVIL STILL FREE?

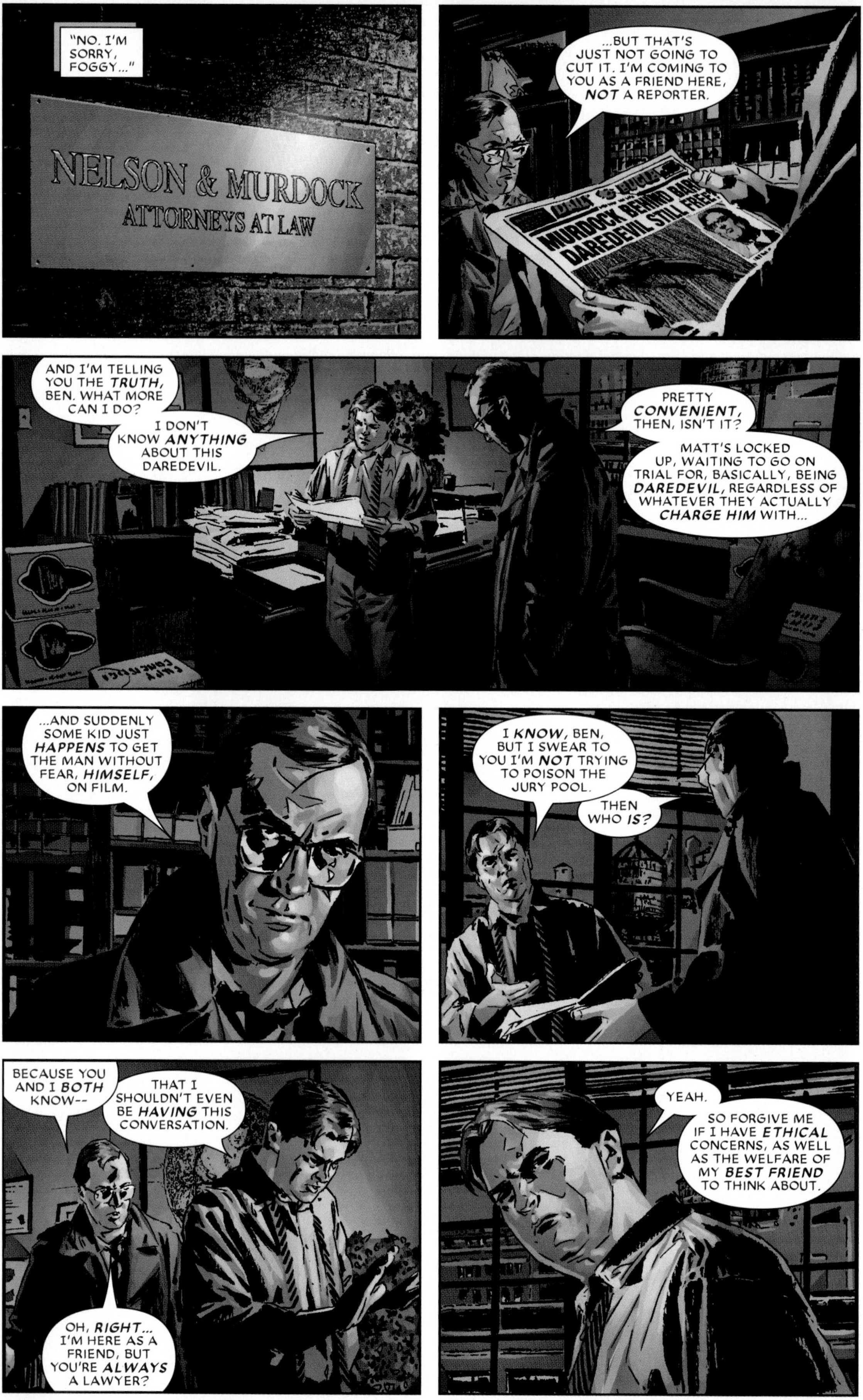
"NO. I'M SORRY, FOGGY..."
NELSON & MURDOCK
ATTORNEYS AT LAW
...BUT THAT'S JUST NOT GOING TO CUT IT. I'M COMING TO YOU AS A FRIEND HERE, NOT A REPORTER.
MURDOCK BEHIND BARS DAREDEVIL STILL FREE!
AND I'M TELLING YOU THE TRUTH, BEN. WHAT MORE CAN I DO?
I DON'T KNOW ANYTHING ABOUT THIS DAREDEVIL.
PRETTY CONVENIENT, THEN, ISN'T IT?
MATT'S LOCKED UP, WAITING TO GO ON TRIAL FOR, BASICALLY, BEING DAREDEVIL, REGARDLESS OF WHATEVER THEY ACTUALLY CHARGE HIM WITH...
...AND SUDDENLY SOME KID JUST HAPPENS TO GET THE MAN WITHOUT FEAR, HIMSELF, ON FILM.
I KNOW, BEN, BUT I SWEAR TO YOU I'M NOT TRYING TO POISON THE JURY POOL.
THEN WHO IS?
BECAUSE YOU AND I BOTH KNOW--
THAT I SHOULDN'T EVEN BE HAVING THIS CONVERSATION.
OH, RIGHT... I'M HERE AS A FRIEND, BUT YOU'RE ALWAYS A LAWYER?
YEAH.
SO FORGIVE ME IF I HAVE ETHICAL CONCERNS, AS WELL AS THE WELFARE OF MY BEST FRIEND TO THINK ABOUT.

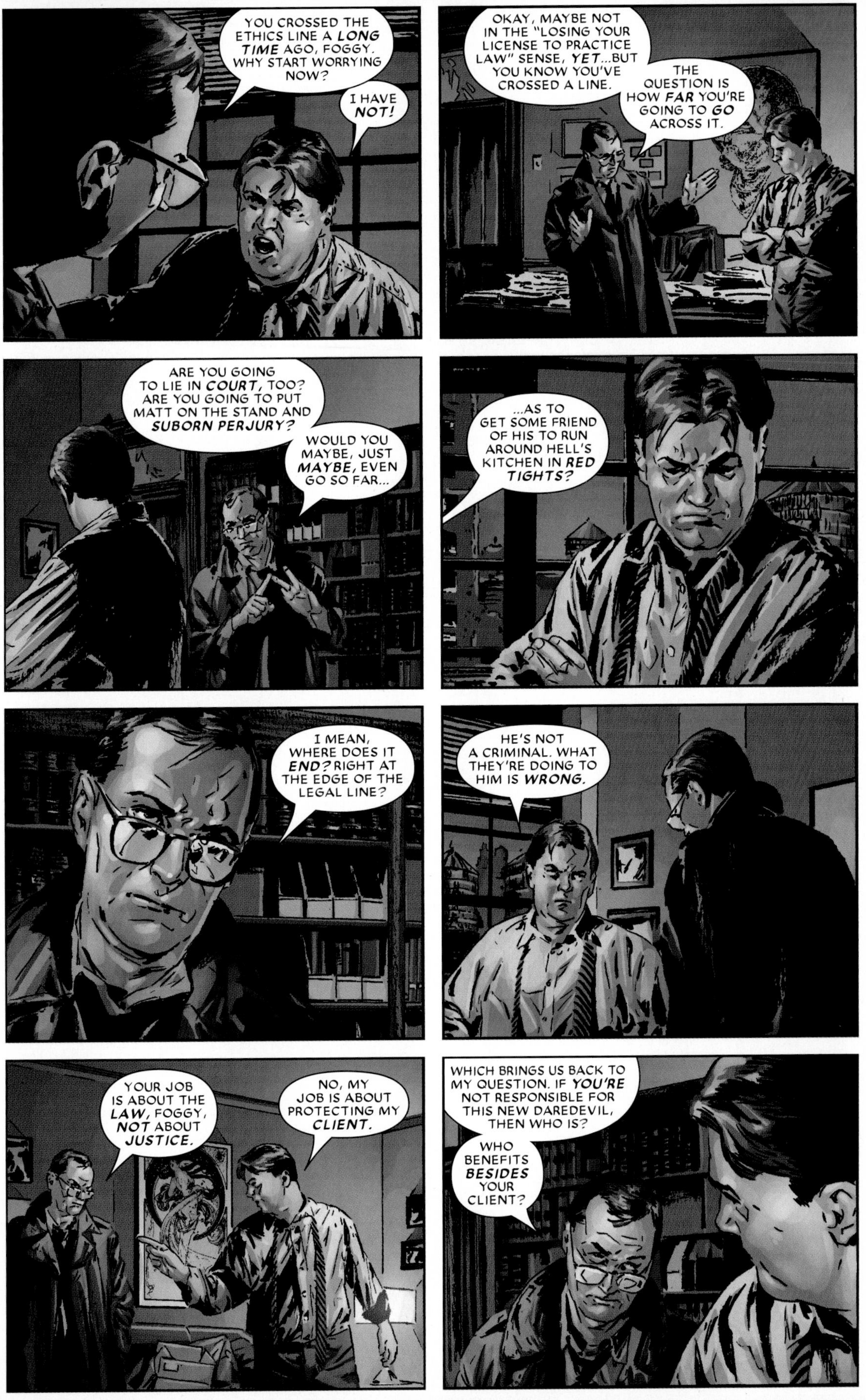
YOU CROSSED THE ETHICS LINE A LONG TIME AGO, FOGGY. WHY START WORRYING NOW?
I HAVE NOT!
OKAY, MAYBE NOT IN THE "LOSING YOUR LICENSE TO PRACTICE LAW" SENSE, YET...BUT YOU KNOW YOU'VE CROSSED A LINE.
THE QUESTION IS HOW FAR YOU'RE GOING TO GO ACROSS IT.
ARE YOU GOING TO LIE IN COURT, TOO? ARE YOU GOING TO PUT MATT ON THE STAND AND SUBORN PERJURY?
WOULD YOU MAYBE, JUST MAYBE, EVEN GO SO FAR...
...AS TO GET SOME FRIEND OF HIS TO RUN AROUND HELL'S KITCHEN IN RED TIGHTS?
I MEAN, WHERE DOES IT END? RIGHT AT THE EDGE OF THE LEGAL LINE?
HE'S NOT A CRIMINAL. WHAT THEY'RE DOING TO HIM IS WRONG.
YOUR JOB IS ABOUT THE LAW, FOGGY, NOT ABOUT JUSTICE.
NO, MY JOB IS ABOUT PROTECTING MY CLIENT.
WHICH BRINGS US BACK TO MY QUESTION. IF YOU'RE NOT RESPONSIBLE FOR THIS NEW DAREDEVIL, THEN WHO IS?
WHO BENEFITS BESIDES YOUR CLIENT?

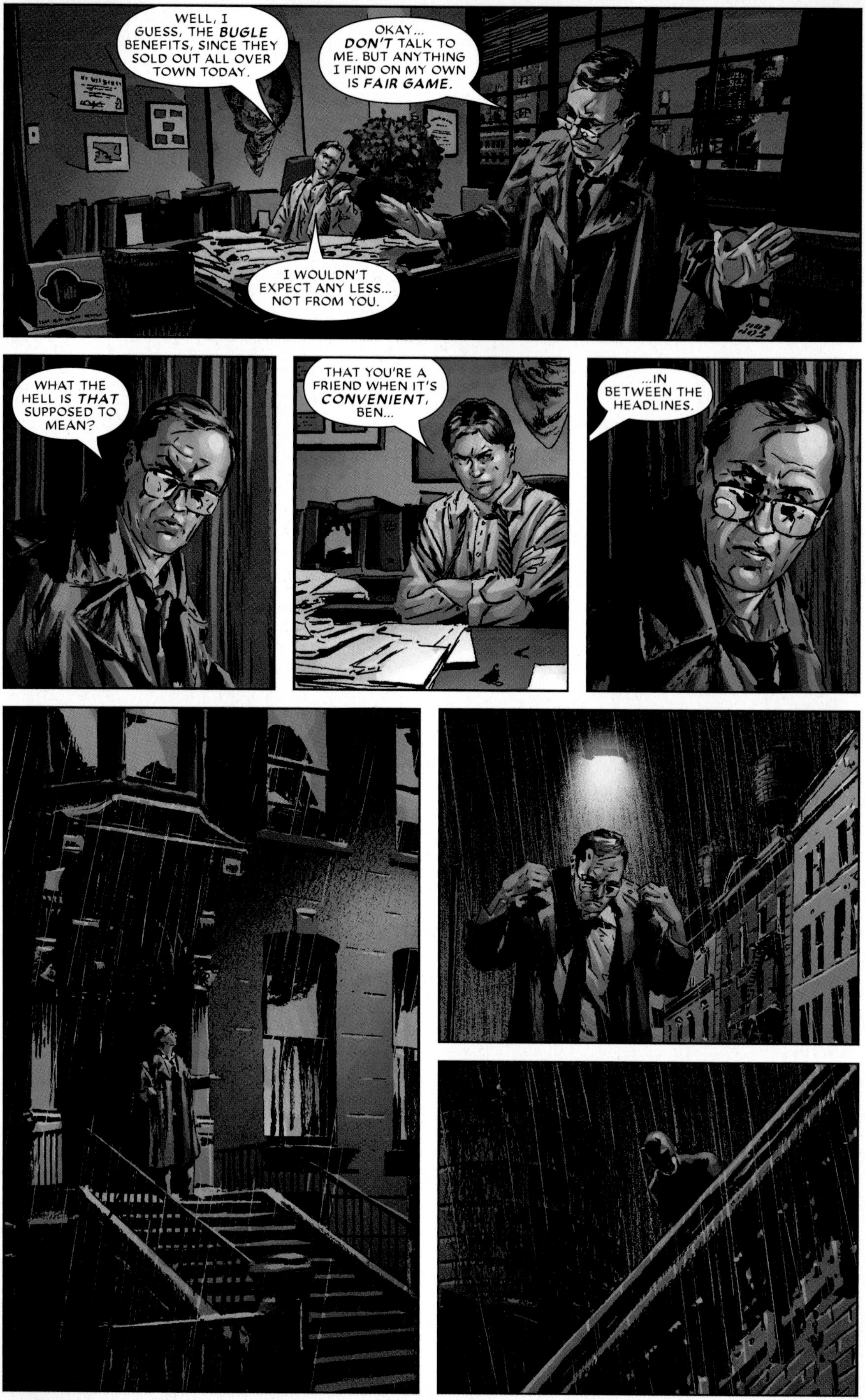
WELL, I GUESS, THE BUGLE BENEFITS, SINCE THEY SOLD OUT ALL OVER TOWN TODAY.
OKAY... DON'T TALK TO ME. BUT ANYTHING I FIND ON MY OWN IS FAIR GAME.
I WOULDN'T EXPECT ANY LESS... NOT FROM YOU.
WHAT THE HELL IS THAT SUPPOSED TO MEAN?
THAT YOU'RE A FRIEND WHEN IT'S CONVENIENT, BEN...
...IN BETWEEN THE HEADLINES.

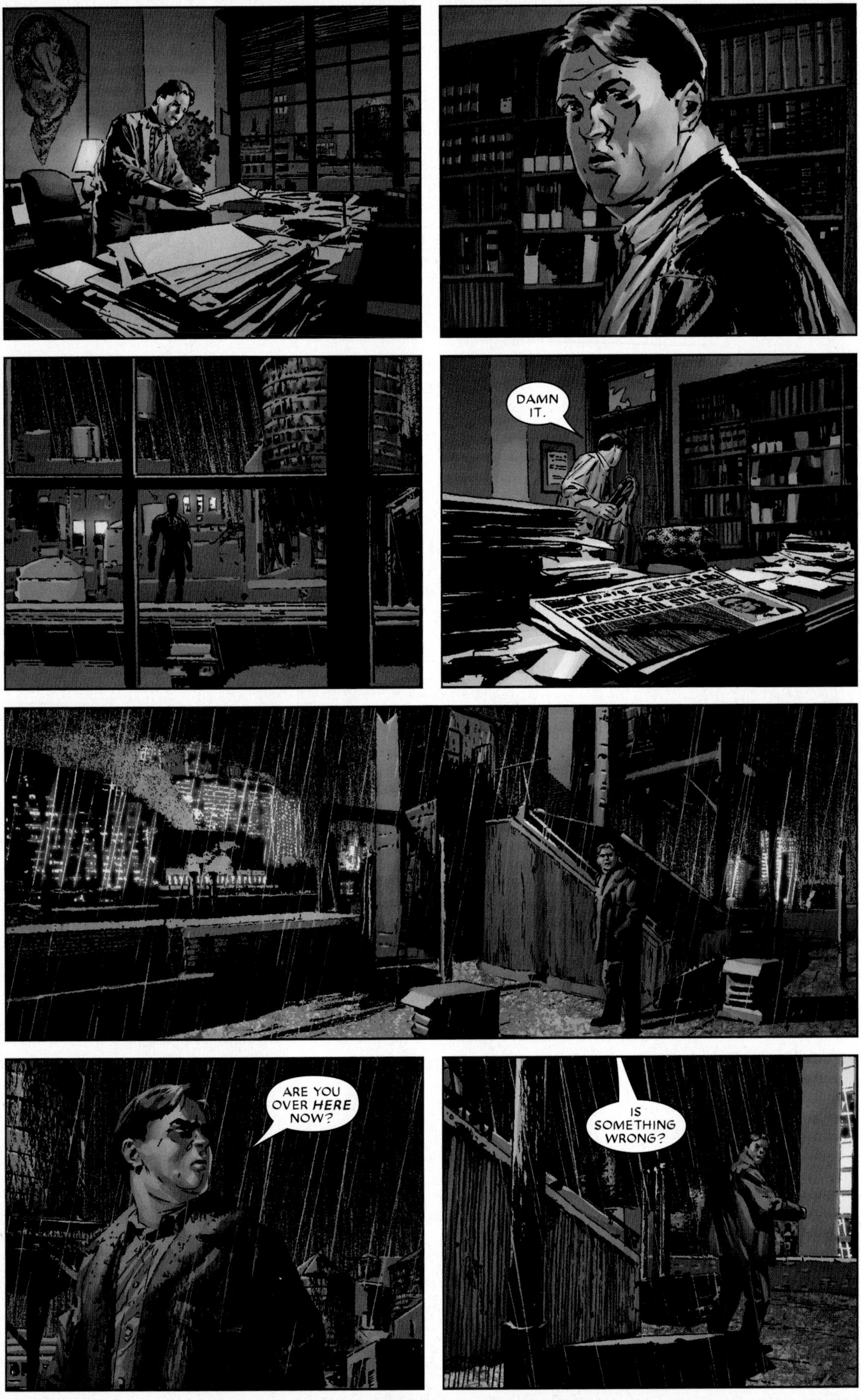
DAMN IT.
MURDOCK BEHIND BARS
DAREDEVIL STILL FREE?
ARE YOU OVER *HERE* NOW?
IS SOMETHING WRONG?

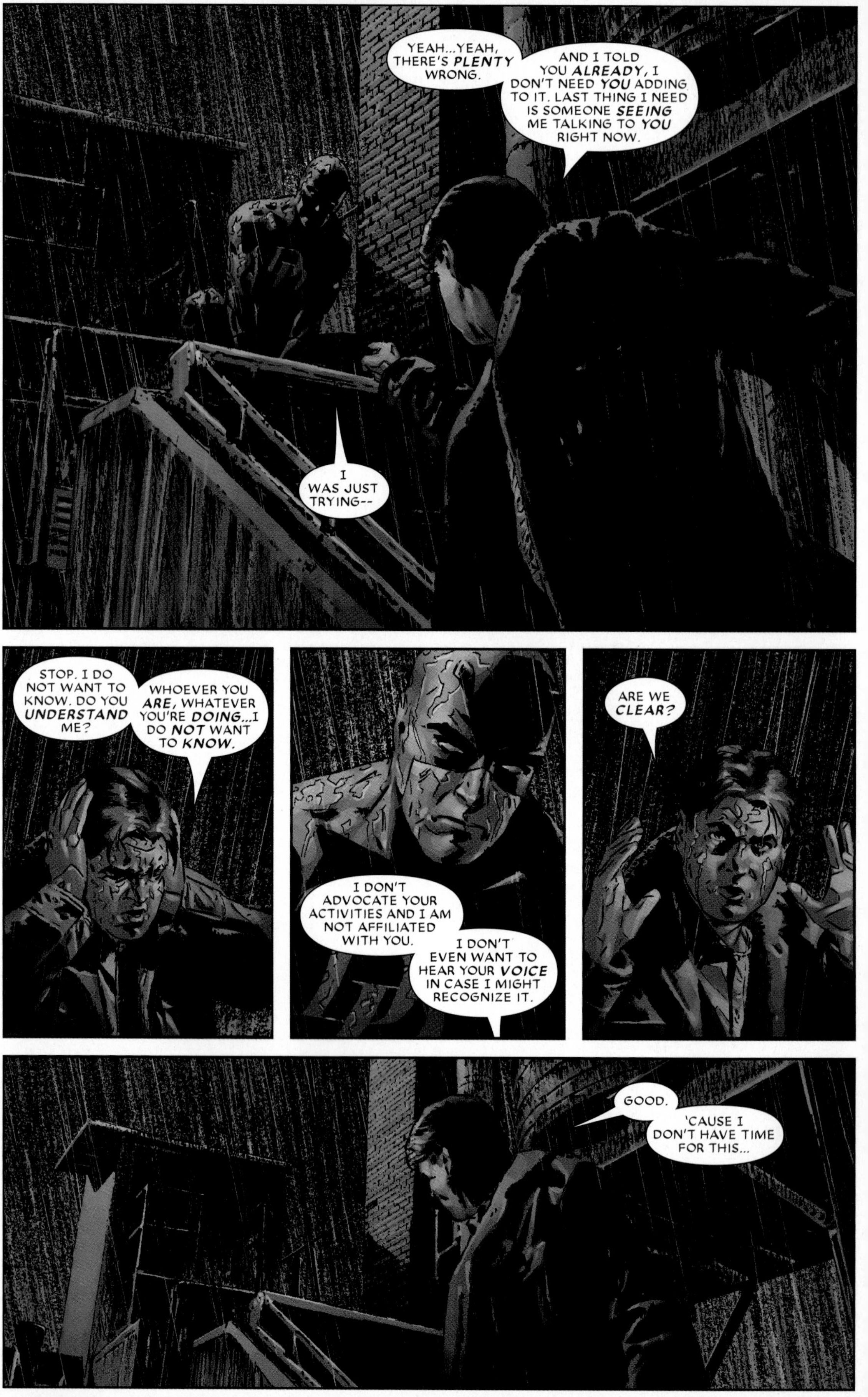
YEAH...YEAH, THERE'S PLENTY WRONG.
AND I TOLD YOU ALREADY, I DON'T NEED YOU ADDING TO IT. LAST THING I NEED IS SOMEONE SEEING ME TALKING TO YOU RIGHT NOW.
I WAS JUST TRYING--
STOP. I DO NOT WANT TO KNOW. DO YOU UNDERSTAND ME?
WHOEVER YOU ARE, WHATEVER YOU'RE DOING...I DO NOT WANT TO KNOW.
I DON'T ADVOCATE YOUR ACTIVITIES AND I AM NOT AFFILIATED WITH YOU.
I DON'T EVEN WANT TO HEAR YOUR VOICE IN CASE I MIGHT RECOGNIZE IT.
ARE WE CLEAR?
GOOD.
'CAUSE I DON'T HAVE TIME FOR THIS...

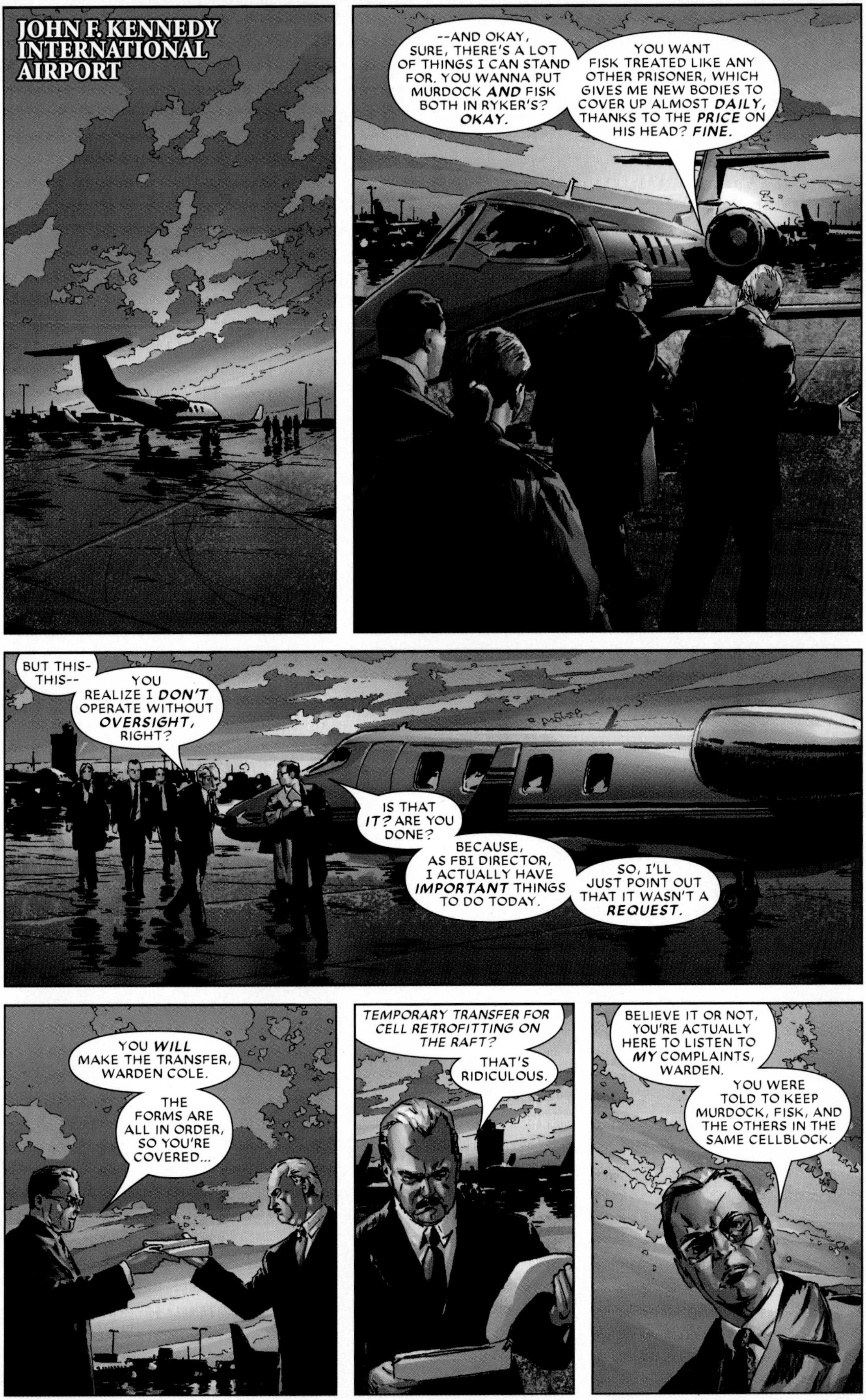
JOHN F. KENNEDY INTERNATIONAL AIRPORT
--AND OKAY, SURE, THERE'S A LOT OF THINGS I CAN STAND FOR. YOU WANNA PUT MURDOCK AND FISK BOTH IN RYKER'S? OKAY.
YOU WANT FISK TREATED LIKE ANY OTHER PRISONER, WHICH GIVES ME NEW BODIES TO COVER UP ALMOST DAILY, THANKS TO THE PRICE ON HIS HEAD? FINE.
BUT THIS- THIS--
YOU REALIZE I DON'T OPERATE WITHOUT OVERSIGHT, RIGHT?
IS THAT IT? ARE YOU DONE?
BECAUSE, AS FBI DIRECTOR, I ACTUALLY HAVE IMPORTANT THINGS TO DO TODAY.
SO, I'LL JUST POINT OUT THAT IT WASN'T A REQUEST.
YOU WILL MAKE THE TRANSFER, WARDEN COLE.
THE FORMS ARE ALL IN ORDER, SO YOU'RE COVERED...
TEMPORARY TRANSFER FOR CELL RETROFITTING ON THE RAFT?
THAT'S RIDICULOUS.
BELIEVE IT OR NOT, YOU'RE ACTUALLY HERE TO LISTEN TO MY COMPLAINTS, WARDEN.
YOU WERE TOLD TO KEEP MURDOCK, FISK, AND THE OTHERS IN THE SAME CELLBLOCK.

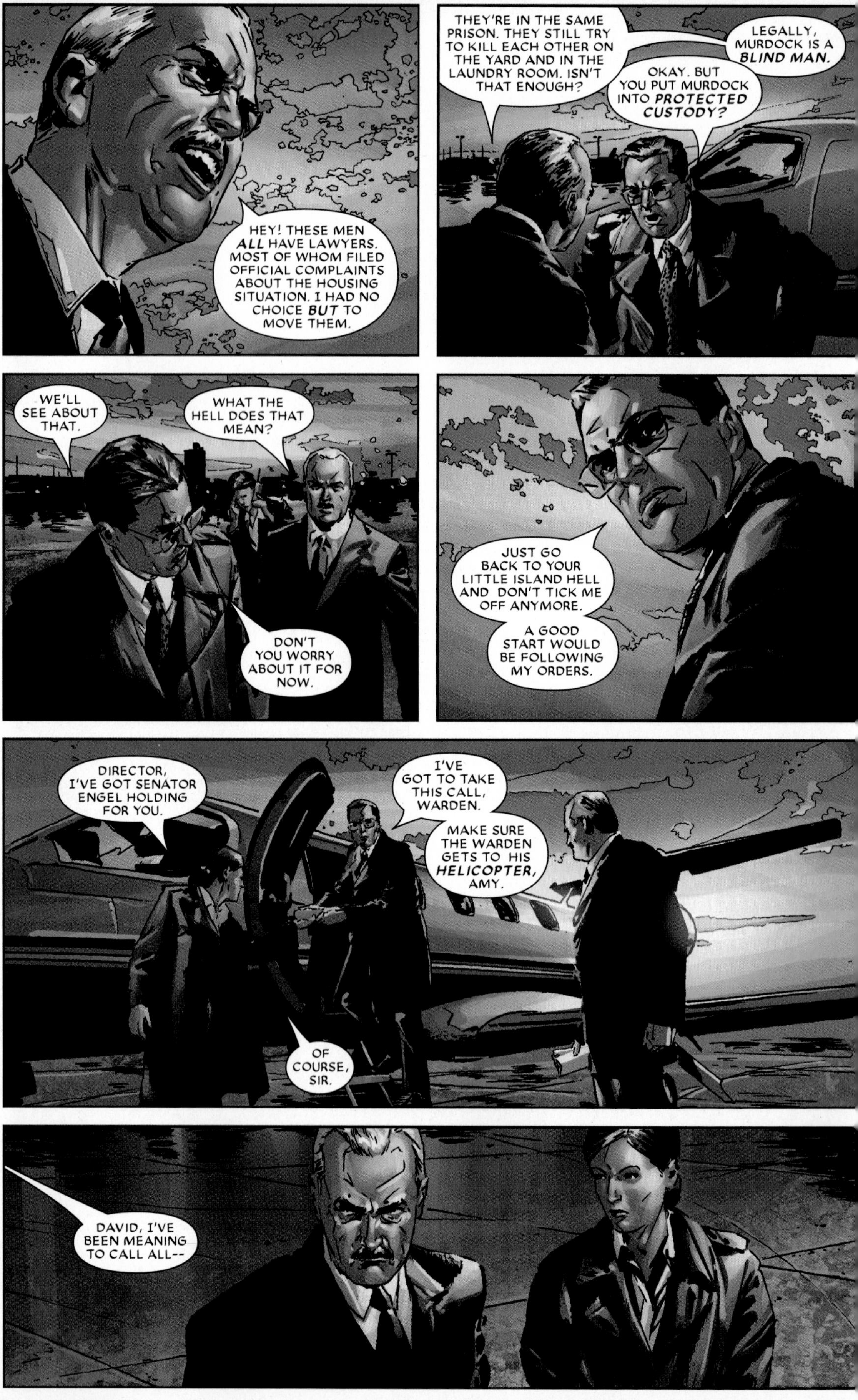
HEY! THESE MEN ALL HAVE LAWYERS. MOST OF WHOM FILED OFFICIAL COMPLAINTS ABOUT THE HOUSING SITUATION. I HAD NO CHOICE BUT TO MOVE THEM.
THEY'RE IN THE SAME PRISON. THEY STILL TRY TO KILL EACH OTHER ON THE YARD AND IN THE LAUNDRY ROOM. ISN'T THAT ENOUGH?
LEGALLY, MURDOCK IS A BLIND MAN.
OKAY. BUT YOU PUT MURDOCK INTO PROTECTED CUSTODY?
WE'LL SEE ABOUT THAT.
WHAT THE HELL DOES THAT MEAN?
DON'T YOU WORRY ABOUT IT FOR NOW.
JUST GO BACK TO YOUR LITTLE ISLAND HELL AND DON'T TICK ME OFF ANYMORE.
A GOOD START WOULD BE FOLLOWING MY ORDERS.
DIRECTOR, I'VE GOT SENATOR ENGEL HOLDING FOR YOU.
I'VE GOT TO TAKE THIS CALL, WARDEN.
MAKE SURE THE WARDEN GETS TO HIS HELICOPTER, AMY.
OF COURSE, SIR.
DAVID, I'VE BEEN MEANING TO CALL ALL--

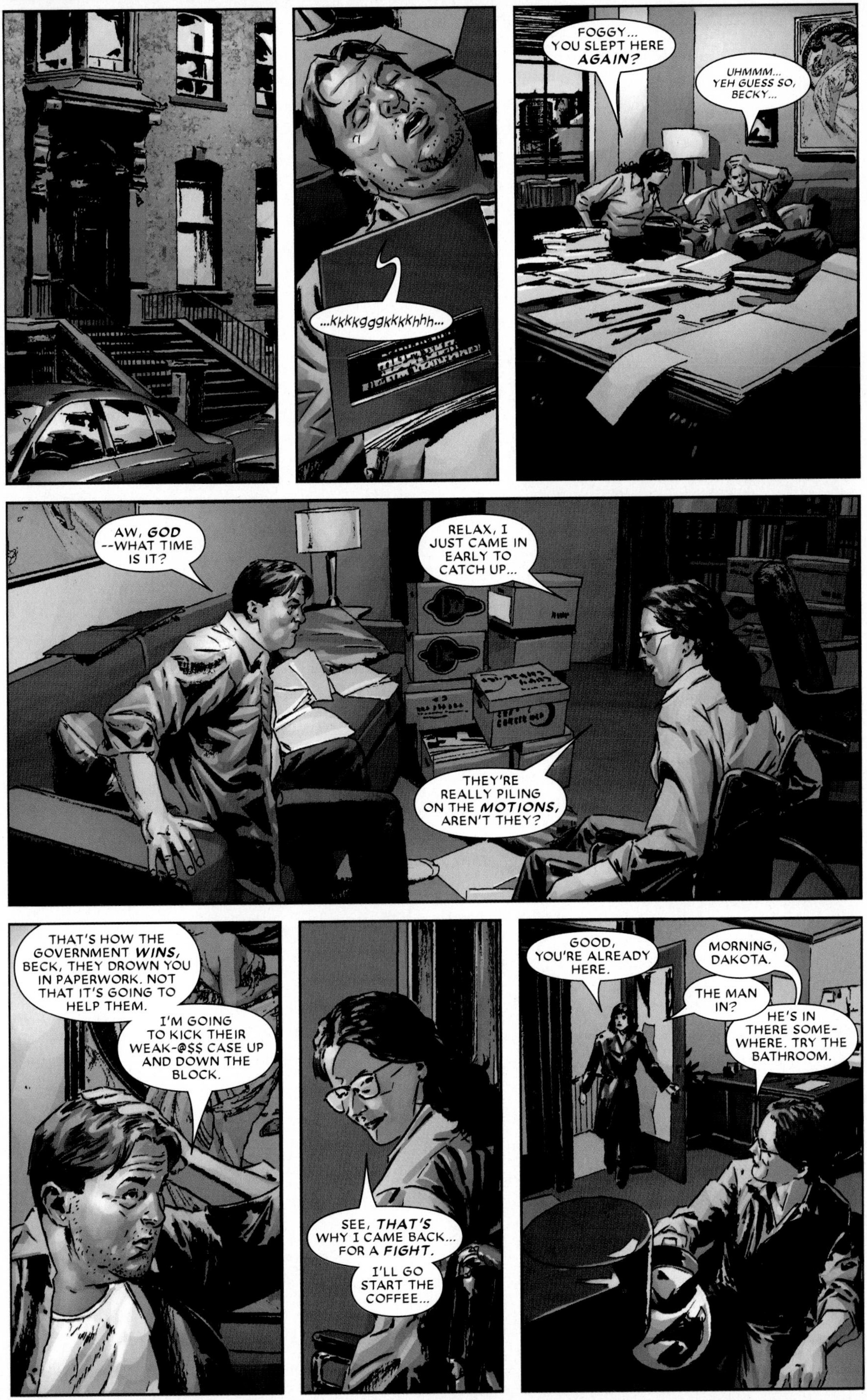
...kkkkggkkkhhh...
FOGGY... YOU SLEPT HERE AGAIN?
UHMMM... YEH GUESS SO, BECKY...
AW, GOD --WHAT TIME IS IT?
RELAX, I JUST CAME IN EARLY TO CATCH UP...
THEY'RE REALLY PILING ON THE MOTIONS, AREN'T THEY?
THAT'S HOW THE GOVERNMENT WINS, BECK, THEY DROWN YOU IN PAPERWORK. NOT THAT IT'S GOING TO HELP THEM.
I'M GOING TO KICK THEIR WEAK-@$$ CASE UP AND DOWN THE BLOCK.
SEE, THAT'S WHY I CAME BACK... FOR A FIGHT.
I'LL GO START THE COFFEE...
GOOD, YOU'RE ALREADY HERE.
MORNING, DAKOTA.
THE MAN IN?
HE'S IN THERE SOME-WHERE. TRY THE BATHROOM.

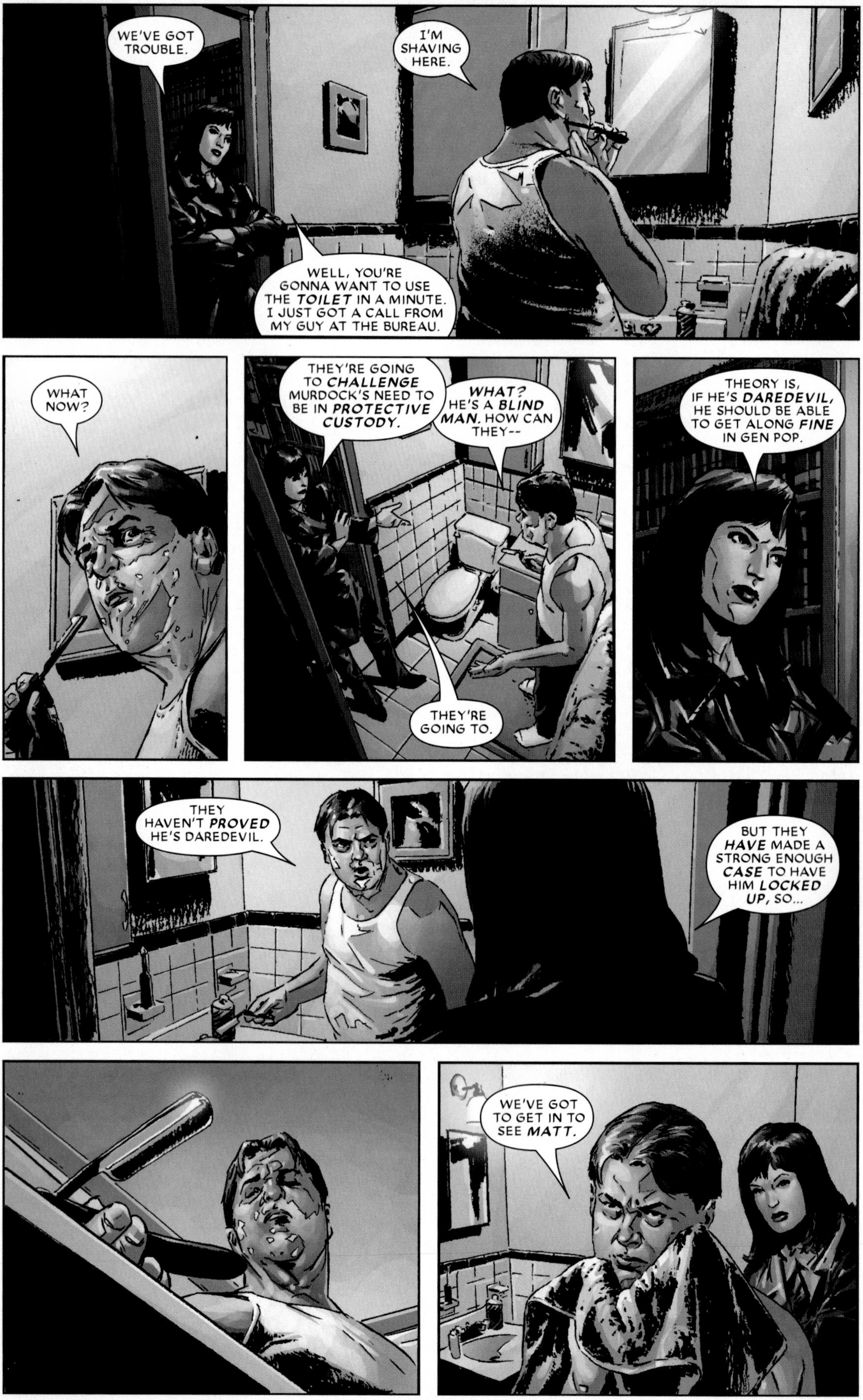

WE'VE GOT TROUBLE.
I'M SHAVING HERE.
WELL, YOU'RE GONNA WANT TO USE THE TOILET IN A MINUTE. I JUST GOT A CALL FROM MY GUY AT THE BUREAU.
WHAT NOW?
THEY'RE GOING TO CHALLENGE MURDOCK'S NEED TO BE IN PROTECTIVE CUSTODY.
WHAT? HE'S A BLIND MAN. HOW CAN THEY--
THEY'RE GOING TO.
THEORY IS, IF HE'S DAREDEVIL, HE SHOULD BE ABLE TO GET ALONG FINE IN GEN POP.
THEY HAVEN'T PROVED HE'S DAREDEVIL.
BUT THEY HAVE MADE A STRONG ENOUGH CASE TO HAVE HIM LOCKED UP, SO...
WE'VE GOT TO GET IN TO SEE MATT.

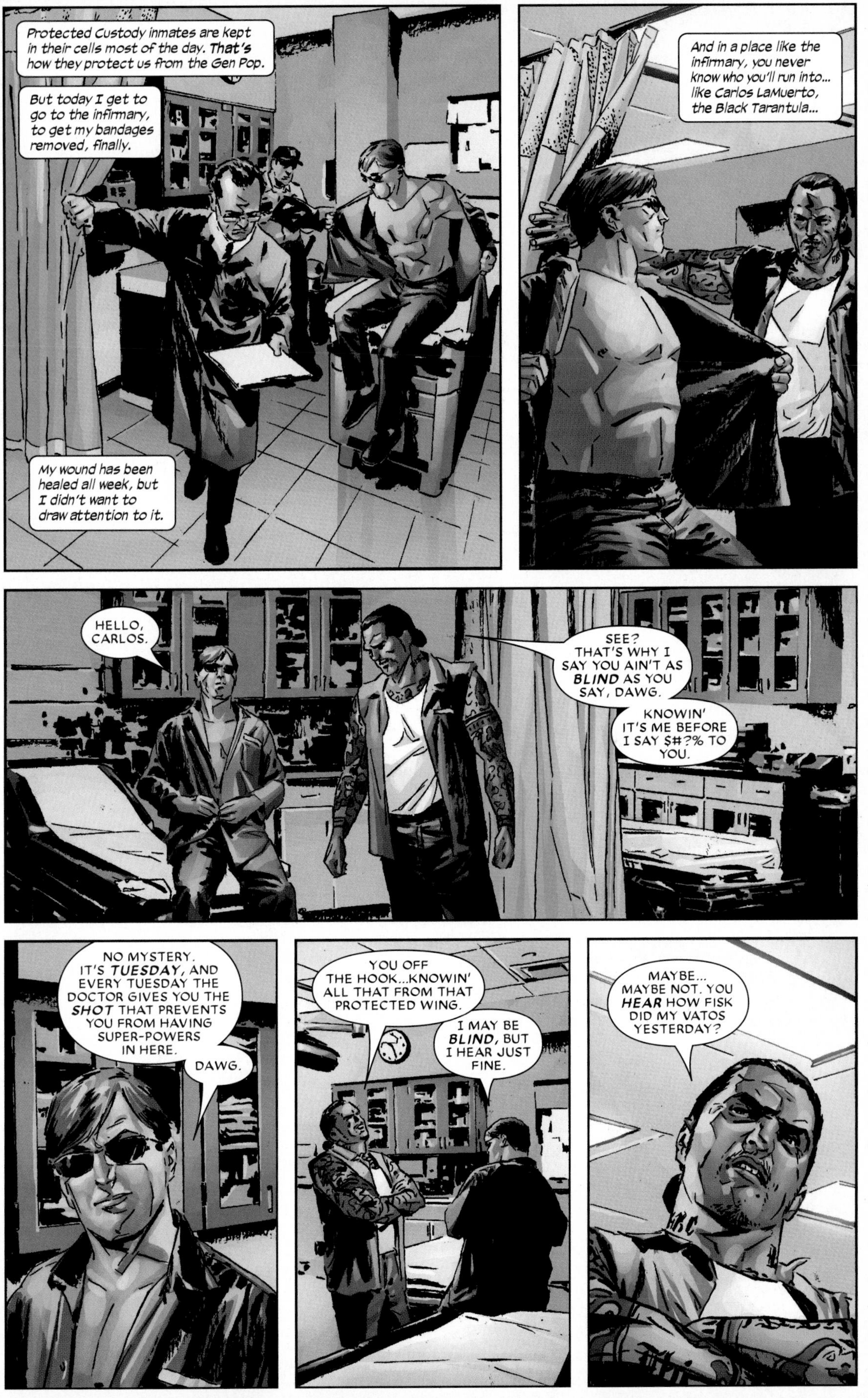
Protected Custody inmates are kept in their cells most of the day. That's how they protect us from the Gen Pop.
But today I get to go to the infirmary, to get my bandages removed, finally.
My wound has been healed all week, but I didn't want to draw attention to it.
And in a place like the infirmary, you never know who you'll run into... like Carlos LaMuerto, the Black Tarantula...
HELLO, CARLOS.
SEE? THAT'S WHY I SAY YOU AIN'T AS BLIND AS YOU SAY, DAWG.
KNOWIN' IT'S ME BEFORE I SAY $#?% TO YOU.
NO MYSTERY. IT'S TUESDAY, AND EVERY TUESDAY THE DOCTOR GIVES YOU THE SHOT THAT PREVENTS YOU FROM HAVING SUPER-POWERS IN HERE.
DAWG.
YOU OFF THE HOOK...KNOWIN' ALL THAT FROM THAT PROTECTED WING.
I MAY BE BLIND, BUT I HEAR JUST FINE.
MAYBE... MAYBE NOT. YOU HEAR HOW FISK DID MY VATOS YESTERDAY?

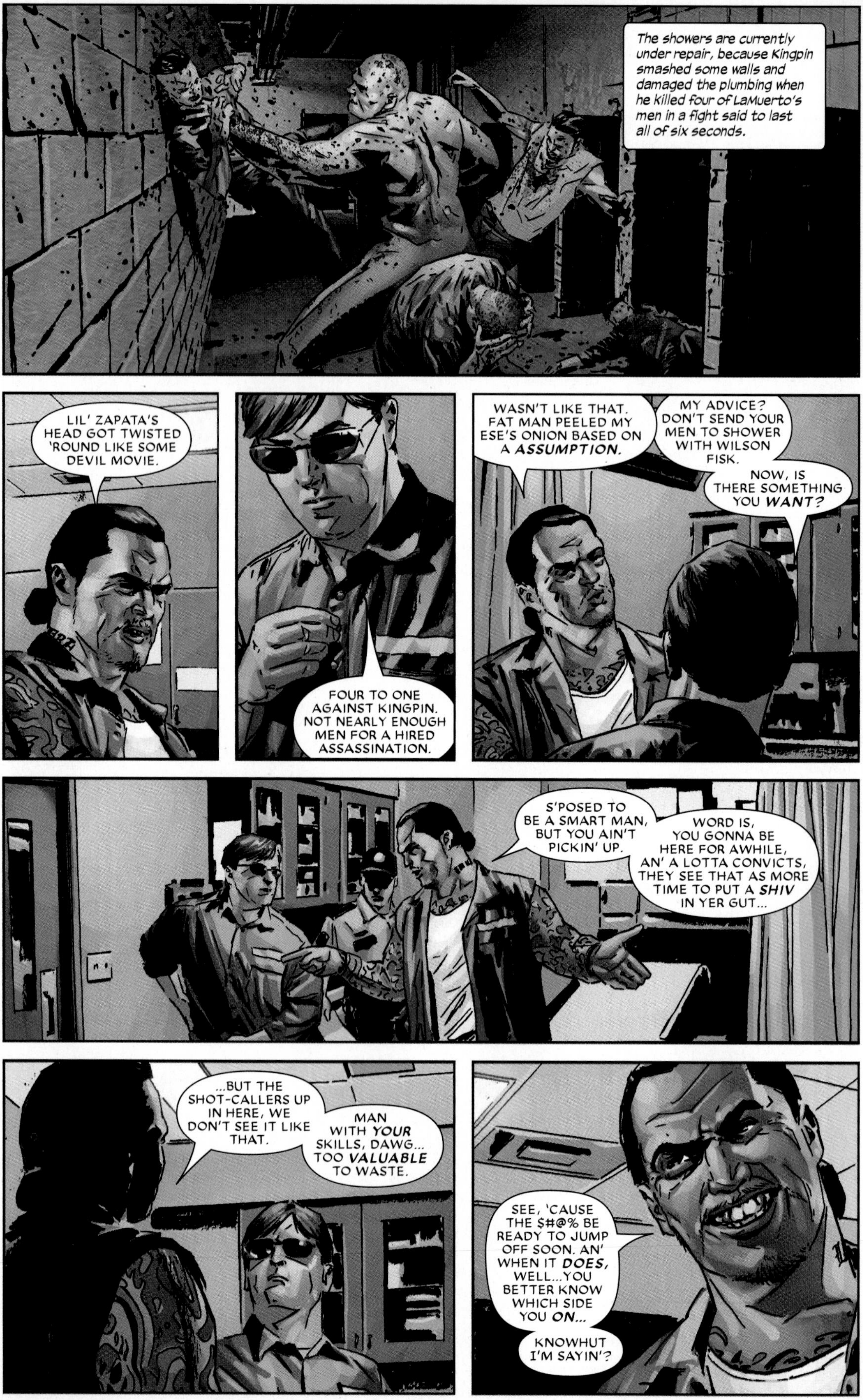
The showers are currently under repair, because Kingpin smashed some walls and damaged the plumbing when he killed four of LaMuerto's men in a fight said to last all of six seconds.
LIL' ZAPATA'S HEAD GOT TWISTED 'ROUND LIKE SOME DEVIL MOVIE.
FOUR TO ONE AGAINST KINGPIN. NOT NEARLY ENOUGH MEN FOR A HIRED ASSASSINATION.
WASN'T LIKE THAT. FAT MAN PEELED MY ESE'S ONION BASED ON A ASSUMPTION.
MY ADVICE? DON'T SEND YOUR MEN TO SHOWER WITH WILSON FISK.
NOW, IS THERE SOMETHING YOU WANT?
S'POSED TO BE A SMART MAN, BUT YOU AIN'T PICKIN' UP.
WORD IS, YOU GONNA BE HERE FOR AWHILE, AN' A LOTTA CONVICTS, THEY SEE THAT AS MORE TIME TO PUT A SHIV IN YER GUT...
...BUT THE SHOT-CALLERS UP IN HERE, WE DON'T SEE IT LIKE THAT.
MAN WITH YOUR SKILLS, DAWG... TOO VALUABLE TO WASTE.
SEE, 'CAUSE THE $#@% BE READY TO JUMP OFF SOON. AN' WHEN IT DOES, WELL...YOU BETTER KNOW WHICH SIDE YOU ON...
KNOWHUT I'M SAYIN'?

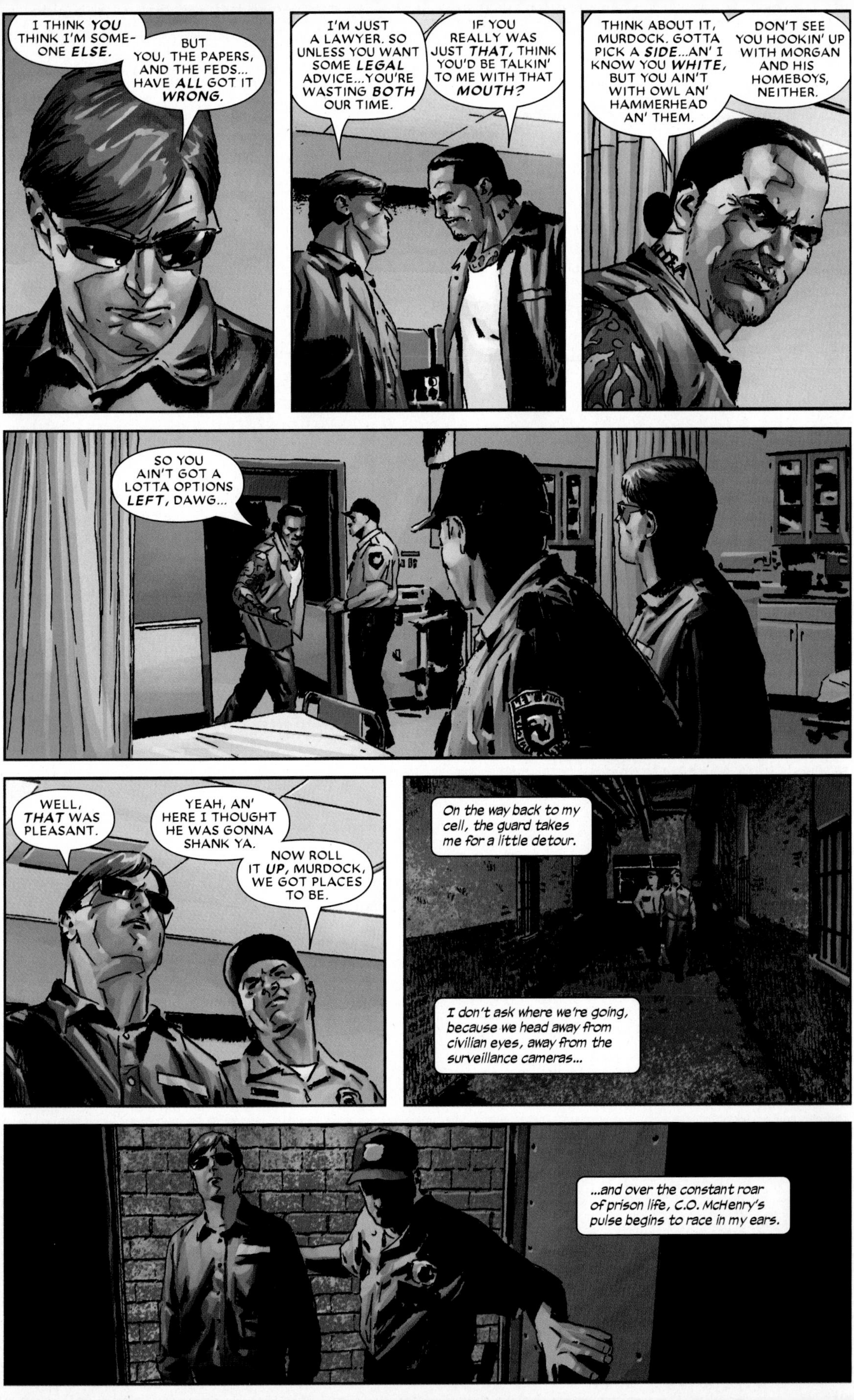
I THINK *YOU* THINK I'M SOME-ONE *ELSE.*
BUT YOU, THE PAPERS, AND THE FEDS... HAVE *ALL* GOT IT *WRONG.*
I'M JUST A LAWYER. SO UNLESS YOU WANT SOME *LEGAL* ADVICE...YOU'RE WASTING *BOTH* OUR TIME.
IF YOU REALLY WAS JUST *THAT,* THINK YOU'D BE TALKIN' TO ME WITH THAT *MOUTH?*
THINK ABOUT IT, MURDOCK. GOTTA PICK A *SIDE*...AN' I KNOW YOU *WHITE,* BUT YOU AIN'T WITH OWL AN' HAMMERHEAD AN' THEM.
DON'T SEE YOU HOOKIN' UP WITH MORGAN AND HIS HOMEBOYS, NEITHER.
SO YOU AIN'T GOT A LOTTA OPTIONS *LEFT,* DAWG...
WELL, *THAT* WAS PLEASANT.
YEAH, AN' HERE I THOUGHT HE WAS GONNA SHANK YA.
NOW ROLL IT *UP,* MURDOCK, WE GOT PLACES TO BE.
On the way back to my cell, the guard takes me for a little detour.
I don't ask where we're going, because we head away from civilian eyes, away from the surveillance cameras...
...and over the constant roar of prison life, C.O. McHenry's pulse begins to race in my ears.

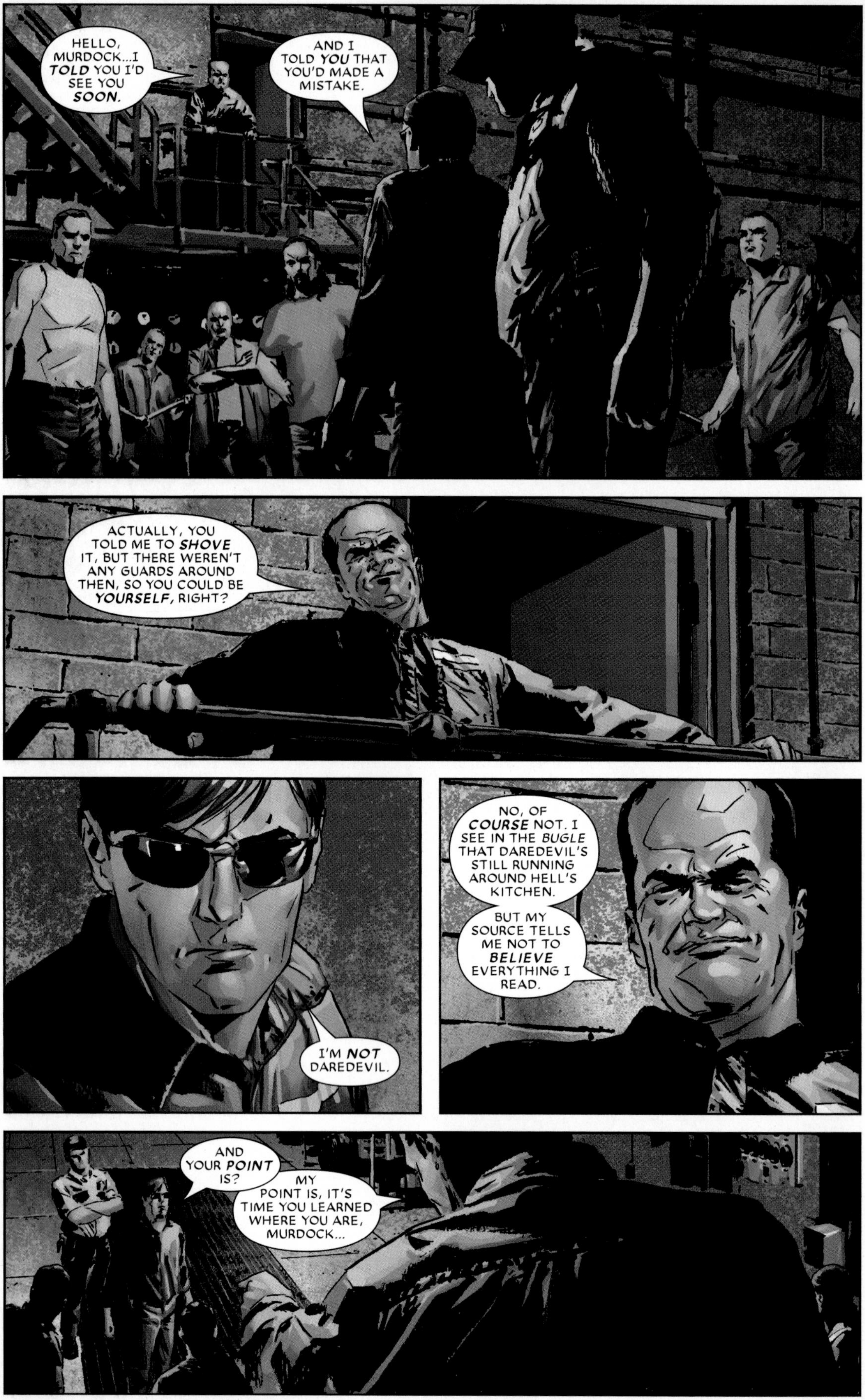
HELLO, MURDOCK...I *TOLD* YOU I'D SEE YOU *SOON.*
AND I TOLD *YOU* THAT YOU'D MADE A MISTAKE.
ACTUALLY, YOU TOLD ME TO *SHOVE* IT, BUT THERE WEREN'T ANY GUARDS AROUND THEN, SO YOU COULD BE *YOURSELF,* RIGHT?
I'M *NOT* DAREDEVIL.
NO, OF *COURSE* NOT. I SEE IN THE *BUGLE* THAT DAREDEVIL'S STILL RUNNING AROUND HELL'S KITCHEN.
BUT MY SOURCE TELLS ME NOT TO *BELIEVE* EVERYTHING I READ.
AND YOUR *POINT* IS?
MY POINT IS, IT'S TIME YOU LEARNED WHERE YOU ARE, MURDOCK...

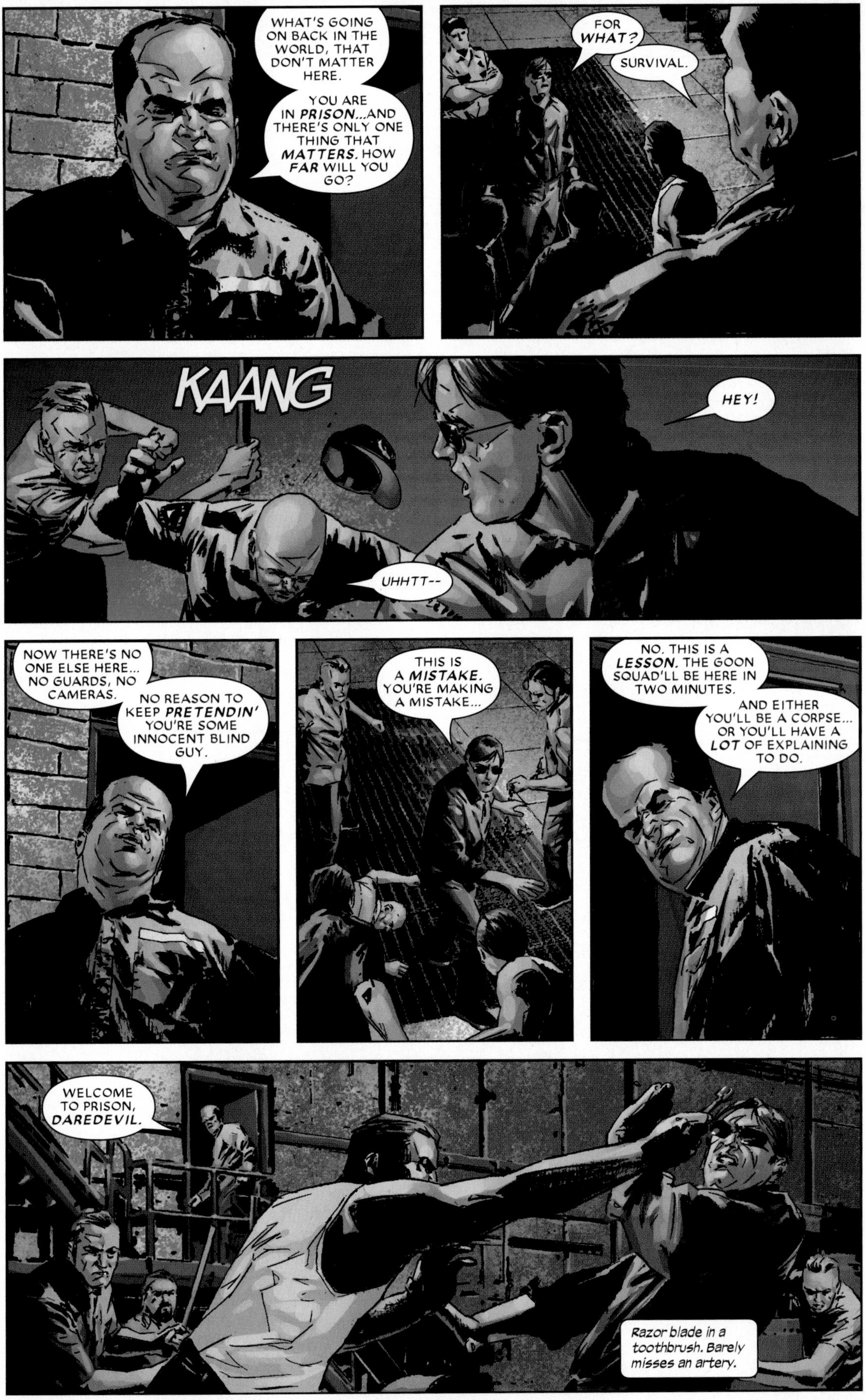
WHAT'S GOING ON BACK IN THE WORLD, THAT DON'T MATTER HERE.
YOU ARE IN **PRISON**...AND THERE'S ONLY ONE THING THAT **MATTERS.** HOW **FAR** WILL YOU GO?
FOR **WHAT?**
SURVIVAL.
KAANG
HEY!
UHHTT--
NOW THERE'S NO ONE ELSE HERE... NO GUARDS, NO CAMERAS.
NO REASON TO KEEP **PRETENDIN'** YOU'RE SOME INNOCENT BLIND GUY.
THIS IS A **MISTAKE.** YOU'RE MAKING A MISTAKE...
NO. THIS IS A **LESSON.** THE GOON SQUAD'LL BE HERE IN TWO MINUTES.
AND EITHER YOU'LL BE A CORPSE... OR YOU'LL HAVE A **LOT** OF EXPLAINING TO DO.
WELCOME TO PRISON, **DAREDEVIL.**
Razor blade in a toothbrush. Barely misses an artery.

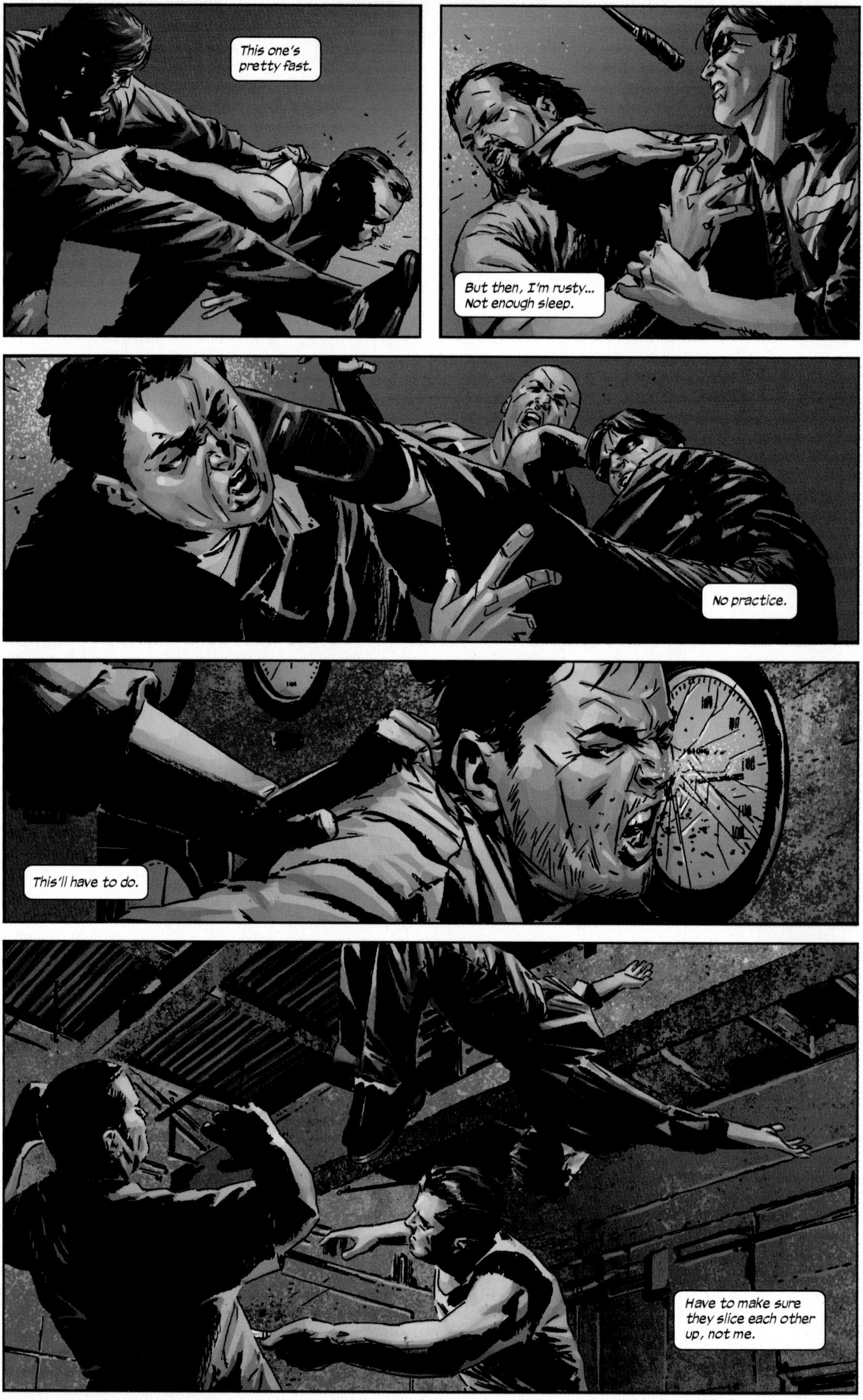

This one's pretty fast.
But then, I'm rusty... Not enough sleep.
No practice.
This'll have to do.
Have to make sure they slice each other up, not me.

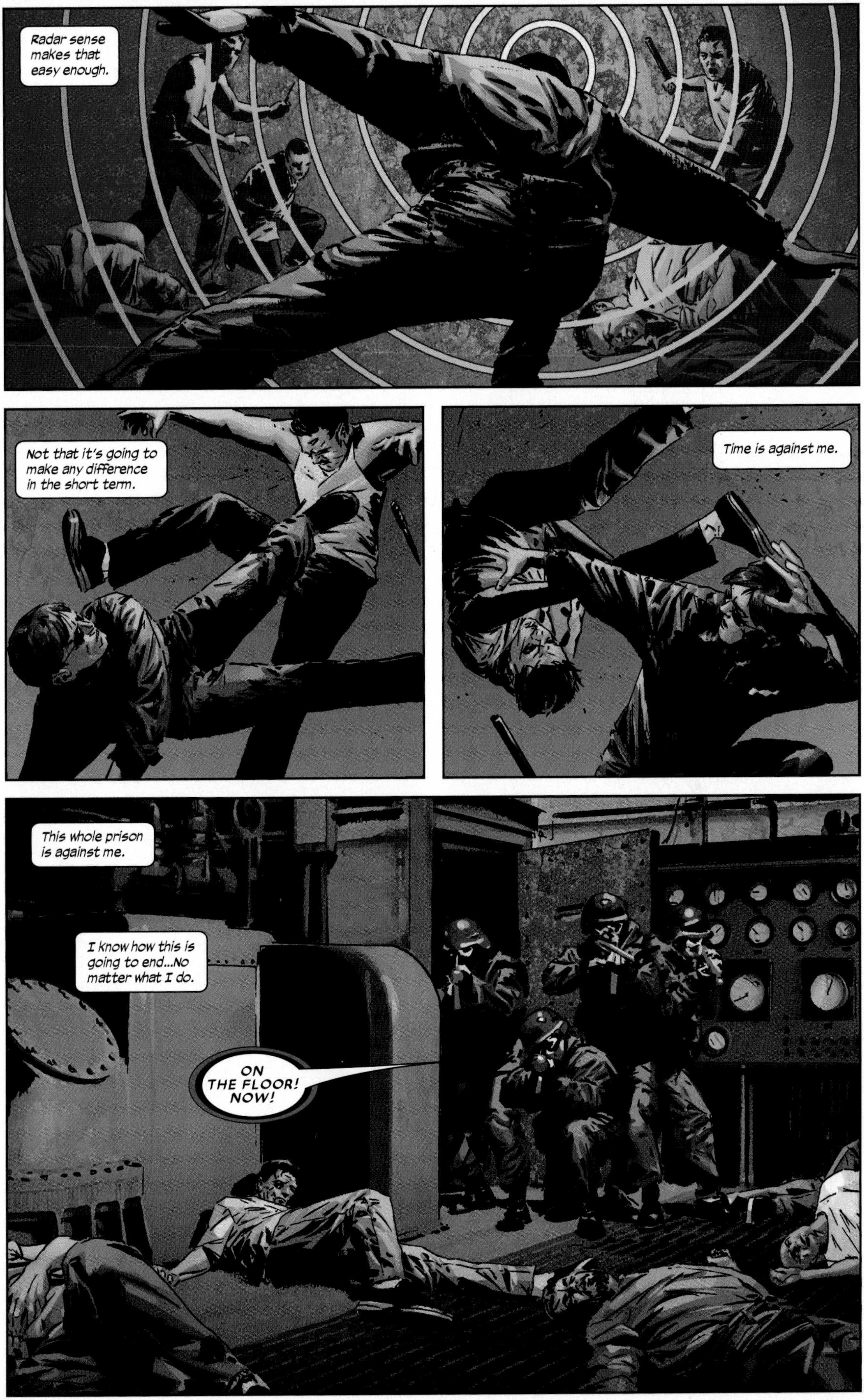
Radar sense makes that easy enough.
Not that it's going to make any difference in the short term.
Time is against me.
This whole prison is against me.
I know how this is going to end...No matter what I do.
ON THE FLOOR! NOW!

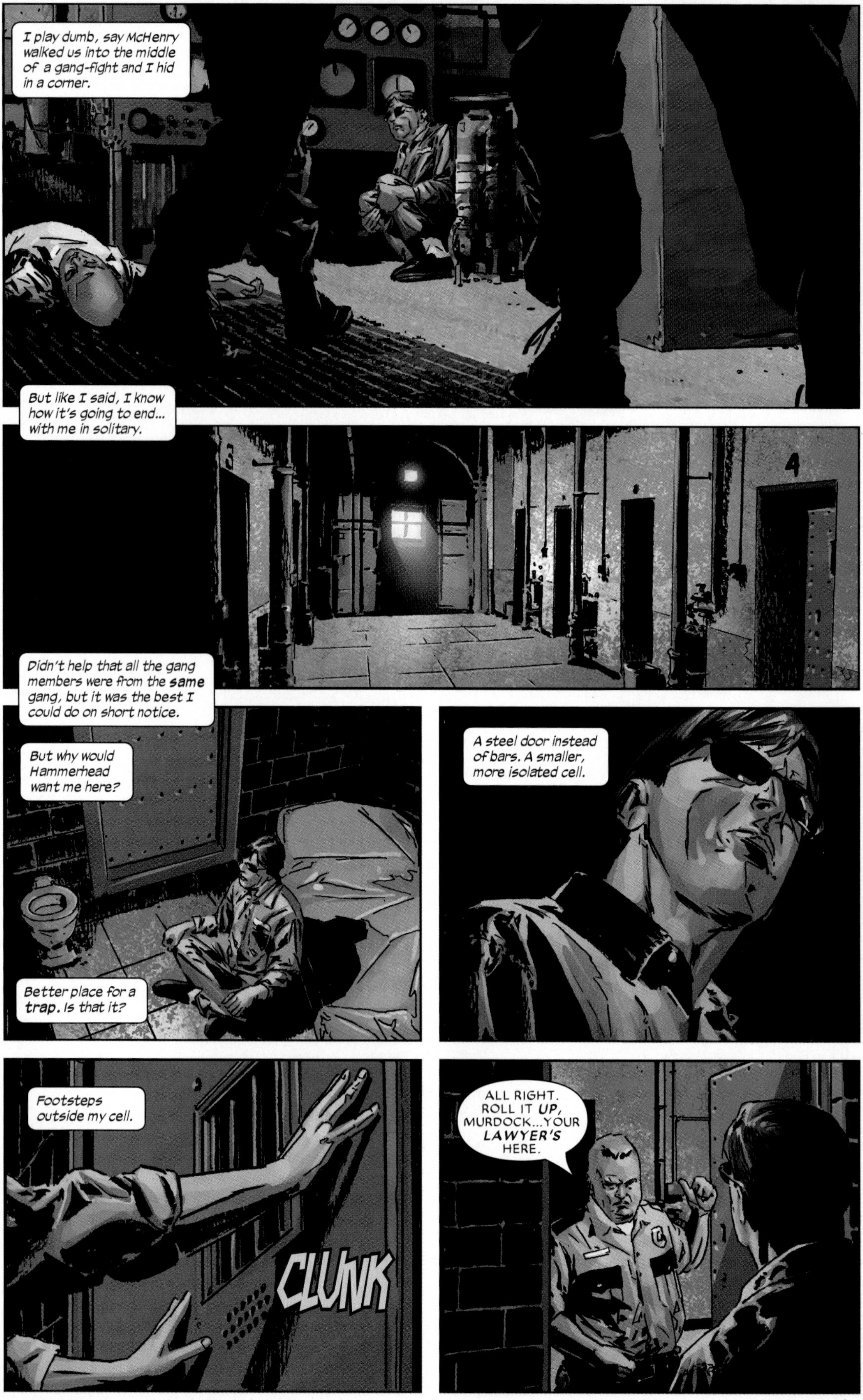
I play dumb, say McHenry walked us into the middle of a gang-fight and I hid in a corner.
But like I said, I know how it's going to end... with me in solitary.
Didn't help that all the gang members were from the **same** gang, but it was the best I could do on short notice.
But why would Hammerhead want me here?
Better place for a **trap.** Is that it?
A steel door instead of bars. A smaller, more isolated cell.
Footsteps outside my cell.
CLUNK
ALL RIGHT. ROLL IT *UP,* MURDOCK... YOUR ***LAWYER'S*** HERE.

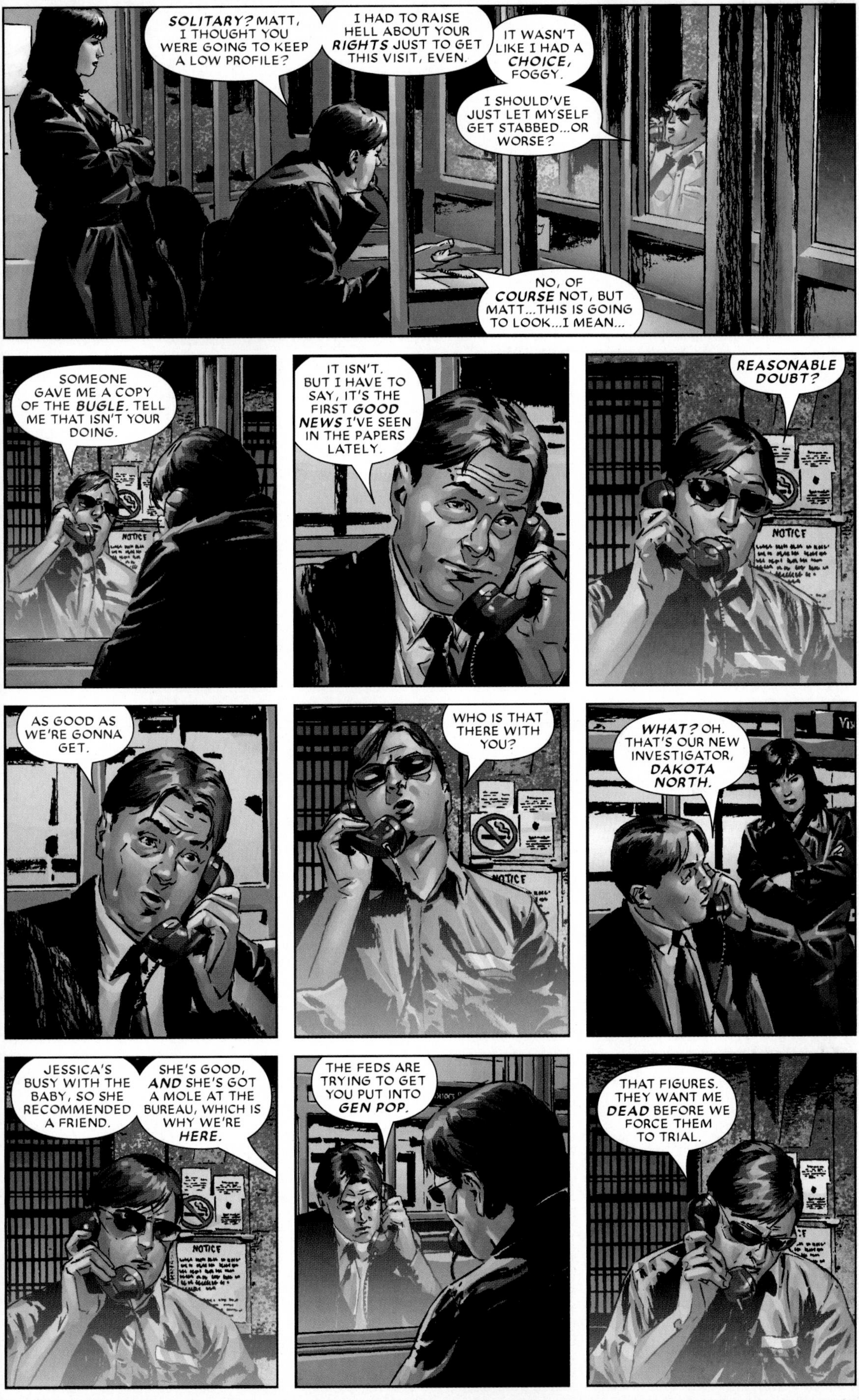
SOLITARY? MATT, I THOUGHT YOU WERE GOING TO KEEP A LOW PROFILE?
I HAD TO RAISE HELL ABOUT YOUR RIGHTS JUST TO GET THIS VISIT, EVEN.
IT WASN'T LIKE I HAD A CHOICE, FOGGY.
I SHOULD'VE JUST LET MYSELF GET STABBED...OR WORSE?
NO, OF COURSE NOT, BUT MATT...THIS IS GOING TO LOOK...I MEAN...
SOMEONE GAVE ME A COPY OF THE BUGLE. TELL ME THAT ISN'T YOUR DOING.
IT ISN'T. BUT I HAVE TO SAY, IT'S THE FIRST GOOD NEWS I'VE SEEN IN THE PAPERS LATELY.
REASONABLE DOUBT?
AS GOOD AS WE'RE GONNA GET.
WHO IS THAT THERE WITH YOU?
WHAT? OH. THAT'S OUR NEW INVESTIGATOR, DAKOTA NORTH.
JESSICA'S BUSY WITH THE BABY, SO SHE RECOMMENDED A FRIEND.
SHE'S GOOD, AND SHE'S GOT A MOLE AT THE BUREAU, WHICH IS WHY WE'RE HERE.
THE FEDS ARE TRYING TO GET YOU PUT INTO GEN POP.
THAT FIGURES. THEY WANT ME DEAD BEFORE WE FORCE THEM TO TRIAL.

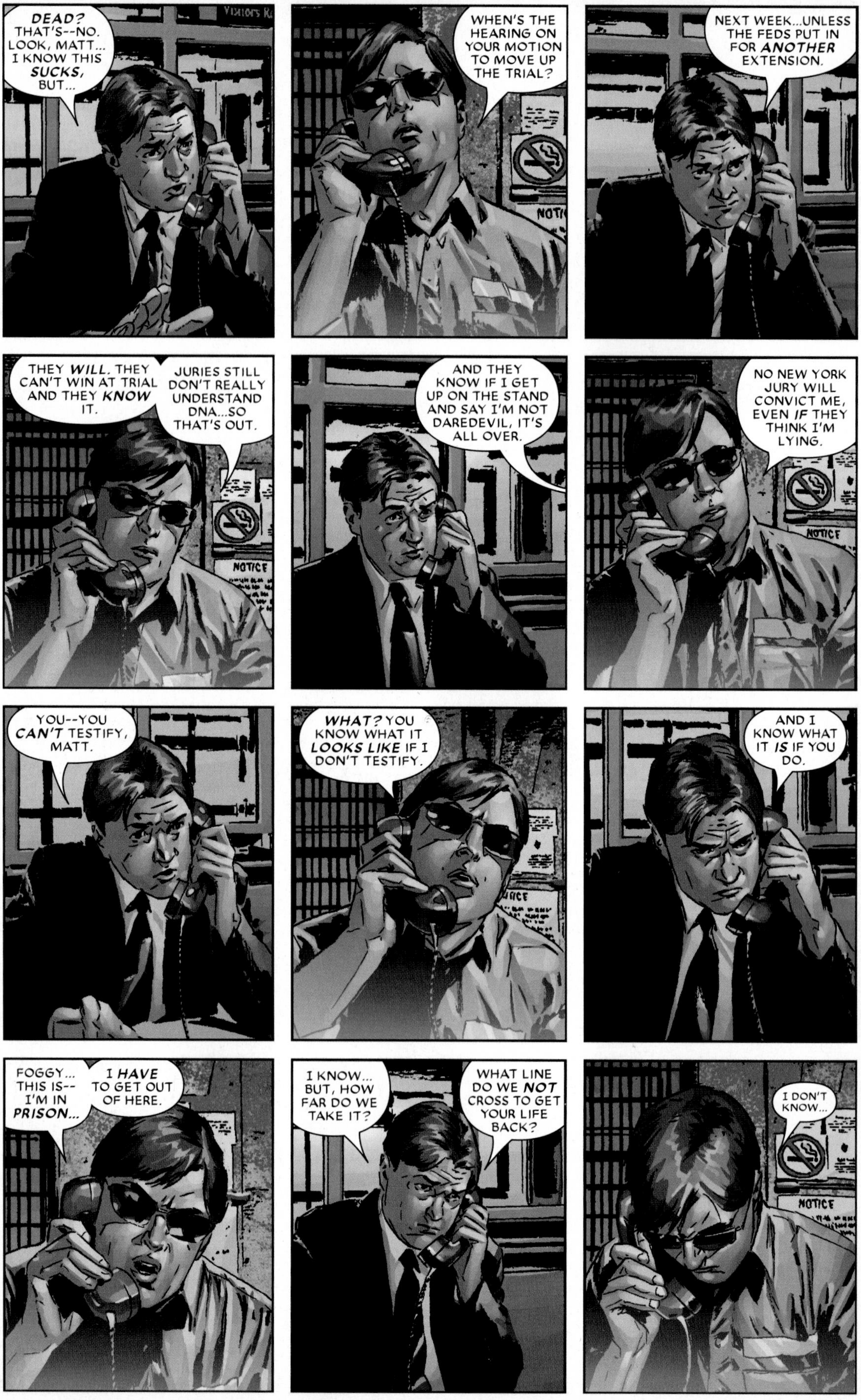
DEAD? THAT'S--NO. LOOK, MATT... I KNOW THIS SUCKS, BUT...
WHEN'S THE HEARING ON YOUR MOTION TO MOVE UP THE TRIAL?
NEXT WEEK...UNLESS THE FEDS PUT IN FOR ANOTHER EXTENSION.
THEY WILL. THEY CAN'T WIN AT TRIAL AND THEY KNOW IT.
JURIES STILL DON'T REALLY UNDERSTAND DNA...SO THAT'S OUT.
AND THEY KNOW IF I GET UP ON THE STAND AND SAY I'M NOT DAREDEVIL, IT'S ALL OVER.
NO NEW YORK JURY WILL CONVICT ME, EVEN IF THEY THINK I'M LYING.
YOU--YOU CAN'T TESTIFY, MATT.
WHAT? YOU KNOW WHAT IT LOOKS LIKE IF I DON'T TESTIFY.
AND I KNOW WHAT IT IS IF YOU DO.
FOGGY... THIS IS-- I'M IN PRISON...
I HAVE TO GET OUT OF HERE.
I KNOW... BUT, HOW FAR DO WE TAKE IT?
WHAT LINE DO WE NOT CROSS TO GET YOUR LIFE BACK?
I DON'T KNOW...

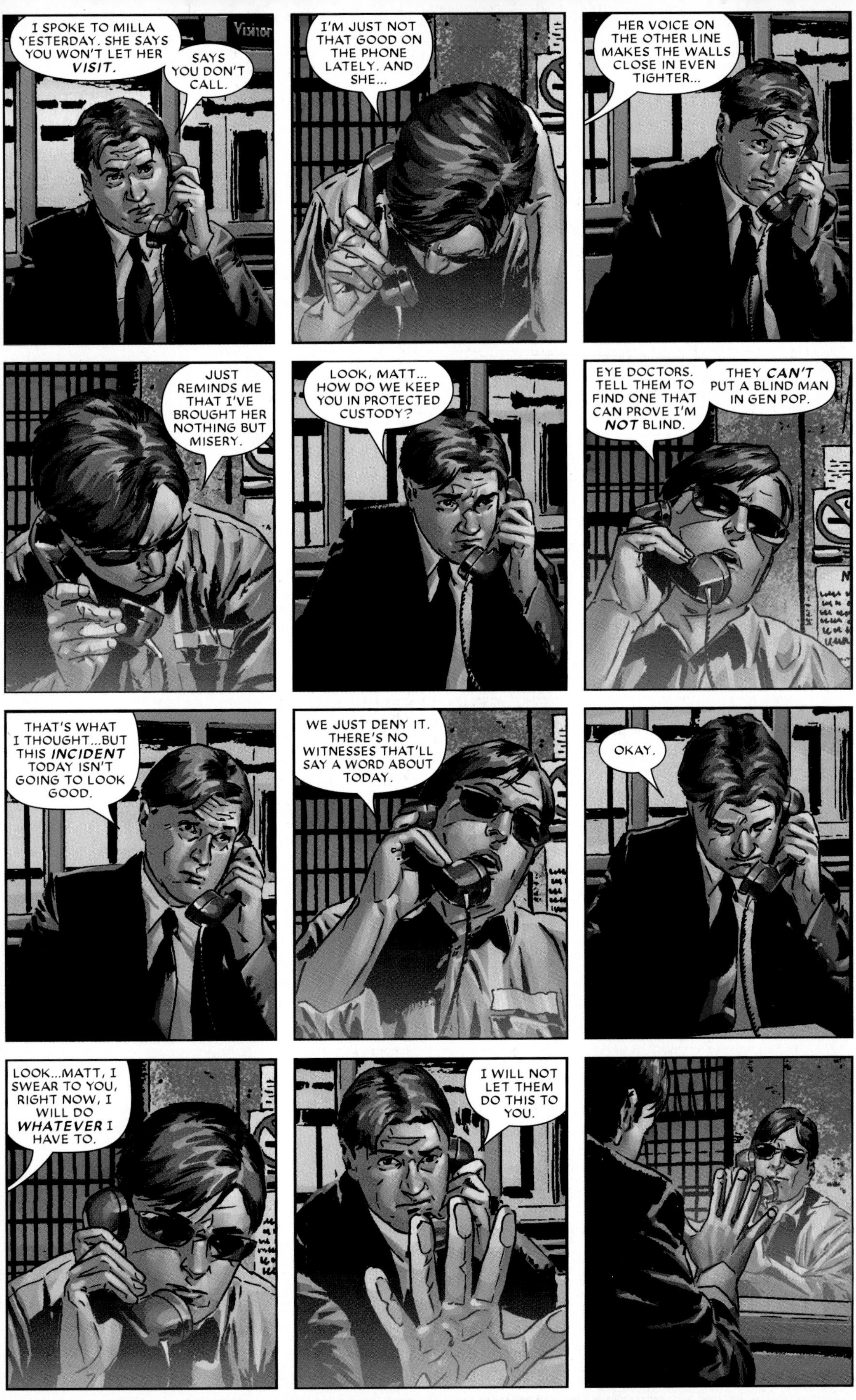
I SPOKE TO MILLA YESTERDAY. SHE SAYS YOU WON'T LET HER VISIT.
SAYS YOU DON'T CALL.
I'M JUST NOT THAT GOOD ON THE PHONE LATELY. AND SHE...
HER VOICE ON THE OTHER LINE MAKES THE WALLS CLOSE IN EVEN TIGHTER...
JUST REMINDS ME THAT I'VE BROUGHT HER NOTHING BUT MISERY.
LOOK, MATT... HOW DO WE KEEP YOU IN PROTECTED CUSTODY?
EYE DOCTORS. TELL THEM TO FIND ONE THAT CAN PROVE I'M NOT BLIND.
THEY CAN'T PUT A BLIND MAN IN GEN POP.
THAT'S WHAT I THOUGHT...BUT THIS INCIDENT TODAY ISN'T GOING TO LOOK GOOD.
WE JUST DENY IT. THERE'S NO WITNESSES THAT'LL SAY A WORD ABOUT TODAY.
OKAY.
LOOK...MATT, I SWEAR TO YOU, RIGHT NOW, I WILL DO WHATEVER I HAVE TO.
I WILL NOT LET THEM DO THIS TO YOU.

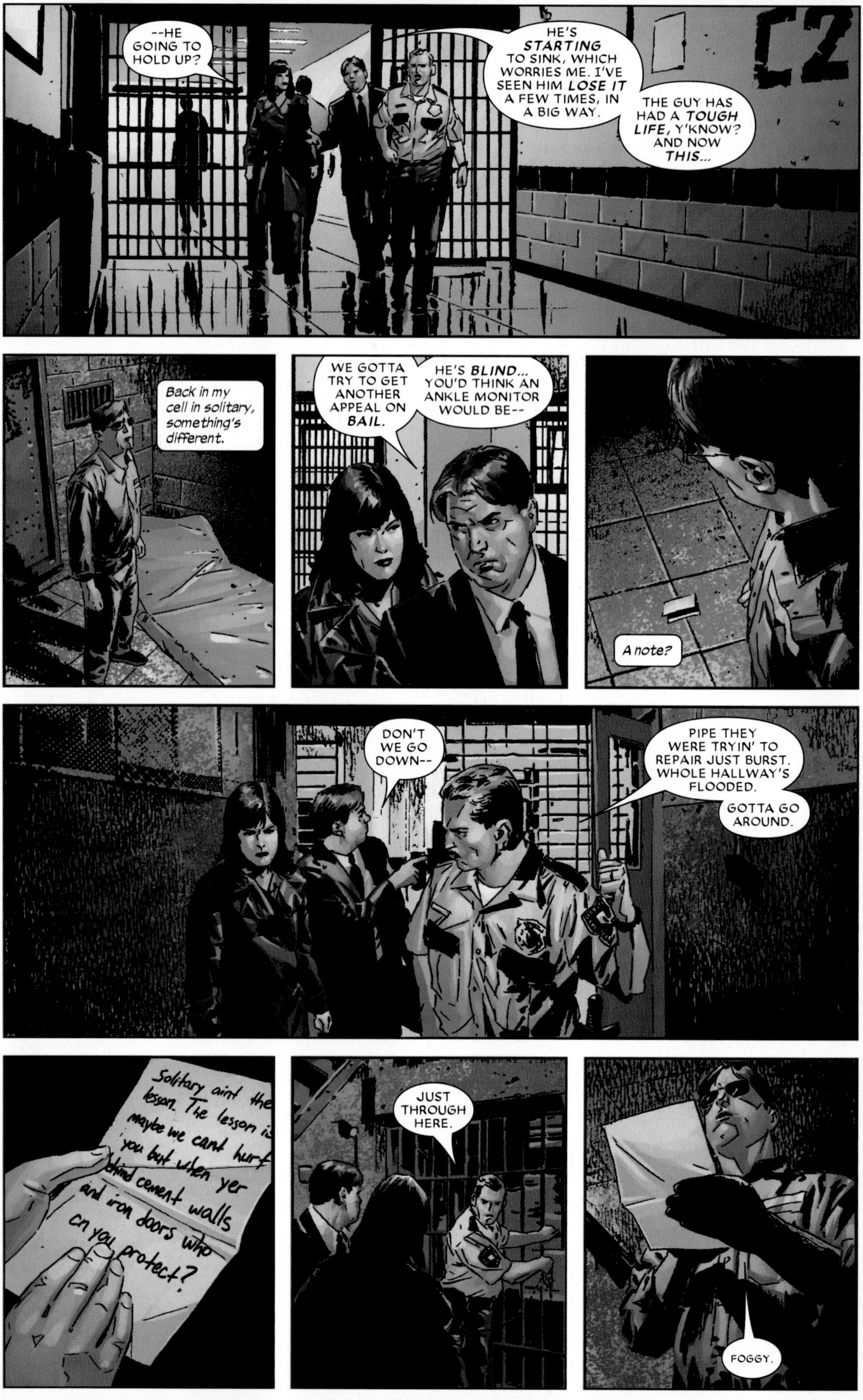
--HE GOING TO HOLD UP?
HE'S STARTING TO SINK, WHICH WORRIES ME. I'VE SEEN HIM LOSE IT A FEW TIMES, IN A BIG WAY.
THE GUY HAS HAD A TOUGH LIFE, Y'KNOW? AND NOW THIS...
C2
Back in my cell in solitary, something's different.
WE GOTTA TRY TO GET ANOTHER APPEAL ON BAIL.
HE'S BLIND... YOU'D THINK AN ANKLE MONITOR WOULD BE--
A note?
DON'T WE GO DOWN--
PIPE THEY WERE TRYIN' TO REPAIR JUST BURST. WHOLE HALLWAY'S FLOODED.
GOTTA GO AROUND.
Solitary aint the lesson. The lesson is maybe we cant hurt you but when yer behind cement walls and iron doors who cn you protect?
JUST THROUGH HERE.
FOGGY.

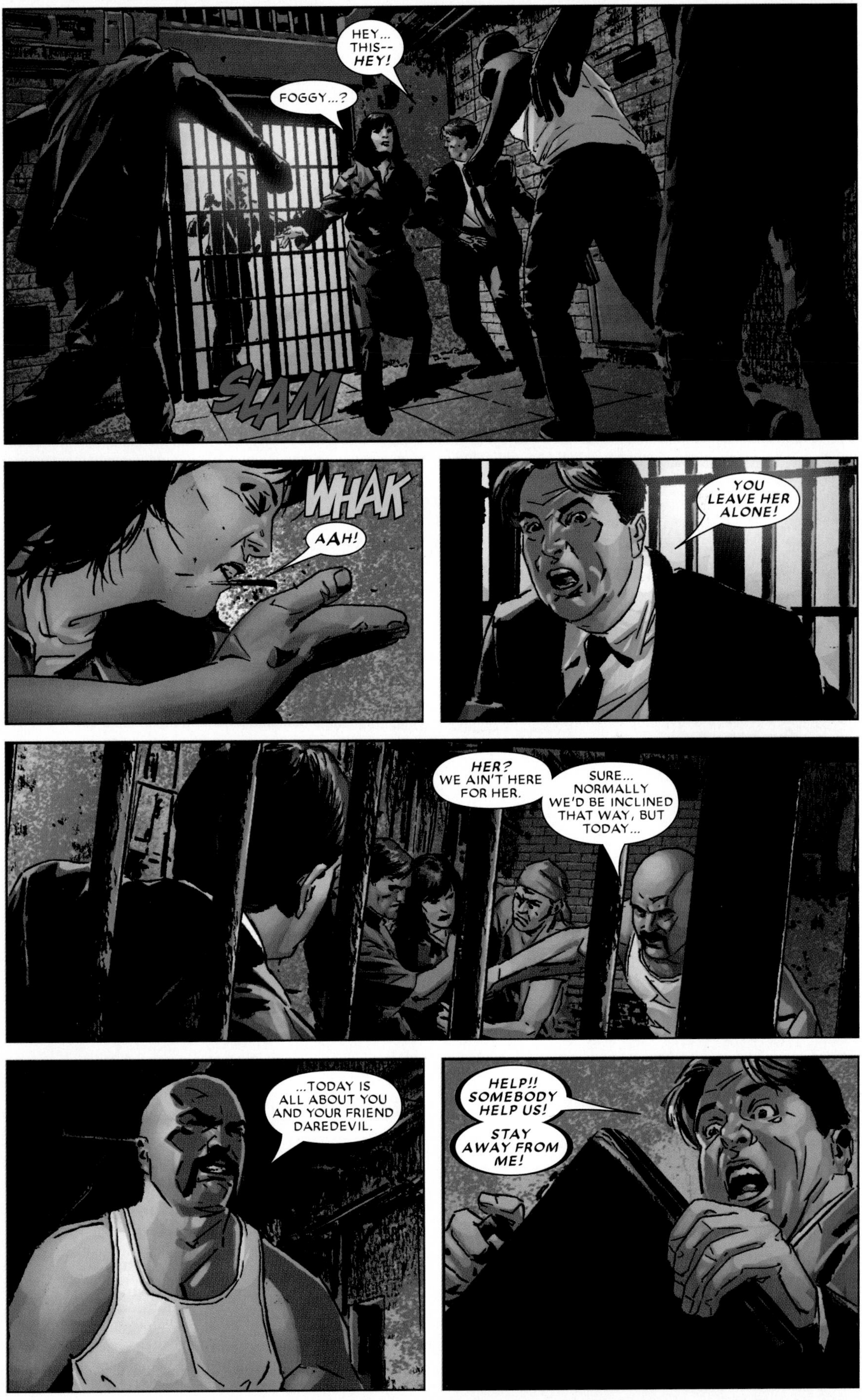
FOGGY...?
HEY... THIS-- HEY!
SLAM
WHAK
AAH!
YOU LEAVE HER ALONE!
HER? WE AIN'T HERE FOR HER.
SURE... NORMALLY WE'D BE INCLINED THAT WAY, BUT TODAY...
...TODAY IS ALL ABOUT YOU AND YOUR FRIEND DAREDEVIL.
HELP!! SOMEBODY HELP US!
STAY AWAY FROM ME!

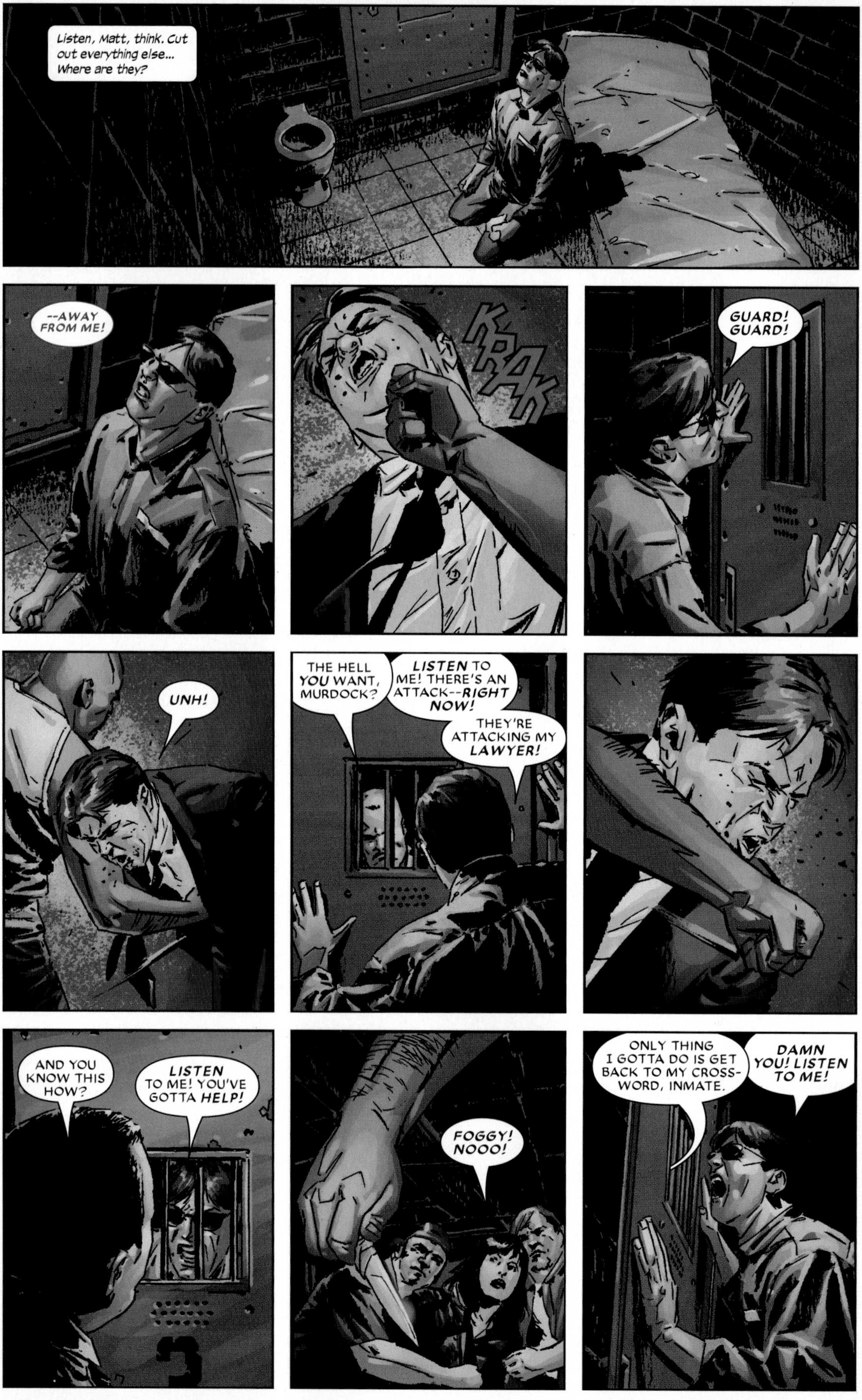
Listen, Matt, think. Cut out everything else... Where are they?
--AWAY FROM ME!
KRAK
GUARD! GUARD!
UNH!
THE HELL YOU WANT, MURDOCK?
LISTEN TO ME! THERE'S AN ATTACK--RIGHT NOW!
THEY'RE ATTACKING MY LAWYER!
AND YOU KNOW THIS HOW?
LISTEN TO ME! YOU'VE GOTTA HELP!
FOGGY! NOOO!
ONLY THING I GOTTA DO IS GET BACK TO MY CROSS-WORD, INMATE.
DAMN YOU! LISTEN TO ME!

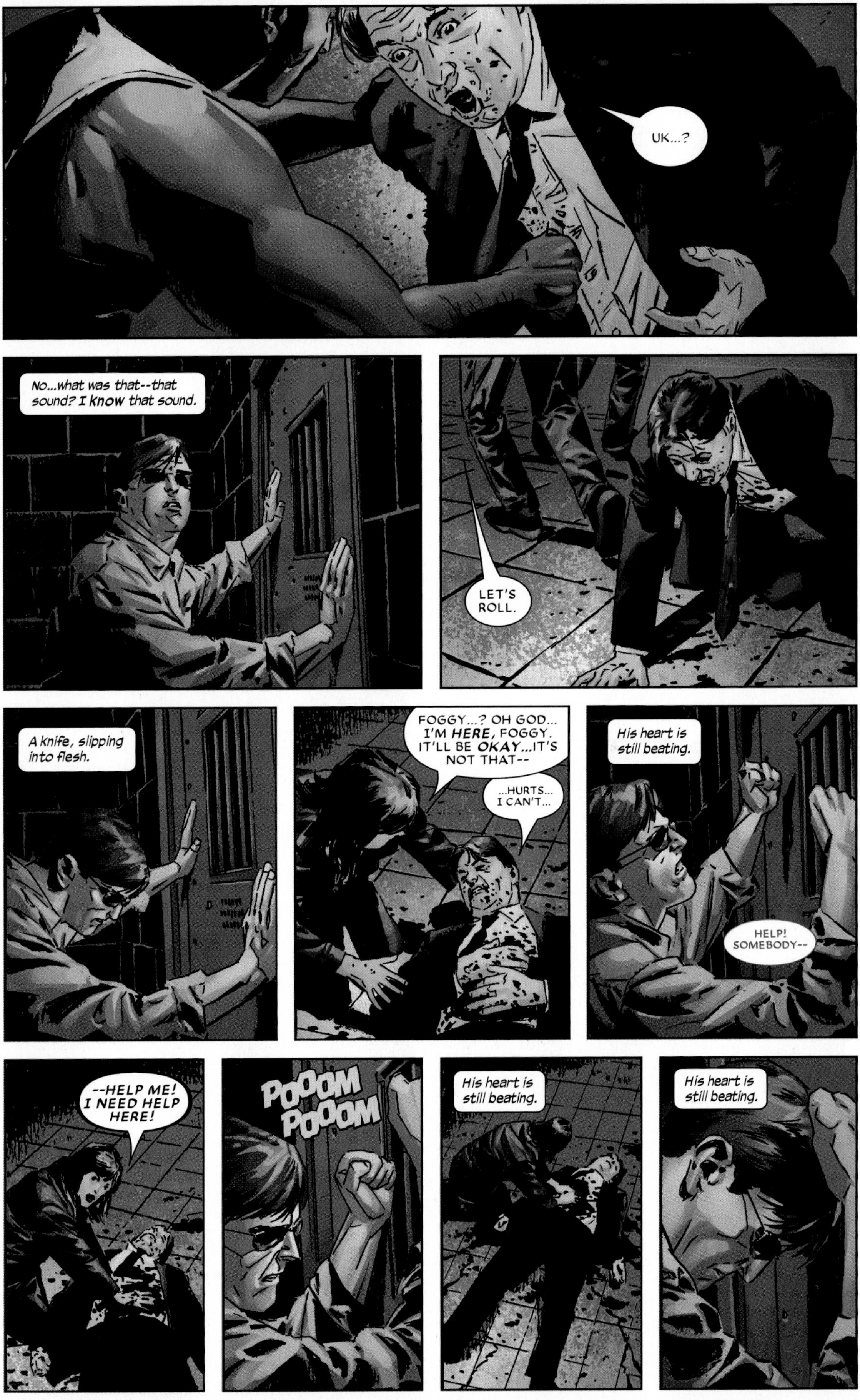

UK...?
No...what was that--that sound? I *know* that sound.
LET'S ROLL.
A knife, slipping into flesh.
FOGGY...? OH GOD... I'M *HERE*, FOGGY. IT'LL BE *OKAY*...IT'S NOT THAT--
...HURTS... I CAN'T...
His heart is still beating.
HELP! SOMEBODY--
--HELP ME! I NEED HELP HERE!
POOOM POOOM
His heart is still beating.
His heart is still beating.

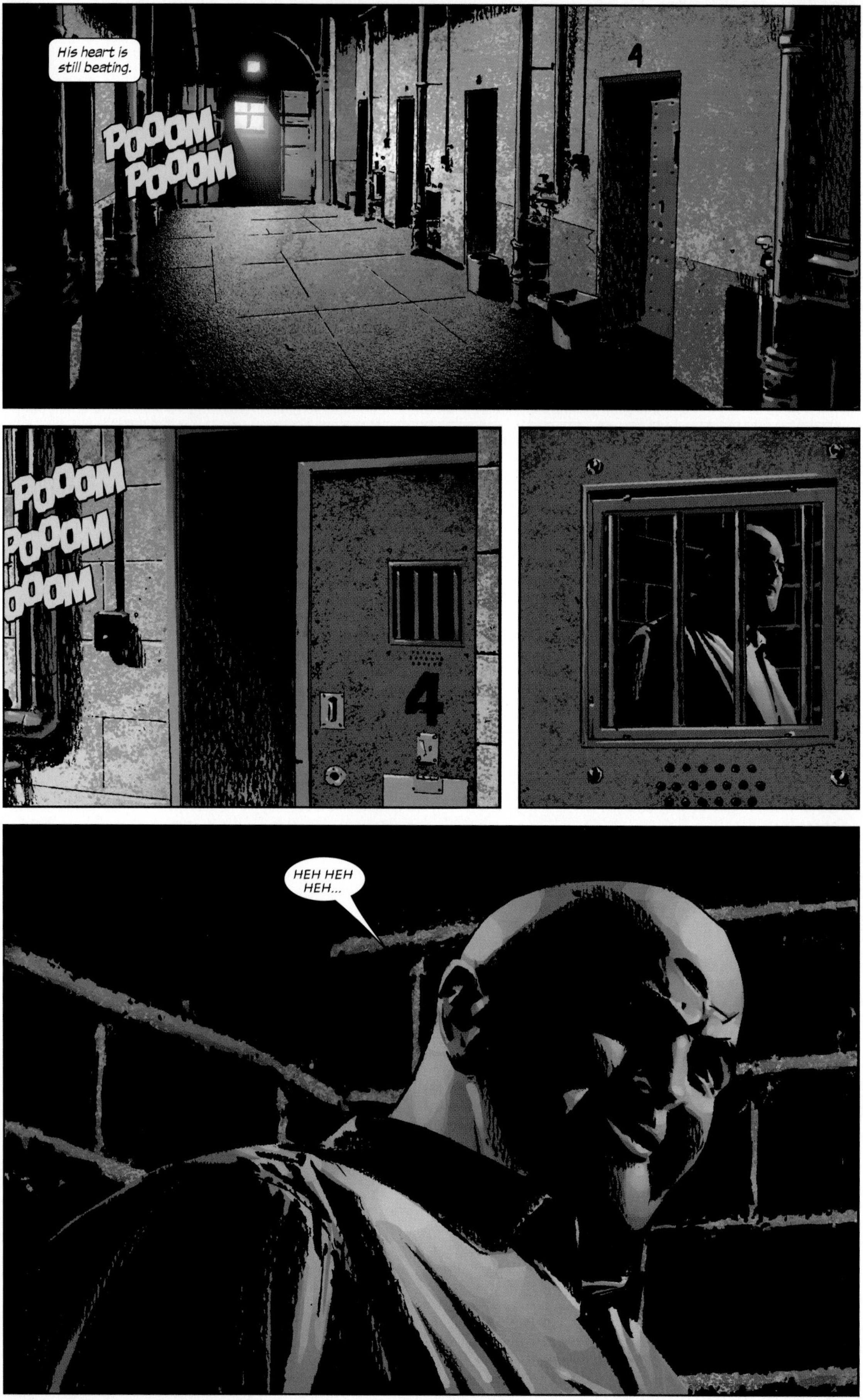
His heart is still beating.
POOOM POOOM
POOOM POOOM OOOM
HEH HEH HEH...

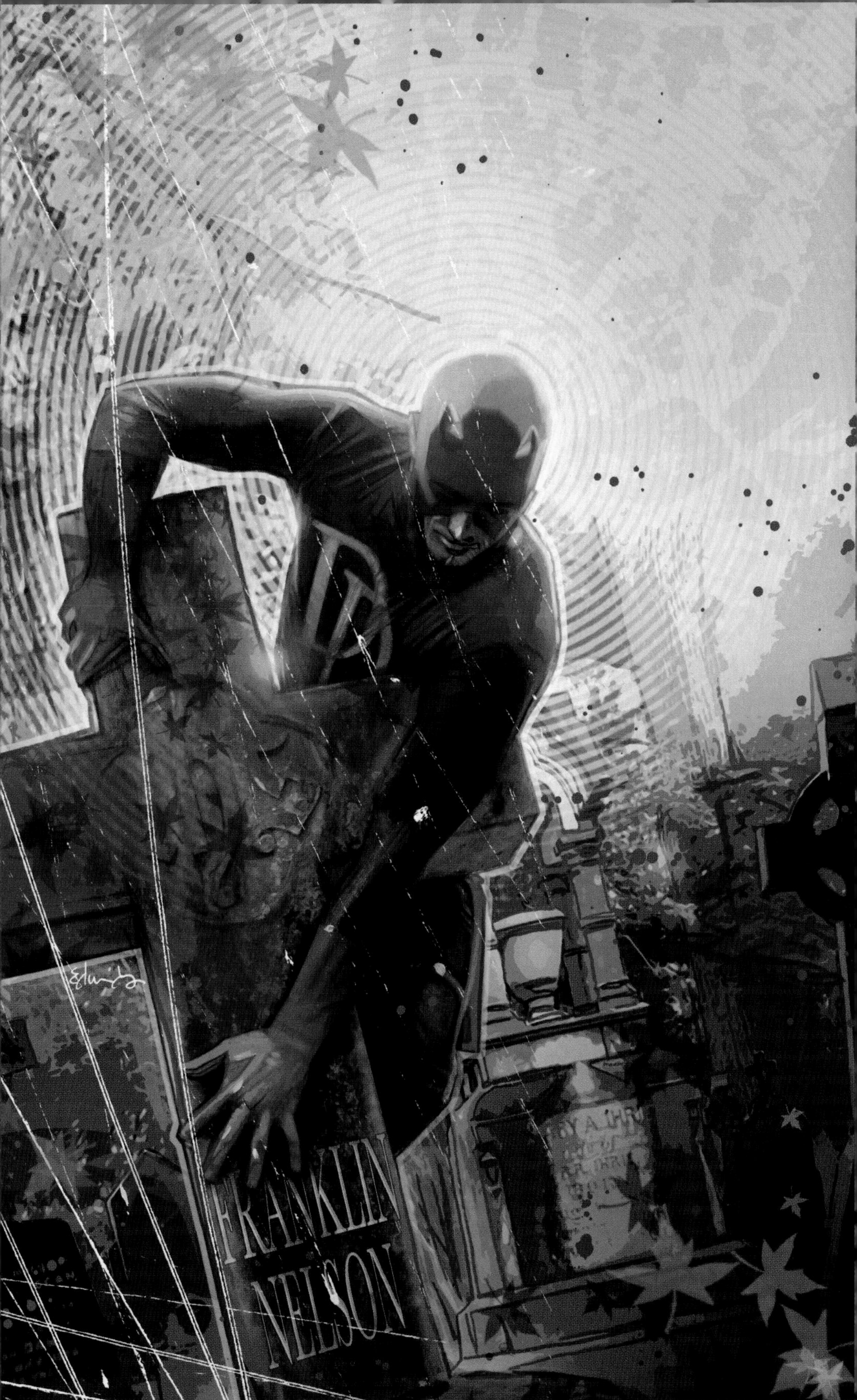
FRANKLIN
NELSON

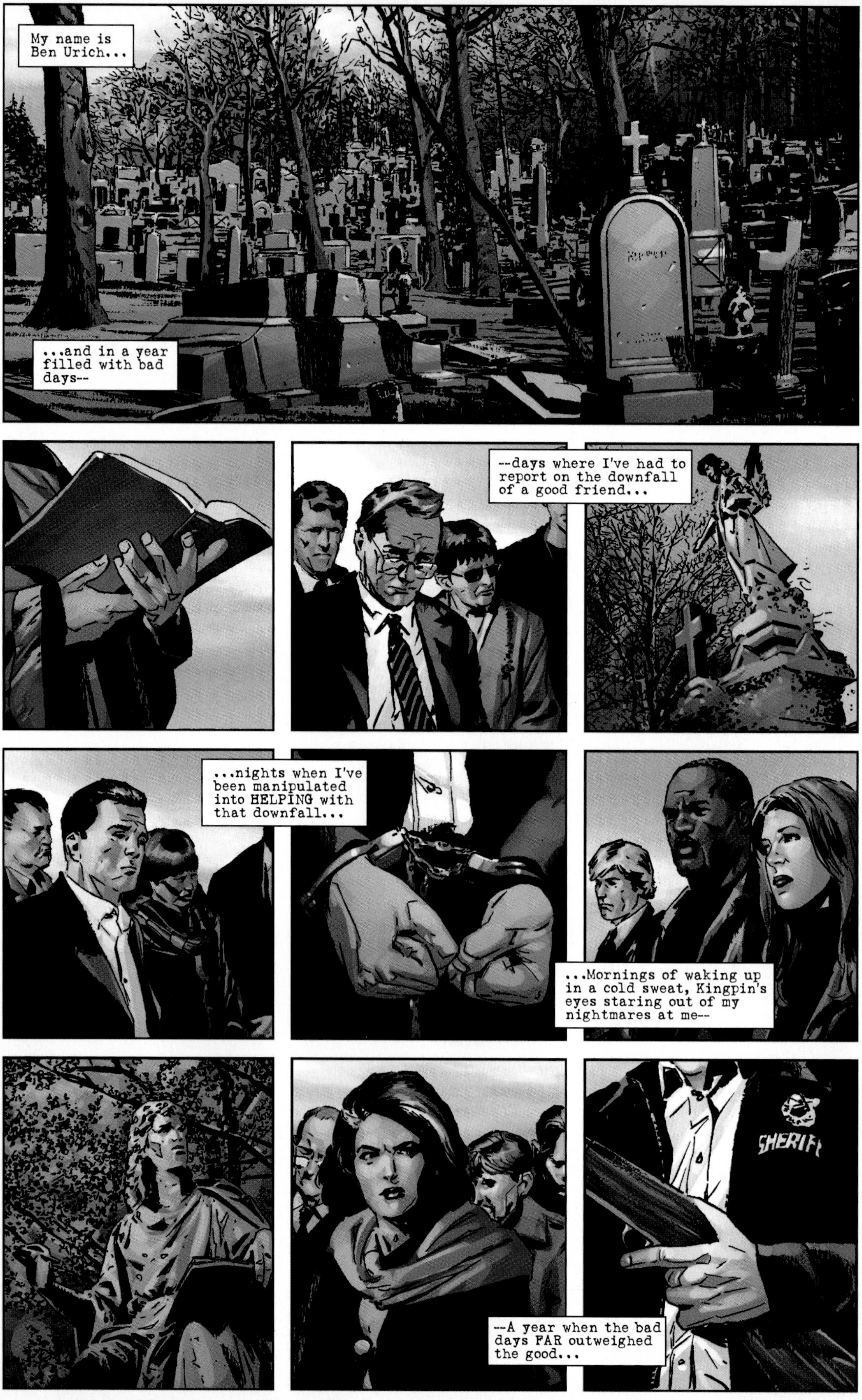
My name is Ben Urich...
...and in a year filled with bad days--
--days where I've had to report on the downfall of a good friend...
...nights when I've been manipulated into HELPING with that downfall...
...Mornings of waking up in a cold sweat, Kingpin's eyes staring out of my nightmares at me--
SHERIFF
--A year when the bad days FAR outweighed the good...

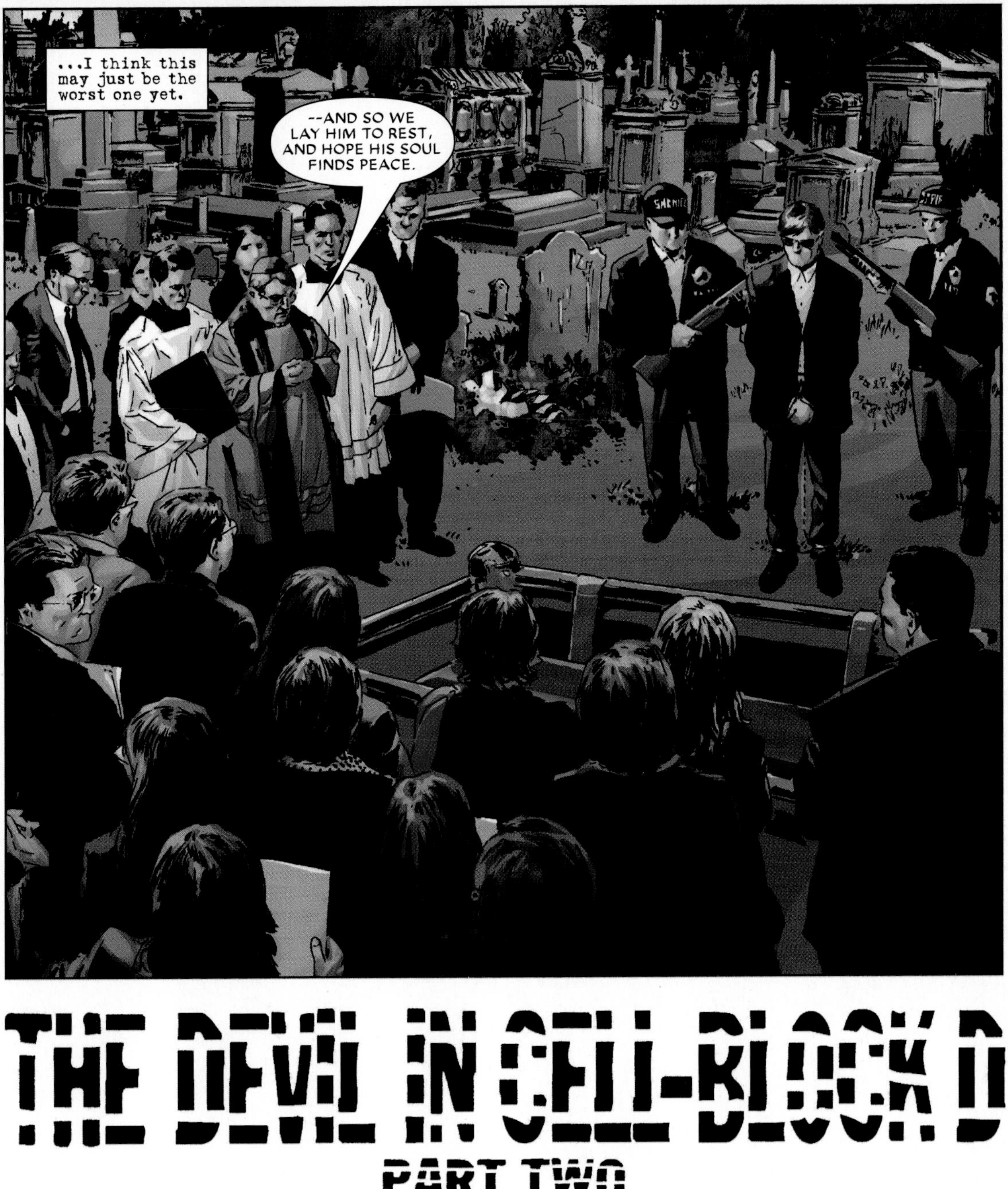
...I think this may just be the worst one yet.
--AND SO WE LAY HIM TO REST, AND HOPE HIS SOUL FINDS PEACE.

THE DEVIL IN CELL-BLOCK D
PART TWO

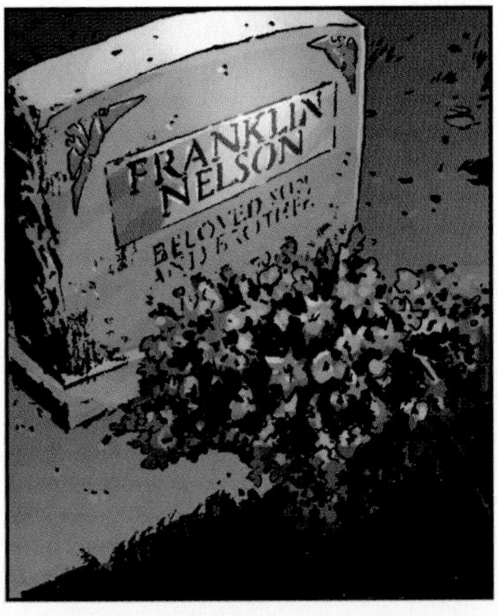
FRANKLIN NELSON

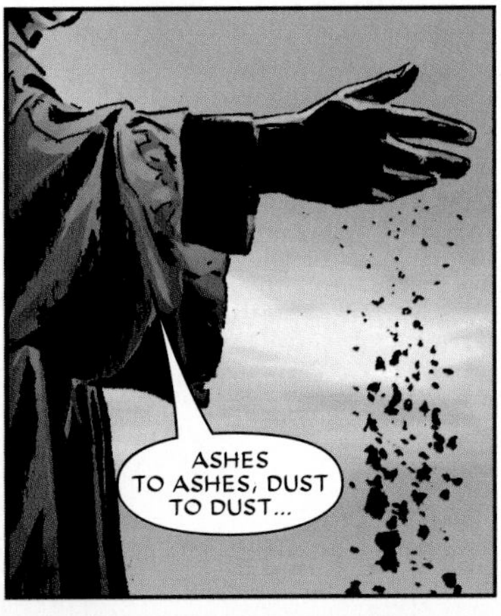
ASHES TO ASHES, DUST TO DUST...

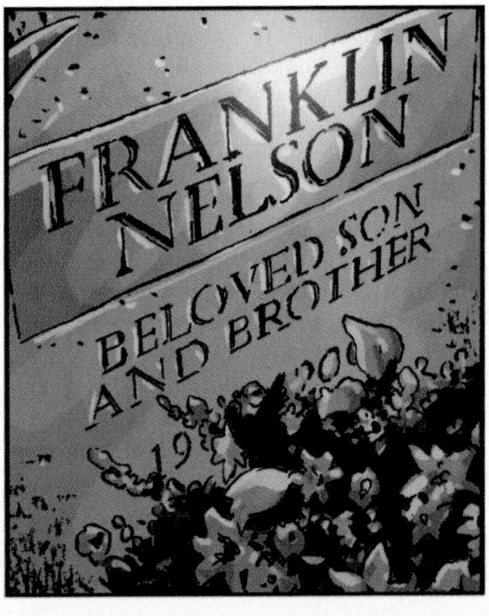
FRANKLIN NELSON
BELOVED SON AND BROTHER

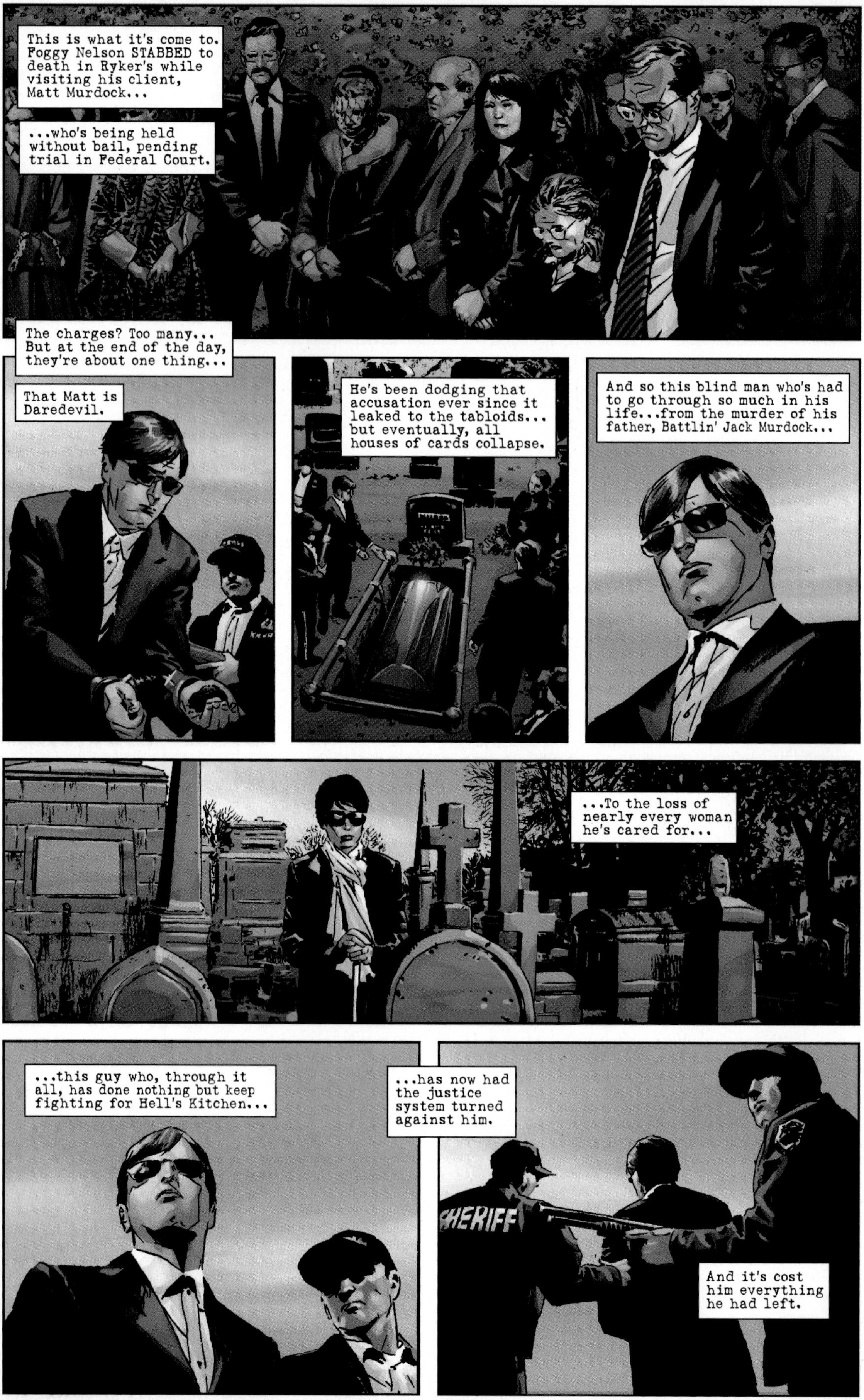
This is what it's come to. Foggy Nelson STABBED to death in Ryker's while visiting his client, Matt Murdock...
...who's being held without bail, pending trial in Federal Court.
The charges? Too many... But at the end of the day, they're about one thing...
That Matt is Daredevil.
He's been dodging that accusation ever since it leaked to the tabloids... but eventually, all houses of cards collapse.
And so this blind man who's had to go through so much in his life...from the murder of his father, Battlin' Jack Murdock...
...To the loss of nearly every woman he's cared for...
...this guy who, through it all, has done nothing but keep fighting for Hell's Kitchen...
...has now had the justice system turned against him.
SHERIFF
And it's cost him everything he had left.

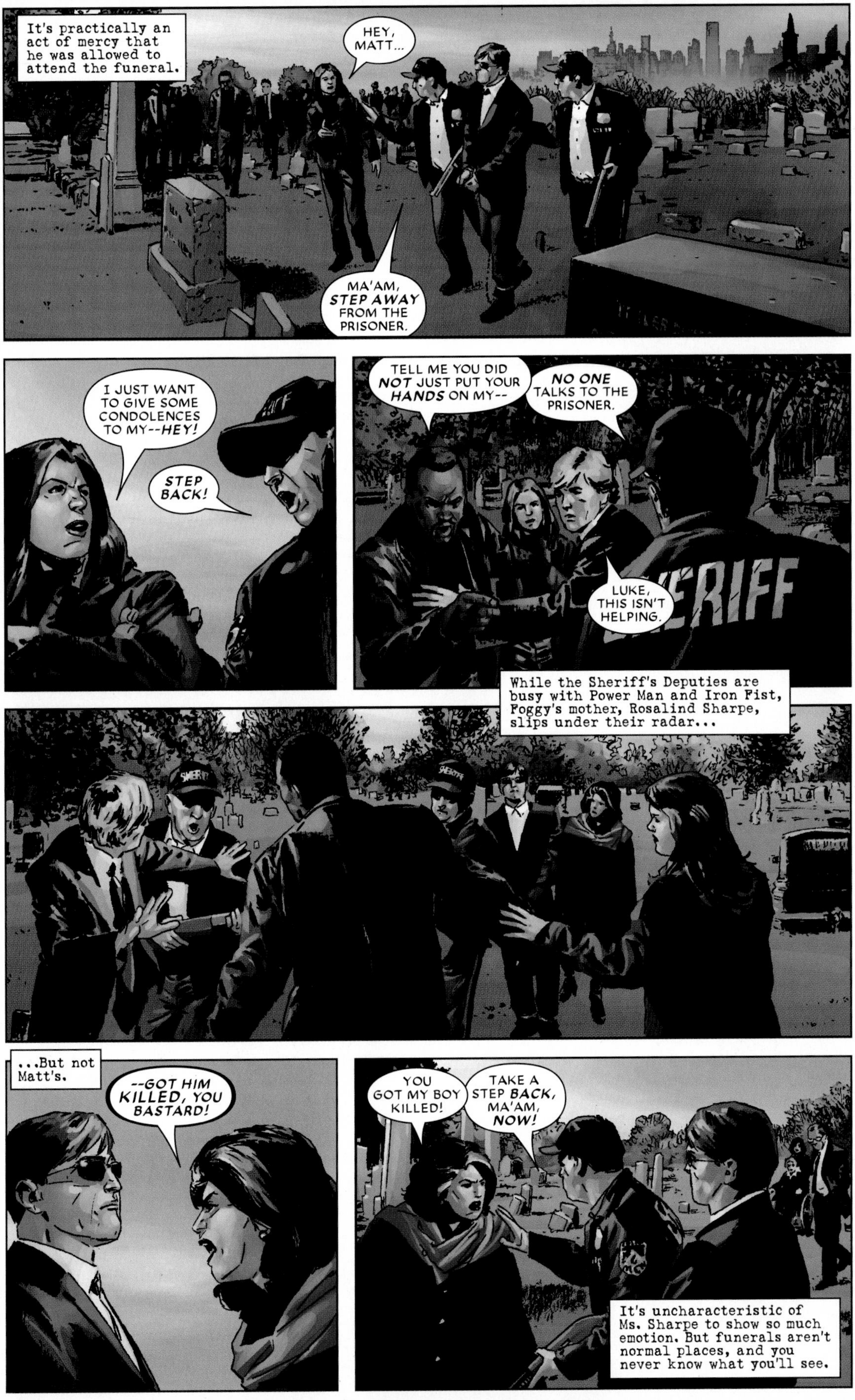
It's practically an act of mercy that he was allowed to attend the funeral.
HEY, MATT...
MA'AM, STEP AWAY FROM THE PRISONER.
I JUST WANT TO GIVE SOME CONDOLENCES TO MY--HEY!
STEP BACK!
TELL ME YOU DID NOT JUST PUT YOUR HANDS ON MY--
NO ONE TALKS TO THE PRISONER.
SHERIFF
LUKE, THIS ISN'T HELPING.
While the Sheriff's Deputies are busy with Power Man and Iron Fist, Foggy's mother, Rosalind Sharpe, slips under their radar...
...But not Matt's.
--GOT HIM KILLED, YOU BASTARD!
YOU GOT MY BOY KILLED!
TAKE A STEP BACK, MA'AM, NOW!
It's uncharacteristic of Ms. Sharpe to show so much emotion. But funerals aren't normal places, and you never know what you'll see.

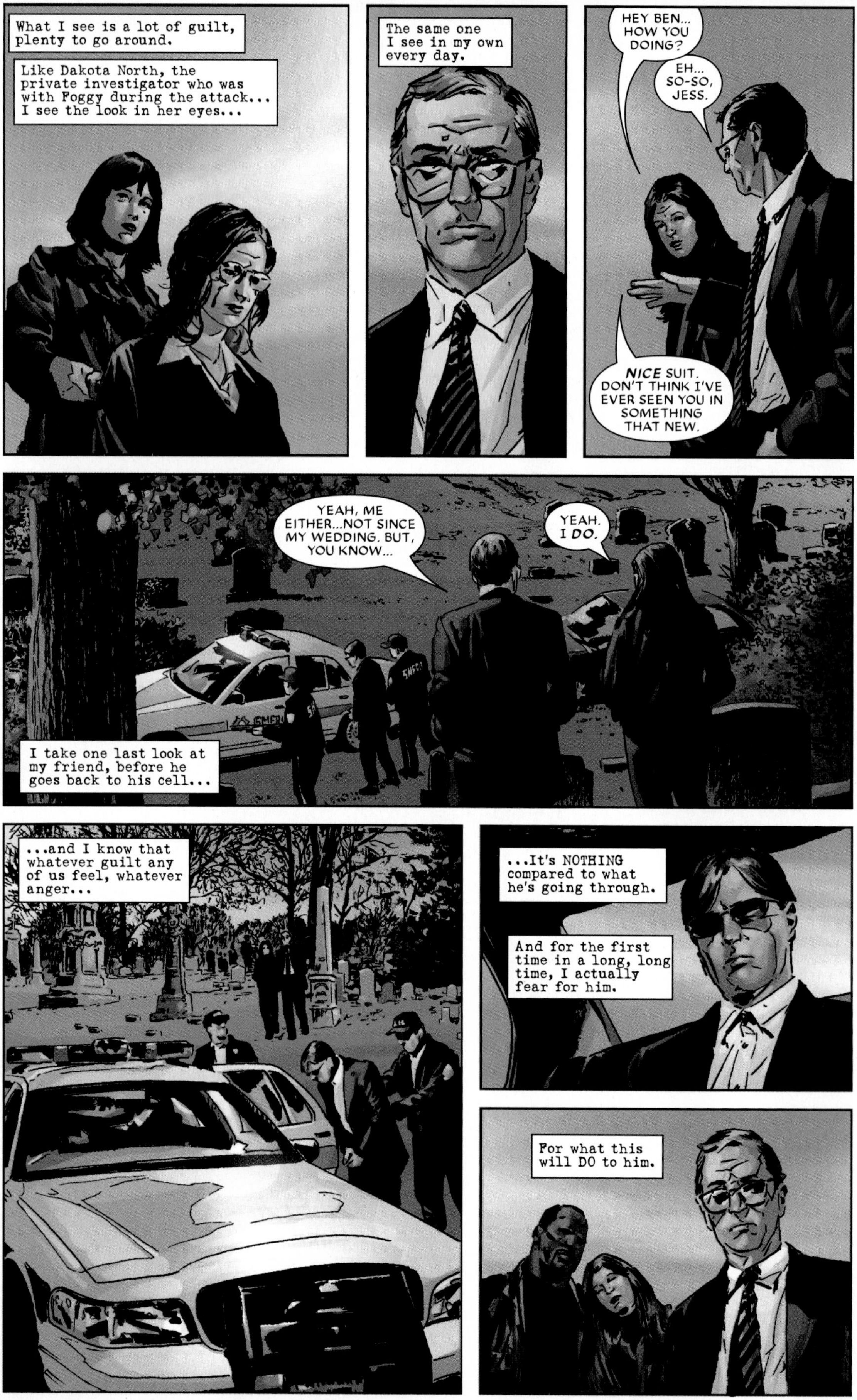

What I see is a lot of guilt, plenty to go around.
Like Dakota North, the private investigator who was with Foggy during the attack... I see the look in her eyes...
The same one I see in my own every day.
HEY BEN... HOW YOU DOING?
EH... SO-SO, JESS.
NICE SUIT. DON'T THINK I'VE EVER SEEN YOU IN SOMETHING THAT NEW.
YEAH, ME EITHER...NOT SINCE MY WEDDING. BUT, YOU KNOW...
YEAH. I DO.
I take one last look at my friend, before he goes back to his cell...
...and I know that whatever guilt any of us feel, whatever anger...
...It's NOTHING compared to what he's going through.
And for the first time in a long, long time, I actually fear for him.
For what this will DO to him.

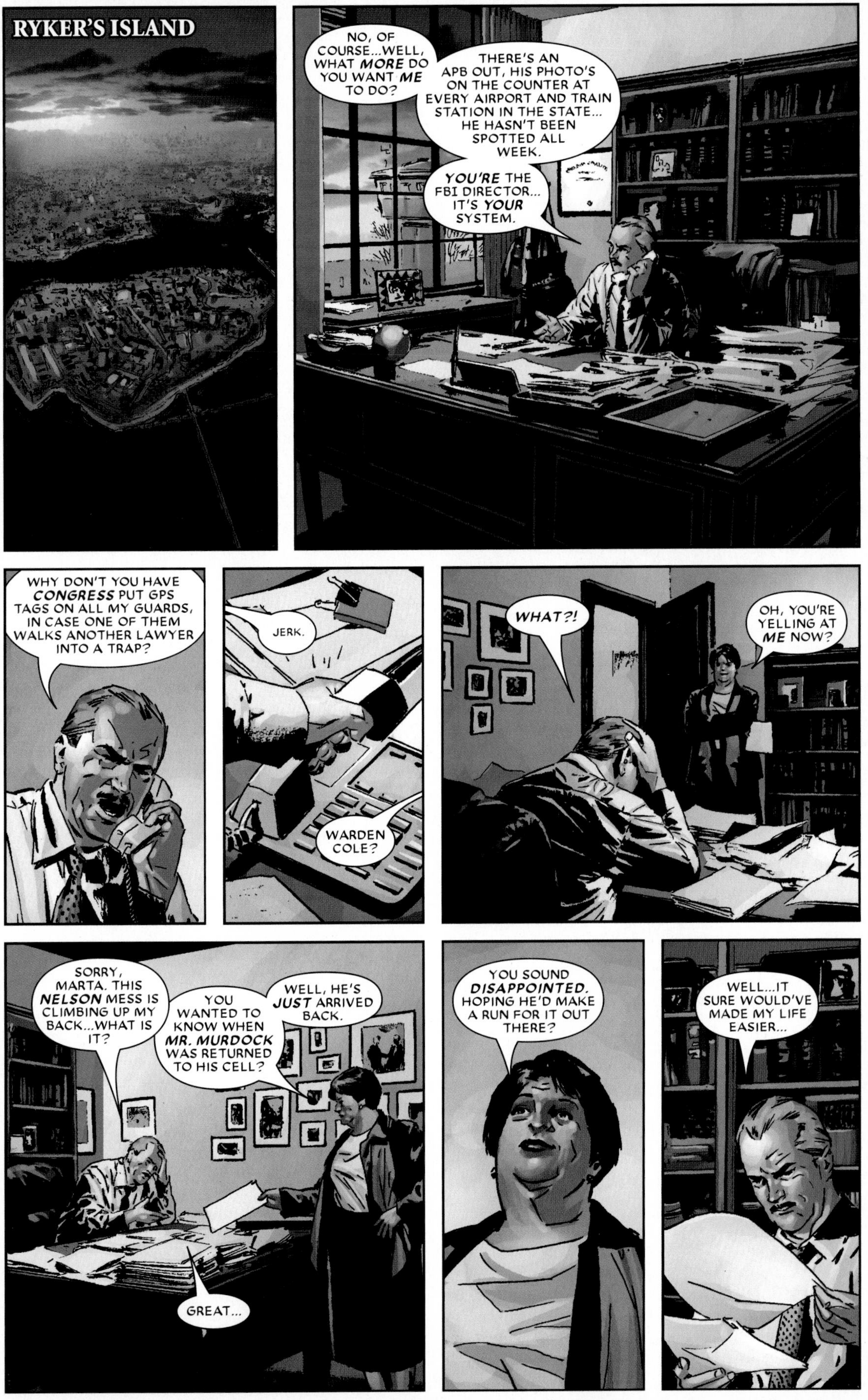
RYKER'S ISLAND
NO, OF COURSE...WELL, WHAT MORE DO YOU WANT ME TO DO?
THERE'S AN APB OUT, HIS PHOTO'S ON THE COUNTER AT EVERY AIRPORT AND TRAIN STATION IN THE STATE... HE HASN'T BEEN SPOTTED ALL WEEK.
YOU'RE THE FBI DIRECTOR... IT'S YOUR SYSTEM.
WHY DON'T YOU HAVE CONGRESS PUT GPS TAGS ON ALL MY GUARDS, IN CASE ONE OF THEM WALKS ANOTHER LAWYER INTO A TRAP?
JERK.
WARDEN COLE?
WHAT?!
OH, YOU'RE YELLING AT ME NOW?
SORRY, MARTA. THIS NELSON MESS IS CLIMBING UP MY BACK...WHAT IS IT?
YOU WANTED TO KNOW WHEN MR. MURDOCK WAS RETURNED TO HIS CELL?
WELL, HE'S JUST ARRIVED BACK.
GREAT...
YOU SOUND DISAPPOINTED. HOPING HE'D MAKE A RUN FOR IT OUT THERE?
WELL...IT SURE WOULD'VE MADE MY LIFE EASIER...

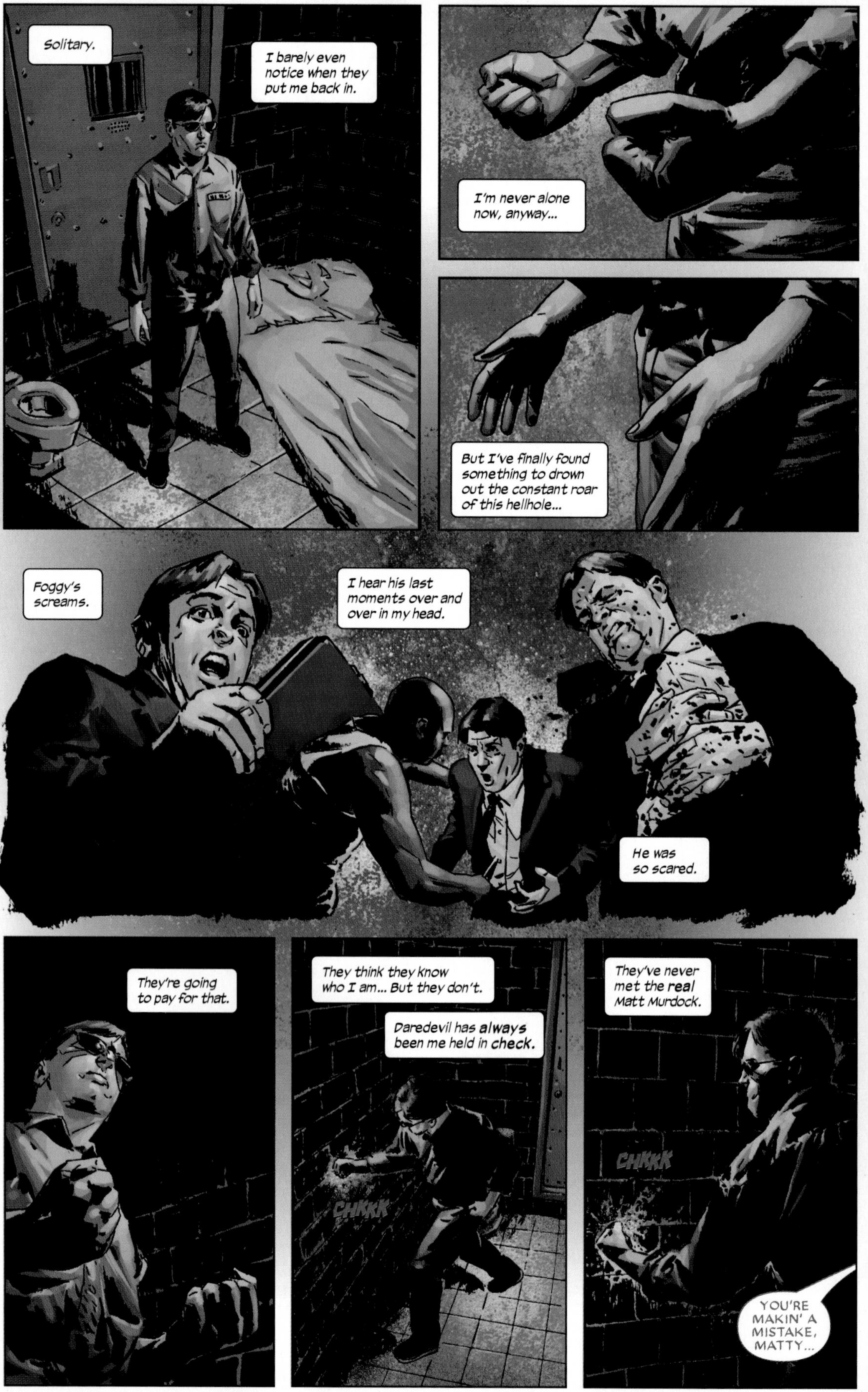
Solitary.
I barely even notice when they put me back in.
I'm never alone now, anyway...
But I've finally found something to drown out the constant roar of this hellhole...
Foggy's screams.
I hear his last moments over and over in my head.
He was so scared.
They're going to pay for that.
They think they know who I am... But they don't.
Daredevil has always been me held in check.
CHKKK
They've never met the real Matt Murdock.
CHKKK
YOU'RE MAKIN' A MISTAKE, MATTY...

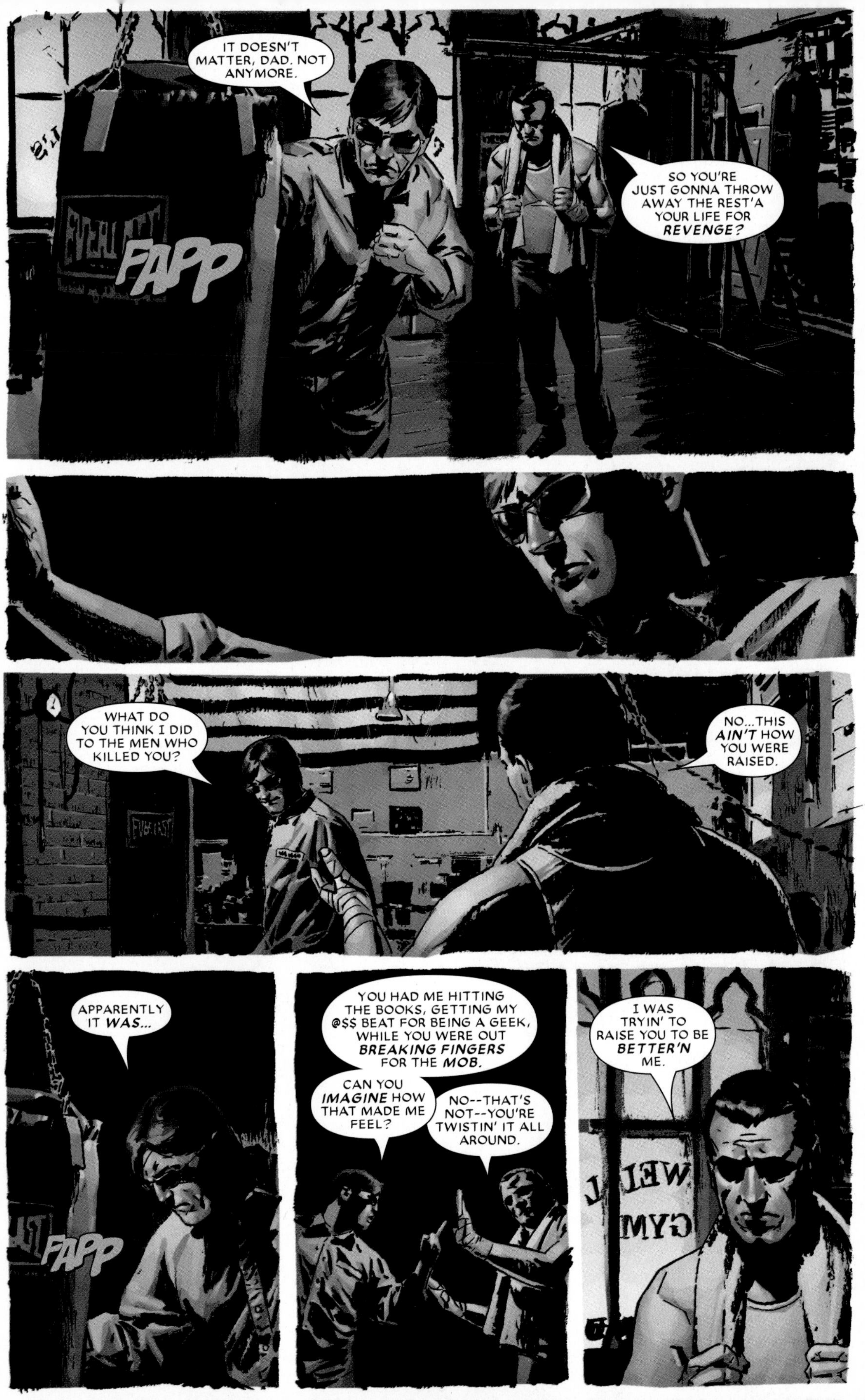
IT DOESN'T MATTER, DAD. NOT ANYMORE.
FAPP
SO YOU'RE JUST GONNA THROW AWAY THE REST'A YOUR LIFE FOR REVENGE?
WHAT DO YOU THINK I DID TO THE MEN WHO KILLED YOU?
NO...THIS AIN'T HOW YOU WERE RAISED.
APPARENTLY IT WAS...
FAPP
YOU HAD ME HITTING THE BOOKS, GETTING MY @$$ BEAT FOR BEING A GEEK, WHILE YOU WERE OUT BREAKING FINGERS FOR THE MOB.
CAN YOU IMAGINE HOW THAT MADE ME FEEL?
NO--THAT'S NOT--YOU'RE TWISTIN' IT ALL AROUND.
I WAS TRYIN' TO RAISE YOU TO BE BETTER'N ME.
WEL
GYM

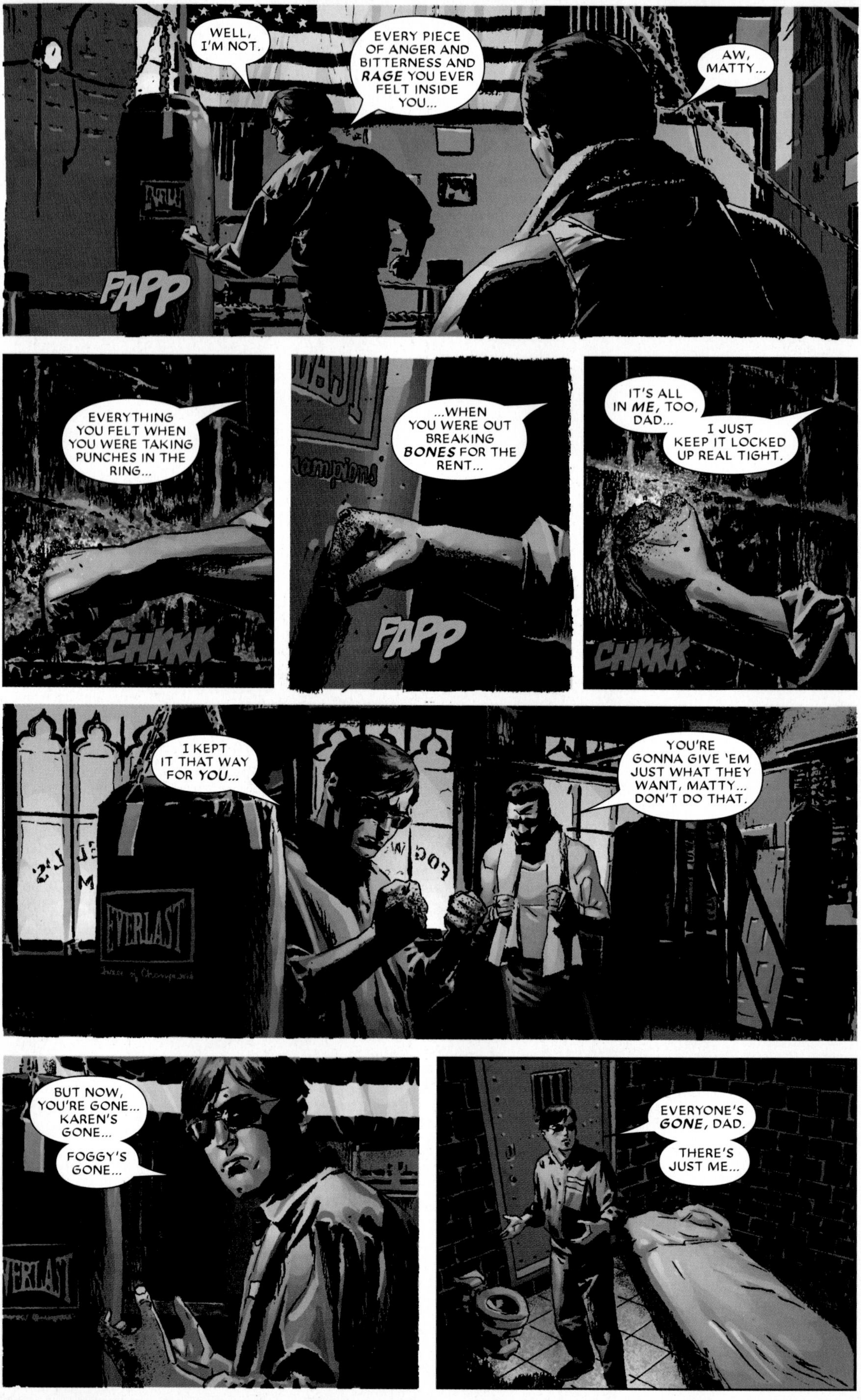
WELL, I'M NOT.
EVERY PIECE OF ANGER AND BITTERNESS AND RAGE YOU EVER FELT INSIDE YOU...
AW, MATTY...
FAPP
EVERYTHING YOU FELT WHEN YOU WERE TAKING PUNCHES IN THE RING...
CHKKK
...WHEN YOU WERE OUT BREAKING BONES FOR THE RENT...
FAPP
IT'S ALL IN ME, TOO, DAD...
I JUST KEEP IT LOCKED UP REAL TIGHT.
CHKKK
I KEPT IT THAT WAY FOR YOU...
YOU'RE GONNA GIVE 'EM JUST WHAT THEY WANT, MATTY... DON'T DO THAT.
EVERLAST
BUT NOW, YOU'RE GONE... KAREN'S GONE...
FOGGY'S GONE...
EVERYONE'S GONE, DAD.
THERE'S JUST ME...

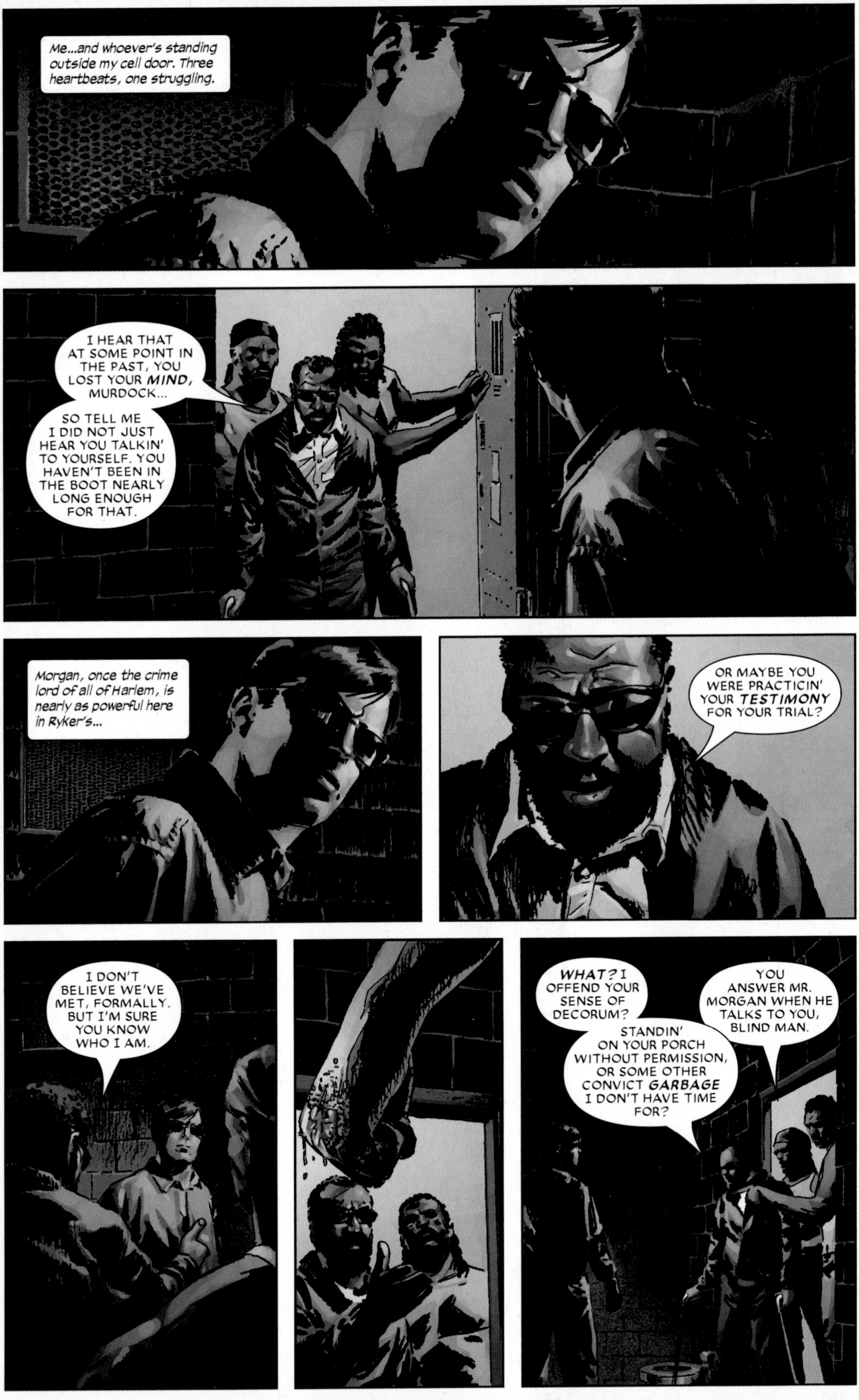
Me...and whoever's standing outside my cell door. Three heartbeats, one struggling.
I HEAR THAT AT SOME POINT IN THE PAST, YOU LOST YOUR MIND, MURDOCK...
SO TELL ME I DID NOT JUST HEAR YOU TALKIN' TO YOURSELF. YOU HAVEN'T BEEN IN THE BOOT NEARLY LONG ENOUGH FOR THAT.
Morgan, once the crime lord of all of Harlem, is nearly as powerful here in Ryker's...
OR MAYBE YOU WERE PRACTICIN' YOUR TESTIMONY FOR YOUR TRIAL?
I DON'T BELIEVE WE'VE MET, FORMALLY. BUT I'M SURE YOU KNOW WHO I AM.
WHAT? I OFFEND YOUR SENSE OF DECORUM?
STANDIN' ON YOUR PORCH WITHOUT PERMISSION, OR SOME OTHER CONVICT GARBAGE I DON'T HAVE TIME FOR?
YOU ANSWER MR. MORGAN WHEN HE TALKS TO YOU, BLIND MAN.

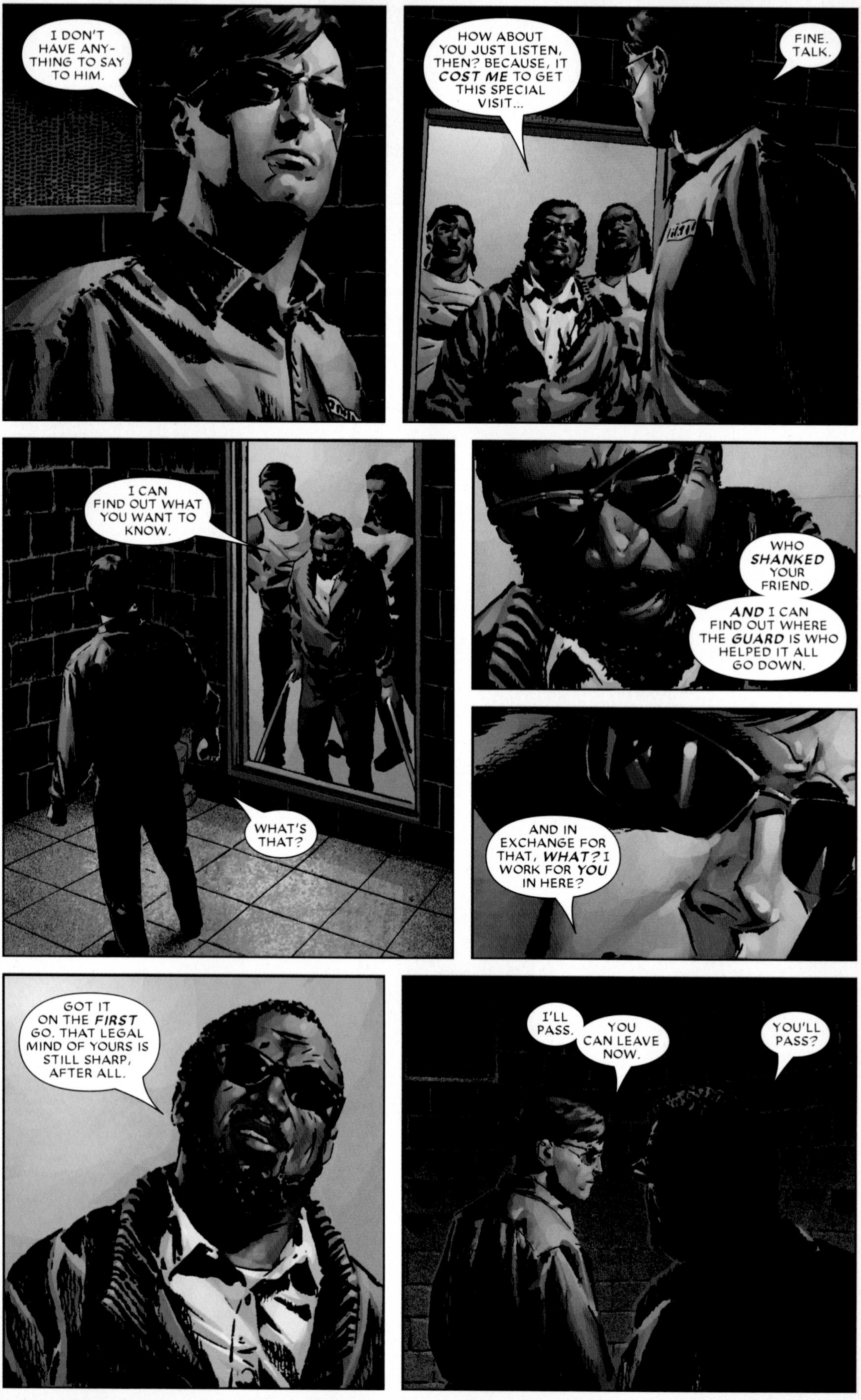
I DON'T HAVE ANY-THING TO SAY TO HIM.
HOW ABOUT YOU JUST LISTEN, THEN? BECAUSE, IT COST ME TO GET THIS SPECIAL VISIT...
FINE. TALK.
I CAN FIND OUT WHAT YOU WANT TO KNOW.
WHAT'S THAT?
WHO SHANKED YOUR FRIEND.
AND I CAN FIND OUT WHERE THE GUARD IS WHO HELPED IT ALL GO DOWN.
AND IN EXCHANGE FOR THAT, WHAT? I WORK FOR YOU IN HERE?
GOT IT ON THE FIRST GO. THAT LEGAL MIND OF YOURS IS STILL SHARP, AFTER ALL.
I'LL PASS.
YOU CAN LEAVE NOW.
YOU'LL PASS?

I DON'T THINK YOU'RE UNDERSTANDIN' ME, MURDOCK... I'M OFFERING YOU A *FAVOR.*

AND YOU *DON'T* WANT TO DISRESPECT THAT. NOT IN *HERE.*

CALL IT WHAT YOU LIKE, MORGAN...BUT I DON'T WANT YOUR HELP.

I'LL GET THE ANSWERS I WANT MY OWN WAY.

YOU... YOU'RE LIVIN' IN A FANTASY WORLD, MAN... HALF A MIND TO LET MY BOYS SHOW YOU THAT.

MY BEST FRIEND WAS *BURIED* TODAY.

IF YOU *REALLY* WANT TO SEND YOUR MEN INTO THIS CELL, KNOWING THAT...

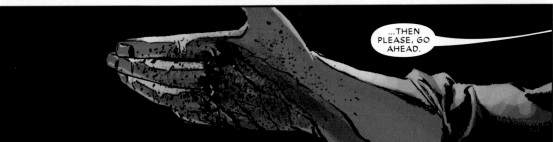

...THEN PLEASE, GO AHEAD.

ANOTHER TIME, MURDOCK... FOR SURE.

YOU HEARIN' ALL THIS, FISK?

LOOKS LIKE YOUR PAL MURDOCK'S GONNA GIVE THE PEOPLE SOMETHING TO WARM UP WITH...

...WHILE WE ALL WAIT FOR *YOUR* FAT @$$ TO GET BACK TO GEN-POP.

My name is Ben Urich and my boss is a complete jackass.

WHAT DID YOU JUST SAY?

GO COVER IT *YOURSELF*, JONAH.

WELL, I *WOULD* COVER IT MYSELF, URICH...

...IF I WASN'T THE ONE WHO SIGNED THE DAMN *PAYCHECKS* AROUND HERE!

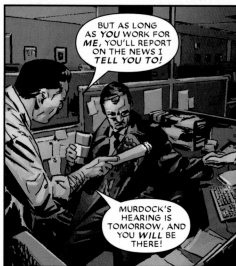

BUT AS LONG AS *YOU* WORK FOR *ME*, YOU'LL REPORT ON THE NEWS I *TELL YOU TO*!

MURDOCK'S HEARING IS TOMORROW, AND YOU *WILL* BE THERE!

JUST SEND KAT OR SOMEBODY... *PLEASE*, JONAH.

I CAN'T DO THIS ANYMORE... HE'S MY *FRIEND*... AND I CAN'T JUST-- I CAN'T BE *PART* OF THIS...

URICH, I'M GONNA SAY THIS *ONE TIME*...AND THEN I WILL *DENY* I EVER SAID IT.

YOU ARE A *GREAT* REPORTER... MAYBE THE BEST I'VE *EVER* KNOWN.

BUT YOU NEED TO PULL YOURSELF TOGETHER, FIND YOUR *OBJECTIVITY*...

...AND GO DO YOUR %@#-ING *JOB*!

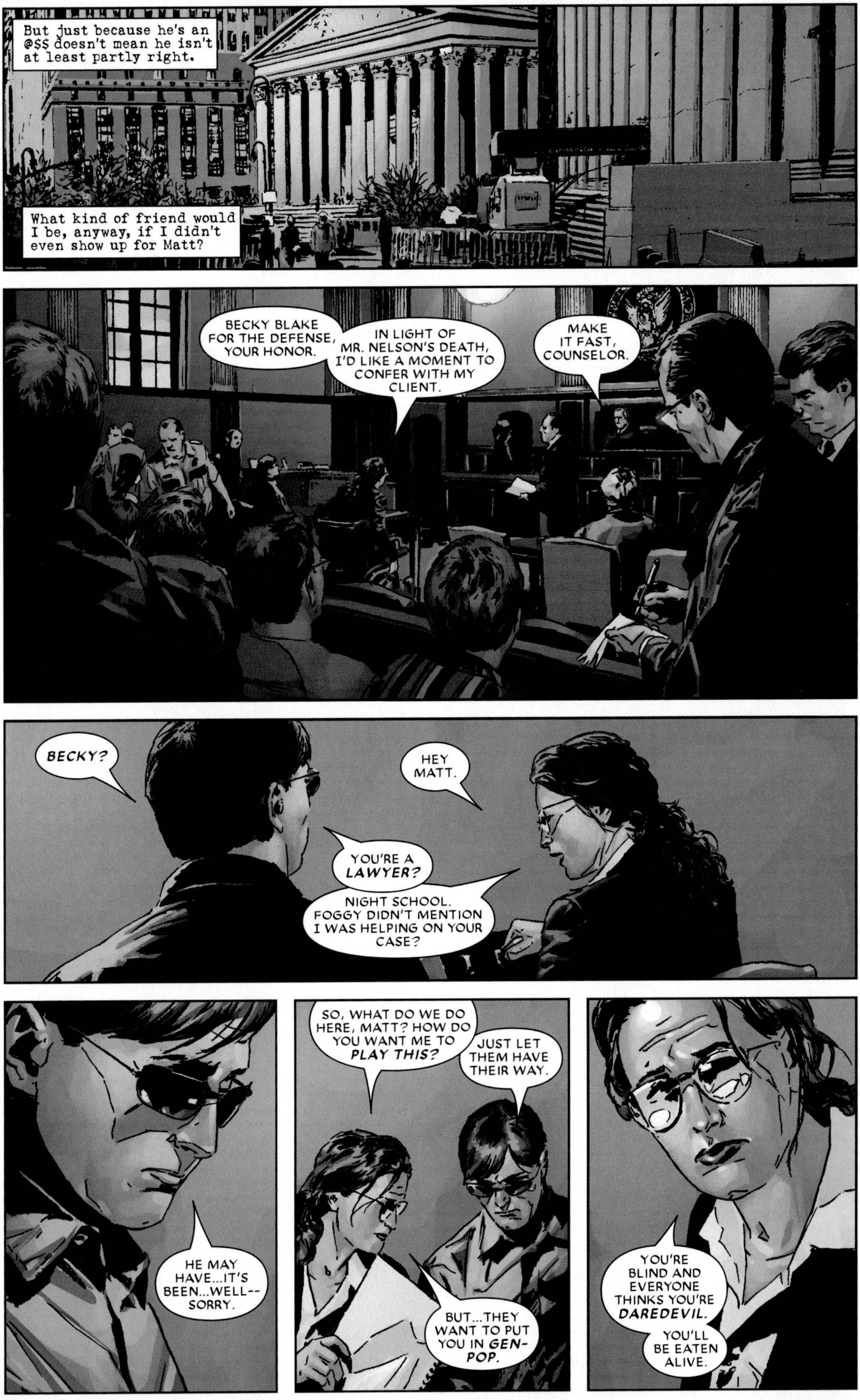
But just because he's an @$$ doesn't mean he isn't at least partly right.
What kind of friend would I be, anyway, if I didn't even show up for Matt?
BECKY BLAKE FOR THE DEFENSE, YOUR HONOR.
IN LIGHT OF MR. NELSON'S DEATH, I'D LIKE A MOMENT TO CONFER WITH MY CLIENT.
MAKE IT FAST, COUNSELOR.
BECKY?
HEY MATT.
YOU'RE A LAWYER?
NIGHT SCHOOL. FOGGY DIDN'T MENTION I WAS HELPING ON YOUR CASE?
HE MAY HAVE...IT'S BEEN...WELL--SORRY.
SO, WHAT DO WE DO HERE, MATT? HOW DO YOU WANT ME TO PLAY THIS?
JUST LET THEM HAVE THEIR WAY.
BUT...THEY WANT TO PUT YOU IN GEN-POP.
YOU'RE BLIND AND EVERYONE THINKS YOU'RE DAREDEVIL.
YOU'LL BE EATEN ALIVE.

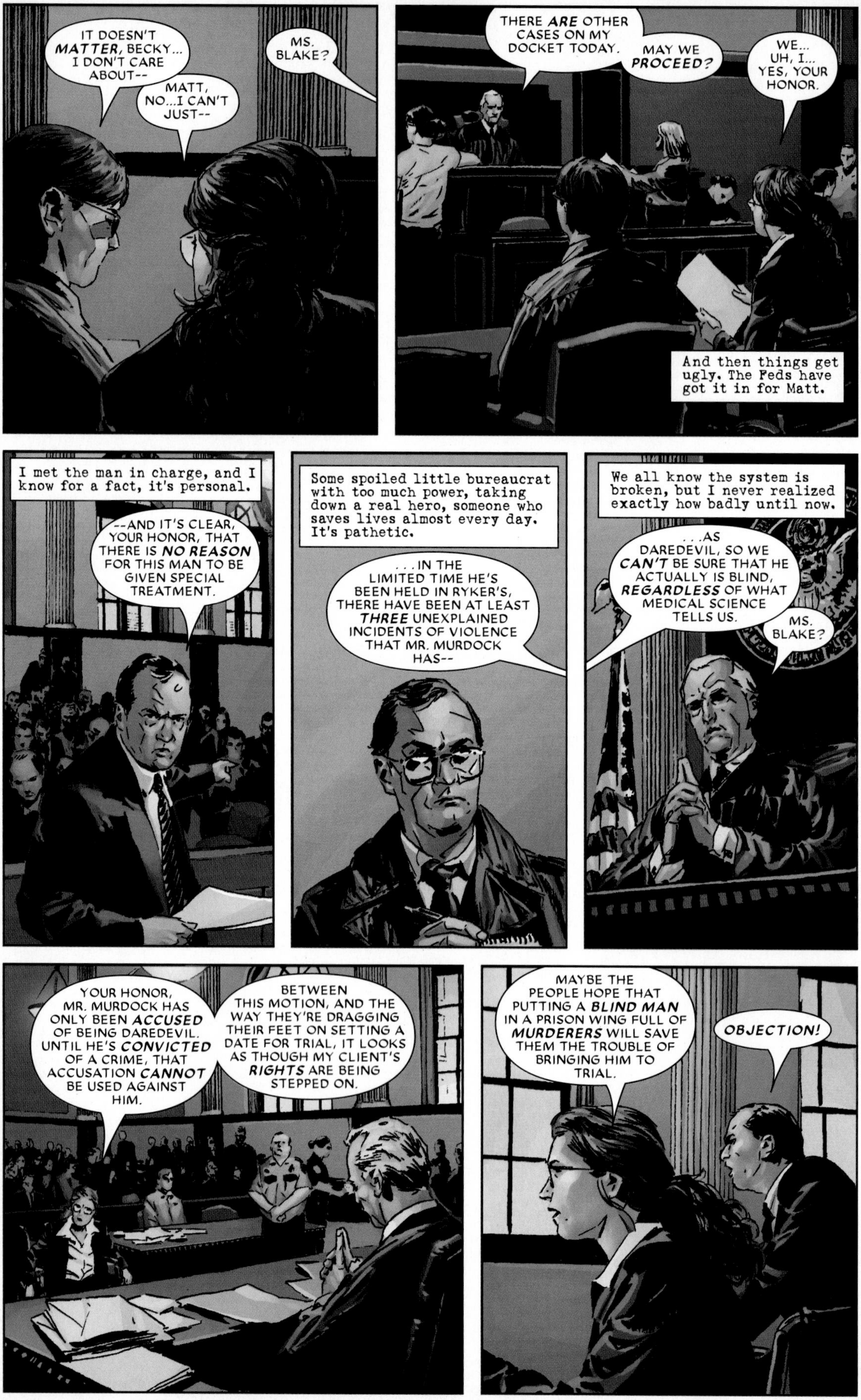
IT DOESN'T MATTER, BECKY... I DON'T CARE ABOUT--
MATT, NO...I CAN'T JUST--
MS. BLAKE?
THERE ARE OTHER CASES ON MY DOCKET TODAY.
MAY WE PROCEED?
WE... UH, I... YES, YOUR HONOR.
And then things get ugly. The Feds have got it in for Matt.
I met the man in charge, and I know for a fact, it's personal.
--AND IT'S CLEAR, YOUR HONOR, THAT THERE IS NO REASON FOR THIS MAN TO BE GIVEN SPECIAL TREATMENT.
Some spoiled little bureaucrat with too much power, taking down a real hero, someone who saves lives almost every day. It's pathetic.
. . .IN THE LIMITED TIME HE'S BEEN HELD IN RYKER'S, THERE HAVE BEEN AT LEAST THREE UNEXPLAINED INCIDENTS OF VIOLENCE THAT MR. MURDOCK HAS--
We all know the system is broken, but I never realized exactly how badly until now.
. . .AS DAREDEVIL, SO WE CAN'T BE SURE THAT HE ACTUALLY IS BLIND, REGARDLESS OF WHAT MEDICAL SCIENCE TELLS US.
MS. BLAKE?
YOUR HONOR, MR. MURDOCK HAS ONLY BEEN ACCUSED OF BEING DAREDEVIL. UNTIL HE'S CONVICTED OF A CRIME, THAT ACCUSATION CANNOT BE USED AGAINST HIM.
BETWEEN THIS MOTION, AND THE WAY THEY'RE DRAGGING THEIR FEET ON SETTING A DATE FOR TRIAL, IT LOOKS AS THOUGH MY CLIENT'S RIGHTS ARE BEING STEPPED ON.
MAYBE THE PEOPLE HOPE THAT PUTTING A BLIND MAN IN A PRISON WING FULL OF MURDERERS WILL SAVE THEM THE TROUBLE OF BRINGING HIM TO TRIAL.
OBJECTION!

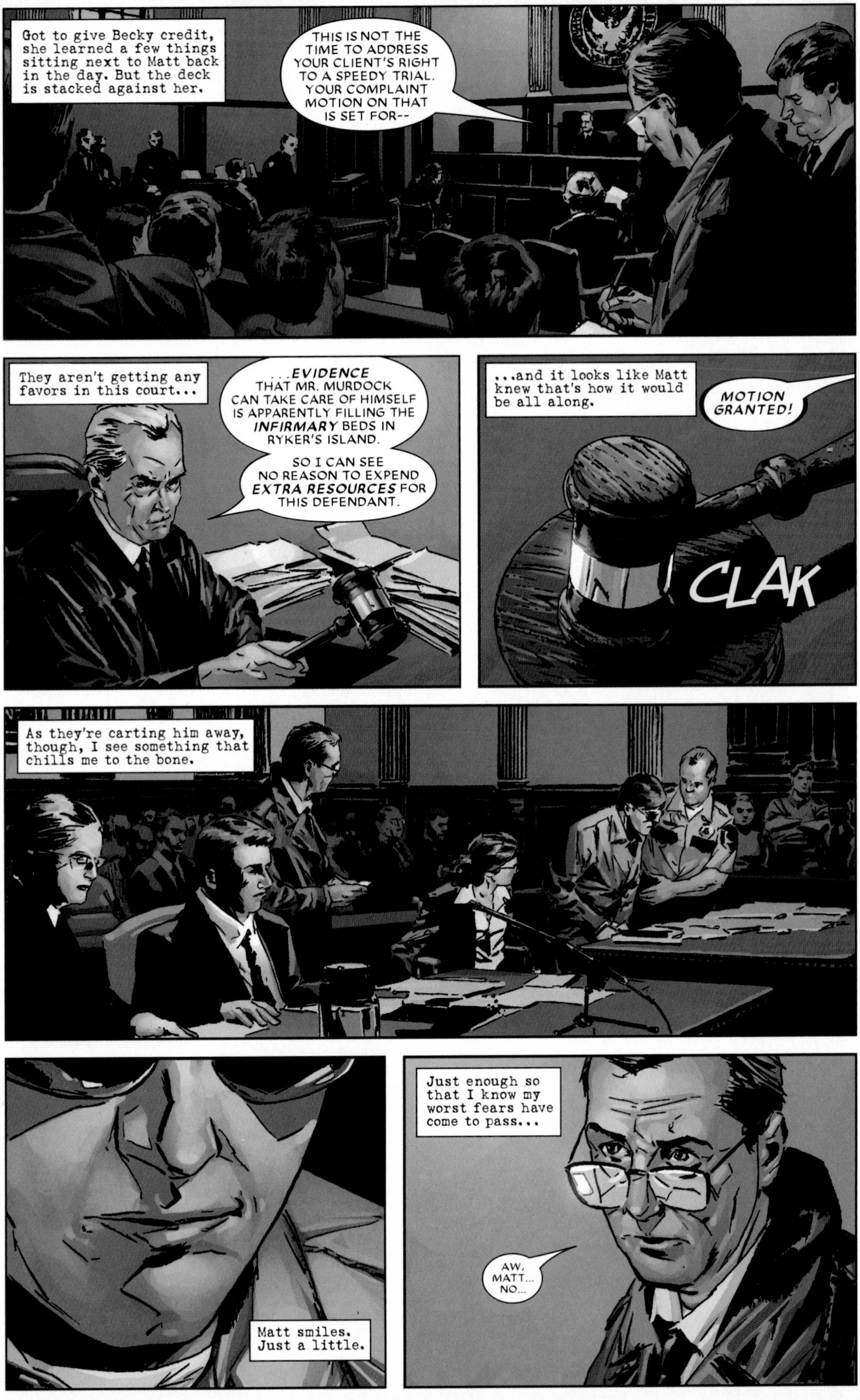

Got to give Becky credit, she learned a few things sitting next to Matt back in the day. But the deck is stacked against her.
THIS IS NOT THE TIME TO ADDRESS YOUR CLIENT'S RIGHT TO A SPEEDY TRIAL. YOUR COMPLAINT MOTION ON THAT IS SET FOR--
They aren't getting any favors in this court...
...EVIDENCE THAT MR. MURDOCK CAN TAKE CARE OF HIMSELF IS APPARENTLY FILLING THE INFIRMARY BEDS IN RYKER'S ISLAND.
SO I CAN SEE NO REASON TO EXPEND EXTRA RESOURCES FOR THIS DEFENDANT.
...and it looks like Matt knew that's how it would be all along.
MOTION GRANTED!
CLAK
As they're carting him away, though, I see something that chills me to the bone.
Matt smiles. Just a little.
Just enough so that I know my worst fears have come to pass...
AW, MATT... NO...

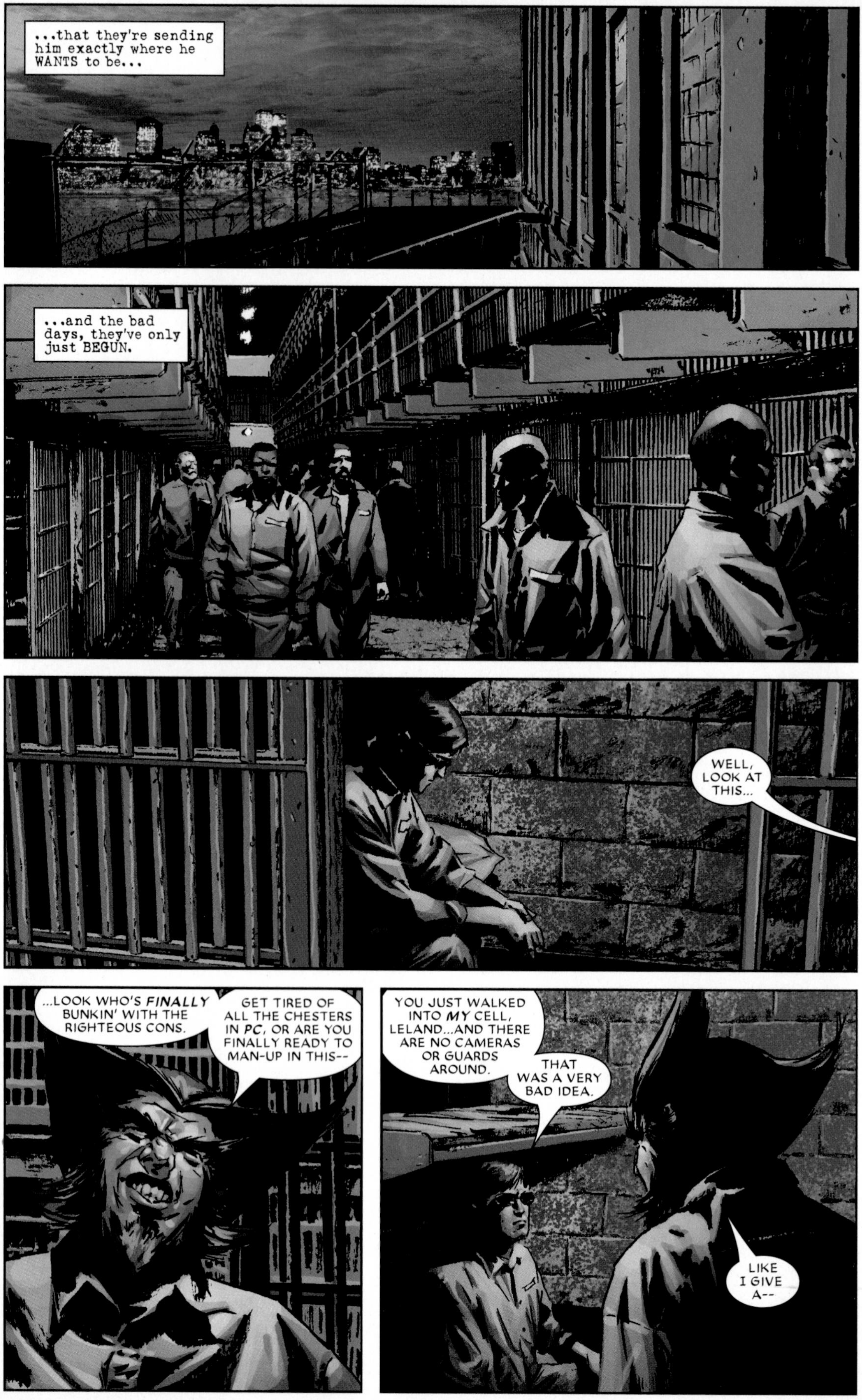
...that they're sending him exactly where he WANTS to be...
...and the bad days, they've only just BEGUN.
WELL, LOOK AT THIS...
...LOOK WHO'S FINALLY BUNKIN' WITH THE RIGHTEOUS CONS.
GET TIRED OF ALL THE CHESTERS IN PC, OR ARE YOU FINALLY READY TO MAN-UP IN THIS--
YOU JUST WALKED INTO MY CELL, LELAND...AND THERE ARE NO CAMERAS OR GUARDS AROUND.
THAT WAS A VERY BAD IDEA.
LIKE I GIVE A--

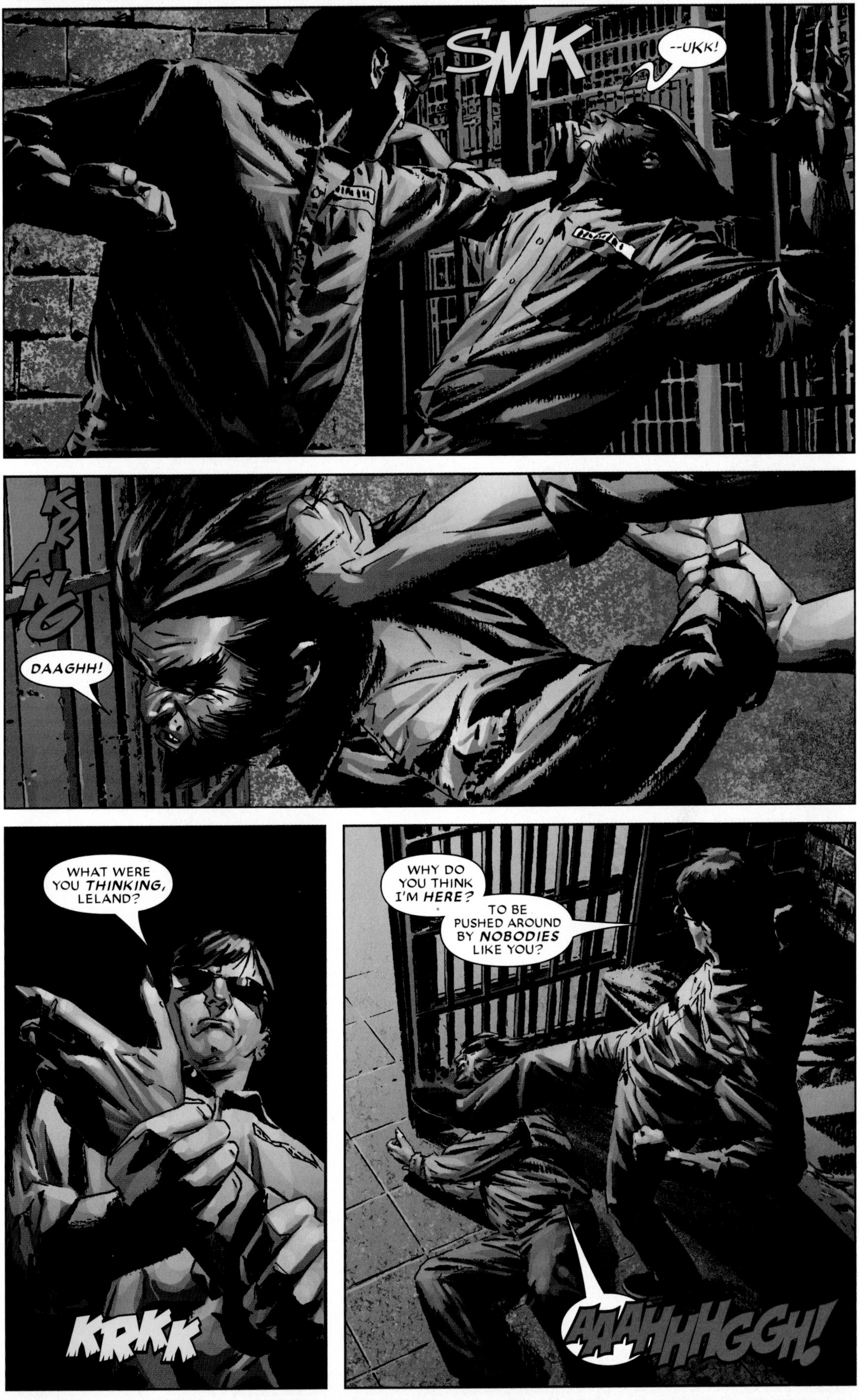
SMK
--UKK!
KRANG
DAAGHH!
WHAT WERE YOU *THINKING*, LELAND?
KRKK
WHY DO YOU THINK I'M *HERE*?
TO BE PUSHED AROUND BY *NOBODIES* LIKE YOU?
AAAHHHGGH!

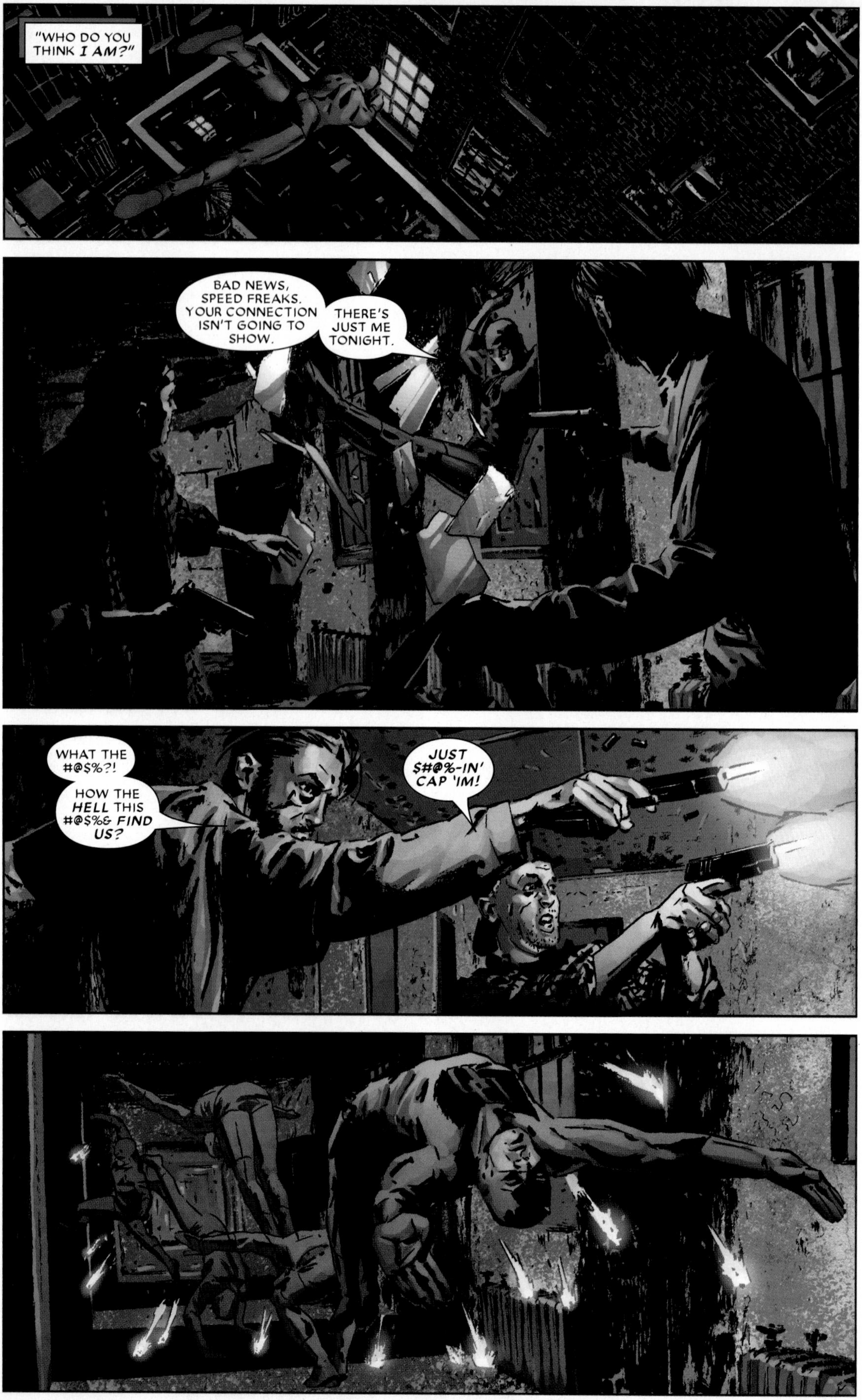
"WHO DO YOU THINK I AM?"
BAD NEWS, SPEED FREAKS. YOUR CONNECTION ISN'T GOING TO SHOW.
THERE'S JUST ME TONIGHT.
WHAT THE #@$%?!
HOW THE HELL THIS #@$%& FIND US?
JUST $#@%-IN' CAP 'IM!

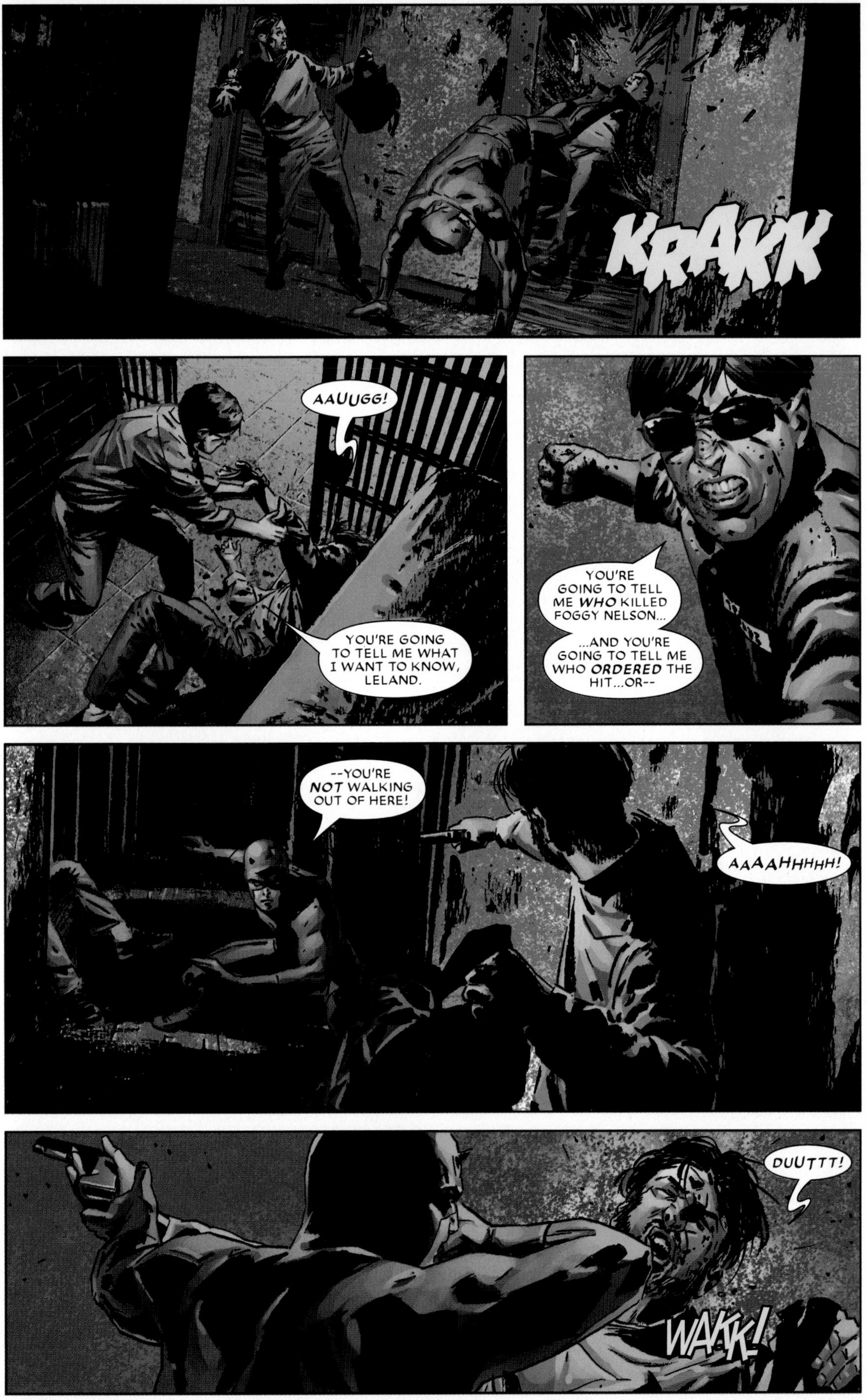
KRAKK
AAUUGG!
YOU'RE GOING TO TELL ME WHAT I WANT TO KNOW, LELAND.
YOU'RE GOING TO TELL ME WHO KILLED FOGGY NELSON...
...AND YOU'RE GOING TO TELL ME WHO ORDERED THE HIT...OR--
--YOU'RE NOT WALKING OUT OF HERE!
AAAAHHHHH!
DUUTTT!
WAKK!

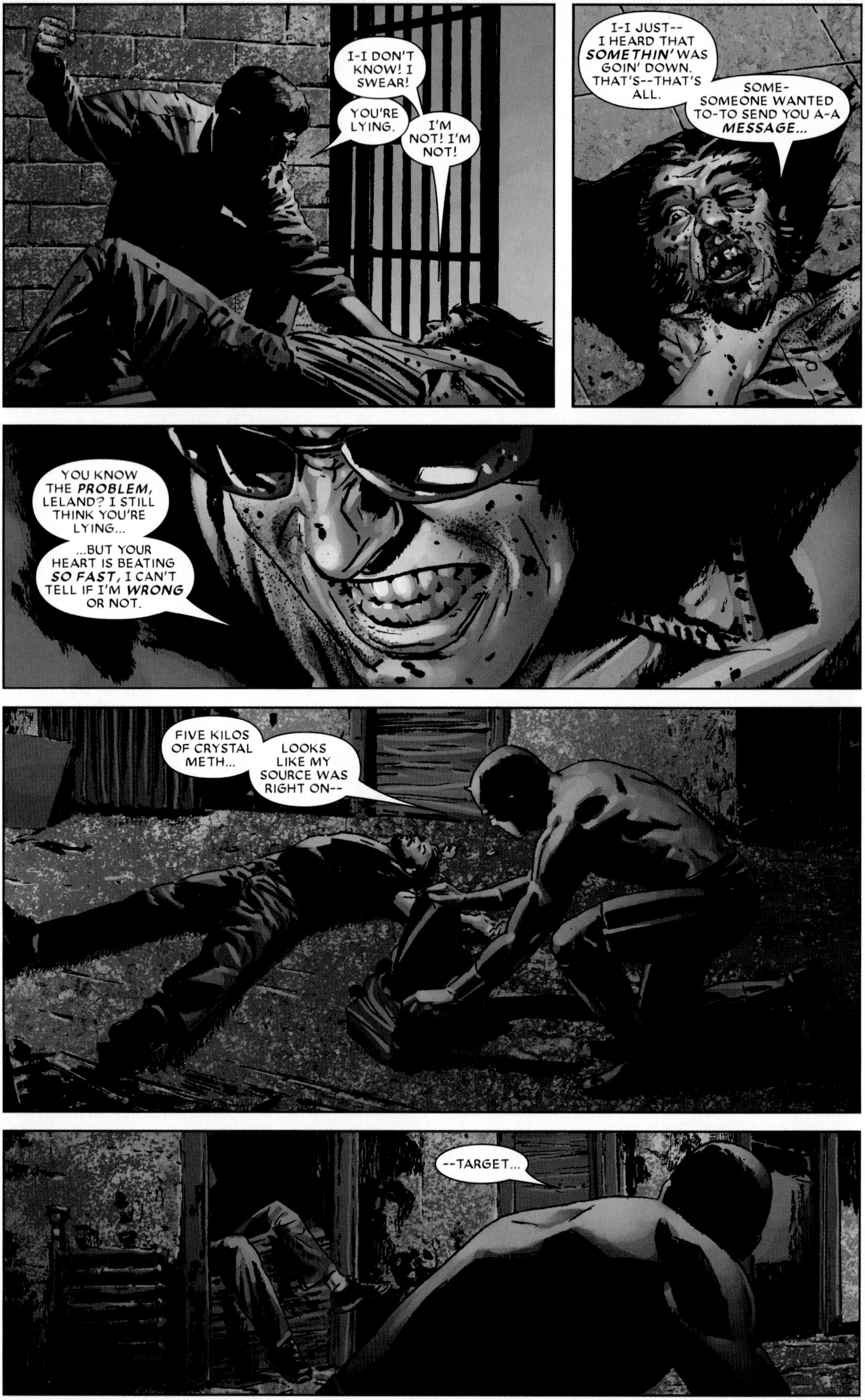
I-I DON'T KNOW! I SWEAR!
YOU'RE LYING.
I'M NOT! I'M NOT!
I-I JUST-- I HEARD THAT SOMETHIN' WAS GOIN' DOWN. THAT'S--THAT'S ALL.
SOME- SOMEONE WANTED TO-TO SEND YOU A-A MESSAGE...
YOU KNOW THE PROBLEM, LELAND? I STILL THINK YOU'RE LYING...
...BUT YOUR HEART IS BEATING SO FAST, I CAN'T TELL IF I'M WRONG OR NOT.
FIVE KILOS OF CRYSTAL METH...
LOOKS LIKE MY SOURCE WAS RIGHT ON--
--TARGET...

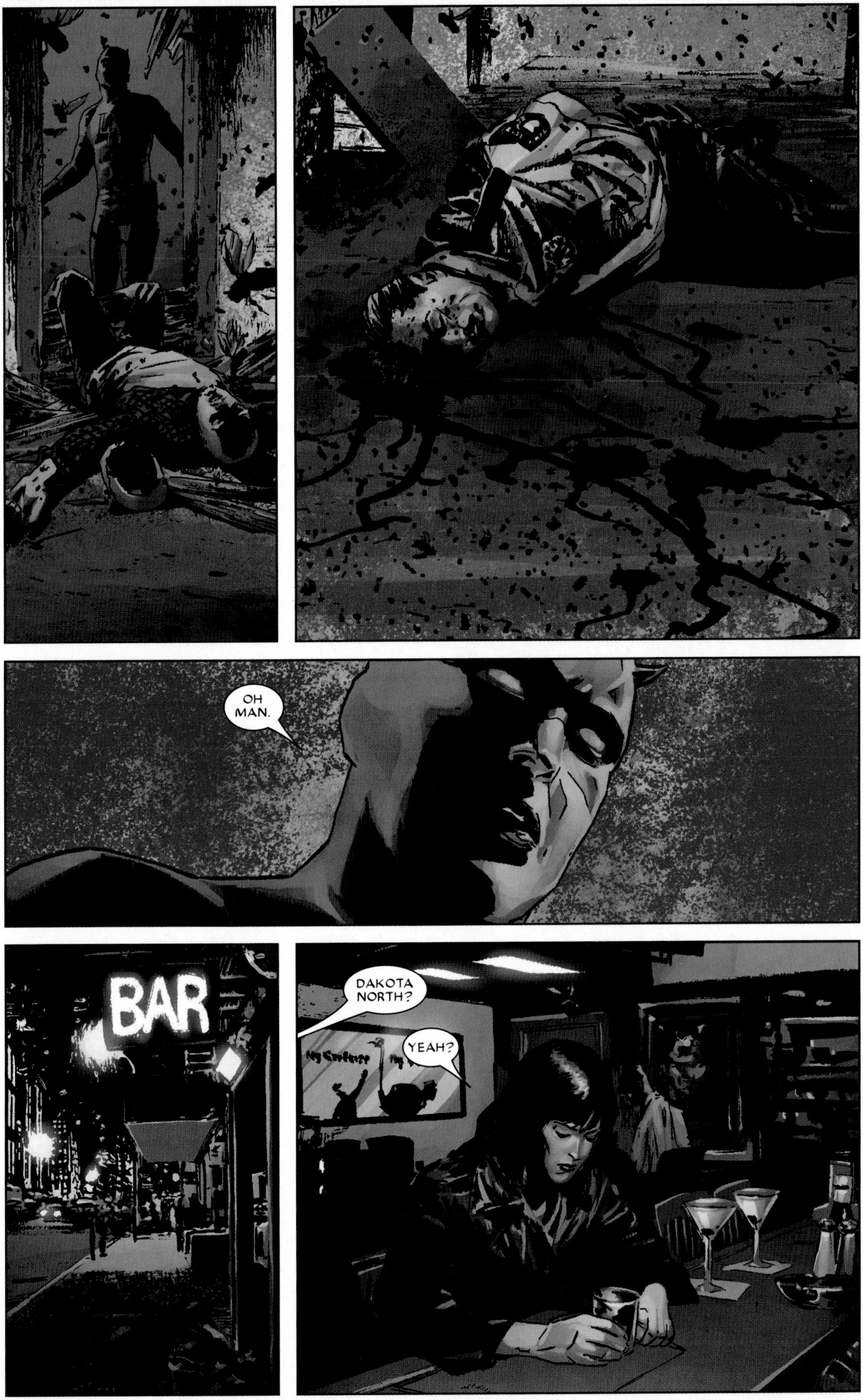
OH MAN.
DAKOTA NORTH?
YEAH?
BAR

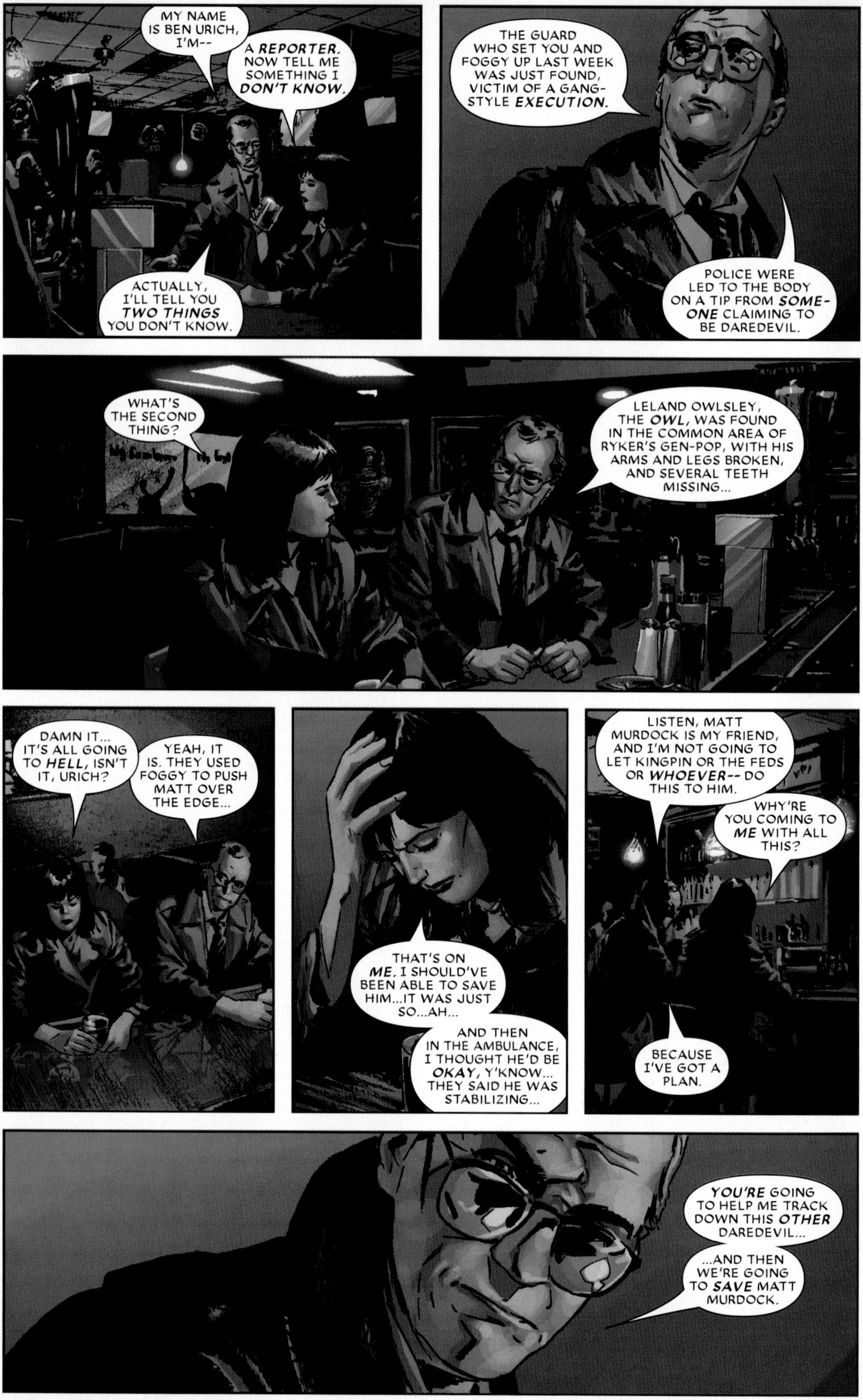
MY NAME IS BEN URICH, I'M--
A *REPORTER.* NOW TELL ME SOMETHING I *DON'T KNOW.*
ACTUALLY, I'LL TELL YOU *TWO THINGS* YOU DON'T KNOW.
THE GUARD WHO SET YOU AND FOGGY UP LAST WEEK WAS JUST FOUND, VICTIM OF A GANG-STYLE *EXECUTION.*
POLICE WERE LED TO THE BODY ON A TIP FROM *SOME-ONE* CLAIMING TO BE DAREDEVIL.
WHAT'S THE SECOND THING?
LELAND OWLSLEY, THE *OWL,* WAS FOUND IN THE COMMON AREA OF RYKER'S GEN-POP, WITH HIS ARMS AND LEGS BROKEN, AND SEVERAL TEETH MISSING...
DAMN IT... IT'S ALL GOING TO *HELL,* ISN'T IT, URICH?
YEAH, IT IS. THEY USED FOGGY TO PUSH MATT OVER THE EDGE...
THAT'S ON *ME.* I SHOULD'VE BEEN ABLE TO SAVE HIM...IT WAS JUST SO...AH...
AND THEN IN THE AMBULANCE, I THOUGHT HE'D BE *OKAY,* Y'KNOW... THEY SAID HE WAS STABILIZING...
LISTEN, MATT MURDOCK IS MY FRIEND, AND I'M NOT GOING TO LET KINGPIN OR THE FEDS OR *WHOEVER--* DO THIS TO HIM.
WHY'RE YOU COMING TO *ME* WITH ALL THIS?
BECAUSE I'VE GOT A PLAN.
YOU'RE GOING TO HELP ME TRACK DOWN THIS *OTHER* DAREDEVIL...
...AND THEN WE'RE GOING TO *SAVE* MATT MURDOCK.

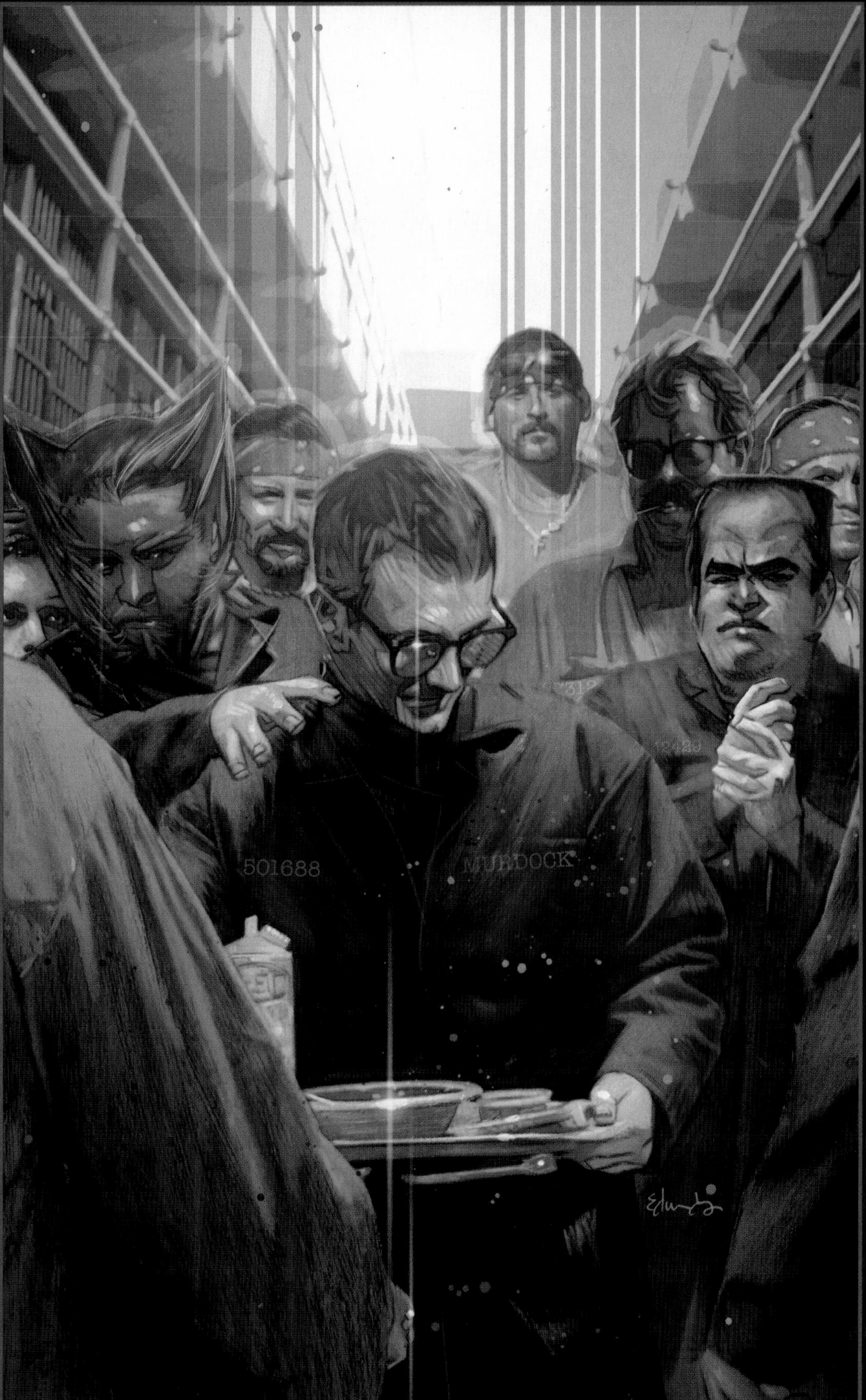
501688
MURDOCK

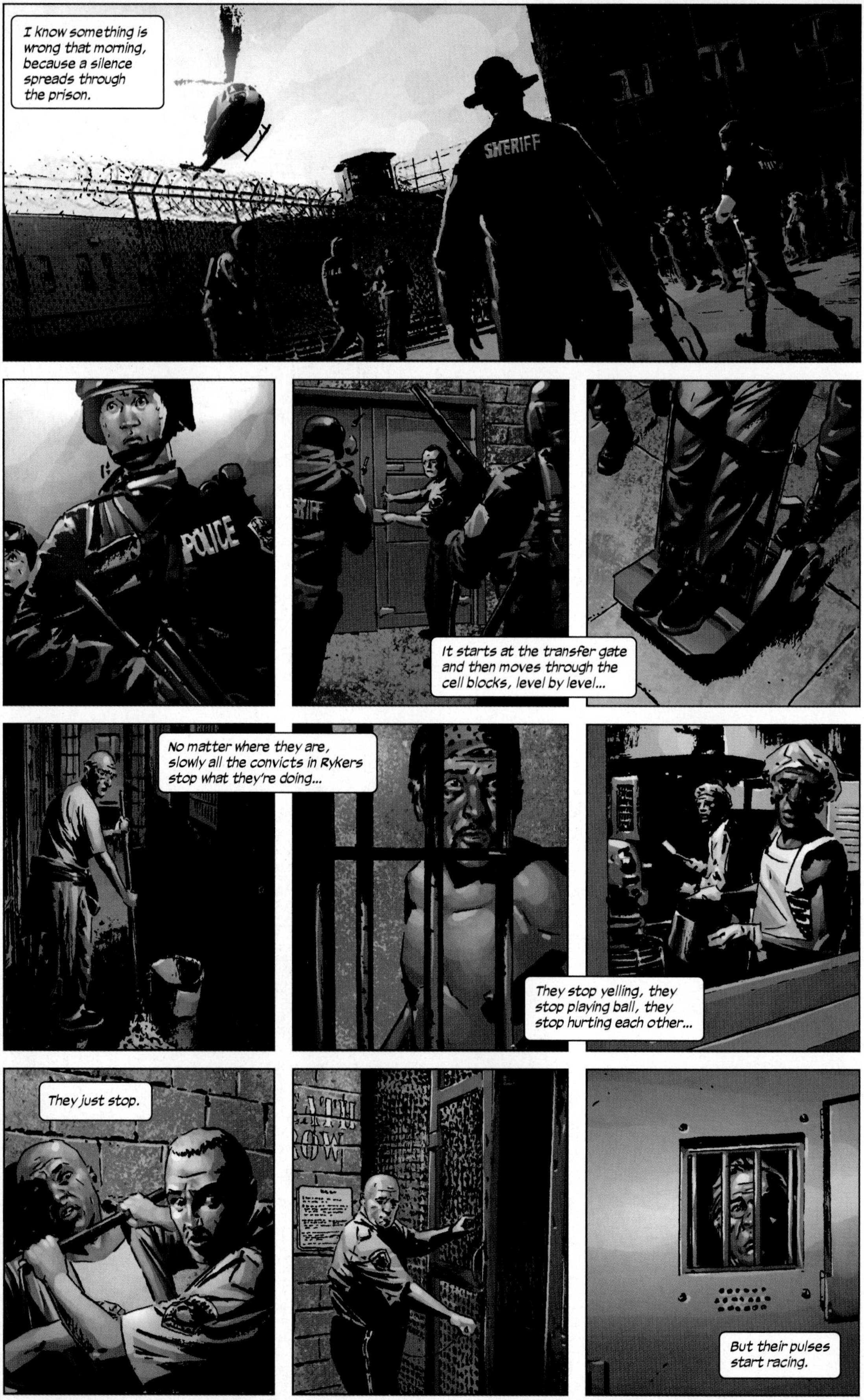
I know something is wrong that morning, because a silence spreads through the prison.
SHERIFF
POLICE
SHERIFF
It starts at the transfer gate and then moves through the cell blocks, level by level...
No matter where they are, slowly all the convicts in Rykers stop what they're doing...
They stop yelling, they stop playing ball, they stop hurting each other...
They just stop.
But their pulses start racing.

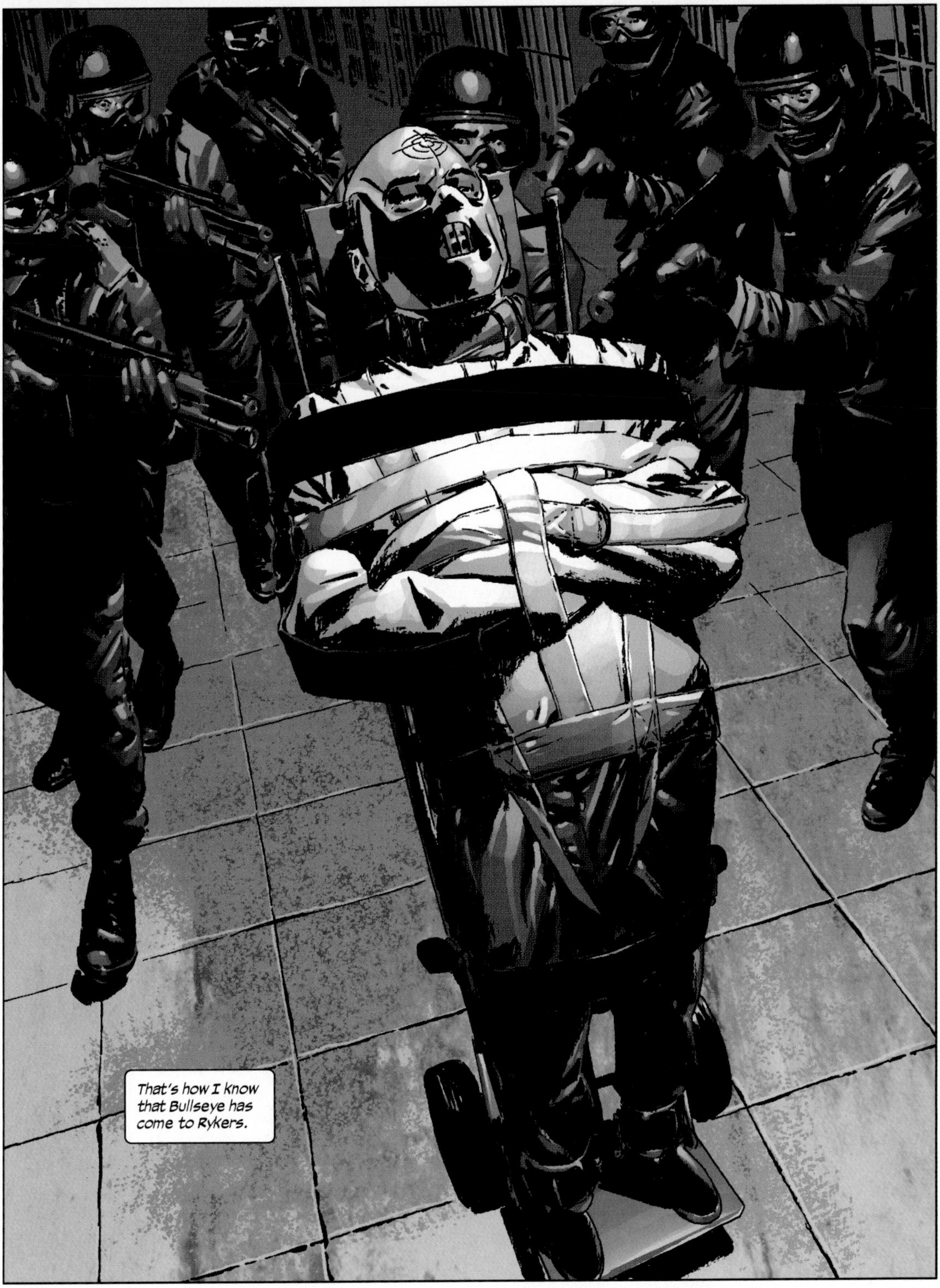
That's how I know that Bullseye has come to Rykers.

THE DEVIL IN CELL-BLOCK D
PART THREE

It's so quiet I barely have to strain to hear C.O. Gruber laying down the law...

YOU WILL BE SERVED LIQUID FOOD, IN PLASTIC BAGS.

YOU WILL NOT BE GIVEN A STRAW, OR EVEN A *SPORK.*

...as the tremor in his voice betrays him.

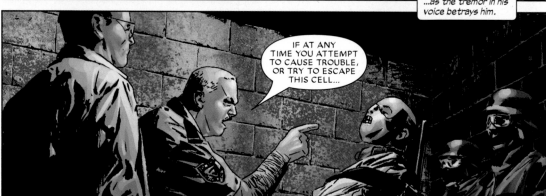

IF AT ANY TIME YOU ATTEMPT TO CAUSE TROUBLE, OR TRY TO ESCAPE THIS CELL...

...VENTS WILL OPEN IN THE CEILING, FILLING THE ROOM WITH GAS, AND WHEN WE ARE SUFFICIENTLY SURE YOU ARE *UNCONSCIOUS...*

...I AND SEVERAL OF MY COLLEAGUES--

--A FEW OF WHO WATCHED YOU *SLAUGHTER* THEIR *FRIENDS* DURING YOUR LAST ESCAPE...

THESE MEN AND I WILL ENTER THIS ROOM AND FIRE BULLETS INTO YOUR HEAD UNTIL WE ARE 100 PERCENT CERTAIN THAT YOU ARE DEAD.

IS THAT UNDERSTOOD?

The whole prison, they're all scared. Even the guards...

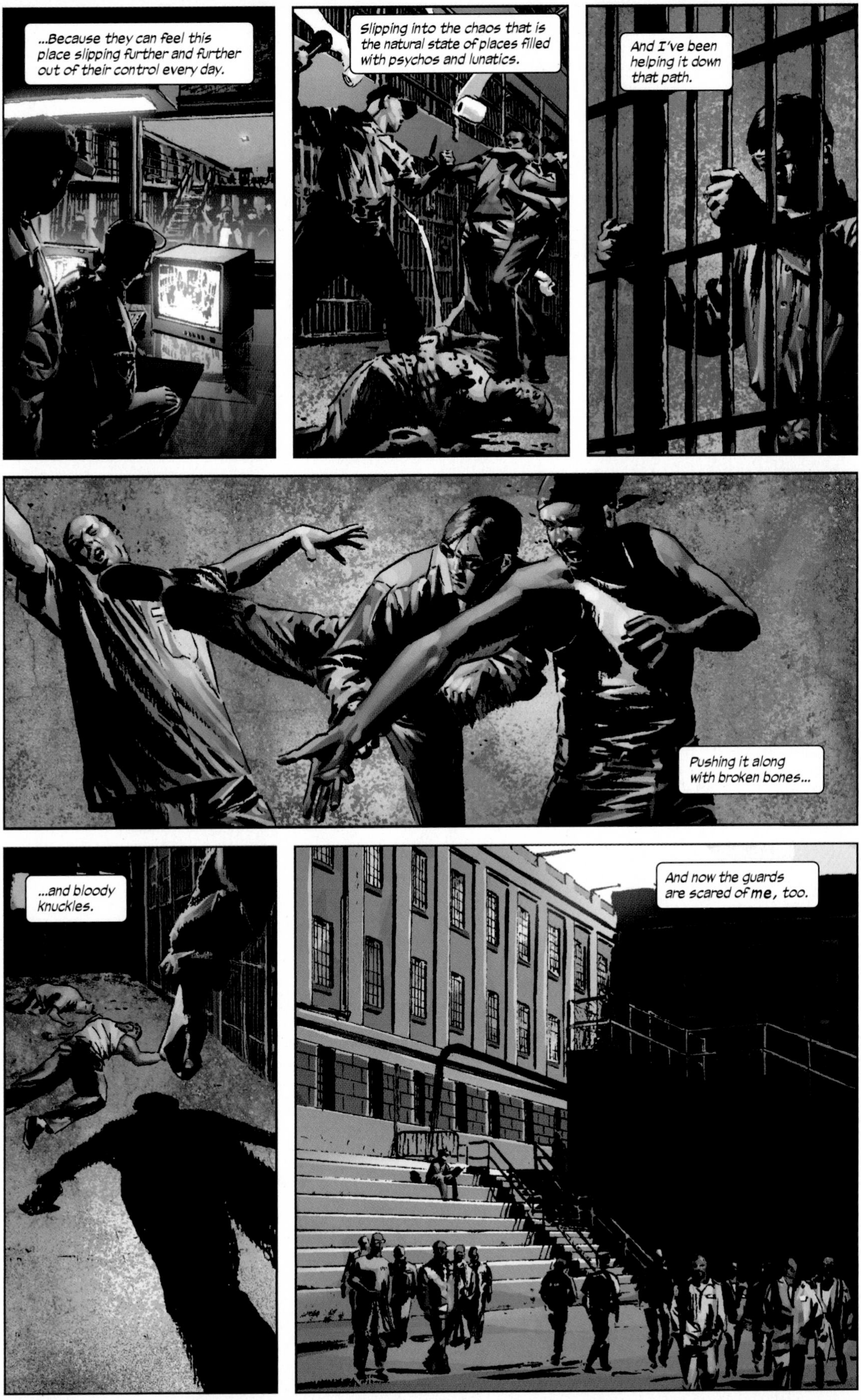
...Because they can feel this place slipping further and further out of their control every day.
Slipping into the chaos that is the natural state of places filled with psychos and lunatics.
And I've been helping it down that path.
Pushing it along with broken bones...
...and bloody knuckles.
And now the guards are scared of me, too.

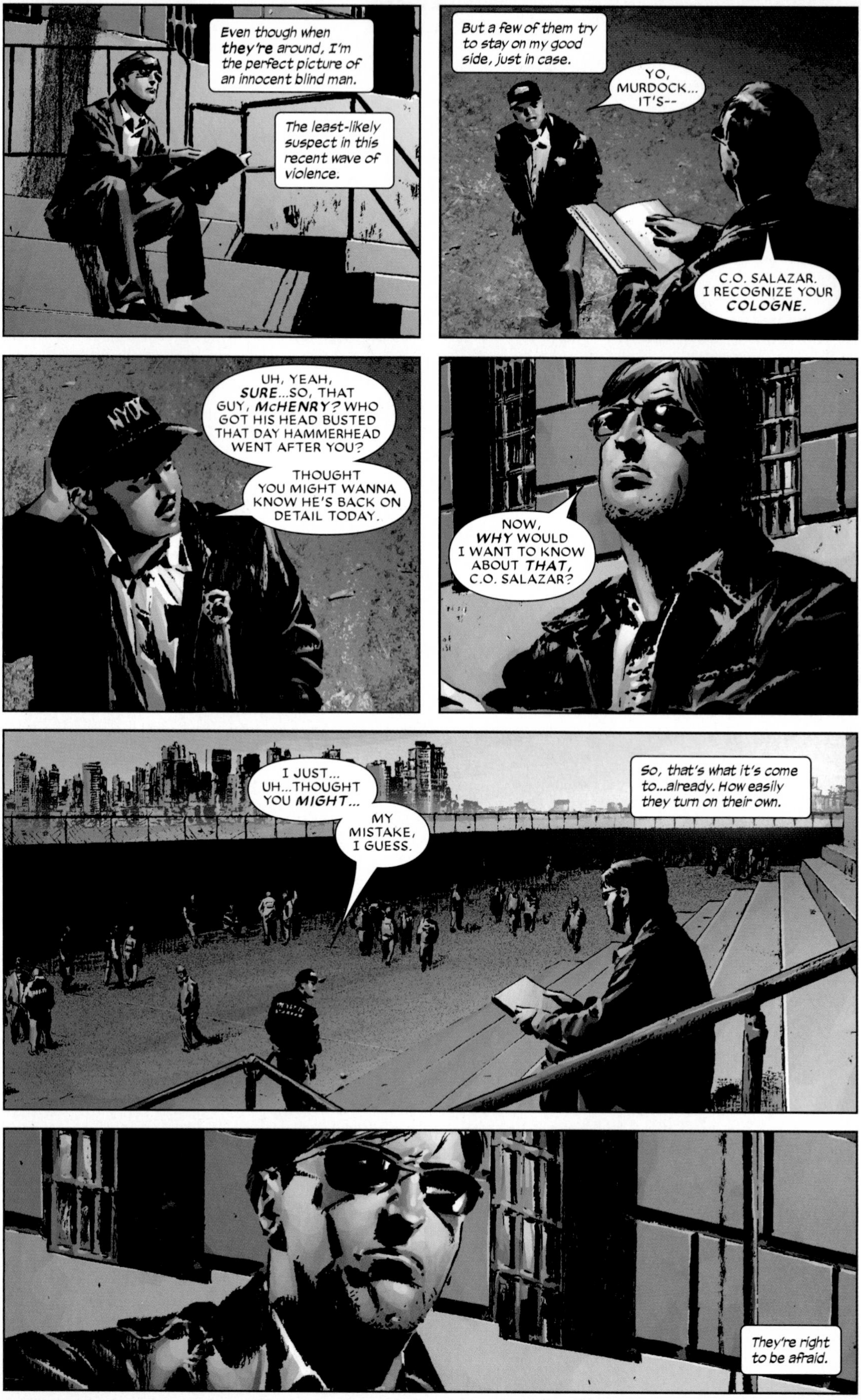
Even though when they're around, I'm the perfect picture of an innocent blind man.
The least-likely suspect in this recent wave of violence.
But a few of them try to stay on my good side, just in case.
YO, MURDOCK... IT'S--
C.O. SALAZAR. I RECOGNIZE YOUR COLOGNE.
UH, YEAH, SURE...SO, THAT GUY, McHENRY? WHO GOT HIS HEAD BUSTED THAT DAY HAMMERHEAD WENT AFTER YOU?
THOUGHT YOU MIGHT WANNA KNOW HE'S BACK ON DETAIL TODAY.
NOW, WHY WOULD I WANT TO KNOW ABOUT THAT, C.O. SALAZAR?
I JUST... UH...THOUGHT YOU MIGHT...
MY MISTAKE, I GUESS.
So, that's what it's come to...already. How easily they turn on their own.
They're right to be afraid.

DAILY BUGLE

VIOLENCE RIPS THROUGH RYKERS

IS MURDOCK RESPONSIBLE?

LEADERS POLL: New Avengers Least Popular Team Yet!

FEDS TO INVESTIGATE BOGART Scandals Loom As Schedules Fall Behind

IS THIS *REALLY* WHAT YOU WANT TO GO WITH, JONAH?

I MEAN, THERE'S ABSOLUTELY *NO PROOF* THAT MATT HAS ANYTHING TO DO WITH WHAT'S GOING ON AT RYKERS.

THAT'S WHY IT'S A *QUESTION,* URICH.

NOT A STATEMENT OF FACT.

YEAH, I GET THAT... I JUST... IT FEELS A BIT *SLANTED.*

AND SINCE *WHEN* EXACTLY HAVE I CONSULTED YOU ON *HEADLINES?*

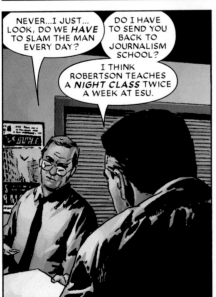

NEVER...I JUST... LOOK, DO WE *HAVE* TO SLAM THE MAN EVERY DAY?

DO I HAVE TO SEND YOU BACK TO JOURNALISM SCHOOL?

I THINK ROBERTSON TEACHES A *NIGHT CLASS* TWICE A WEEK AT ESU.

WE ARE IN THE BUSINESS OF REPORTING THE NEWS AND SELLING *PAPERS,* URICH!

WE ARE *NOT* IN THE BUSINESS OF BEING *NICE* TO YOUR *FRIENDS!*

I KNOW THAT, JONAH... *BELIEVE ME.* I UNDERSTAND THAT.

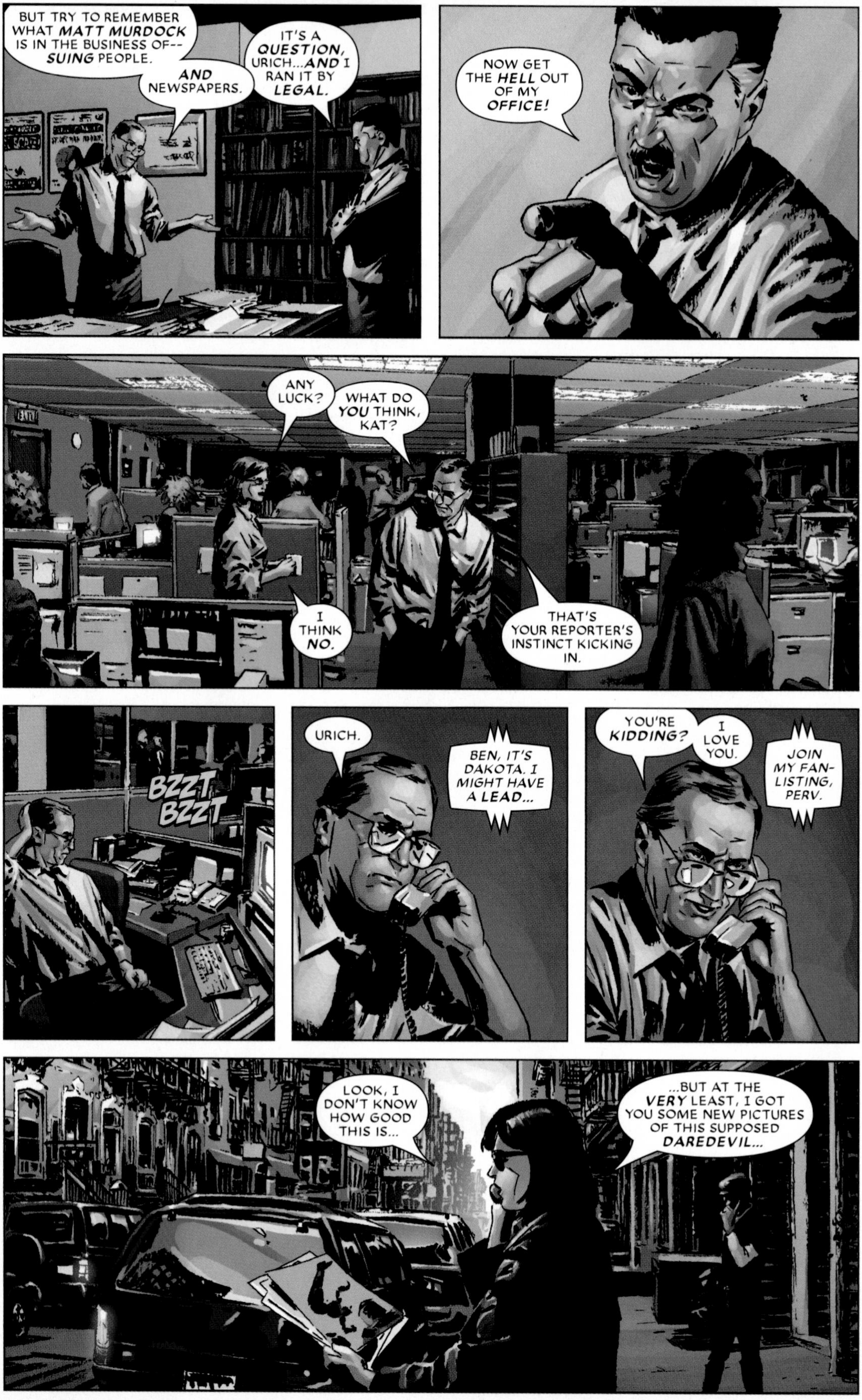
BUT TRY TO REMEMBER WHAT MATT MURDOCK IS IN THE BUSINESS OF-- SUING PEOPLE.
AND NEWSPAPERS.
IT'S A QUESTION, URICH...AND I RAN IT BY LEGAL.
NOW GET THE HELL OUT OF MY OFFICE!
ANY LUCK?
WHAT DO YOU THINK, KAT?
I THINK NO.
THAT'S YOUR REPORTER'S INSTINCT KICKING IN.
BZZT BZZT
URICH.
BEN, IT'S DAKOTA. I MIGHT HAVE A LEAD...
YOU'RE KIDDING?
I LOVE YOU.
JOIN MY FAN-LISTING, PERV.
LOOK, I DON'T KNOW HOW GOOD THIS IS...
...BUT AT THE VERY LEAST, I GOT YOU SOME NEW PICTURES OF THIS SUPPOSED DAREDEVIL...

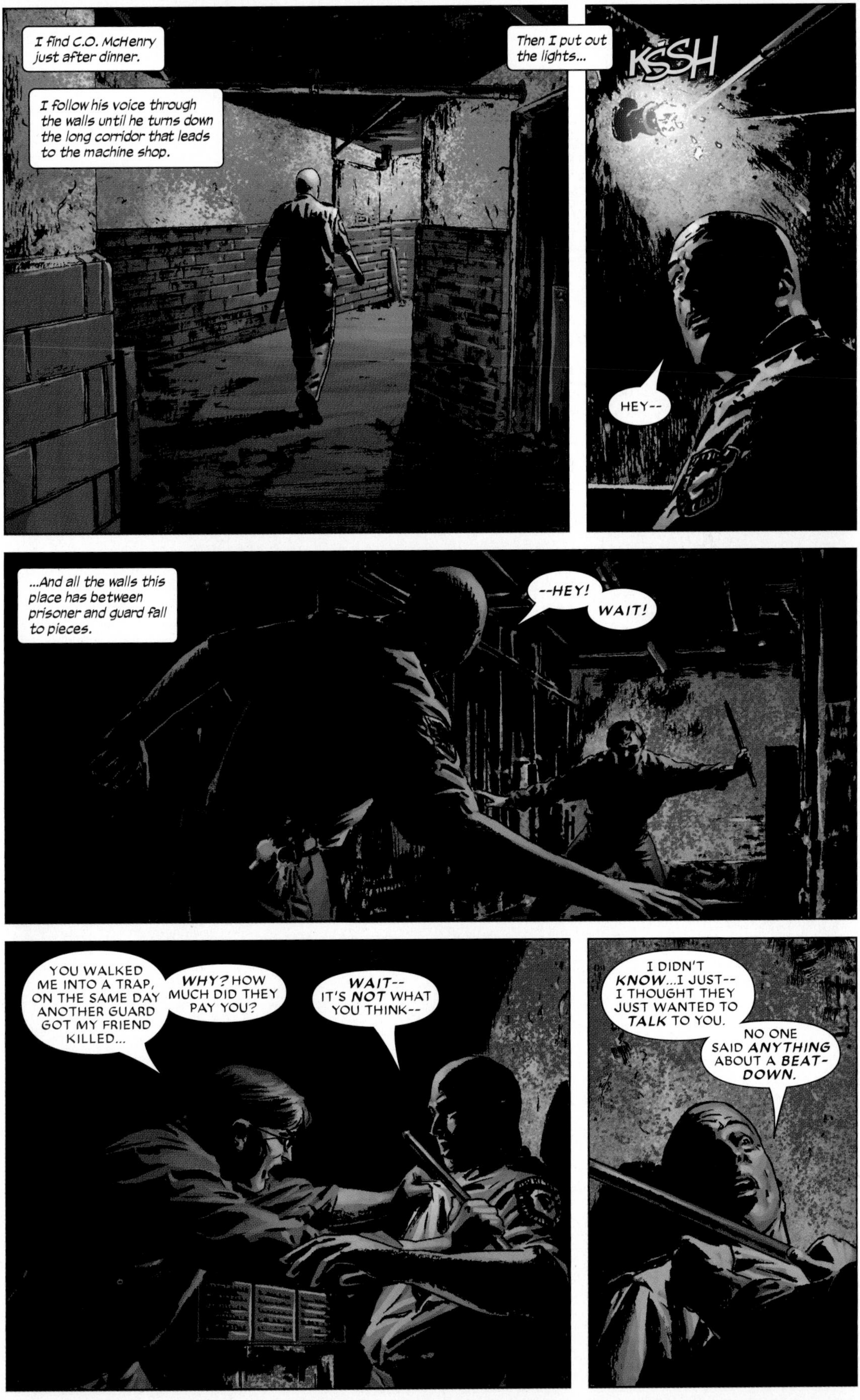

I find C.O. McHenry just after dinner.
I follow his voice through the walls until he turns down the long corridor that leads to the machine shop.
Then I put out the lights...
KSSH
HEY--
...And all the walls this place has between prisoner and guard fall to pieces.
--HEY!
WAIT!
YOU WALKED ME INTO A TRAP, ON THE SAME DAY ANOTHER GUARD GOT MY FRIEND KILLED...
WHY? HOW MUCH DID THEY PAY YOU?
WAIT-- IT'S NOT WHAT YOU THINK--
I DIDN'T KNOW...I JUST-- I THOUGHT THEY JUST WANTED TO TALK TO YOU.
NO ONE SAID ANYTHING ABOUT A BEAT-DOWN.

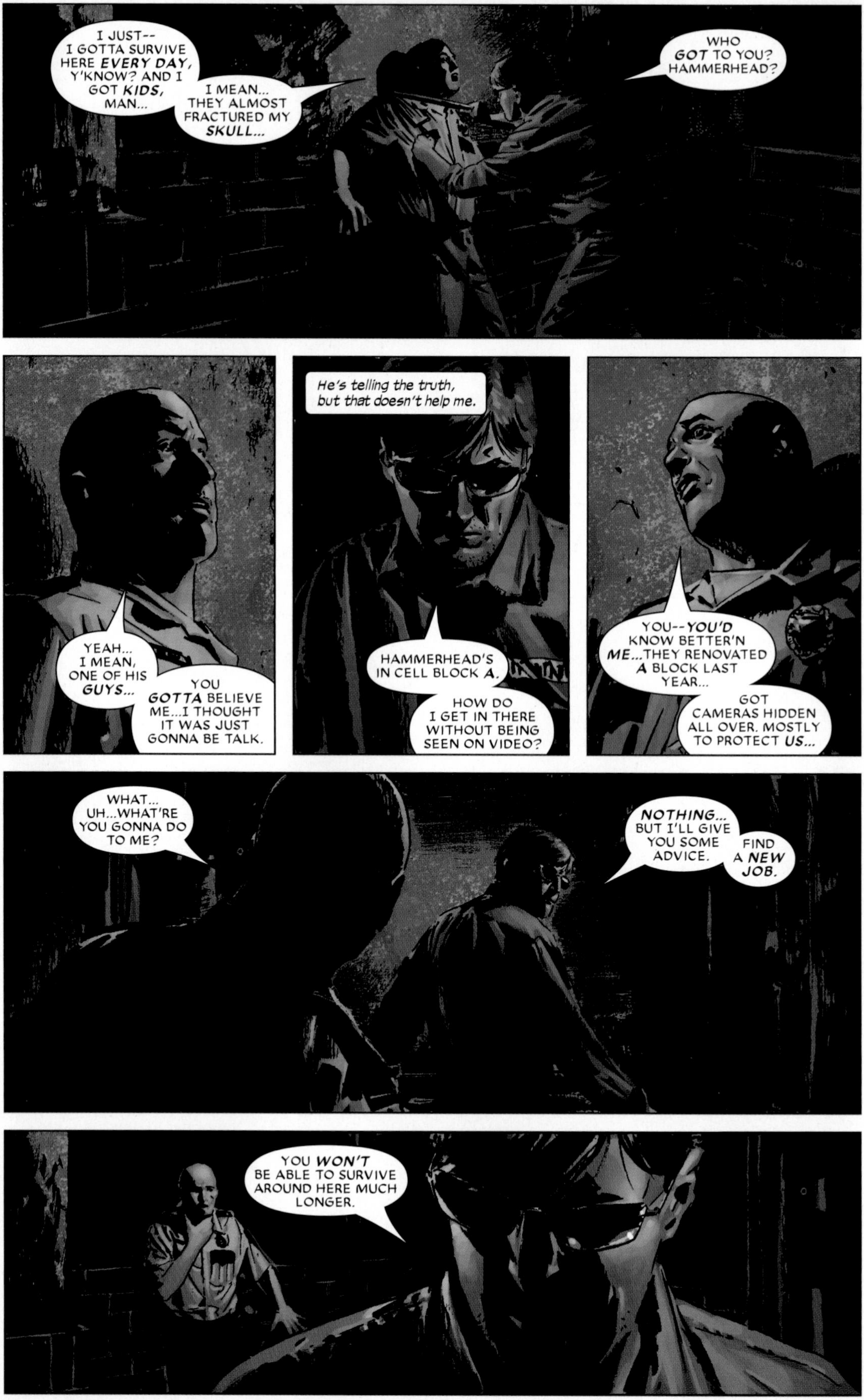
I JUST-- I GOTTA SURVIVE HERE EVERY DAY, Y'KNOW? AND I GOT KIDS, MAN...
I MEAN... THEY ALMOST FRACTURED MY SKULL...
WHO GOT TO YOU? HAMMERHEAD?
YEAH... I MEAN, ONE OF HIS GUYS...
YOU GOTTA BELIEVE ME...I THOUGHT IT WAS JUST GONNA BE TALK.
He's telling the truth, but that doesn't help me.
HAMMERHEAD'S IN CELL BLOCK A.
HOW DO I GET IN THERE WITHOUT BEING SEEN ON VIDEO?
YOU--YOU'D KNOW BETTER'N ME...THEY RENOVATED A BLOCK LAST YEAR...
GOT CAMERAS HIDDEN ALL OVER. MOSTLY TO PROTECT US...
WHAT... UH...WHAT'RE YOU GONNA DO TO ME?
NOTHING... BUT I'LL GIVE YOU SOME ADVICE.
FIND A NEW JOB.
YOU WON'T BE ABLE TO SURVIVE AROUND HERE MUCH LONGER.

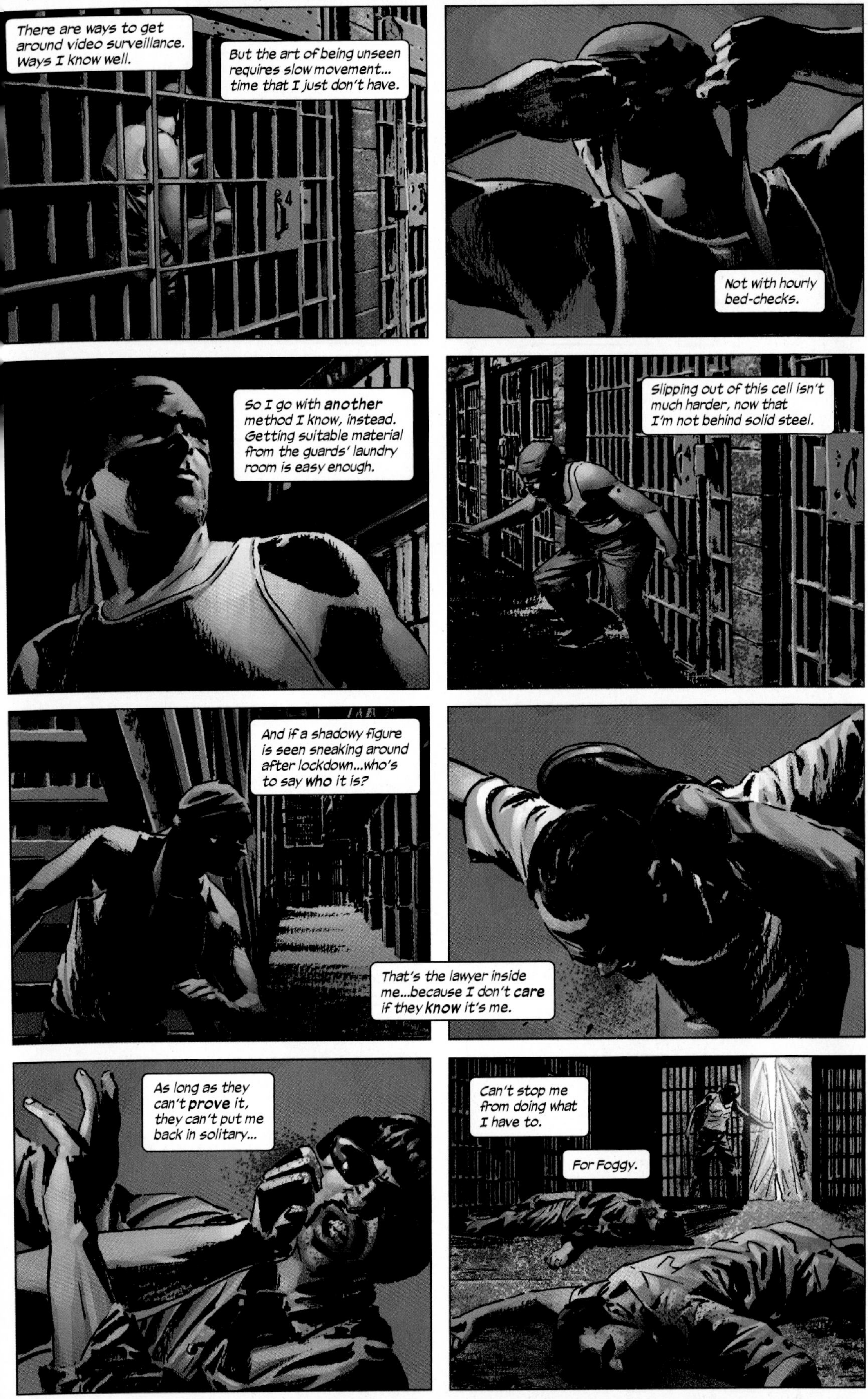
There are ways to get around video surveillance. Ways I know well.
But the art of being unseen requires slow movement... time that I just don't have.
Not with hourly bed-checks.
So I go with another method I know, instead. Getting suitable material from the guards' laundry room is easy enough.
Slipping out of this cell isn't much harder, now that I'm not behind solid steel.
And if a shadowy figure is seen sneaking around after lockdown...who's to say who it is?
That's the lawyer inside me...because I don't care if they know it's me.
As long as they can't prove it, they can't put me back in solitary...
Can't stop me from doing what I have to.
For Foggy.

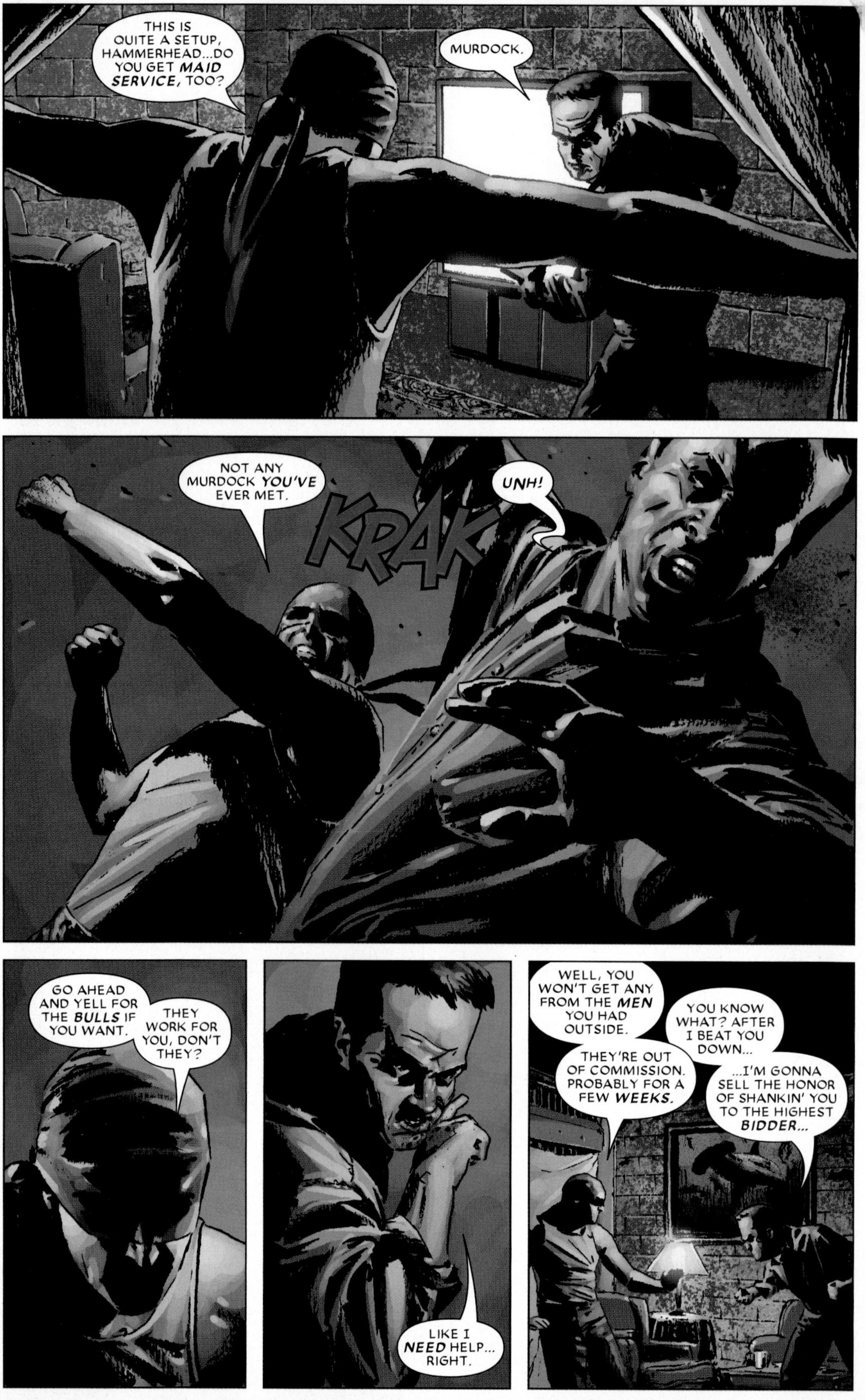
THIS IS QUITE A SETUP, HAMMERHEAD...DO YOU GET MAID SERVICE, TOO?
MURDOCK.
NOT ANY MURDOCK YOU'VE EVER MET.
KRAK
UNH!
GO AHEAD AND YELL FOR THE BULLS IF YOU WANT.
THEY WORK FOR YOU, DON'T THEY?
LIKE I NEED HELP... RIGHT.
WELL, YOU WON'T GET ANY FROM THE MEN YOU HAD OUTSIDE.
THEY'RE OUT OF COMMISSION. PROBABLY FOR A FEW WEEKS.
YOU KNOW WHAT? AFTER I BEAT YOU DOWN...
...I'M GONNA SELL THE HONOR OF SHANKIN' YOU TO THE HIGHEST BIDDER...

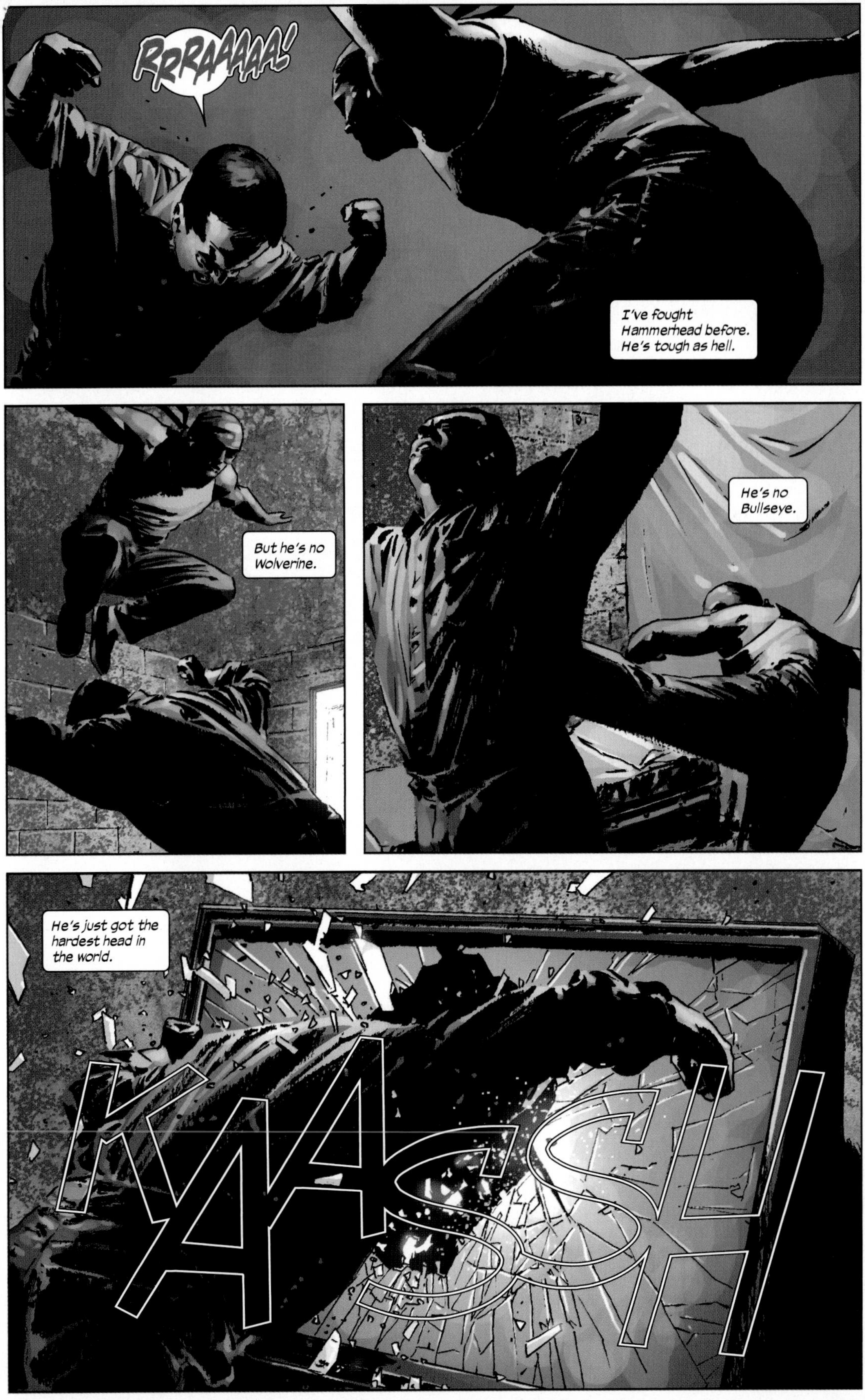
RRRAAAAA!
I've fought Hammerhead before. He's tough as hell.
But he's no Wolverine.
He's no Bullseye.
He's just got the hardest head in the world.
KKAASSHH

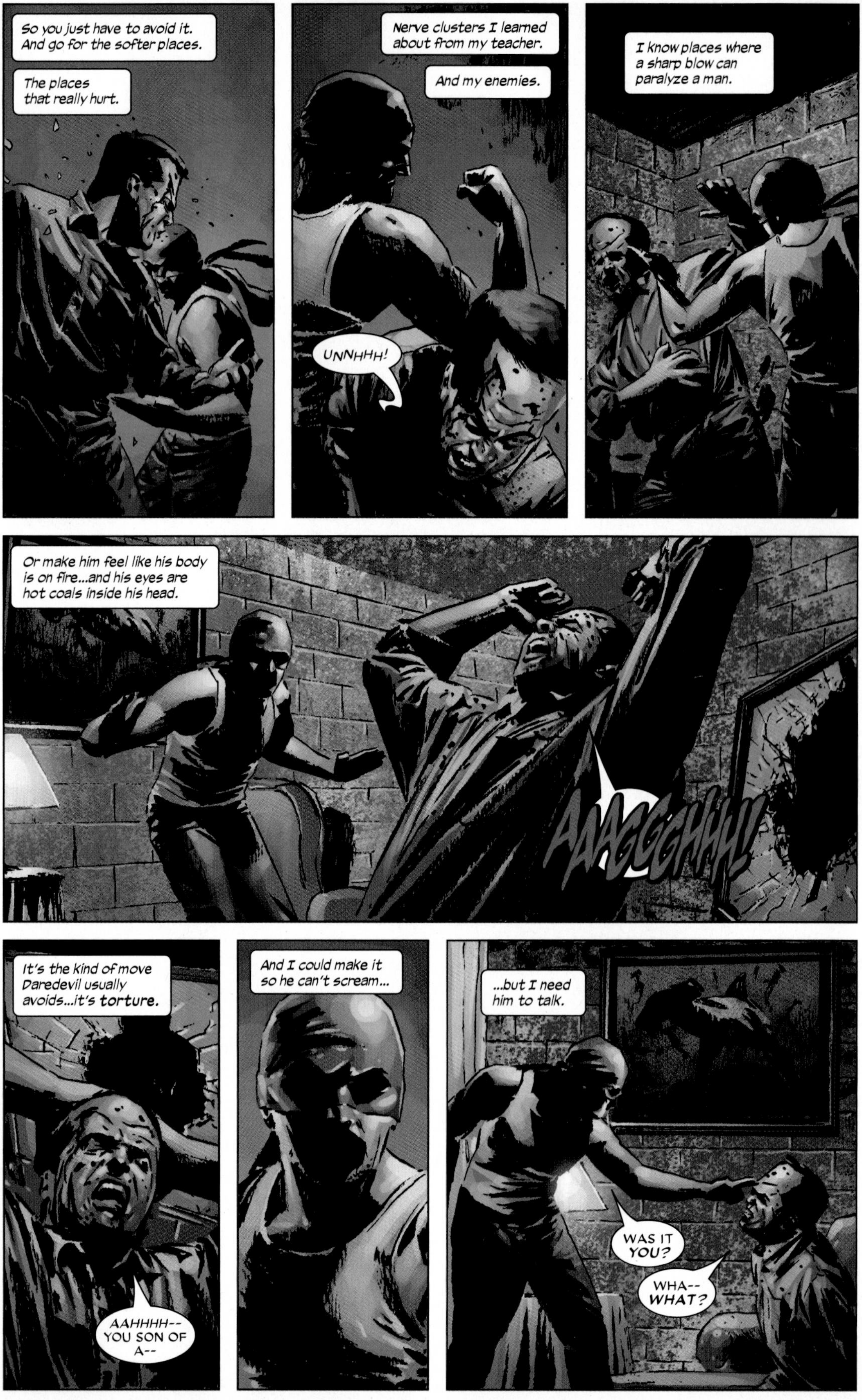
So you just have to avoid it. And go for the softer places.
The places that really hurt.
Nerve clusters I learned about from my teacher.
And my enemies.
UNNHHH!
I know places where a sharp blow can paralyze a man.
Or make him feel like his body is on fire...and his eyes are hot coals inside his head.
AAAGGHHH!
It's the kind of move Daredevil usually avoids...it's torture.
AAHHHH-- YOU SON OF A--
And I could make it so he can't scream...
...but I need him to talk.
WAS IT YOU?
WHA-- WHAT?

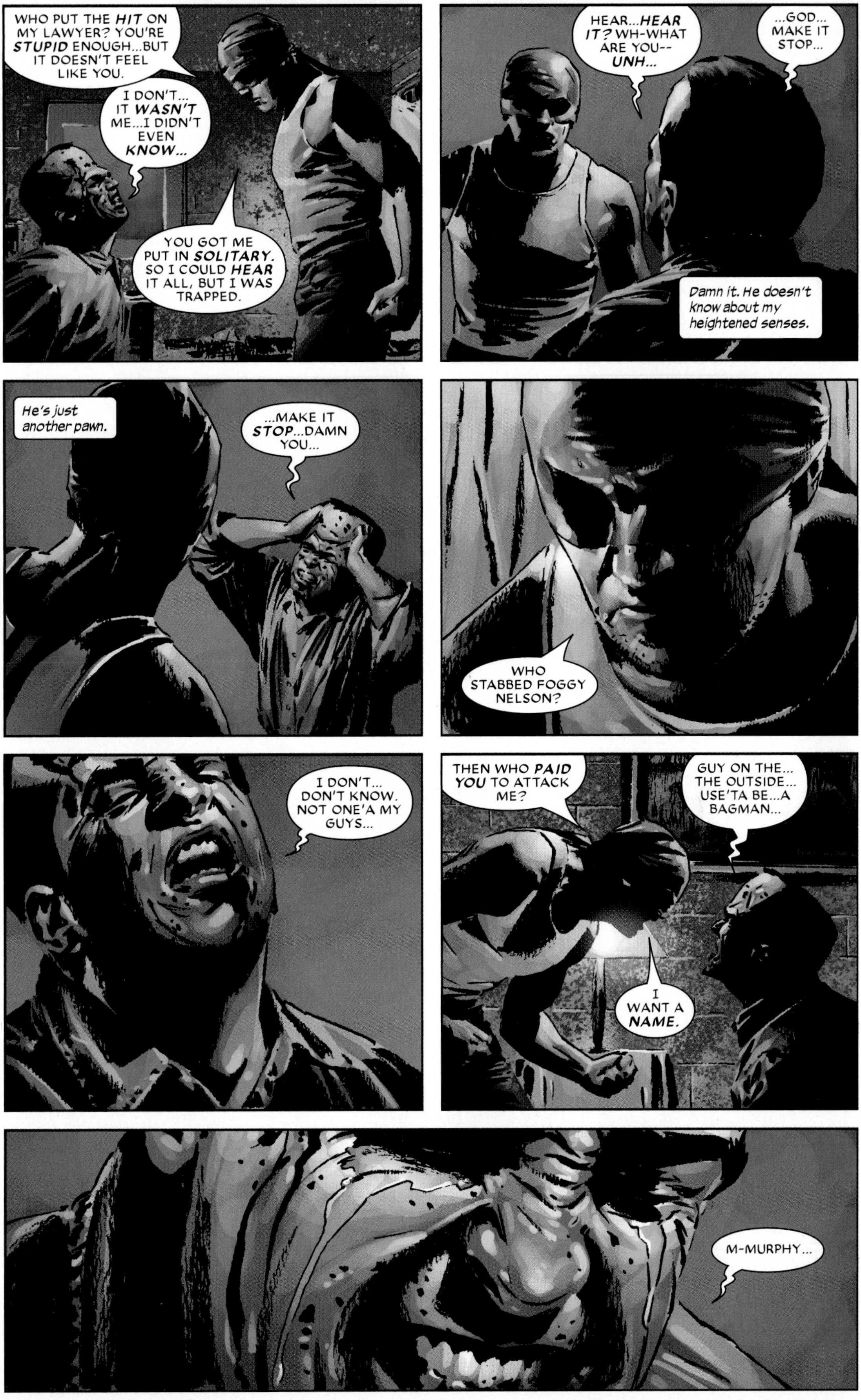
WHO PUT THE HIT ON MY LAWYER? YOU'RE STUPID ENOUGH...BUT IT DOESN'T FEEL LIKE YOU.
I DON'T... IT WASN'T ME...I DIDN'T EVEN KNOW...
YOU GOT ME PUT IN SOLITARY. SO I COULD HEAR IT ALL, BUT I WAS TRAPPED.
HEAR...HEAR IT? WH-WHAT ARE YOU-- UNH...
...GOD... MAKE IT STOP...
Damn it. He doesn't know about my heightened senses.
He's just another pawn.
...MAKE IT STOP...DAMN YOU...
WHO STABBED FOGGY NELSON?
I DON'T... DON'T KNOW. NOT ONE'A MY GUYS...
THEN WHO PAID YOU TO ATTACK ME?
GUY ON THE... THE OUTSIDE... USE'TA BE...A BAGMAN...
I WANT A NAME.
M-MURPHY...

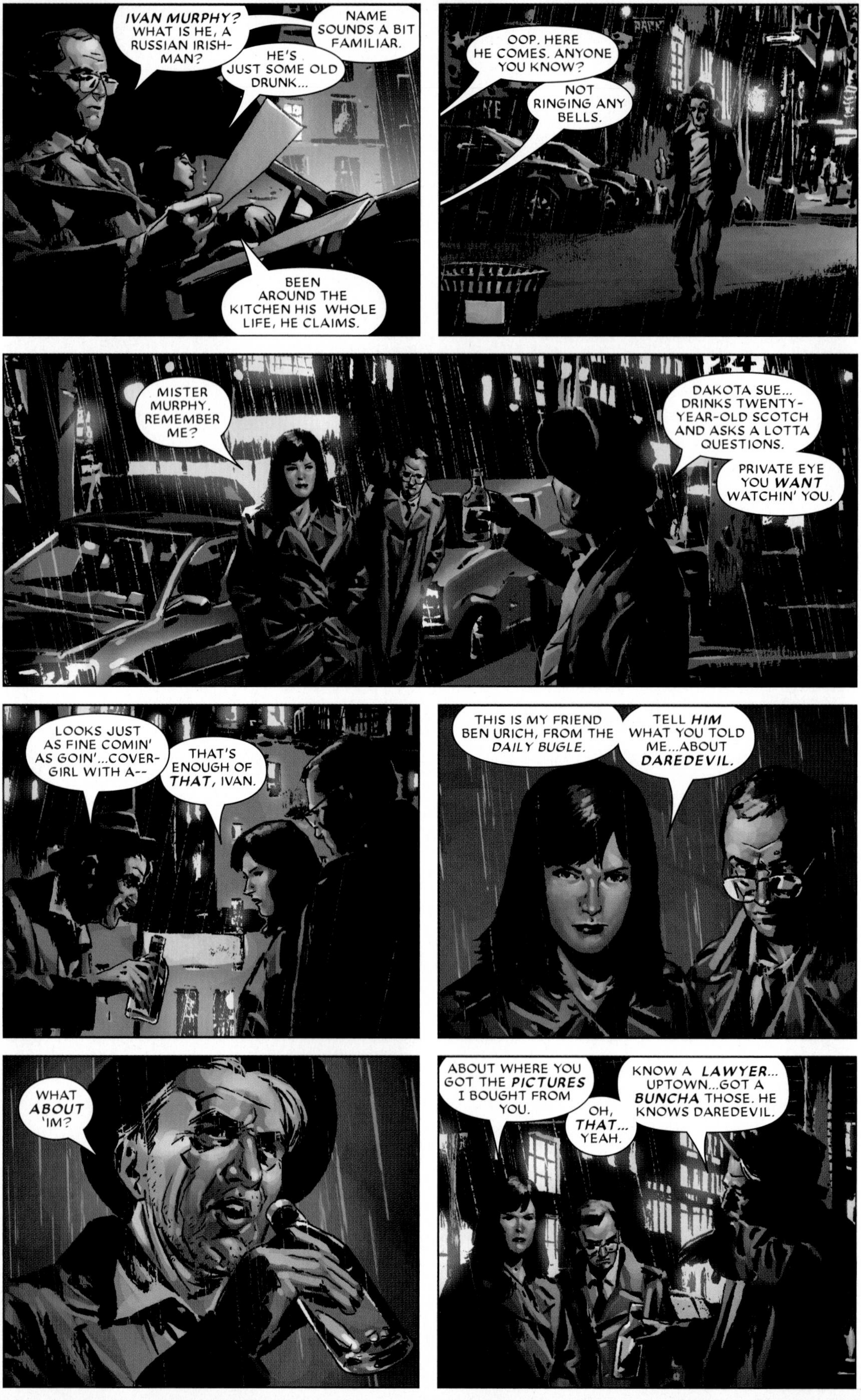
IVAN MURPHY? WHAT IS HE, A RUSSIAN IRISH-MAN?
NAME SOUNDS A BIT FAMILIAR.
HE'S JUST SOME OLD DRUNK...
BEEN AROUND THE KITCHEN HIS WHOLE LIFE, HE CLAIMS.
OOP. HERE HE COMES. ANYONE YOU KNOW?
NOT RINGING ANY BELLS.
MISTER MURPHY. REMEMBER ME?
DAKOTA SUE... DRINKS TWENTY-YEAR-OLD SCOTCH AND ASKS A LOTTA QUESTIONS.
PRIVATE EYE YOU WANT WATCHIN' YOU.
LOOKS JUST AS FINE COMIN' AS GOIN'...COVER-GIRL WITH A--
THAT'S ENOUGH OF THAT, IVAN.
THIS IS MY FRIEND BEN URICH, FROM THE DAILY BUGLE.
TELL HIM WHAT YOU TOLD ME...ABOUT DAREDEVIL.
WHAT ABOUT 'IM?
ABOUT WHERE YOU GOT THE PICTURES I BOUGHT FROM YOU.
OH, THAT... YEAH.
KNOW A LAWYER... UPTOWN...GOT A BUNCHA THOSE. HE KNOWS DAREDEVIL.

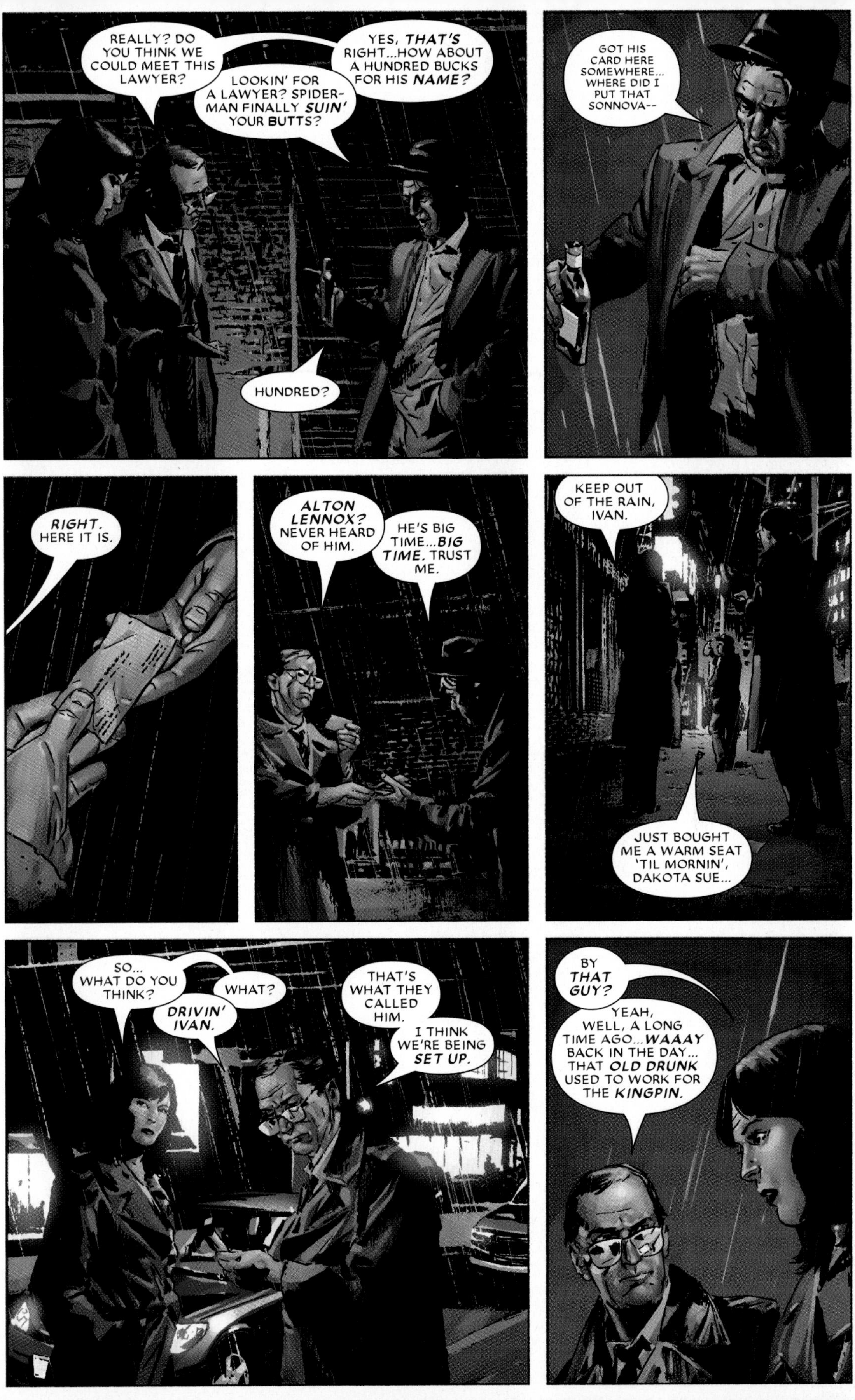
REALLY? DO YOU THINK WE COULD MEET THIS LAWYER?
LOOKIN' FOR A LAWYER? SPIDER-MAN FINALLY SUIN' YOUR BUTTS?
YES, THAT'S RIGHT...HOW ABOUT A HUNDRED BUCKS FOR HIS NAME?
HUNDRED?
GOT HIS CARD HERE SOMEWHERE... WHERE DID I PUT THAT SONNOVA--
RIGHT. HERE IT IS.
ALTON LENNOX? NEVER HEARD OF HIM.
HE'S BIG TIME...BIG TIME. TRUST ME.
KEEP OUT OF THE RAIN, IVAN.
JUST BOUGHT ME A WARM SEAT 'TIL MORNIN', DAKOTA SUE...
SO... WHAT DO YOU THINK?
WHAT?
DRIVIN' IVAN.
THAT'S WHAT THEY CALLED HIM.
I THINK WE'RE BEING SET UP.
BY THAT GUY?
YEAH, WELL, A LONG TIME AGO...WAAAY BACK IN THE DAY... THAT OLD DRUNK USED TO WORK FOR THE KINGPIN.

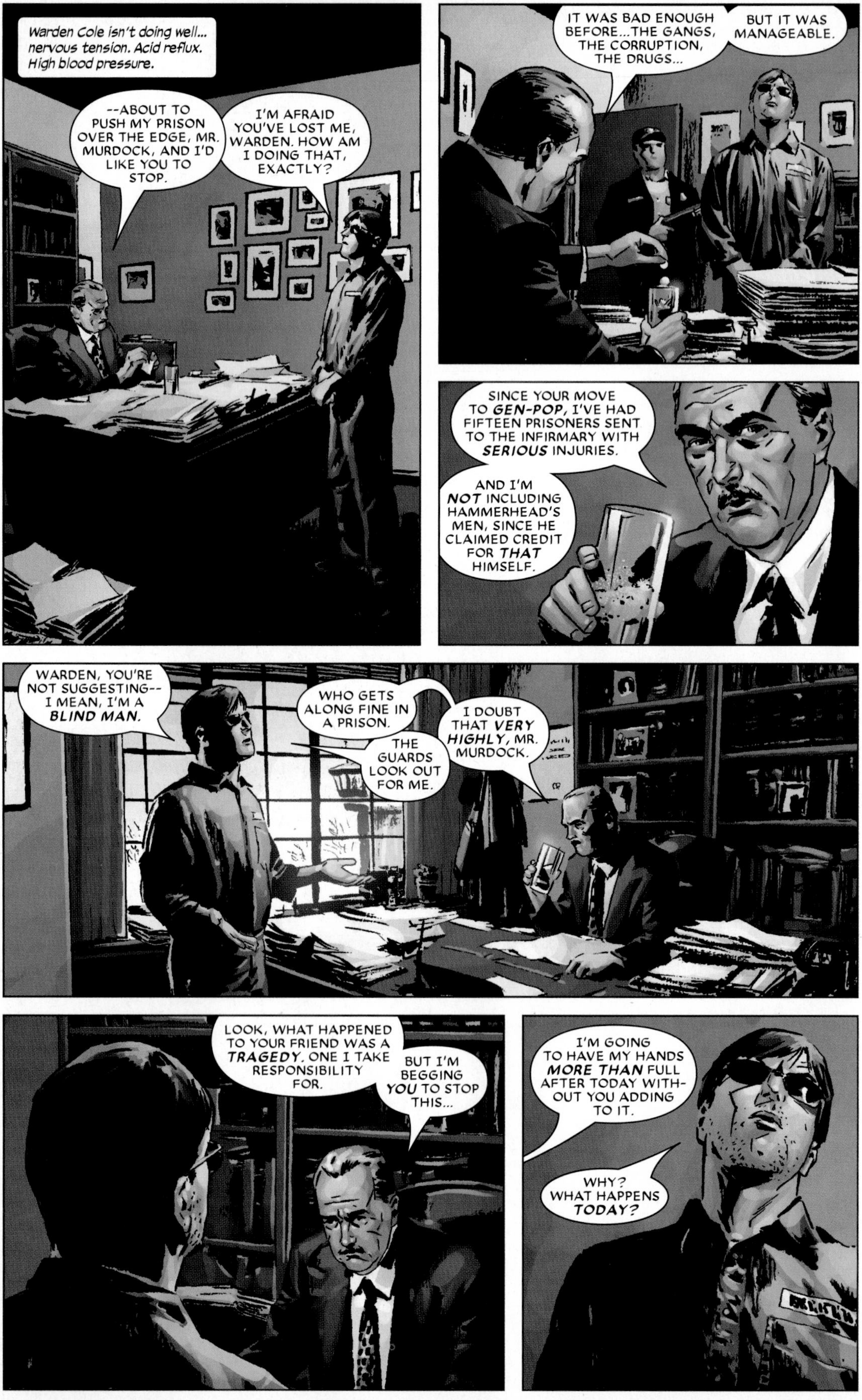
Warden Cole isn't doing well... nervous tension. Acid reflux. High blood pressure.
--ABOUT TO PUSH MY PRISON OVER THE EDGE, MR. MURDOCK, AND I'D LIKE YOU TO STOP.
I'M AFRAID YOU'VE LOST ME, WARDEN. HOW AM I DOING THAT, EXACTLY?
IT WAS BAD ENOUGH BEFORE...THE GANGS, THE CORRUPTION, THE DRUGS...
BUT IT WAS MANAGEABLE.
SINCE YOUR MOVE TO GEN-POP, I'VE HAD FIFTEEN PRISONERS SENT TO THE INFIRMARY WITH SERIOUS INJURIES.
AND I'M NOT INCLUDING HAMMERHEAD'S MEN, SINCE HE CLAIMED CREDIT FOR THAT HIMSELF.
WARDEN, YOU'RE NOT SUGGESTING-- I MEAN, I'M A BLIND MAN.
WHO GETS ALONG FINE IN A PRISON.
THE GUARDS LOOK OUT FOR ME.
I DOUBT THAT VERY HIGHLY, MR. MURDOCK.
LOOK, WHAT HAPPENED TO YOUR FRIEND WAS A TRAGEDY. ONE I TAKE RESPONSIBILITY FOR.
BUT I'M BEGGING YOU TO STOP THIS...
I'M GOING TO HAVE MY HANDS MORE THAN FULL AFTER TODAY WITHOUT YOU ADDING TO IT.
WHY? WHAT HAPPENS TODAY?

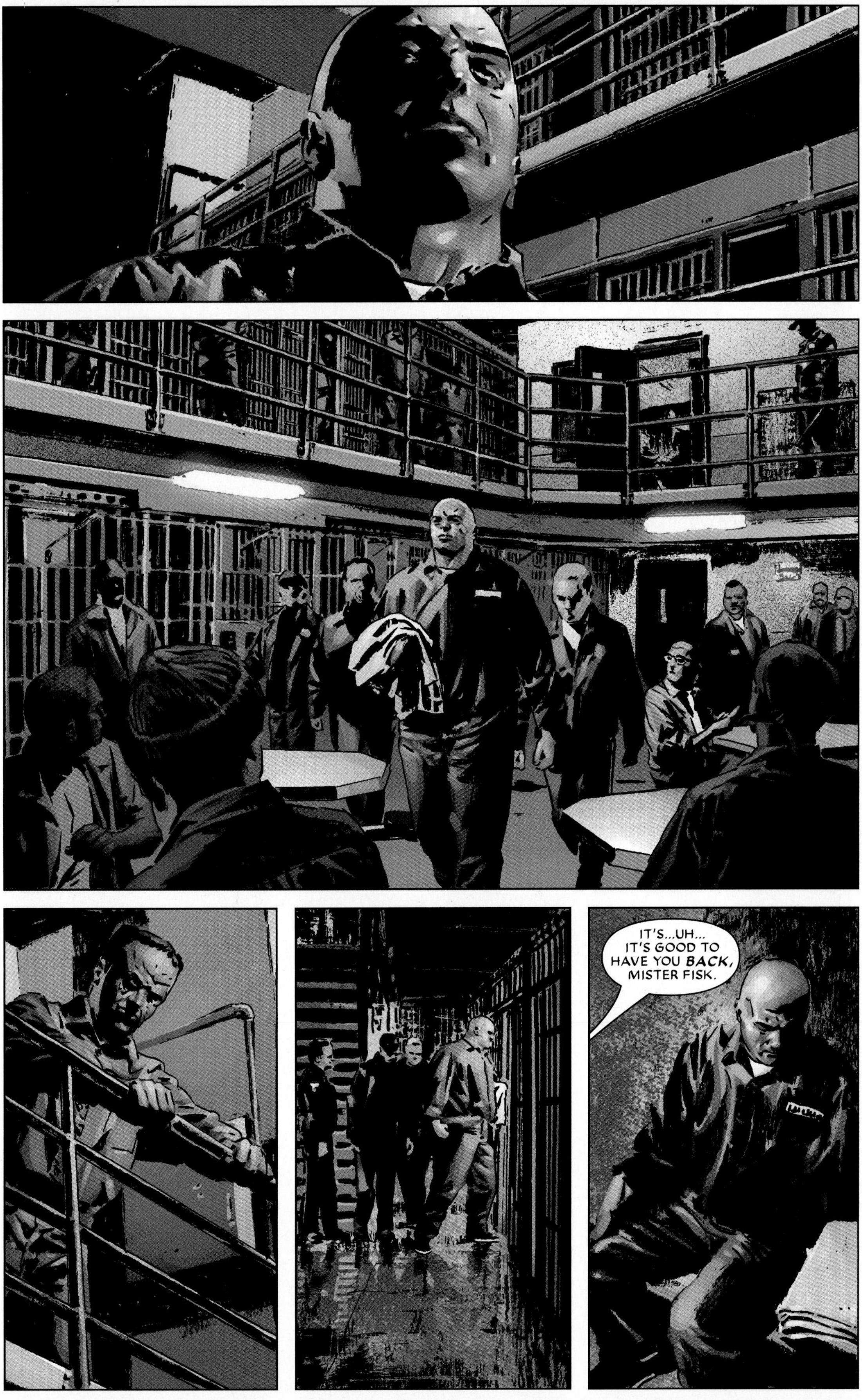
IT'S...UH...
IT'S GOOD TO HAVE YOU BACK, MISTER FISK.

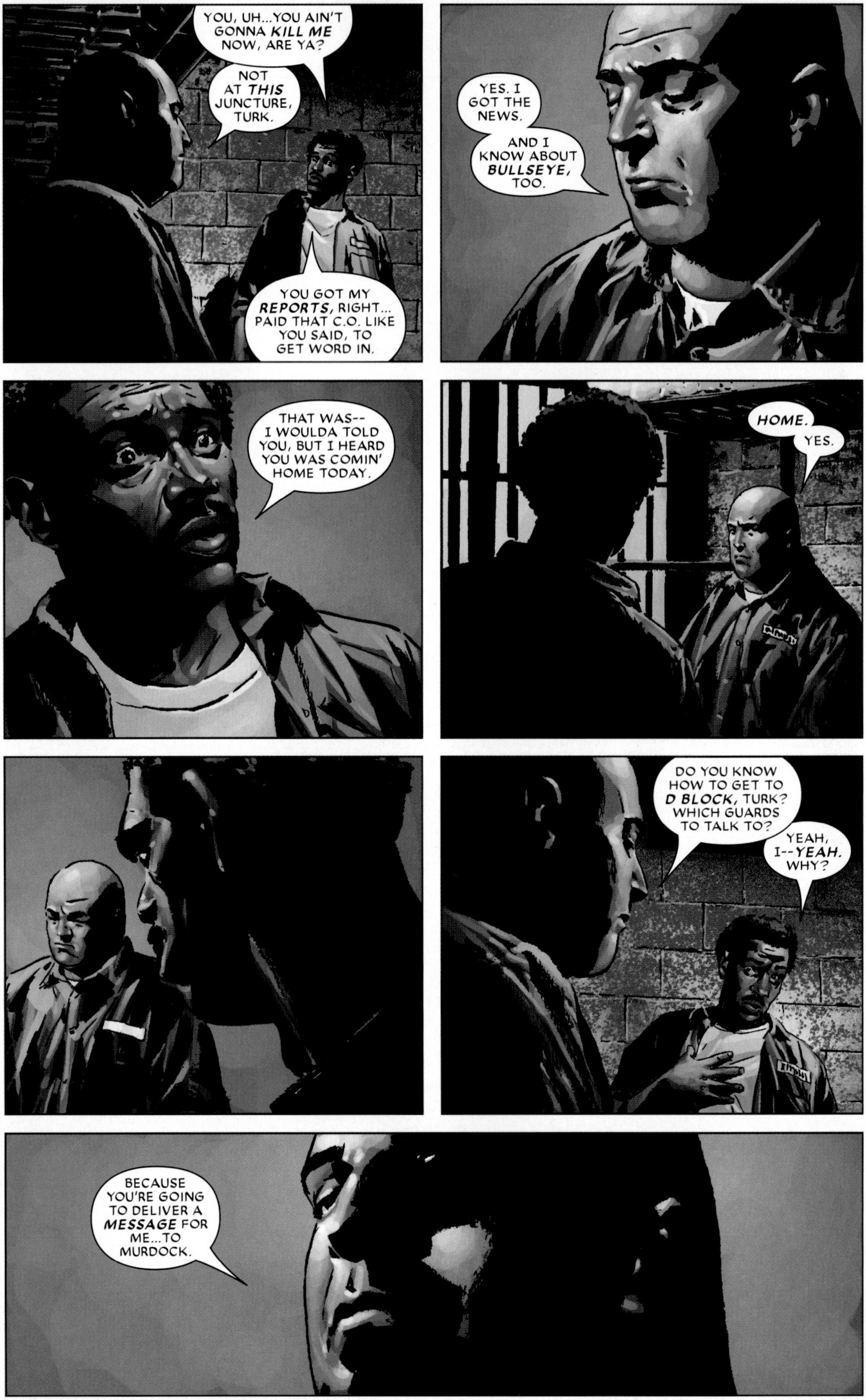
YOU, UH...YOU AIN'T GONNA KILL ME NOW, ARE YA?
NOT AT THIS JUNCTURE, TURK.
YOU GOT MY REPORTS, RIGHT... PAID THAT C.O. LIKE YOU SAID, TO GET WORD IN.
YES. I GOT THE NEWS.
AND I KNOW ABOUT BULLSEYE, TOO.
THAT WAS-- I WOULDA TOLD YOU, BUT I HEARD YOU WAS COMIN' HOME TODAY.
HOME.
YES.
DO YOU KNOW HOW TO GET TO D BLOCK, TURK? WHICH GUARDS TO TALK TO?
YEAH, I--YEAH. WHY?
BECAUSE YOU'RE GOING TO DELIVER A MESSAGE FOR ME...TO MURDOCK.

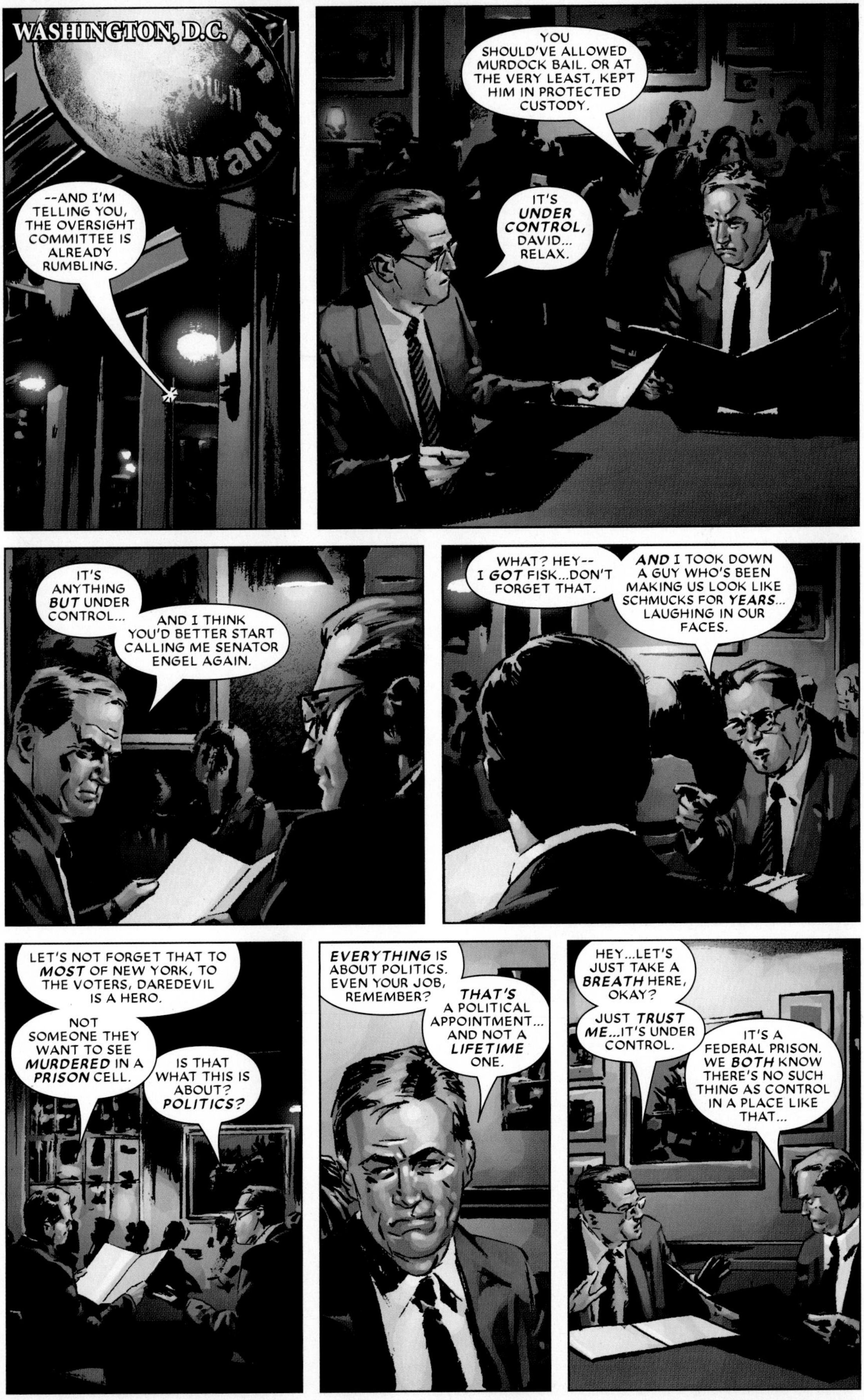
WASHINGTON, D.C.
--AND I'M TELLING YOU, THE OVERSIGHT COMMITTEE IS ALREADY RUMBLING.
YOU SHOULD'VE ALLOWED MURDOCK BAIL. OR AT THE VERY LEAST, KEPT HIM IN PROTECTED CUSTODY.
IT'S UNDER CONTROL, DAVID... RELAX.
IT'S ANYTHING BUT UNDER CONTROL...
AND I THINK YOU'D BETTER START CALLING ME SENATOR ENGEL AGAIN.
WHAT? HEY-- I GOT FISK...DON'T FORGET THAT.
AND I TOOK DOWN A GUY WHO'S BEEN MAKING US LOOK LIKE SCHMUCKS FOR YEARS... LAUGHING IN OUR FACES.
LET'S NOT FORGET THAT TO MOST OF NEW YORK, TO THE VOTERS, DAREDEVIL IS A HERO.
NOT SOMEONE THEY WANT TO SEE MURDERED IN A PRISON CELL.
IS THAT WHAT THIS IS ABOUT? POLITICS?
EVERYTHING IS ABOUT POLITICS. EVEN YOUR JOB, REMEMBER?
THAT'S A POLITICAL APPOINTMENT... AND NOT A LIFETIME ONE.
HEY...LET'S JUST TAKE A BREATH HERE, OKAY?
JUST TRUST ME...IT'S UNDER CONTROL.
IT'S A FEDERAL PRISON. WE BOTH KNOW THERE'S NO SUCH THING AS CONTROL IN A PLACE LIKE THAT...

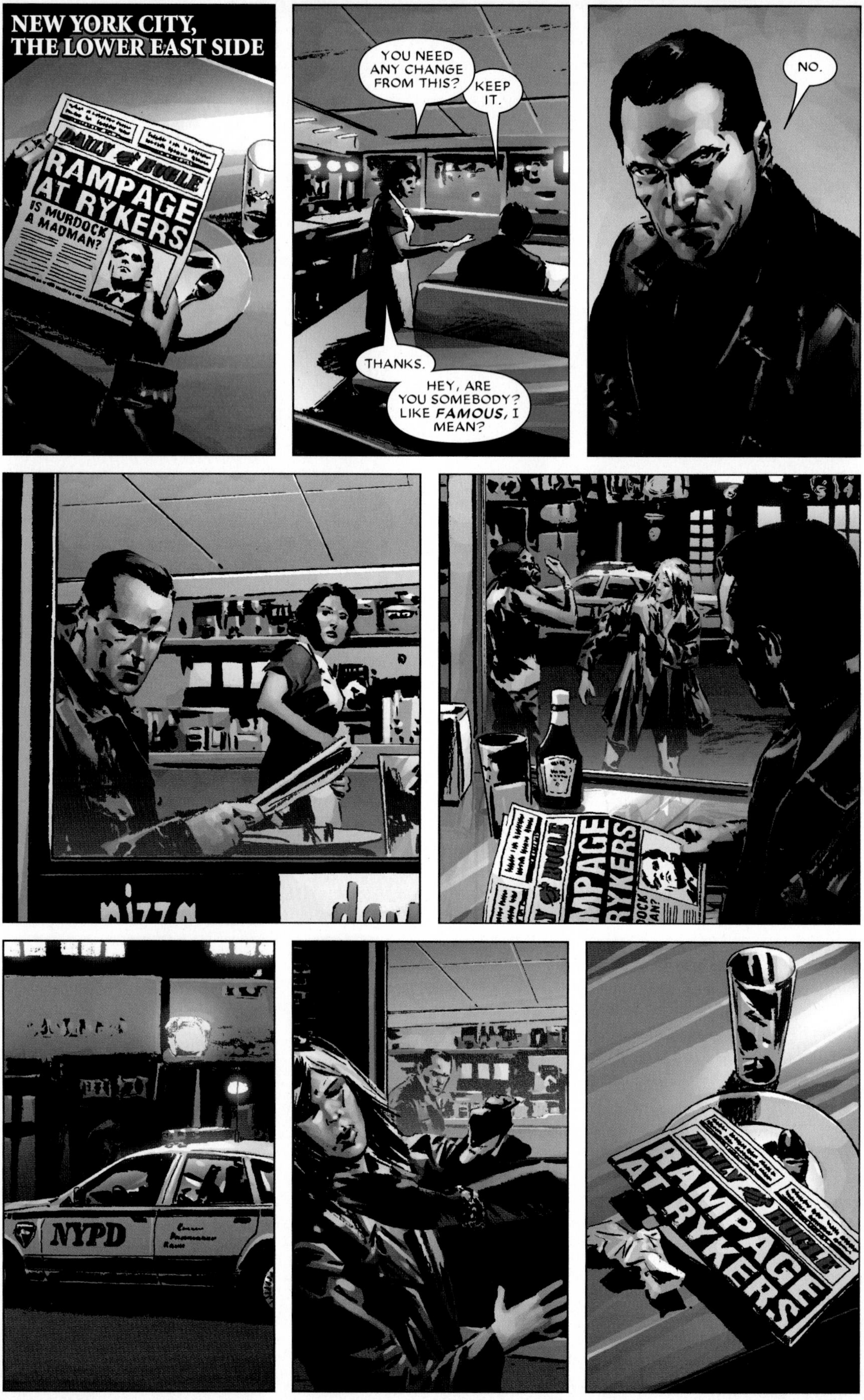

NEW YORK CITY, THE LOWER EAST SIDE
DAILY BUGLE
RAMPAGE AT RYKERS
IS MURDOCK A MADMAN?
YOU NEED ANY CHANGE FROM THIS?
KEEP IT.
THANKS.
HEY, ARE YOU SOMEBODY? LIKE *FAMOUS*, I MEAN?
NO.
pizza
NYPD
RAMPAGE AT RYKERS

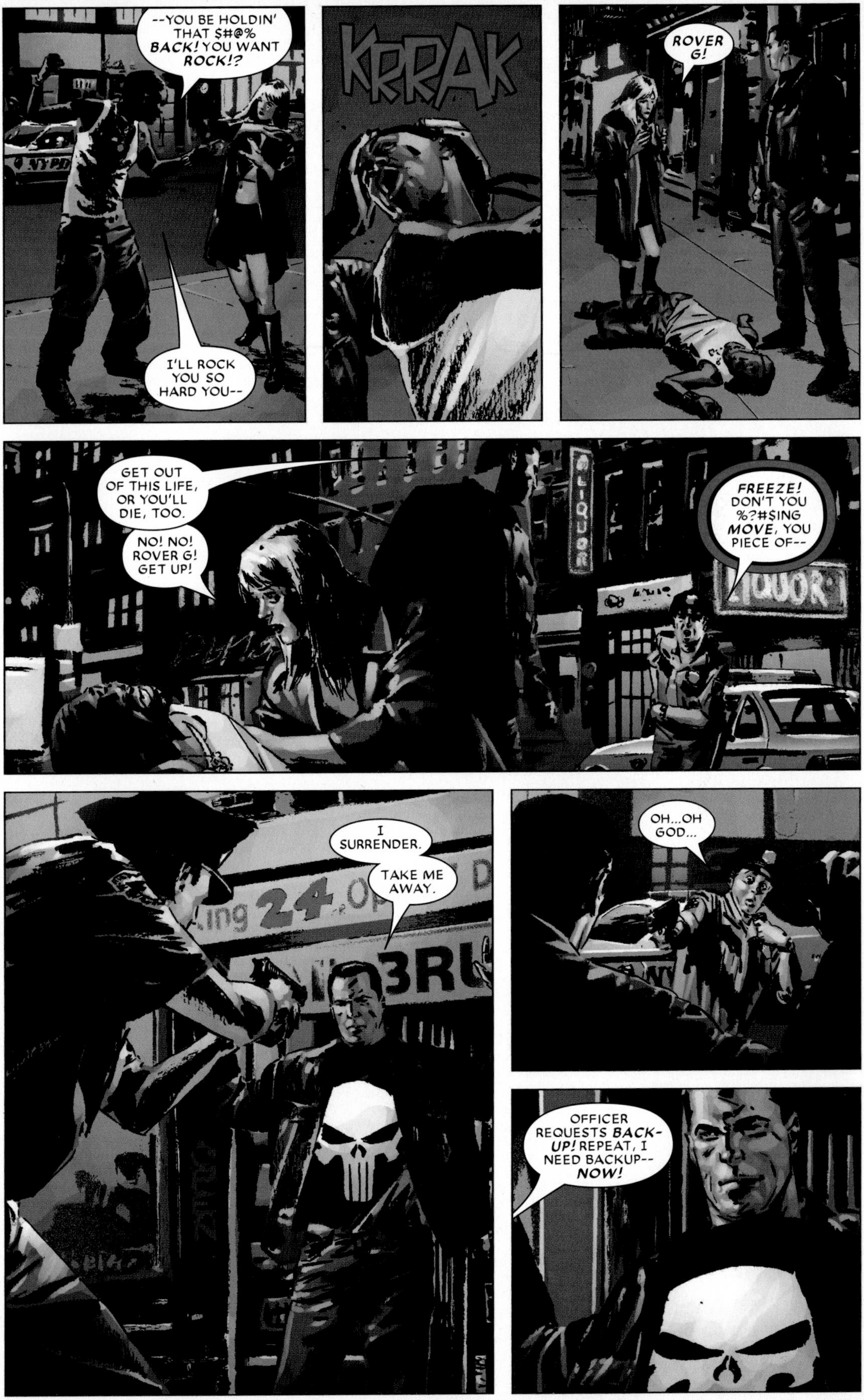
--YOU BE HOLDIN' THAT $#@% BACK! YOU WANT ROCK!?
NYPD
I'LL ROCK YOU SO HARD YOU--
KRRAK
ROVER G!
GET OUT OF THIS LIFE, OR YOU'LL DIE, TOO.
NO! NO! ROVER G! GET UP!
LIQUOR
FREEZE! DON'T YOU %?#$ING MOVE, YOU PIECE OF--
LIQUOR
I SURRENDER.
TAKE ME AWAY.
OH...OH GOD...
OFFICER REQUESTS BACK-UP! REPEAT, I NEED BACKUP-- NOW!

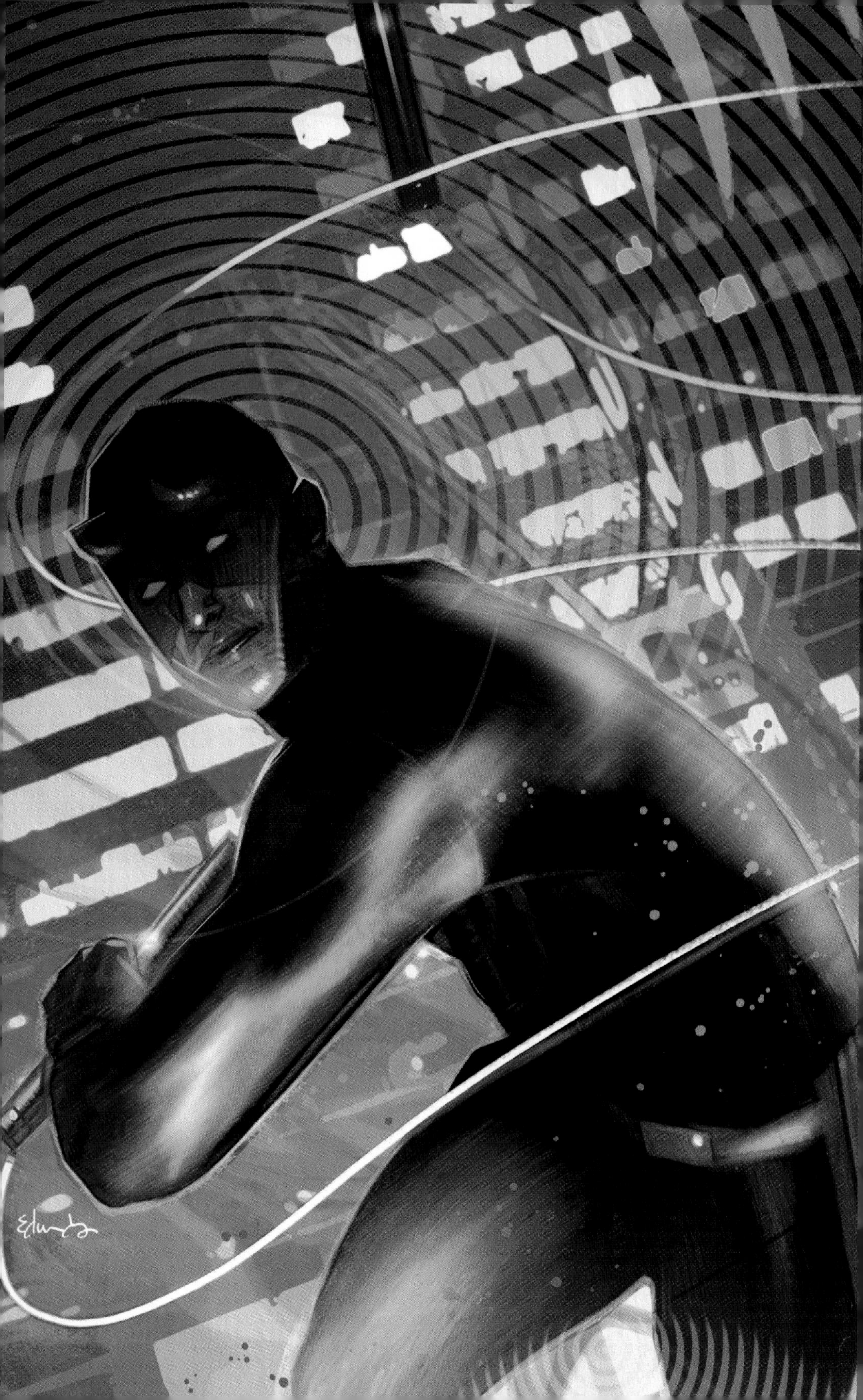

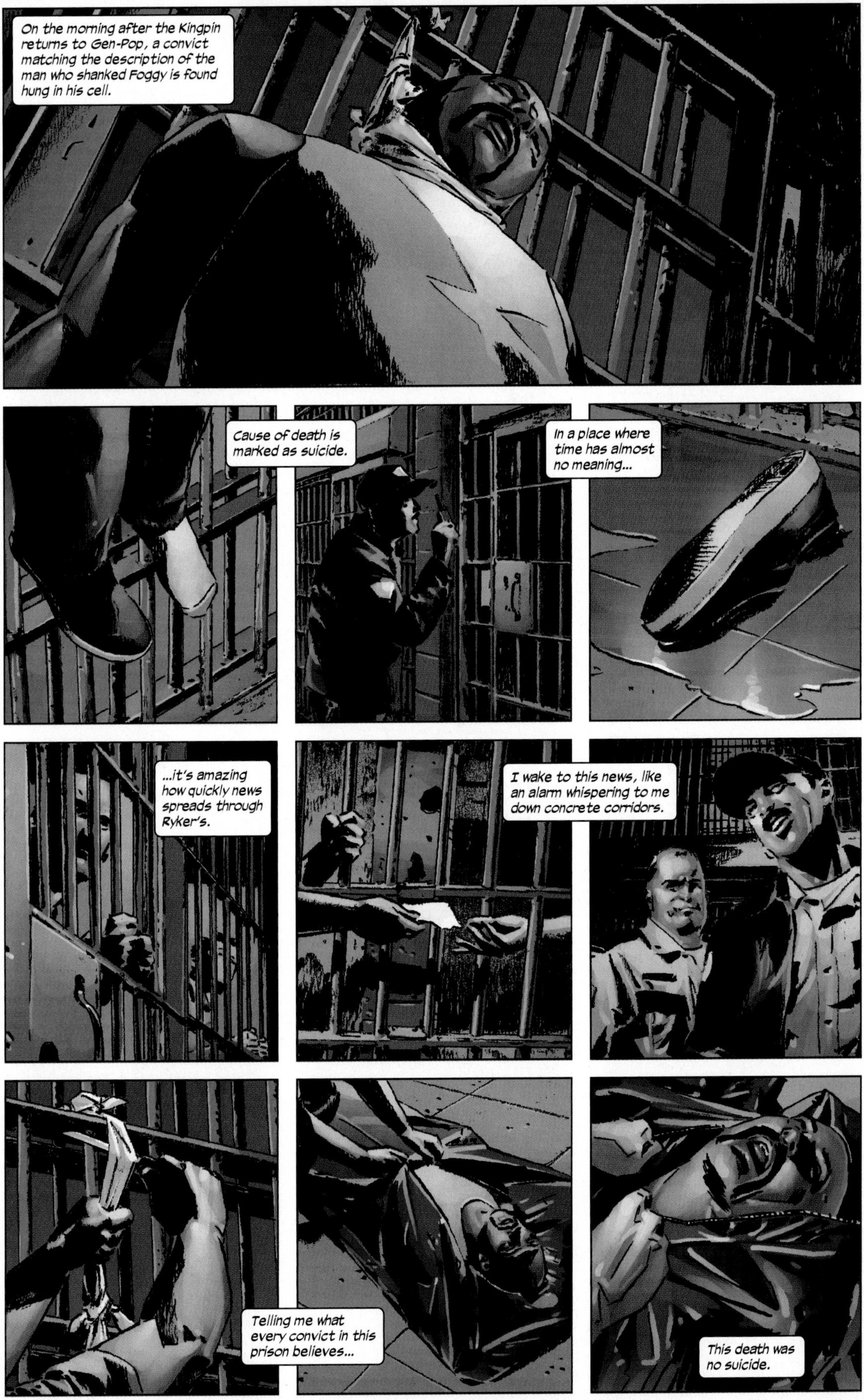
On the morning after the Kingpin returns to Gen-Pop, a convict matching the description of the man who shanked Foggy is found hung in his cell.
Cause of death is marked as suicide.
In a place where time has almost no meaning...
...it's amazing how quickly news spreads through Ryker's.
I wake to this news, like an alarm whispering to me down concrete corridors.
Telling me what every convict in this prison believes...
This death was no suicide.

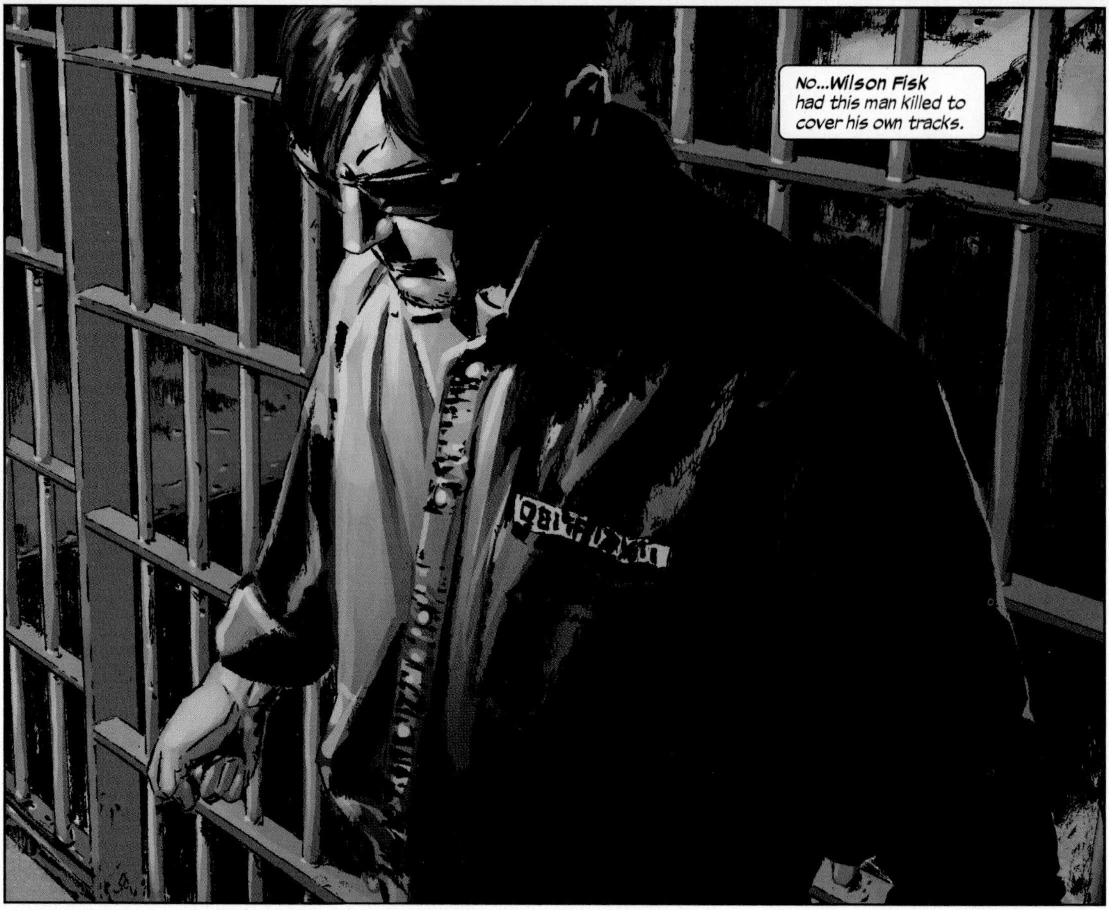
No...Wilson Fisk had this man killed to cover his own tracks.

THE DEVIL IN CELL-BLOCK D
PART FOUR

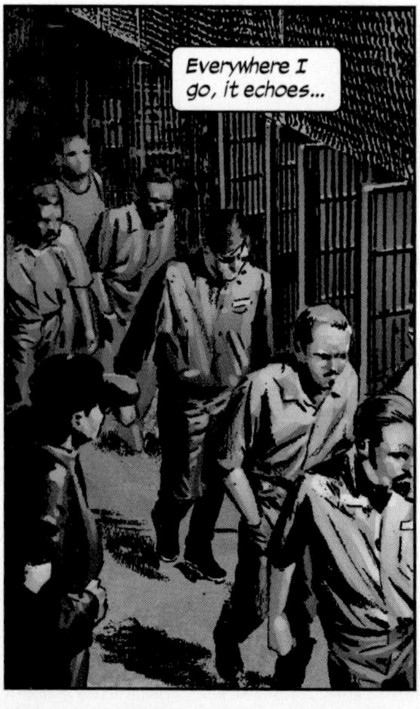
Everywhere I go, it echoes...

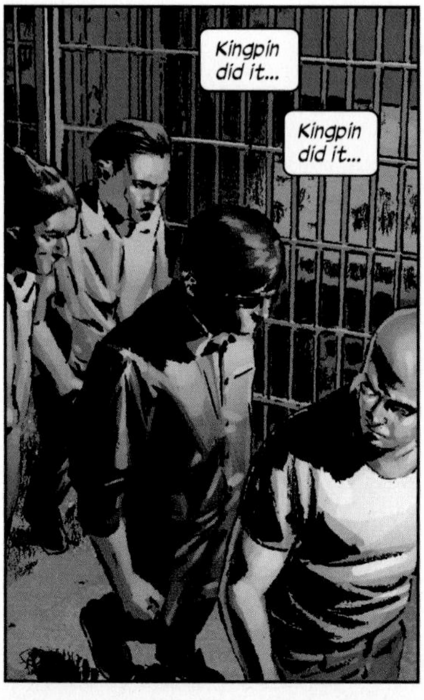
Kingpin did it...
Kingpin did it...

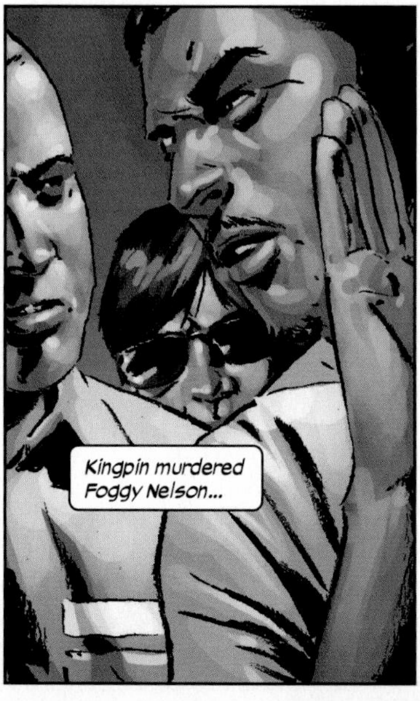
Kingpin murdered Foggy Nelson...

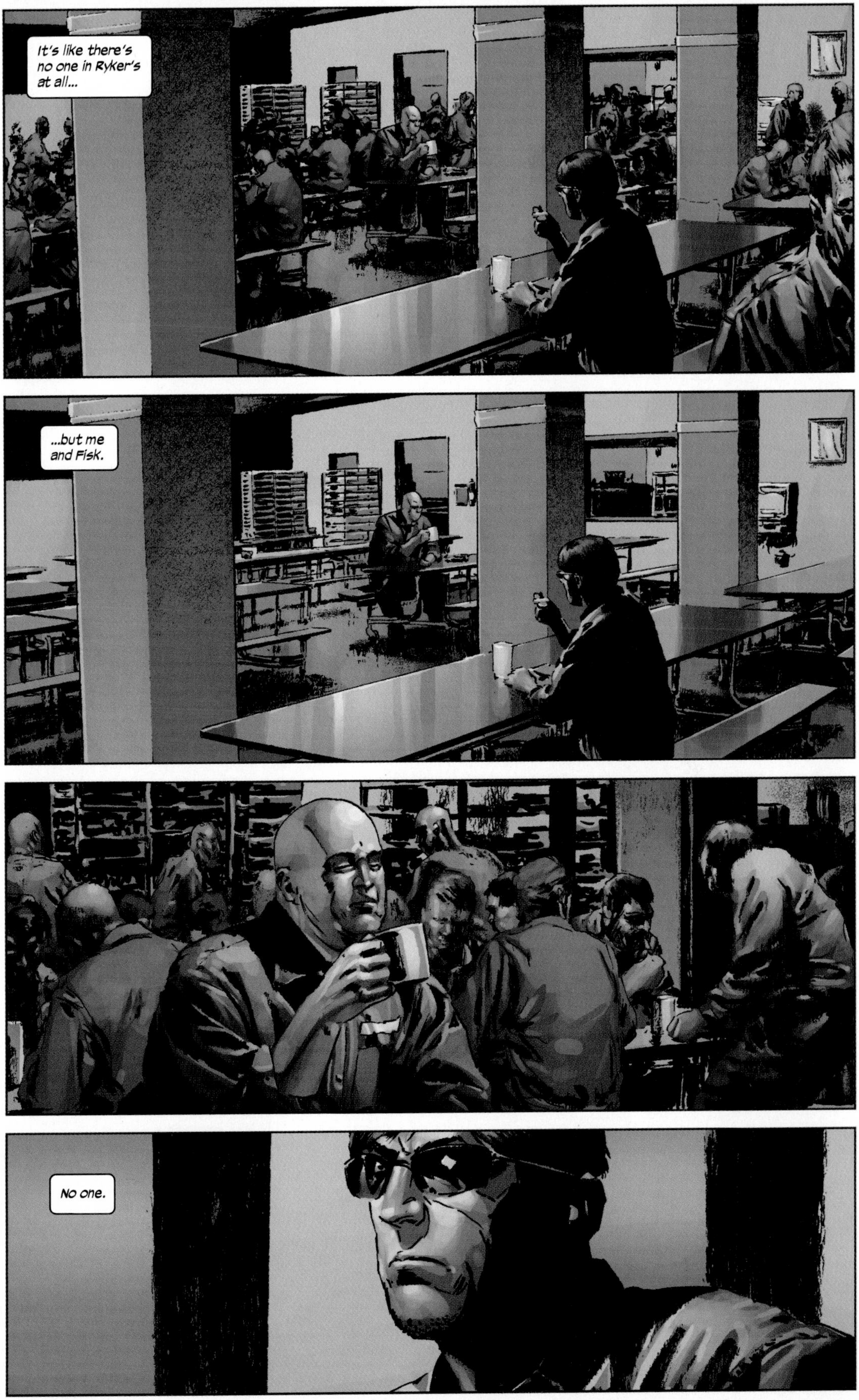
It's like there's no one in Ryker's at all...
...but me and Fisk.
No one.

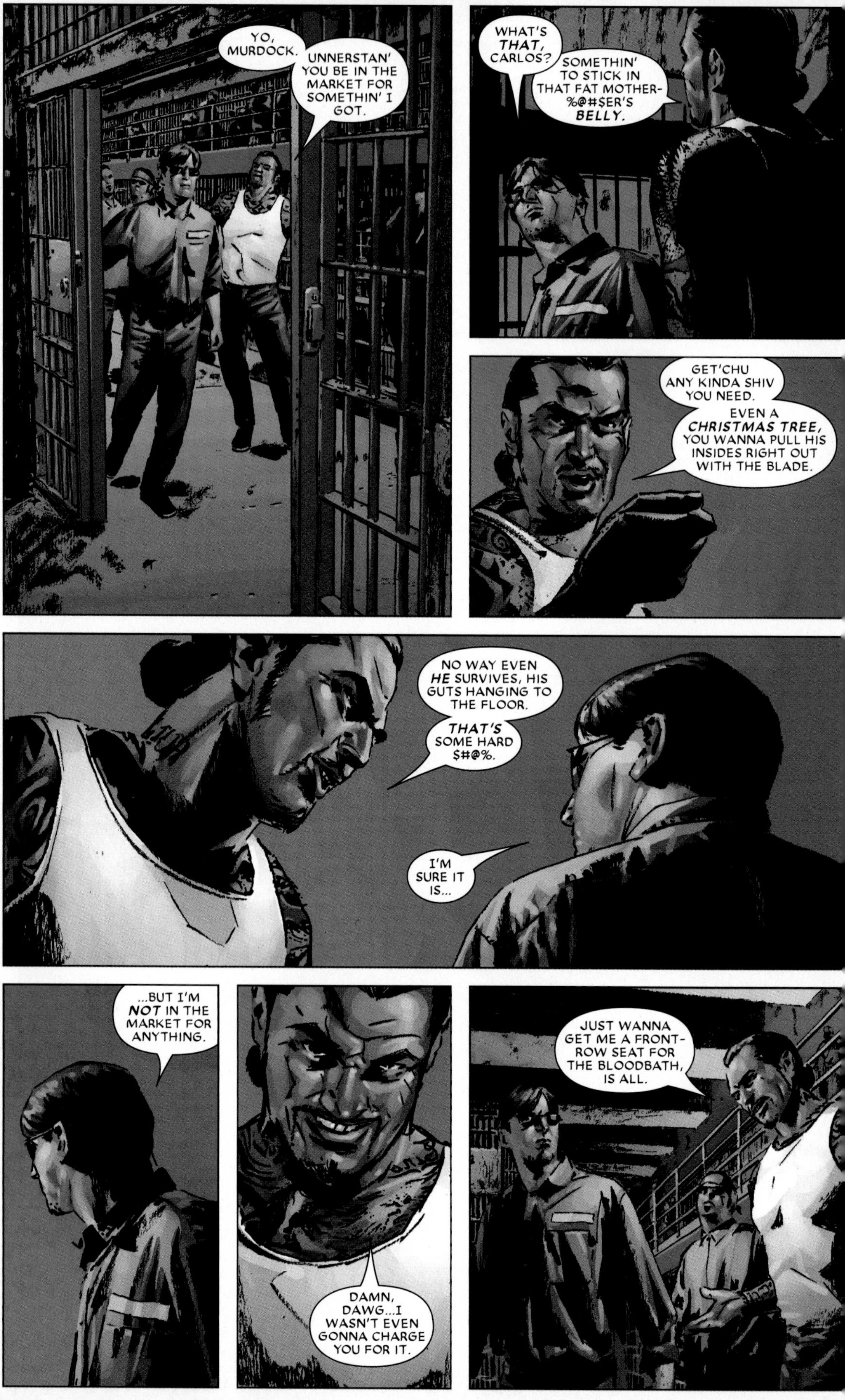

YO, MURDOCK.
UNNERSTAN' YOU BE IN THE MARKET FOR SOMETHIN' I GOT.
WHAT'S *THAT*, CARLOS?
SOMETHIN' TO STICK IN THAT FAT MOTHER-%@#$ER'S *BELLY.*
GET'CHU ANY KINDA SHIV YOU NEED.
EVEN A *CHRISTMAS TREE*, YOU WANNA PULL HIS INSIDES RIGHT OUT WITH THE BLADE.
NO WAY EVEN *HE* SURVIVES, HIS GUTS HANGING TO THE FLOOR.
THAT'S SOME HARD $#@%.
I'M SURE IT IS...
...BUT I'M *NOT* IN THE MARKET FOR ANYTHING.
DAMN, DAWG...I WASN'T EVEN GONNA CHARGE YOU FOR IT.
JUST WANNA GET ME A FRONT-ROW SEAT FOR THE BLOODBATH, IS ALL.

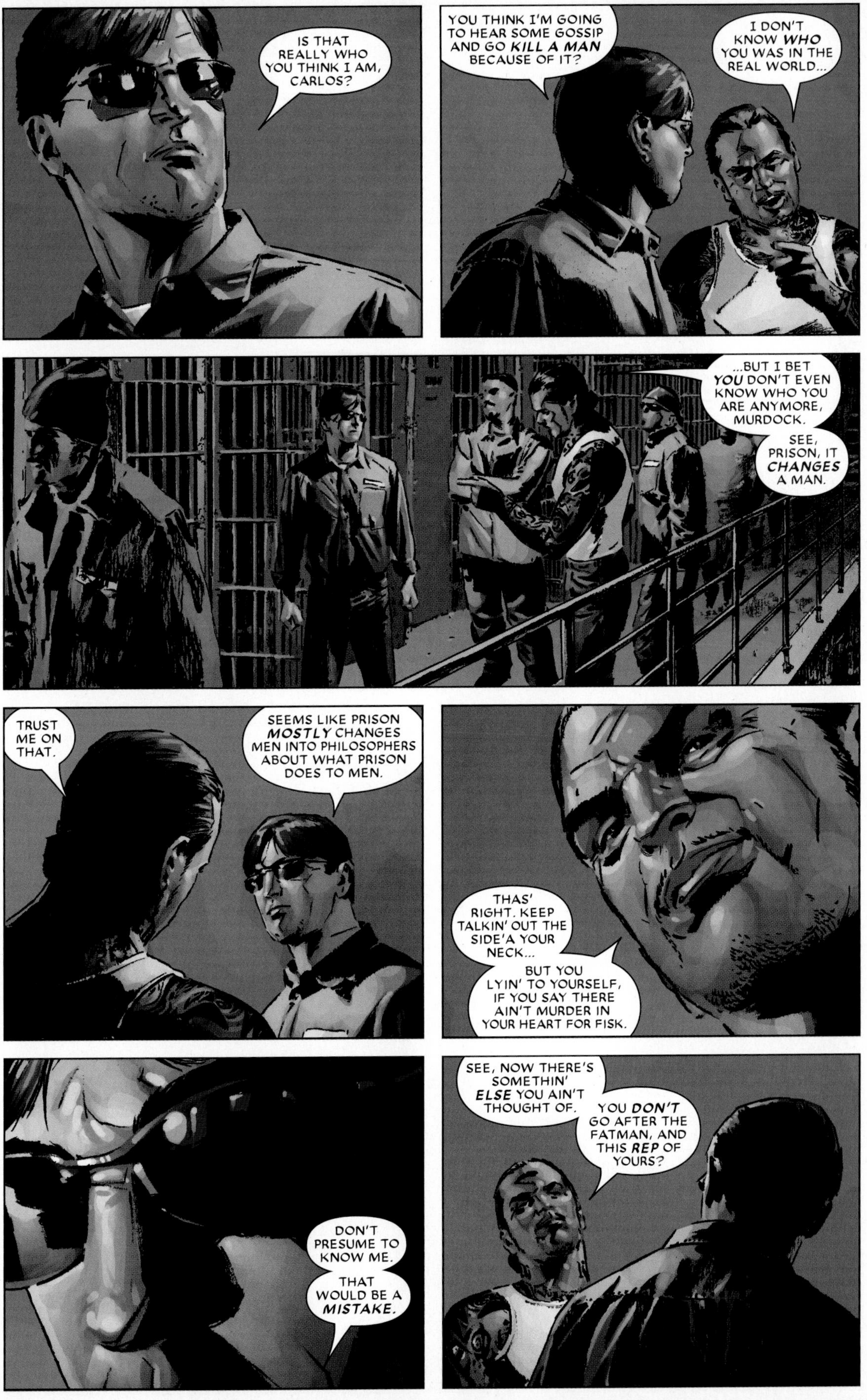
IS THAT REALLY WHO YOU THINK I AM, CARLOS?
YOU THINK I'M GOING TO HEAR SOME GOSSIP AND GO *KILL A MAN* BECAUSE OF IT?
I DON'T KNOW *WHO* YOU WAS IN THE REAL WORLD...
...BUT I BET *YOU* DON'T EVEN KNOW WHO YOU ARE ANYMORE, MURDOCK.
SEE, PRISON, IT *CHANGES* A MAN.
TRUST ME ON THAT.
SEEMS LIKE PRISON *MOSTLY* CHANGES MEN INTO PHILOSOPHERS ABOUT WHAT PRISON DOES TO MEN.
THAS' RIGHT. KEEP TALKIN' OUT THE SIDE'A YOUR NECK...
BUT YOU LYIN' TO YOURSELF, IF YOU SAY THERE AIN'T MURDER IN YOUR HEART FOR FISK.
DON'T PRESUME TO KNOW ME.
THAT WOULD BE A *MISTAKE.*
SEE, NOW THERE'S SOMETHIN' *ELSE* YOU AIN'T THOUGHT OF.
YOU *DON'T* GO AFTER THE FATMAN, AND THIS *REP* OF YOURS?

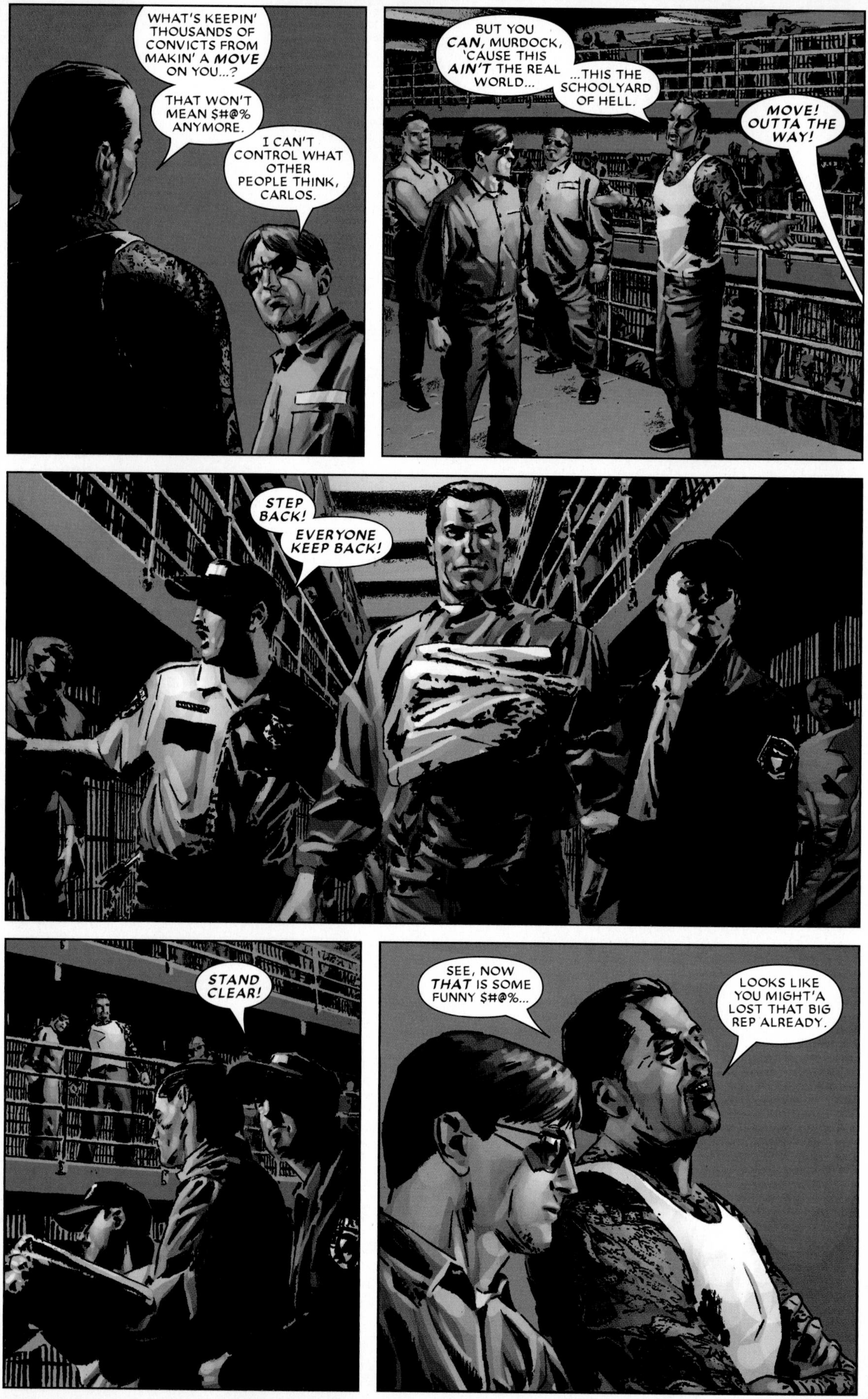
WHAT'S KEEPIN' THOUSANDS OF CONVICTS FROM MAKIN' A MOVE ON YOU...?
THAT WON'T MEAN $#@% ANYMORE.
I CAN'T CONTROL WHAT OTHER PEOPLE THINK, CARLOS.
BUT YOU CAN, MURDOCK, 'CAUSE THIS AIN'T THE REAL WORLD...
...THIS THE SCHOOLYARD OF HELL.
MOVE! OUTTA THE WAY!
STEP BACK!
EVERYONE KEEP BACK!
STAND CLEAR!
SEE, NOW THAT IS SOME FUNNY $#@%...
LOOKS LIKE YOU MIGHT'A LOST THAT BIG REP ALREADY.

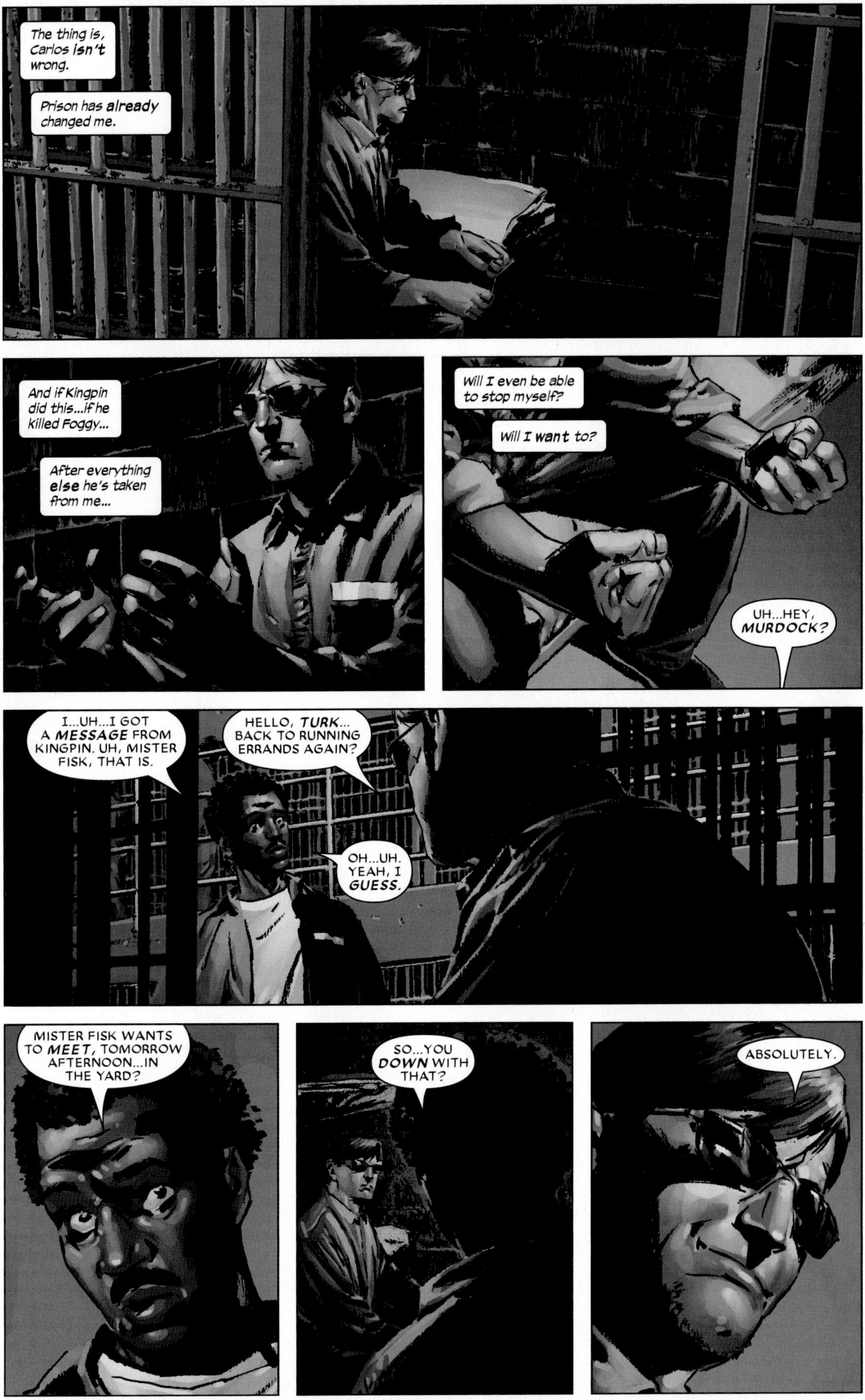
The thing is, Carlos isn't wrong.
Prison has already changed me.
And if Kingpin did this...if he killed Foggy...
After everything else he's taken from me...
Will I even be able to stop myself?
Will I want to?
UH...HEY, MURDOCK?
I...UH...I GOT A MESSAGE FROM KINGPIN. UH, MISTER FISK, THAT IS.
HELLO, TURK... BACK TO RUNNING ERRANDS AGAIN?
OH...UH. YEAH, I GUESS.
MISTER FISK WANTS TO MEET, TOMORROW AFTERNOON...IN THE YARD?
SO...YOU DOWN WITH THAT?
ABSOLUTELY.

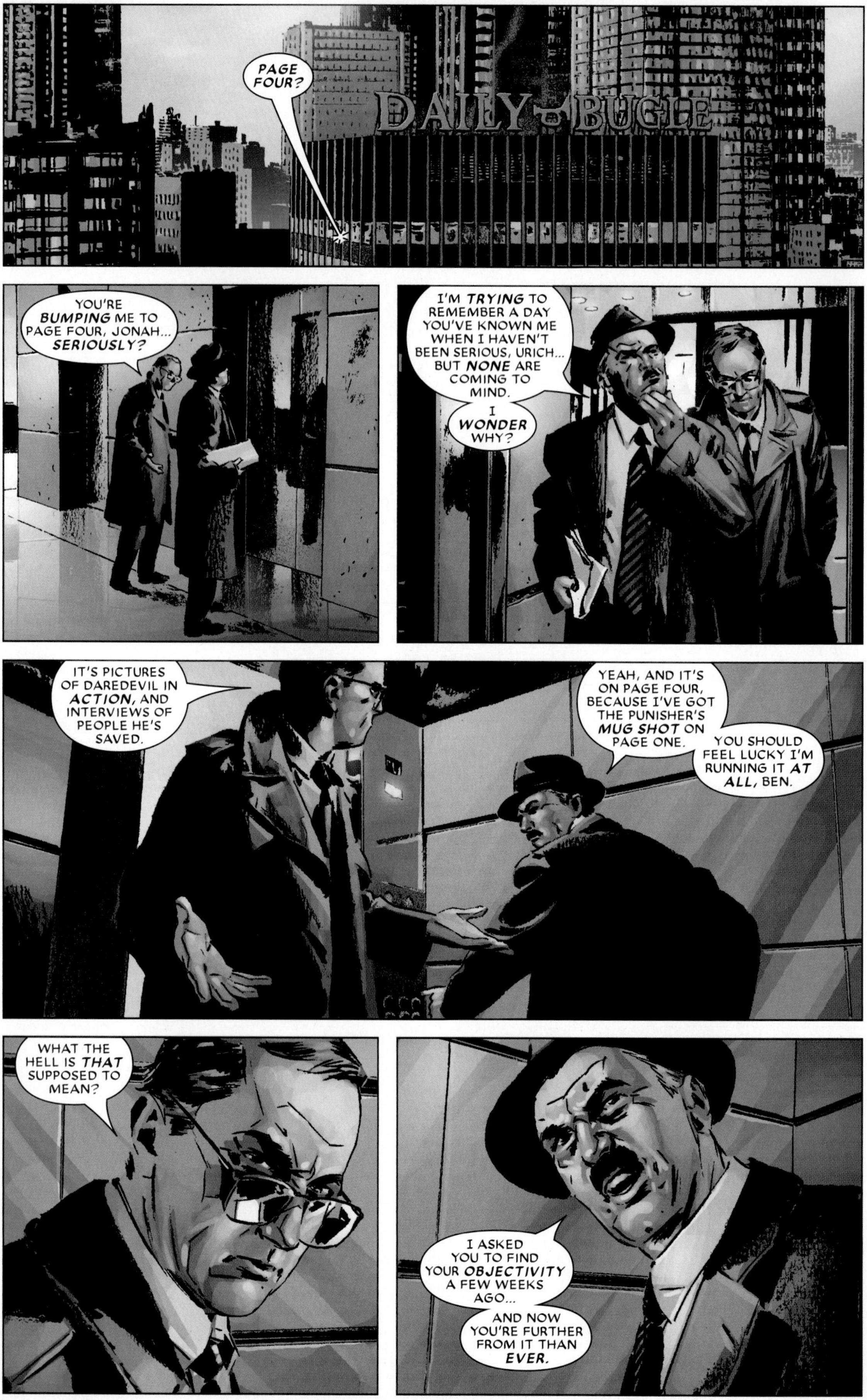
PAGE FOUR?
DAILY BUGLE
YOU'RE BUMPING ME TO PAGE FOUR, JONAH... SERIOUSLY?
I'M TRYING TO REMEMBER A DAY YOU'VE KNOWN ME WHEN I HAVEN'T BEEN SERIOUS, URICH... BUT NONE ARE COMING TO MIND.
I WONDER WHY?
IT'S PICTURES OF DAREDEVIL IN ACTION, AND INTERVIEWS OF PEOPLE HE'S SAVED.
YEAH, AND IT'S ON PAGE FOUR, BECAUSE I'VE GOT THE PUNISHER'S MUG SHOT ON PAGE ONE.
YOU SHOULD FEEL LUCKY I'M RUNNING IT AT ALL, BEN.
WHAT THE HELL IS THAT SUPPOSED TO MEAN?
I ASKED YOU TO FIND YOUR OBJECTIVITY A FEW WEEKS AGO...
AND NOW YOU'RE FURTHER FROM IT THAN EVER.

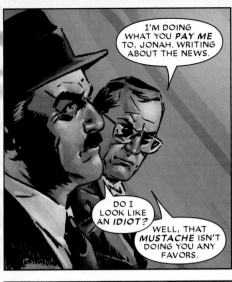

I'M DOING WHAT YOU *PAY ME* TO, JONAH. WRITING ABOUT THE NEWS.

DO I LOOK LIKE AN *IDIOT?*

WELL, THAT *MUSTACHE* ISN'T DOING YOU ANY FAVORS.

HAR-DEE-HAR-HAR, FUNNY GUY.

BUT THAT *DOESN'T* CHANGE THE FACT THAT YOU'RE *NOT* COVERING THE NEWS, YOU'RE ON A *CRUSADE.*

YOU'RE TRYING TO USE MY PAPER TO CLEAR YOUR FRIEND'S *NAME.*

I'M NOT *MAKING UP* A SINGLE THING.

THE PICTURES ARE *REAL.* THE PEOPLE INTERVIEWED ARE REAL.

AND SO IS YOUR *SLANTED* VIEWPOINT.

SAYS THE GUY WHO SLAMMED THE *AVENGERS* FOR LETTING *SPIDER-MAN* JOIN.

IT'S ON PAGE FOUR, URICH...AND *ONLY* BECAUSE IT HELPS SELL PAPERS.

TAKE IT AS A VICTORY.

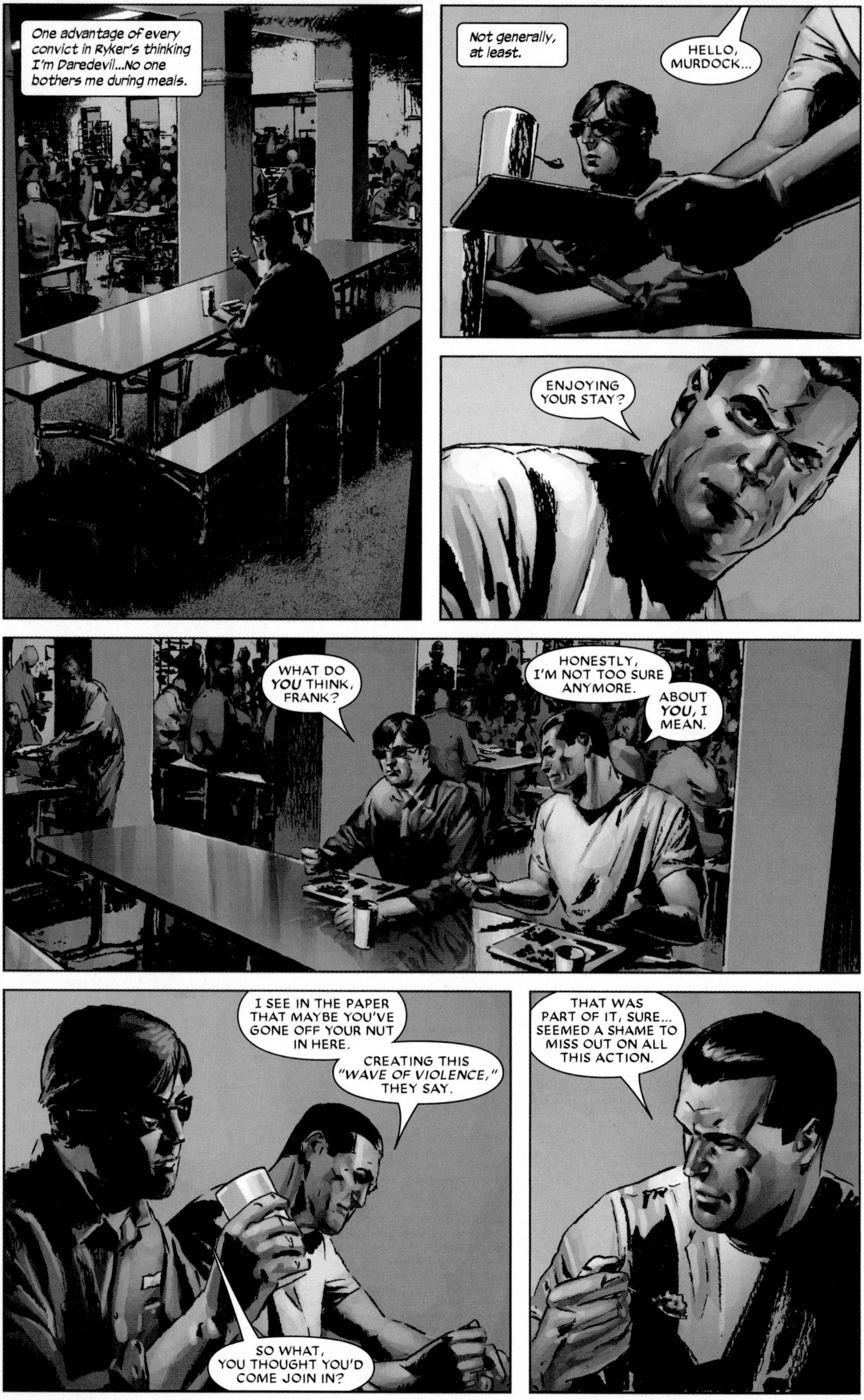
One advantage of every convict in Ryker's thinking I'm Daredevil...No one bothers me during meals.
Not generally, at least.
HELLO, MURDOCK...
ENJOYING YOUR STAY?
WHAT DO YOU THINK, FRANK?
HONESTLY, I'M NOT TOO SURE ANYMORE.
ABOUT YOU, I MEAN.
I SEE IN THE PAPER THAT MAYBE YOU'VE GONE OFF YOUR NUT IN HERE.
CREATING THIS "WAVE OF VIOLENCE," THEY SAY.
SO WHAT, YOU THOUGHT YOU'D COME JOIN IN?
THAT WAS PART OF IT, SURE... SEEMED A SHAME TO MISS OUT ON ALL THIS ACTION.

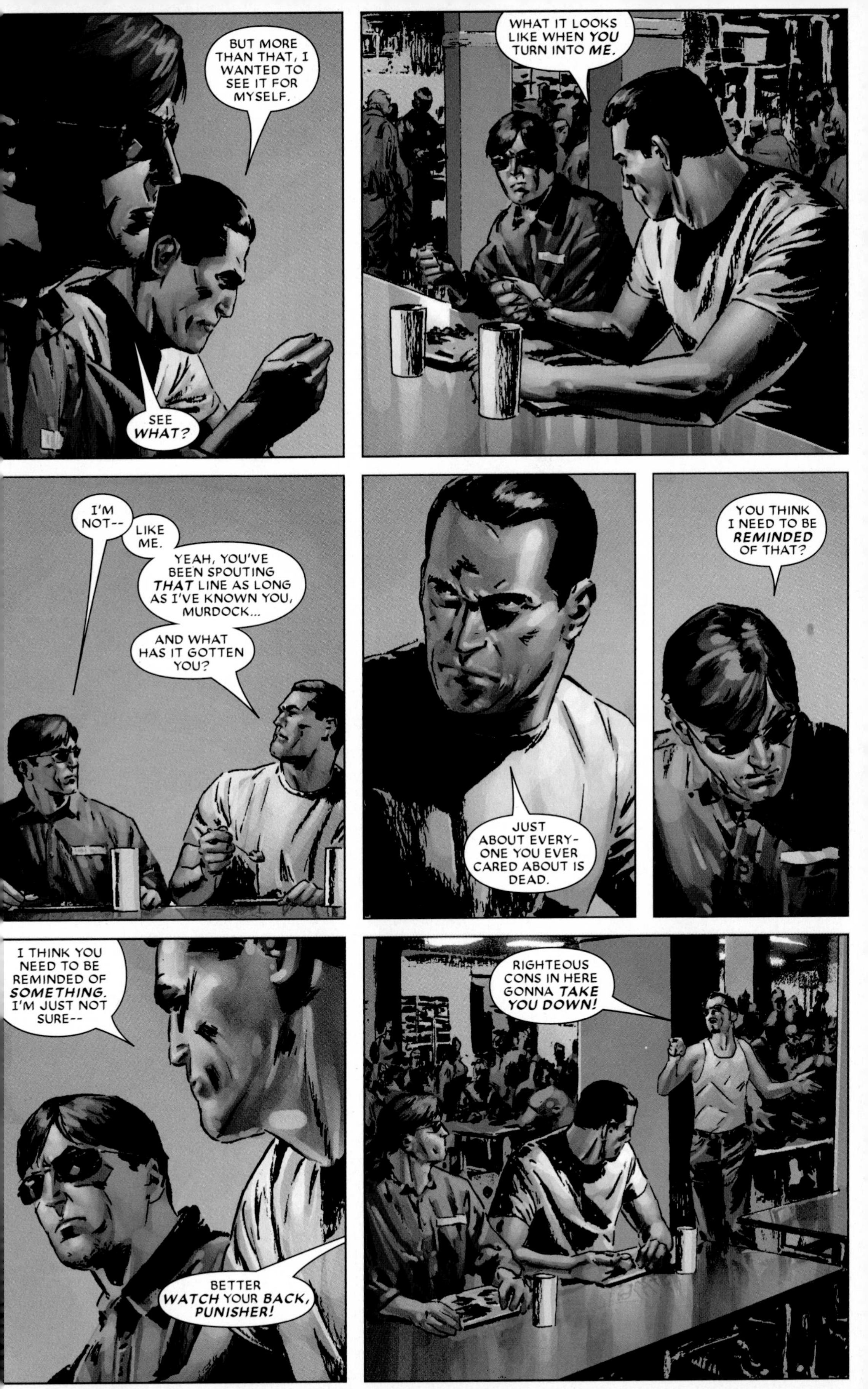

BUT MORE THAN THAT, I WANTED TO SEE IT FOR MYSELF.
SEE *WHAT?*
WHAT IT LOOKS LIKE WHEN *YOU* TURN INTO *ME.*
I'M NOT--
LIKE ME.
YEAH, YOU'VE BEEN SPOUTING *THAT* LINE AS LONG AS I'VE KNOWN YOU, MURDOCK...
AND WHAT HAS IT GOTTEN YOU?
JUST ABOUT EVERY-ONE YOU EVER CARED ABOUT IS DEAD.
YOU THINK I NEED TO BE *REMINDED* OF THAT?
I THINK YOU NEED TO BE REMINDED OF *SOMETHING.* I'M JUST NOT SURE--
BETTER *WATCH* YOUR *BACK, PUNISHER!*
RIGHTEOUS CONS IN HERE GONNA *TAKE YOU DOWN!*

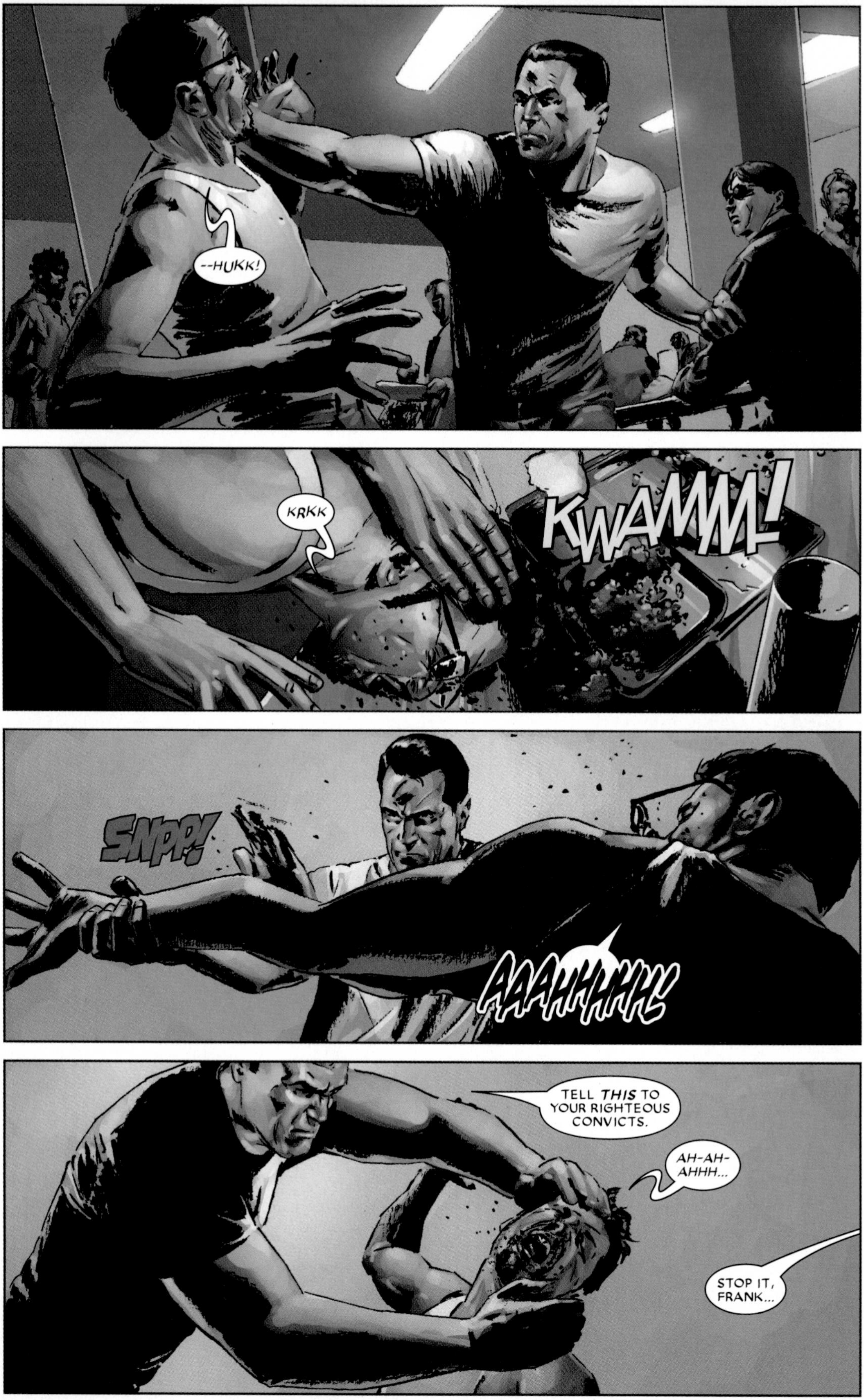
--HUKK!
KRKK
KWAMM!
SNPP!
AAAHHHH!
TELL THIS TO YOUR RIGHTEOUS CONVICTS.
AH-AH-AHHH...
STOP IT, FRANK...

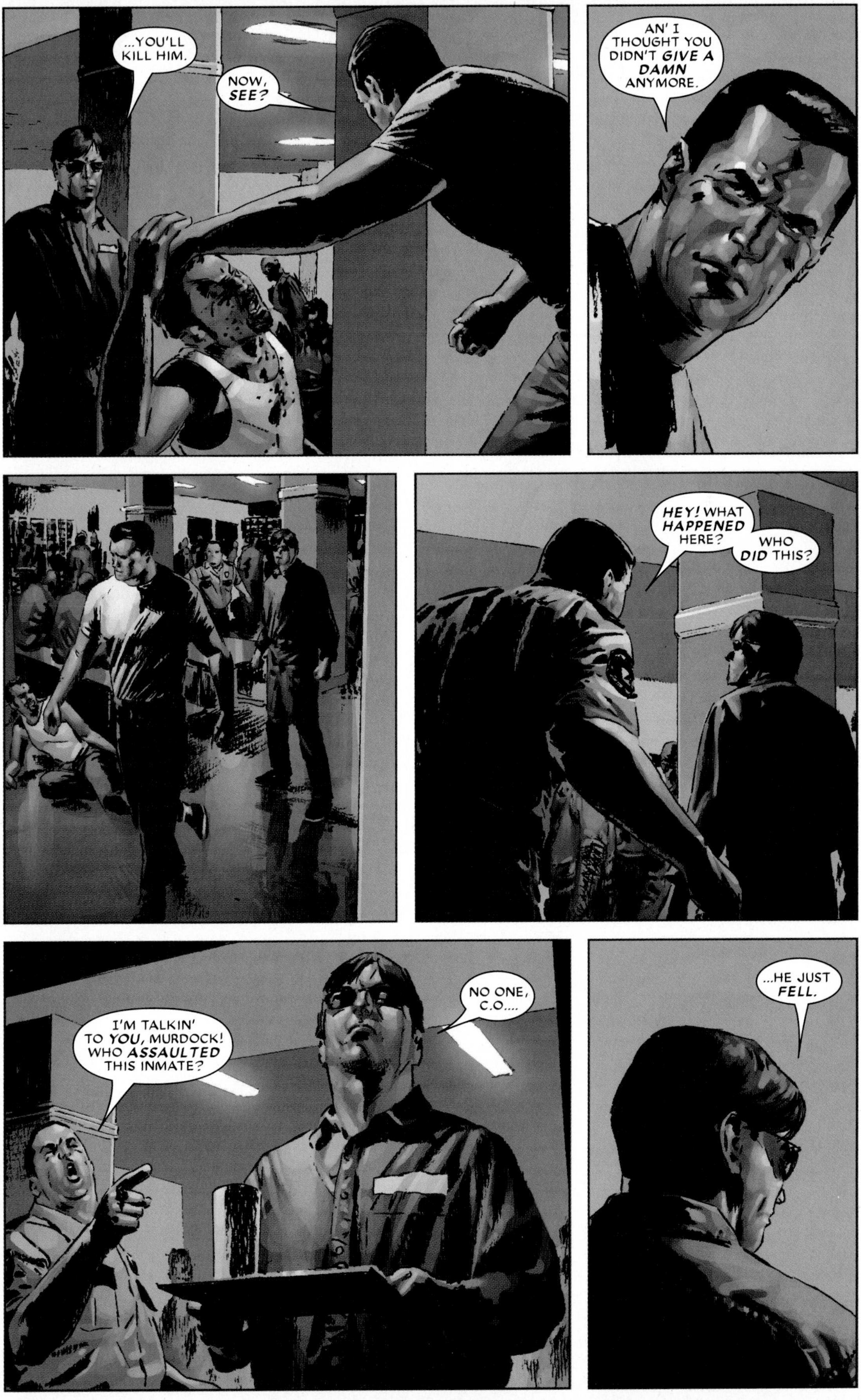
...YOU'LL KILL HIM.
NOW, *SEE?*
AN' I THOUGHT YOU DIDN'T *GIVE A DAMN* ANYMORE.
HEY! WHAT *HAPPENED* HERE?
WHO *DID* THIS?
I'M TALKIN' TO *YOU,* MURDOCK! WHO *ASSAULTED* THIS INMATE?
NO ONE, C.O....
...HE JUST *FELL.*

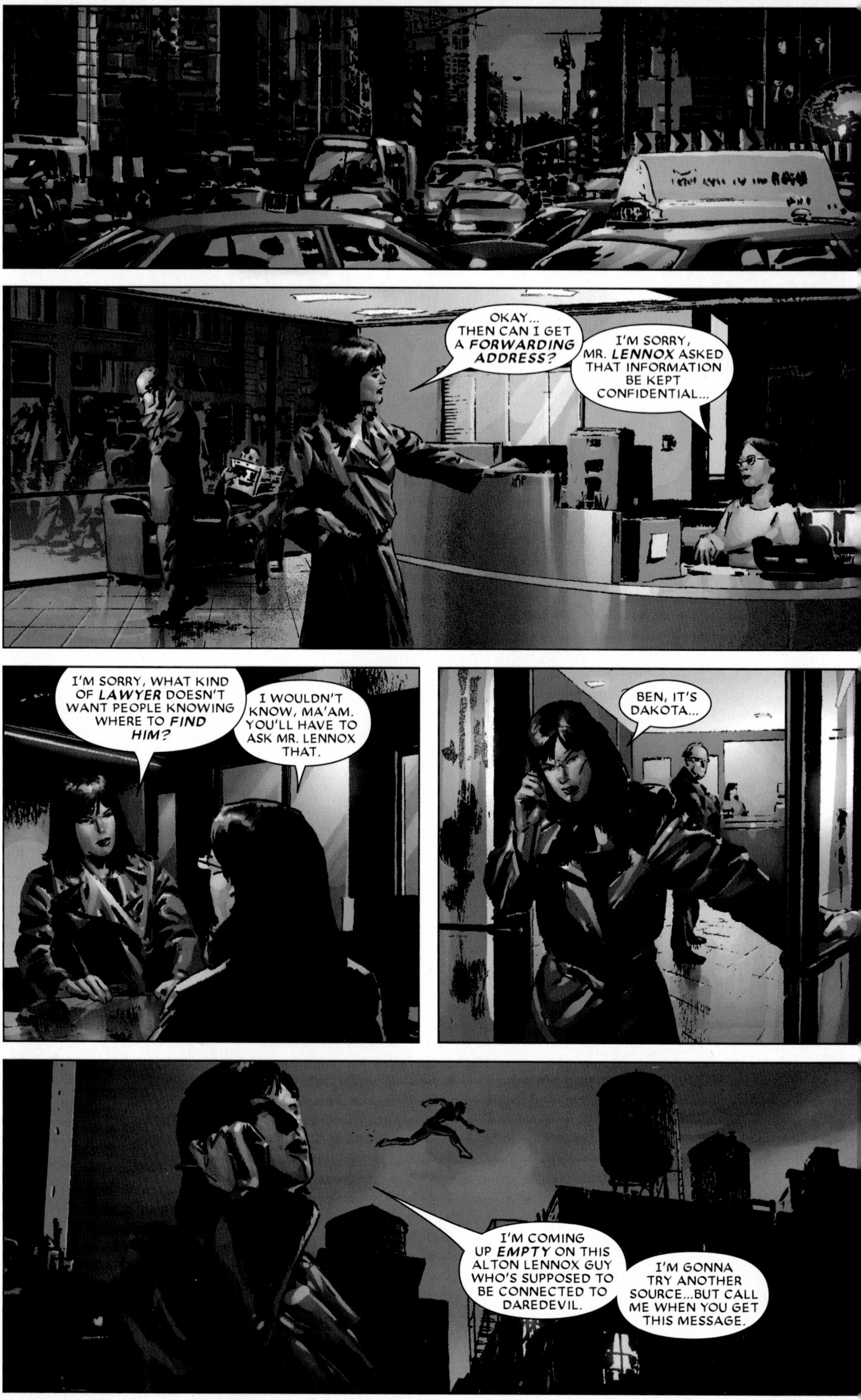
OKAY... THEN CAN I GET A FORWARDING ADDRESS?
I'M SORRY, MR. LENNOX ASKED THAT INFORMATION BE KEPT CONFIDENTIAL...
I'M SORRY, WHAT KIND OF LAWYER DOESN'T WANT PEOPLE KNOWING WHERE TO FIND HIM?
I WOULDN'T KNOW, MA'AM. YOU'LL HAVE TO ASK MR. LENNOX THAT.
BEN, IT'S DAKOTA...
I'M COMING UP EMPTY ON THIS ALTON LENNOX GUY WHO'S SUPPOSED TO BE CONNECTED TO DAREDEVIL.
I'M GONNA TRY ANOTHER SOURCE...BUT CALL ME WHEN YOU GET THIS MESSAGE.

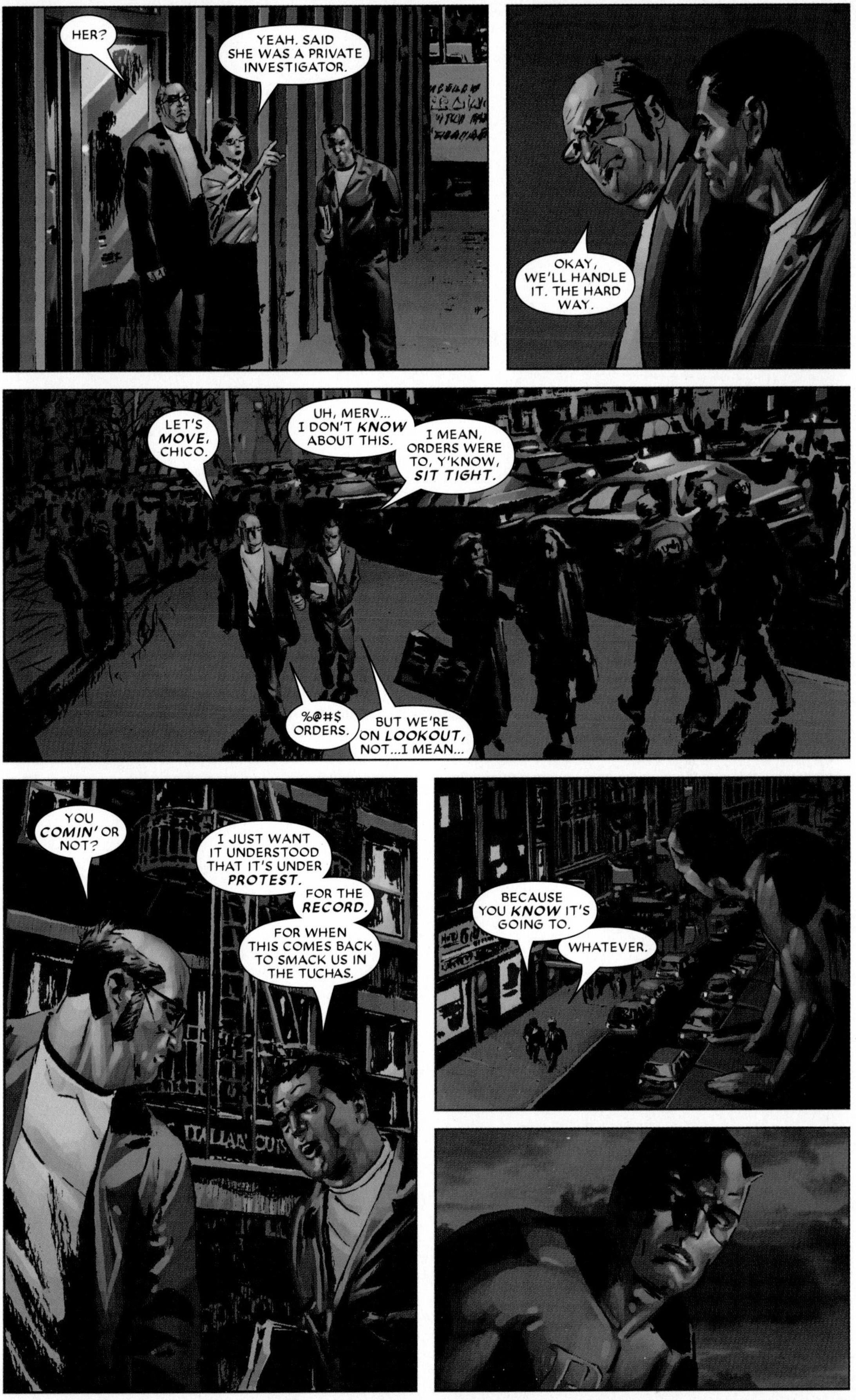
HER?
YEAH. SAID SHE WAS A PRIVATE INVESTIGATOR.
OKAY, WE'LL HANDLE IT. THE HARD WAY.
LET'S **MOVE**, CHICO.
UH, MERV... I DON'T **KNOW** ABOUT THIS.
I MEAN, ORDERS WERE TO, Y'KNOW, **SIT TIGHT**.
%@#$ ORDERS.
BUT WE'RE ON **LOOKOUT**, NOT...I MEAN...
YOU **COMIN'** OR NOT?
I JUST WANT IT UNDERSTOOD THAT IT'S UNDER **PROTEST**.
FOR THE **RECORD**.
FOR WHEN THIS COMES BACK TO SMACK US IN THE TUCHAS.
BECAUSE YOU **KNOW** IT'S GOING TO.
WHATEVER.

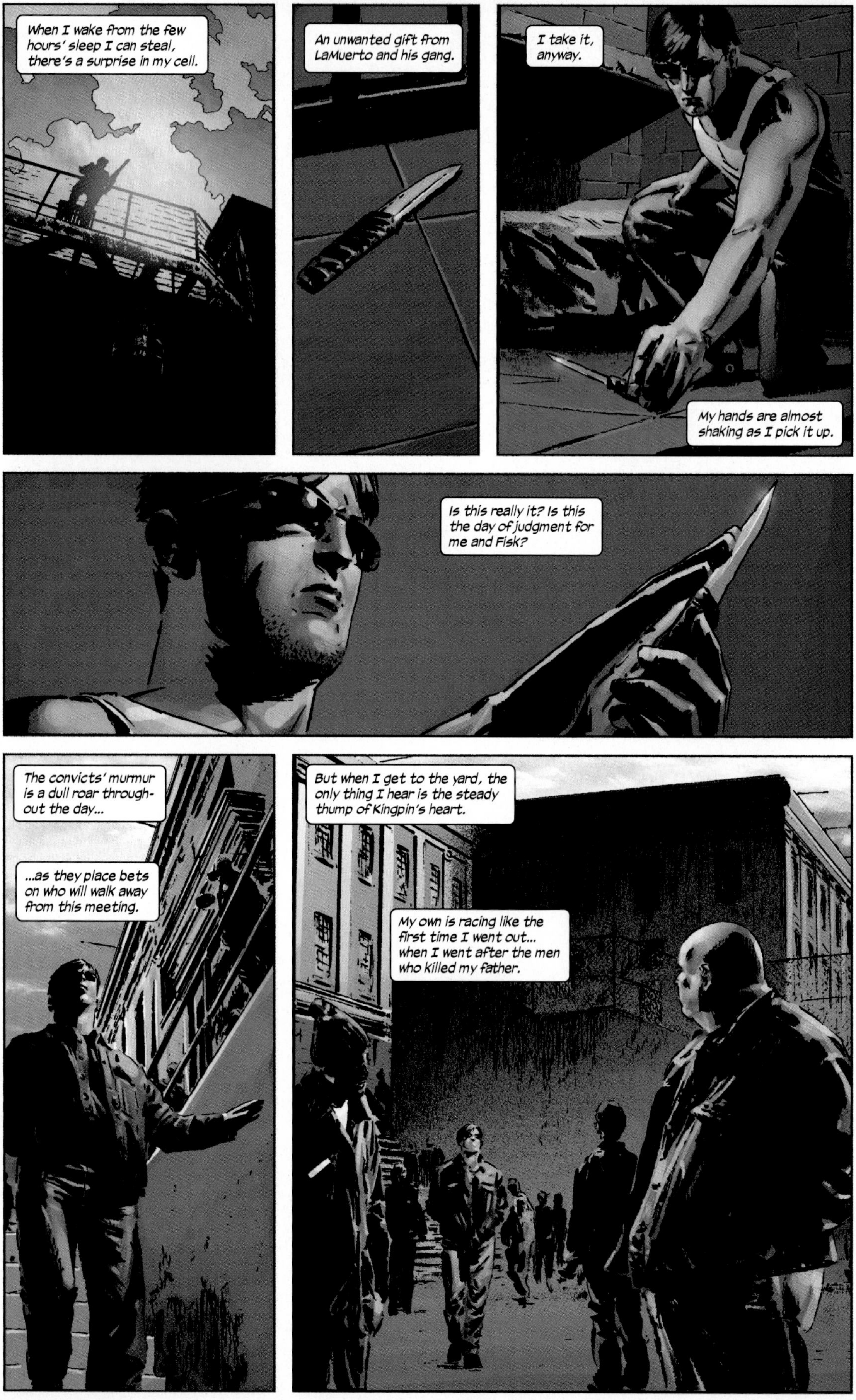
When I wake from the few hours' sleep I can steal, there's a surprise in my cell.
An unwanted gift from LaMuerto and his gang.
I take it, anyway.
My hands are almost shaking as I pick it up.
Is this really it? Is this the day of judgment for me and Fisk?
The convicts' murmur is a dull roar through-out the day...
...as they place bets on who will walk away from this meeting.
But when I get to the yard, the only thing I hear is the steady thump of Kingpin's heart.
My own is racing like the first time I went out... when I went after the men who killed my father.

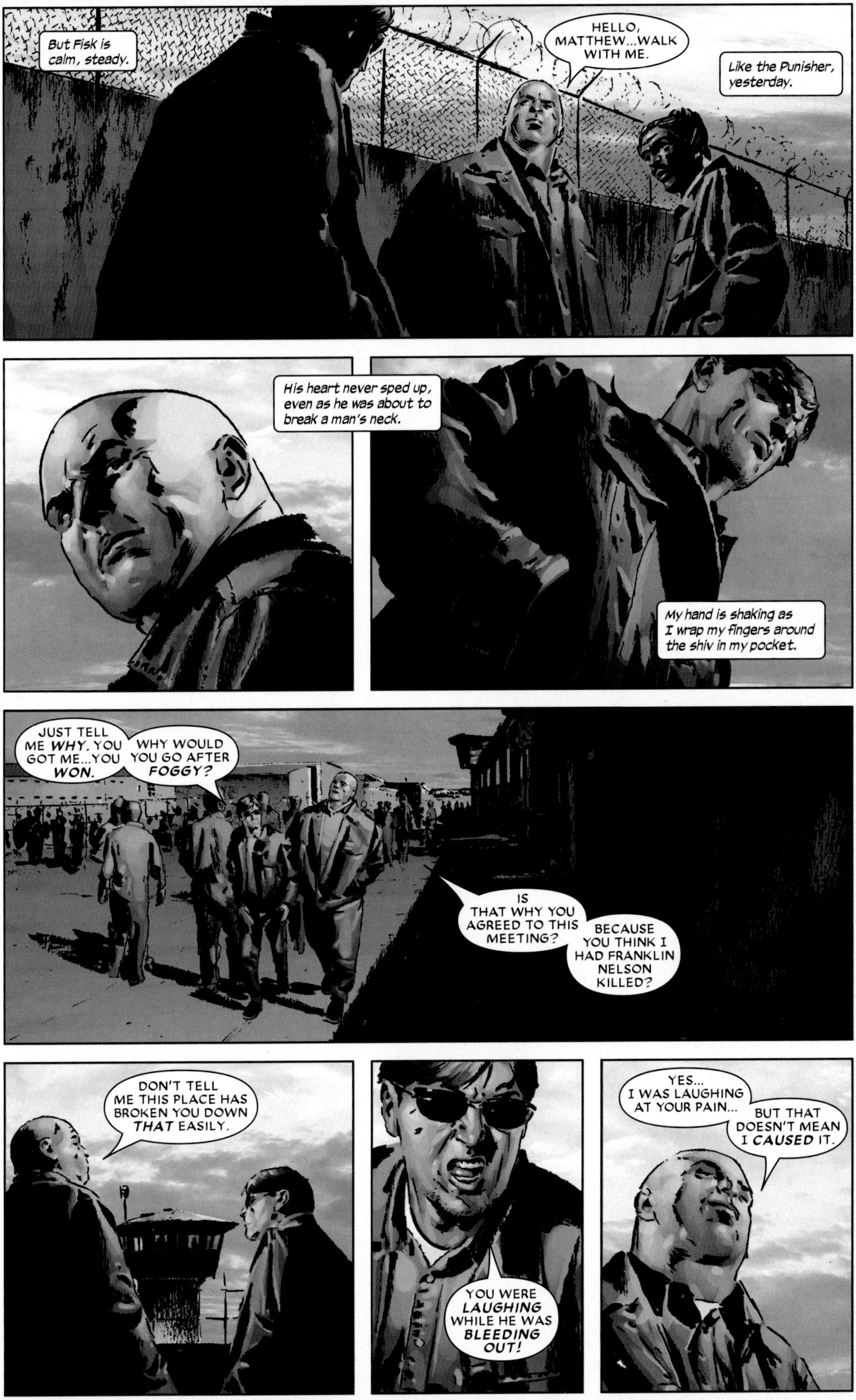
But Fisk is calm, steady.
HELLO, MATTHEW...WALK WITH ME.
Like the Punisher, yesterday.
His heart never sped up, even as he was about to break a man's neck.
My hand is shaking as I wrap my fingers around the shiv in my pocket.
JUST TELL ME WHY. YOU GOT ME...YOU WON.
WHY WOULD YOU GO AFTER FOGGY?
IS THAT WHY YOU AGREED TO THIS MEETING?
BECAUSE YOU THINK I HAD FRANKLIN NELSON KILLED?
DON'T TELL ME THIS PLACE HAS BROKEN YOU DOWN THAT EASILY.
YOU WERE LAUGHING WHILE HE WAS BLEEDING OUT!
YES... I WAS LAUGHING AT YOUR PAIN...
BUT THAT DOESN'T MEAN I CAUSED IT.

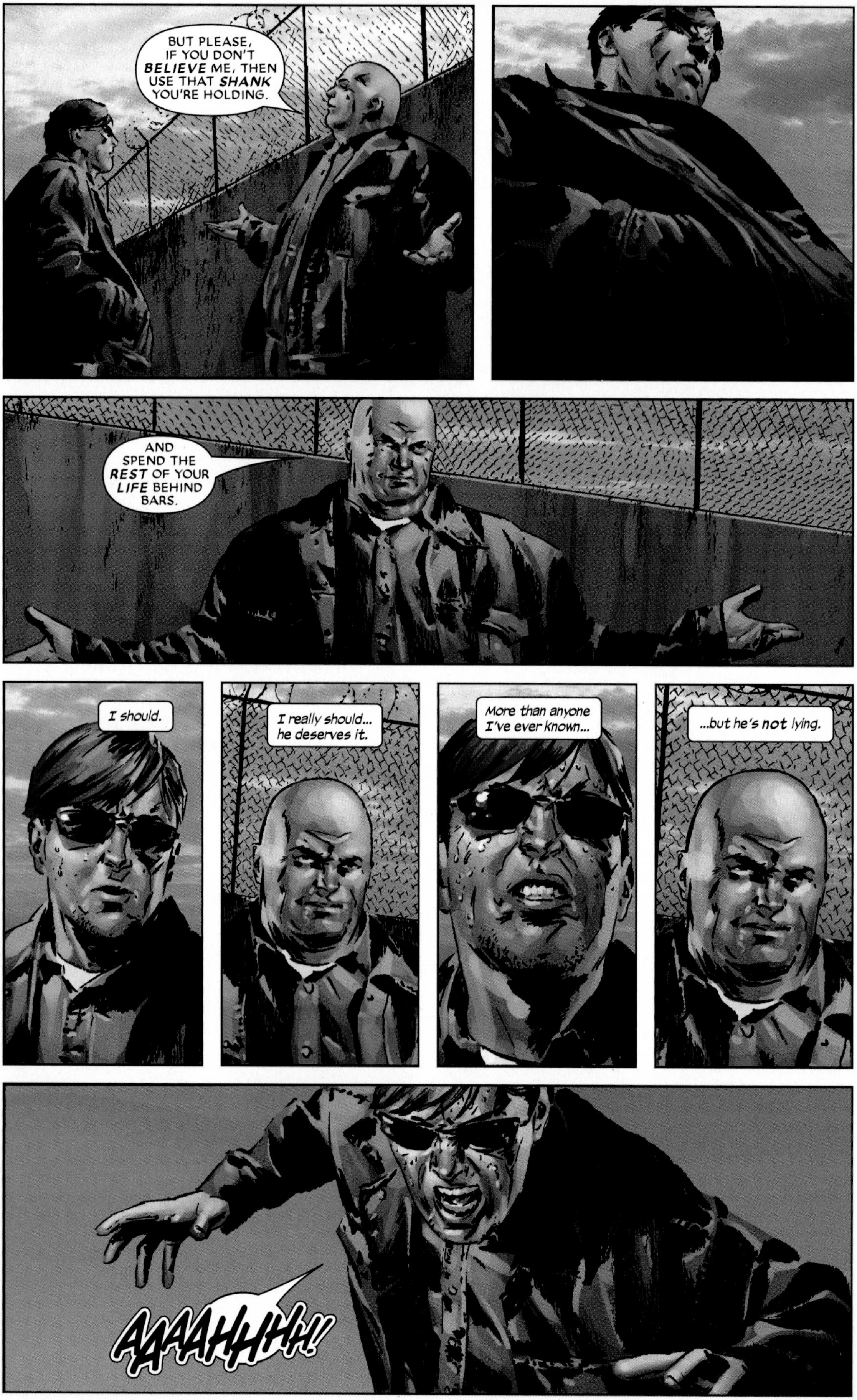
BUT PLEASE, IF YOU DON'T BELIEVE ME, THEN USE THAT SHANK YOU'RE HOLDING.
AND SPEND THE REST OF YOUR LIFE BEHIND BARS.
I should.
I really should... he deserves it.
More than anyone I've ever known...
...but he's not lying.
AAAAHHHH!

And I hate him even more for that.

DAMN YOU! DAMN YOU TO HELL!

WHO DID IT! TELL ME!

USE YOUR *HEAD*, MATTHEW... YOU USED TO BE *GOOD* AT THAT.

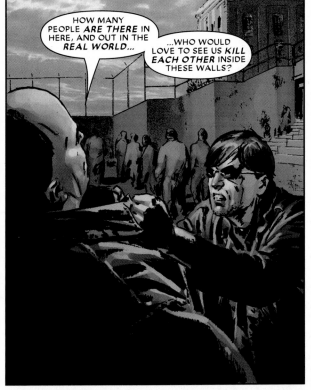

HOW MANY PEOPLE *ARE THERE* IN HERE, AND OUT IN THE *REAL WORLD*...

...WHO WOULD LOVE TO SEE US *KILL EACH OTHER* INSIDE THESE WALLS?

HAVEN'T YOU BEEN *MANIPULATED* ENOUGH TIMES TO REMEMBER WHAT IT *FEELS LIKE?*

OR HAVE YOU JUST GONE *NATIVE?*

DAMN IT...

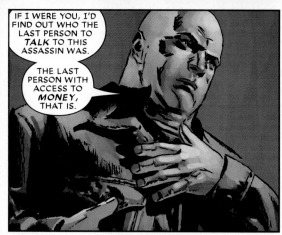

IF I WERE YOU, I'D FIND OUT WHO THE LAST PERSON TO *TALK* TO THIS ASSASSIN WAS.

THE LAST PERSON WITH ACCESS TO *MONEY*, THAT IS.

IT'S STILL YOUR FAULT... IF I WASN'T *IN* HERE...

THAT'S A *CHICKEN-AND-EGG* ARGUMENT AT THIS POINT, *ISN'T IT?*

YOU AND I ARE *ENEMIES...* WE ALWAYS *WILL* BE.

BUT RIGHT NOW WE NEED TO RISE *ABOVE* THAT.

THE HELL WE DO.

YES. THE HELL WE *DO,* IN CASE YOU HAVEN'T *NOTICED,* THERE'S A *WAR* BREWING IN RYKER'S...

AND WHEN IT *BLOWS,* IT'S GOING TO BLOW RIGHT AT YOU AND ME.

AND I, FOR ONE, DO NOT INTEND TO *DIE* BEHIND BARS...

DO *YOU?*

WHEN THE *ANSWERS* YOU SEEK ARE LIKELY BACK IN THE REAL WORLD?

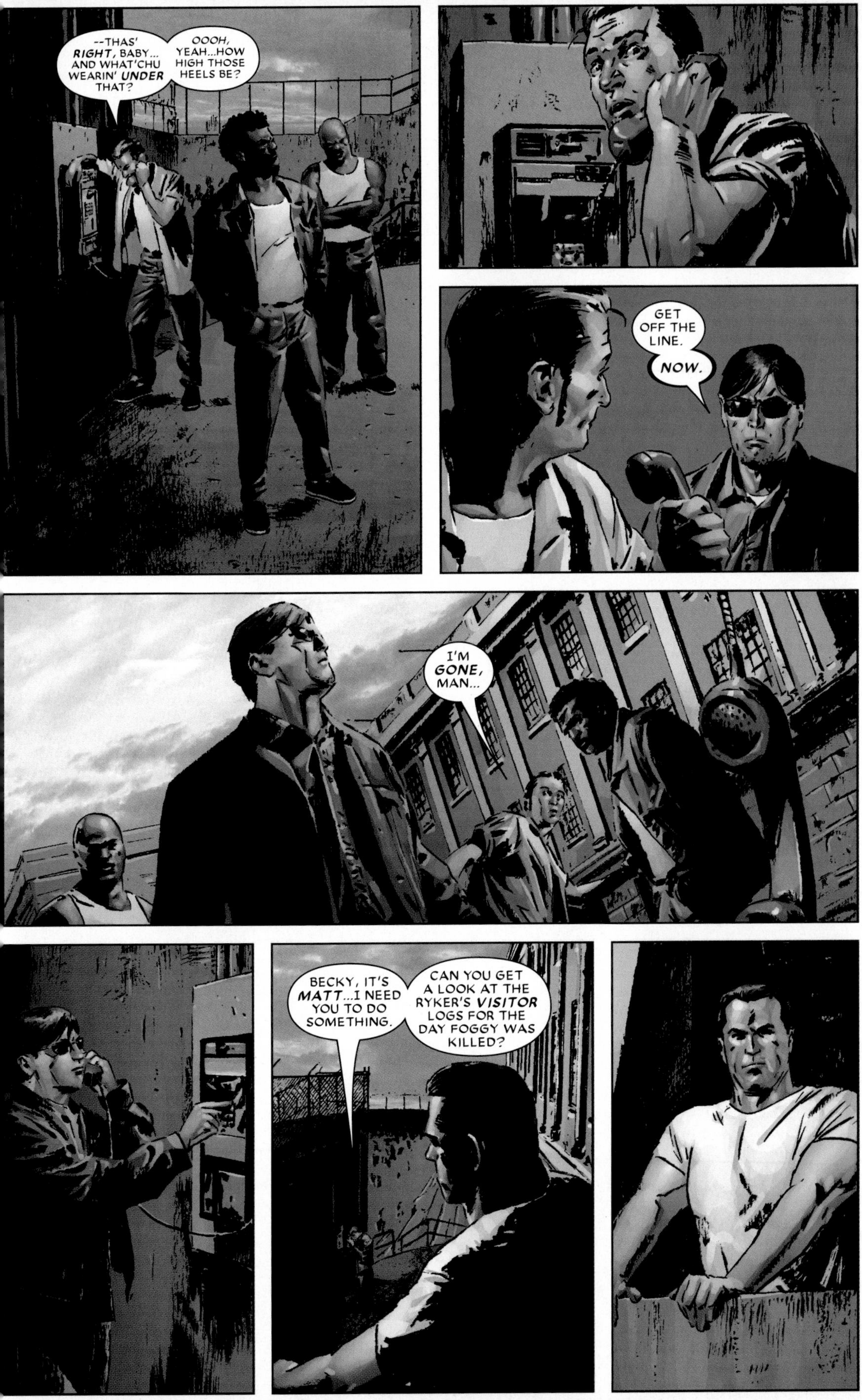
--THAS' *RIGHT*, BABY... AND WHAT'CHU WEARIN' *UNDER* THAT?
OOOH, YEAH...HOW HIGH THOSE HEELS BE?
GET OFF THE LINE.
NOW.
I'M *GONE*, MAN...
BECKY, IT'S *MATT*...I NEED YOU TO DO SOMETHING.
CAN YOU GET A LOOK AT THE RYKER'S *VISITOR* LOGS FOR THE DAY FOGGY WAS KILLED?

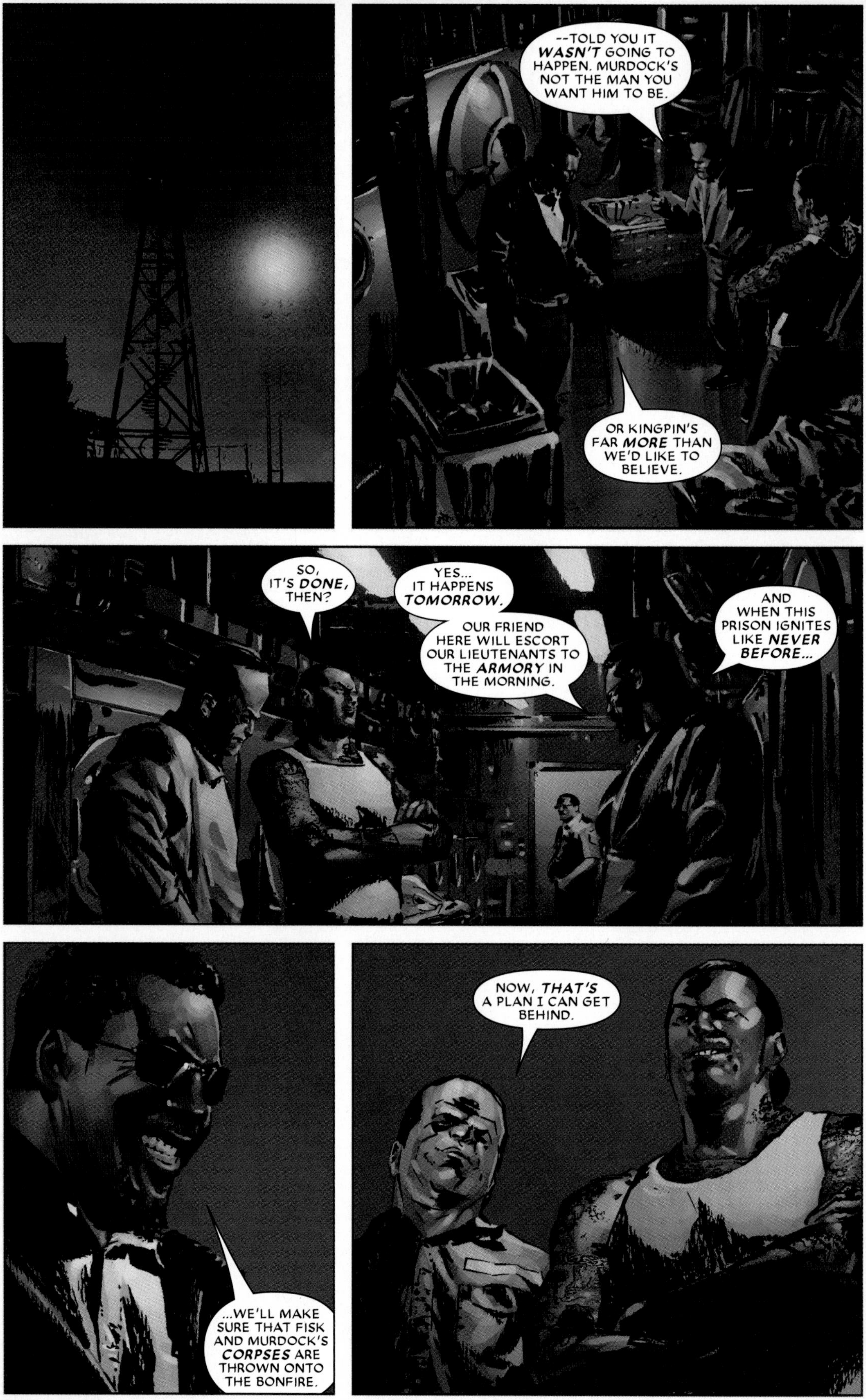
--TOLD YOU IT WASN'T GOING TO HAPPEN. MURDOCK'S NOT THE MAN YOU WANT HIM TO BE.
OR KINGPIN'S FAR MORE THAN WE'D LIKE TO BELIEVE.
SO, IT'S DONE, THEN?
YES... IT HAPPENS TOMORROW.
OUR FRIEND HERE WILL ESCORT OUR LIEUTENANTS TO THE ARMORY IN THE MORNING.
AND WHEN THIS PRISON IGNITES LIKE NEVER BEFORE...
...WE'LL MAKE SURE THAT FISK AND MURDOCK'S CORPSES ARE THROWN ONTO THE BONFIRE.
NOW, THAT'S A PLAN I CAN GET BEHIND.

#86

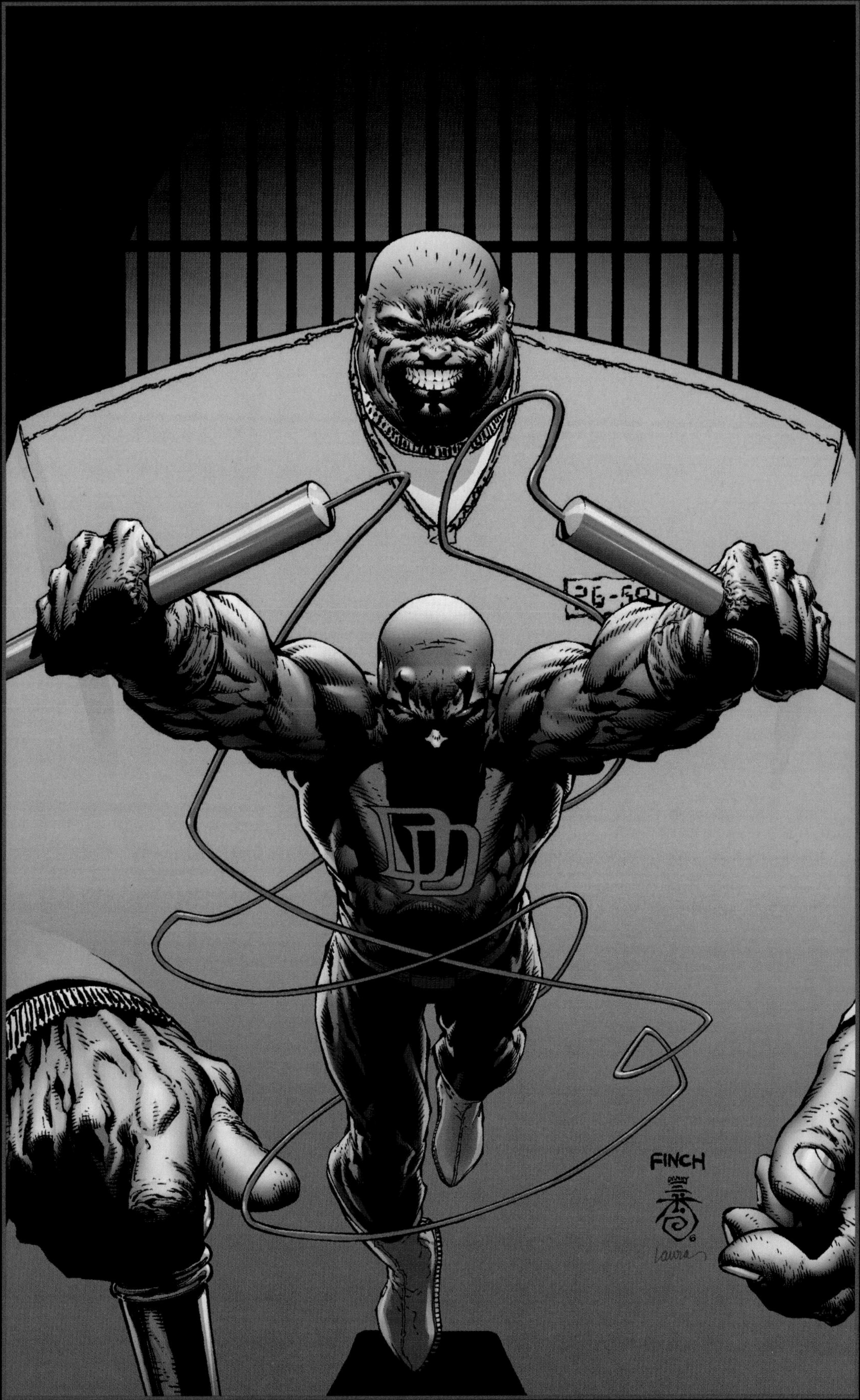
FINCH

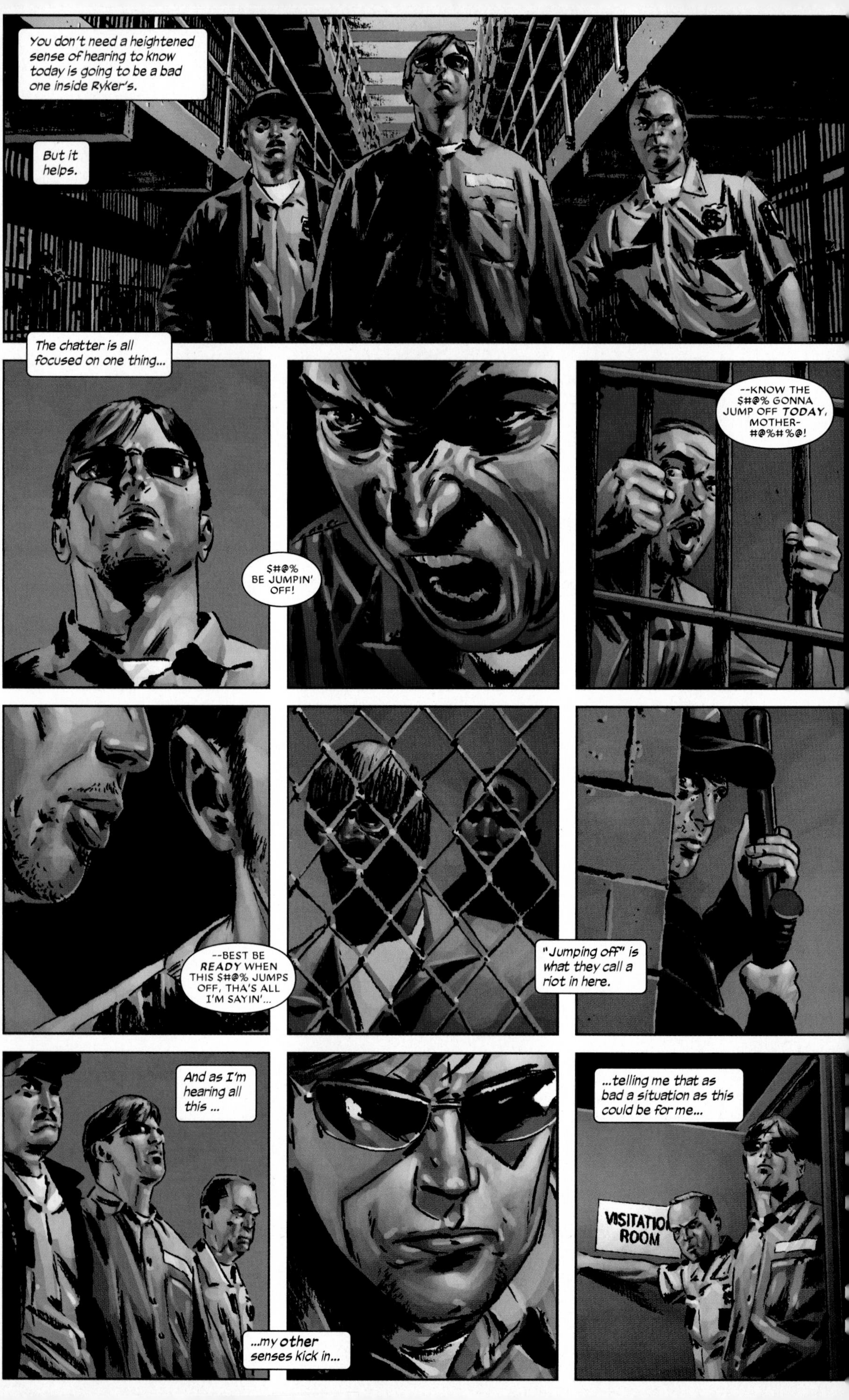

You don't need a heightened sense of hearing to know today is going to be a bad one inside Ryker's.
But it helps.
The chatter is all focused on one thing...
$#@% BE JUMPIN' OFF!
--KNOW THE $#@% GONNA JUMP OFF TODAY, MOTHER-#@%#%@!
--BEST BE READY WHEN THIS $#@% JUMPS OFF, THA'S ALL I'M SAYIN'...
"Jumping off" is what they call a riot in here.
And as I'm hearing all this ...
...my other senses kick in...
...telling me that as bad a situation as this could be for me...
VISITATION ROOM

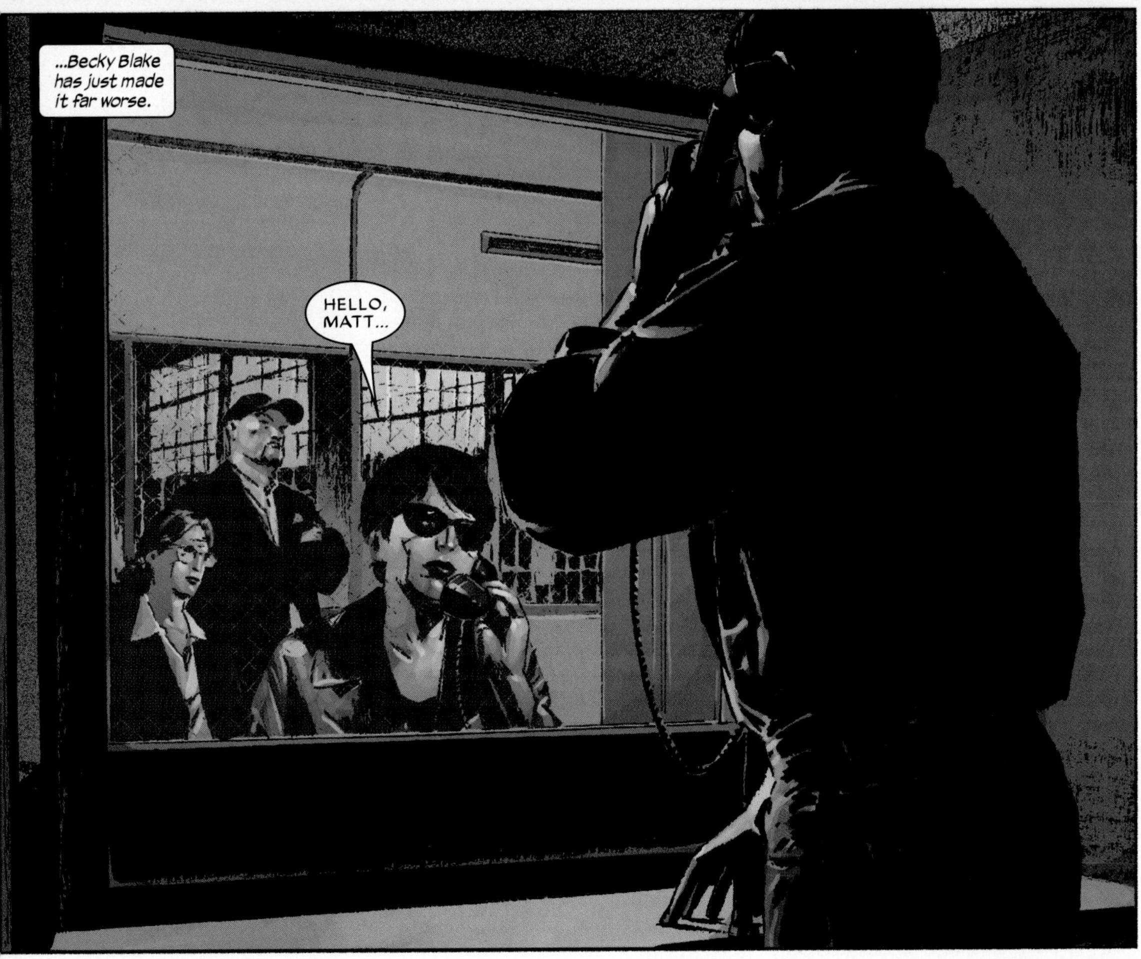
...Becky Blake has just made it far worse.
HELLO, MATT...

THE DEVIL IN CELL BLOCK D

PART FIVE

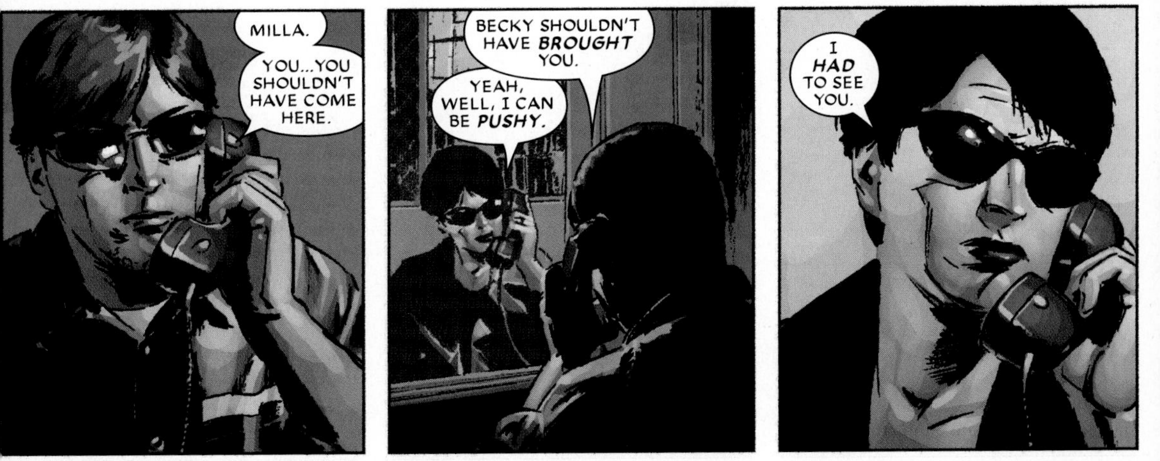
MILLA.
YOU...YOU SHOULDN'T HAVE COME HERE.
BECKY SHOULDN'T HAVE *BROUGHT* YOU.
YEAH, WELL, I CAN BE *PUSHY*.
I *HAD* TO SEE YOU.

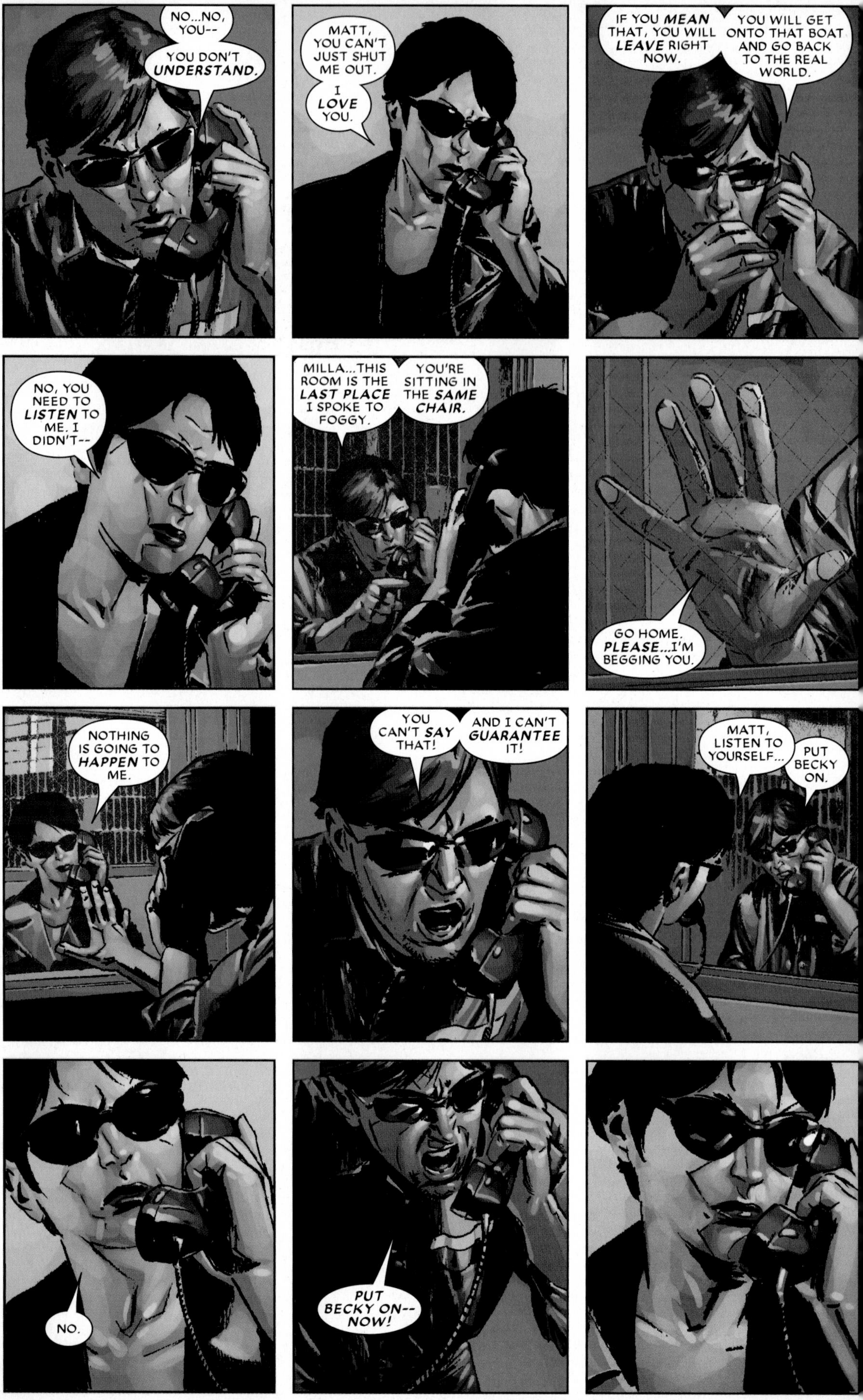
NO...NO, YOU--
YOU DON'T UNDERSTAND.
MATT, YOU CAN'T JUST SHUT ME OUT.
I LOVE YOU.
IF YOU MEAN THAT, YOU WILL LEAVE RIGHT NOW.
YOU WILL GET ONTO THAT BOAT AND GO BACK TO THE REAL WORLD.
NO, YOU NEED TO LISTEN TO ME. I DIDN'T--
MILLA...THIS ROOM IS THE LAST PLACE I SPOKE TO FOGGY.
YOU'RE SITTING IN THE SAME CHAIR.
GO HOME. PLEASE...I'M BEGGING YOU.
NOTHING IS GOING TO HAPPEN TO ME.
YOU CAN'T SAY THAT!
AND I CAN'T GUARANTEE IT!
MATT, LISTEN TO YOURSELF...
PUT BECKY ON.
NO.
PUT BECKY ON-- NOW!

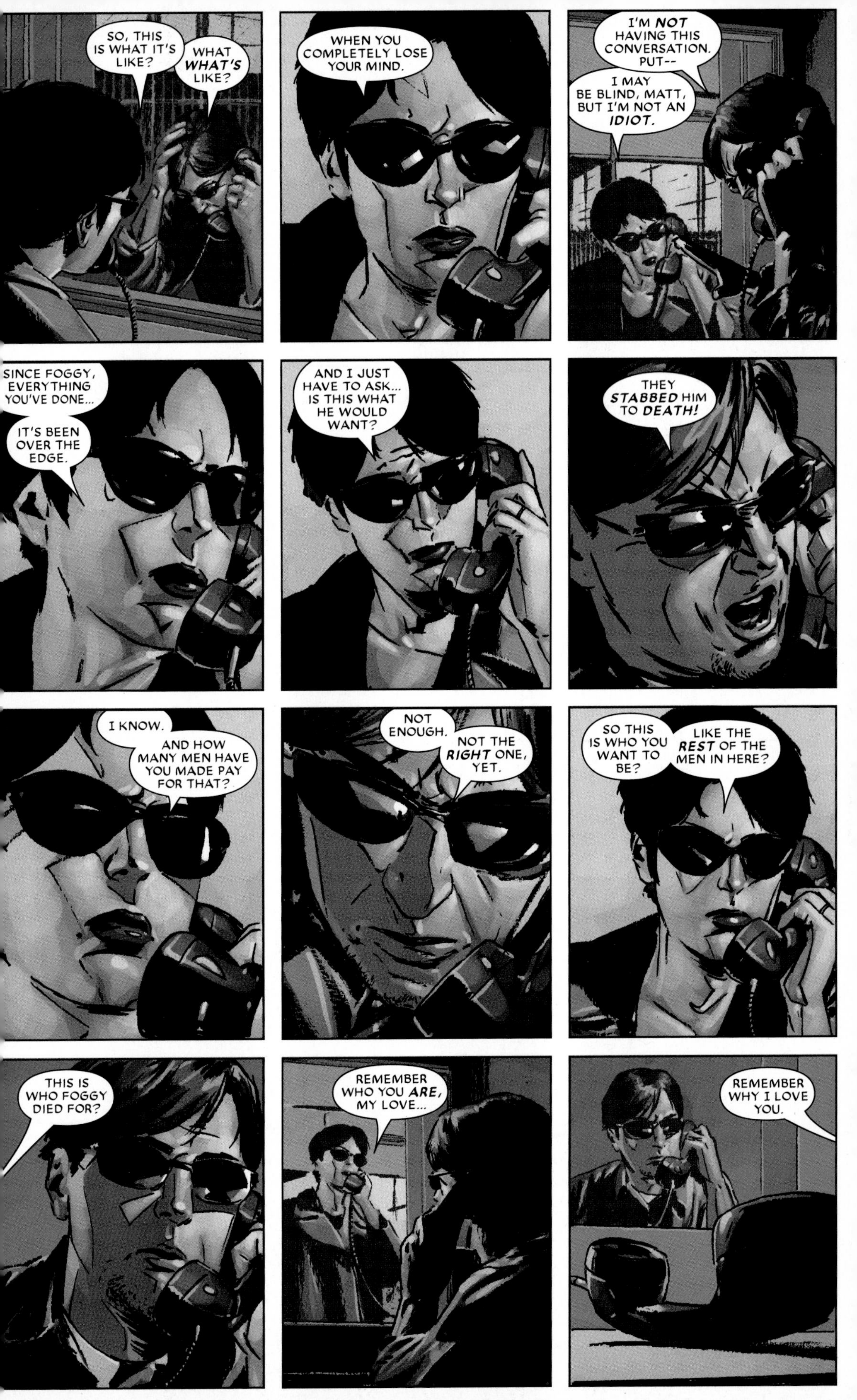
SO, THIS IS WHAT IT'S LIKE?
WHAT *WHAT'S* LIKE?
WHEN YOU COMPLETELY LOSE YOUR MIND.
I'M *NOT* HAVING THIS CONVERSATION. PUT--
I MAY BE BLIND, MATT, BUT I'M NOT AN *IDIOT.*
SINCE FOGGY, EVERYTHING YOU'VE DONE...
IT'S BEEN OVER THE EDGE.
AND I JUST HAVE TO ASK... IS THIS WHAT HE WOULD WANT?
THEY *STABBED* HIM TO *DEATH!*
I KNOW.
AND HOW MANY MEN HAVE YOU MADE PAY FOR THAT?
NOT ENOUGH.
NOT THE *RIGHT* ONE, YET.
SO THIS IS WHO YOU WANT TO BE?
LIKE THE *REST* OF THE MEN IN HERE?
THIS IS WHO FOGGY DIED FOR?
REMEMBER WHO YOU *ARE,* MY LOVE...
REMEMBER WHY I LOVE YOU.

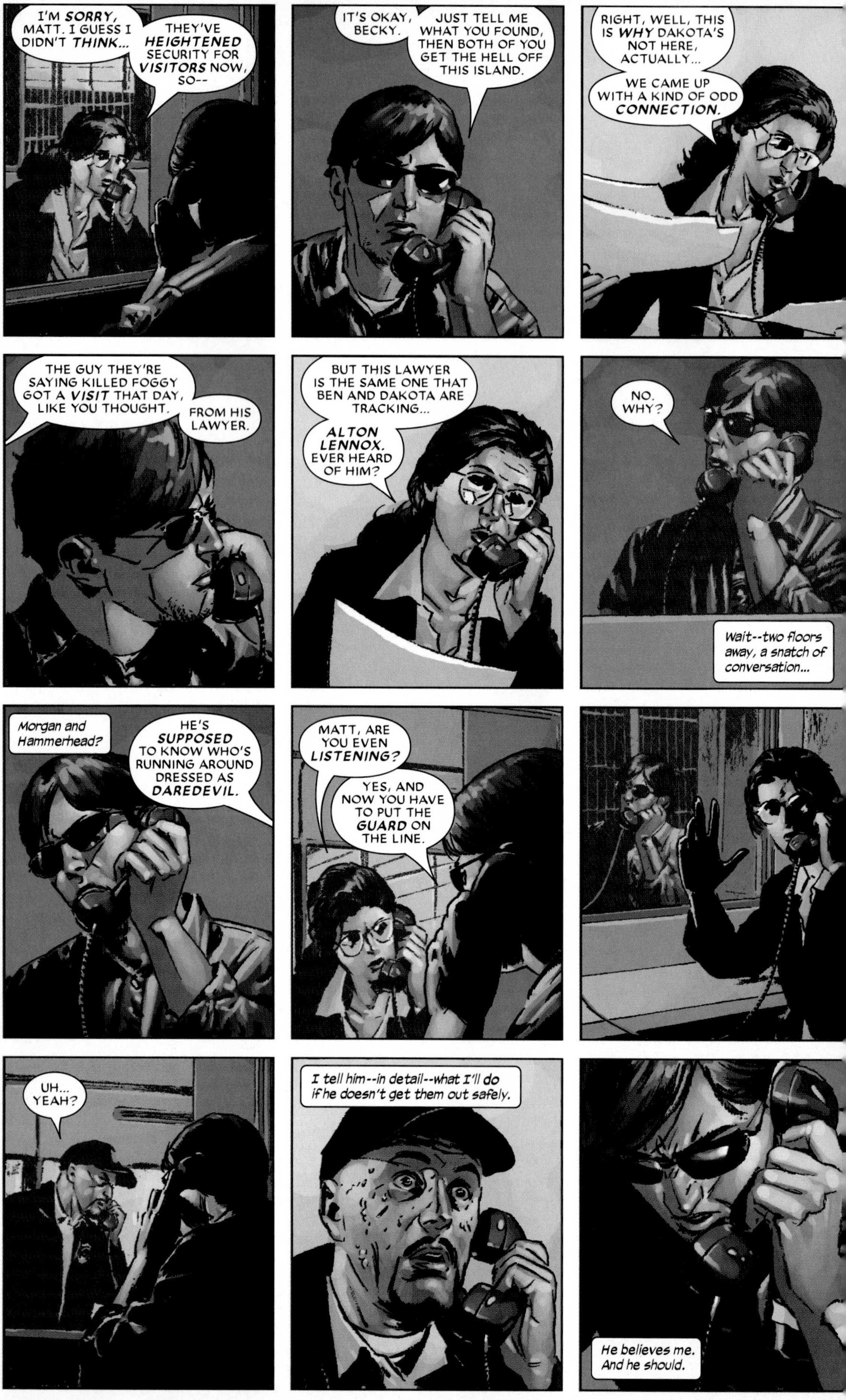

I'M SORRY, MATT. I GUESS I DIDN'T THINK...
THEY'VE HEIGHTENED SECURITY FOR VISITORS NOW, SO--
IT'S OKAY, BECKY.
JUST TELL ME WHAT YOU FOUND, THEN BOTH OF YOU GET THE HELL OFF THIS ISLAND.
RIGHT, WELL, THIS IS WHY DAKOTA'S NOT HERE, ACTUALLY...
WE CAME UP WITH A KIND OF ODD CONNECTION.
THE GUY THEY'RE SAYING KILLED FOGGY GOT A VISIT THAT DAY, LIKE YOU THOUGHT.
FROM HIS LAWYER.
BUT THIS LAWYER IS THE SAME ONE THAT BEN AND DAKOTA ARE TRACKING...
ALTON LENNOX. EVER HEARD OF HIM?
NO. WHY?
Wait--two floors away, a snatch of conversation...
Morgan and Hammerhead?
HE'S SUPPOSED TO KNOW WHO'S RUNNING AROUND DRESSED AS DAREDEVIL.
MATT, ARE YOU EVEN LISTENING?
YES, AND NOW YOU HAVE TO PUT THE GUARD ON THE LINE.
UH... YEAH?
I tell him--in detail--what I'll do if he doesn't get them out safely.
He believes me. And he should.

THE OTHER INMATES ARE KEEPING AN UNUSUAL DISTANCE THIS MORNING, WOULDN'T YOU SAY, TURK?

UH... YEAH, I GUESS.

WE HAD BETTER DO THAT *THING* WE TALKED ABOUT.

R--*REALLY?* I MEAN, I'M *SURE* IT AIN'T WHAT YOU--

TURK. I *THINK*, YOU *DO*. THAT'S WHY YOU'RE HERE.

AND NOT AT THE BOTTOM OF THE OCEAN.

TALK TO THE MEN, AND BE READY AT THE FIRST SIGN.

OH--*OKAY*...

I MEAN, *YES*, MISTER FISK. YES, SIR.

AND BE SURE YOU GIVE HIM *THESE*...

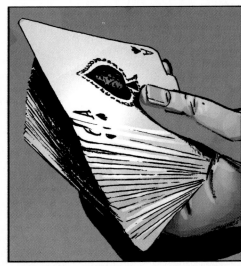

--HELL IS YOUR PROBLEM, MURDOCK? YOU SLOW-WALKIN' ME?

NO, C.O. GRUBER...JUST... NOT FEELING TOO WELL TODAY.

But I am stalling...

Because I need to make sure Milla and Becky are safely out of Ryker's before I do what I have to.

WELL, GET YER @$$ IN GEAR, INMATE.

So as Gruber rants at me, I'm listening to everything but him.

I'm hearing the gate closing behind Milla.

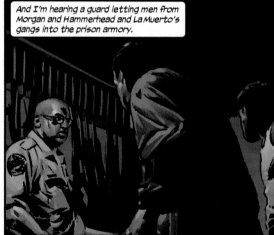

And I'm hearing a guard letting men from Morgan and Hammerhead and La Muerto's gangs into the prison armory.

I'm hearing shotguns cocked and loaded.

And I'm hearing a ferry leave the dock, heading back to the city.

Carrying the people I care about away from the nightmare this place is about to become.

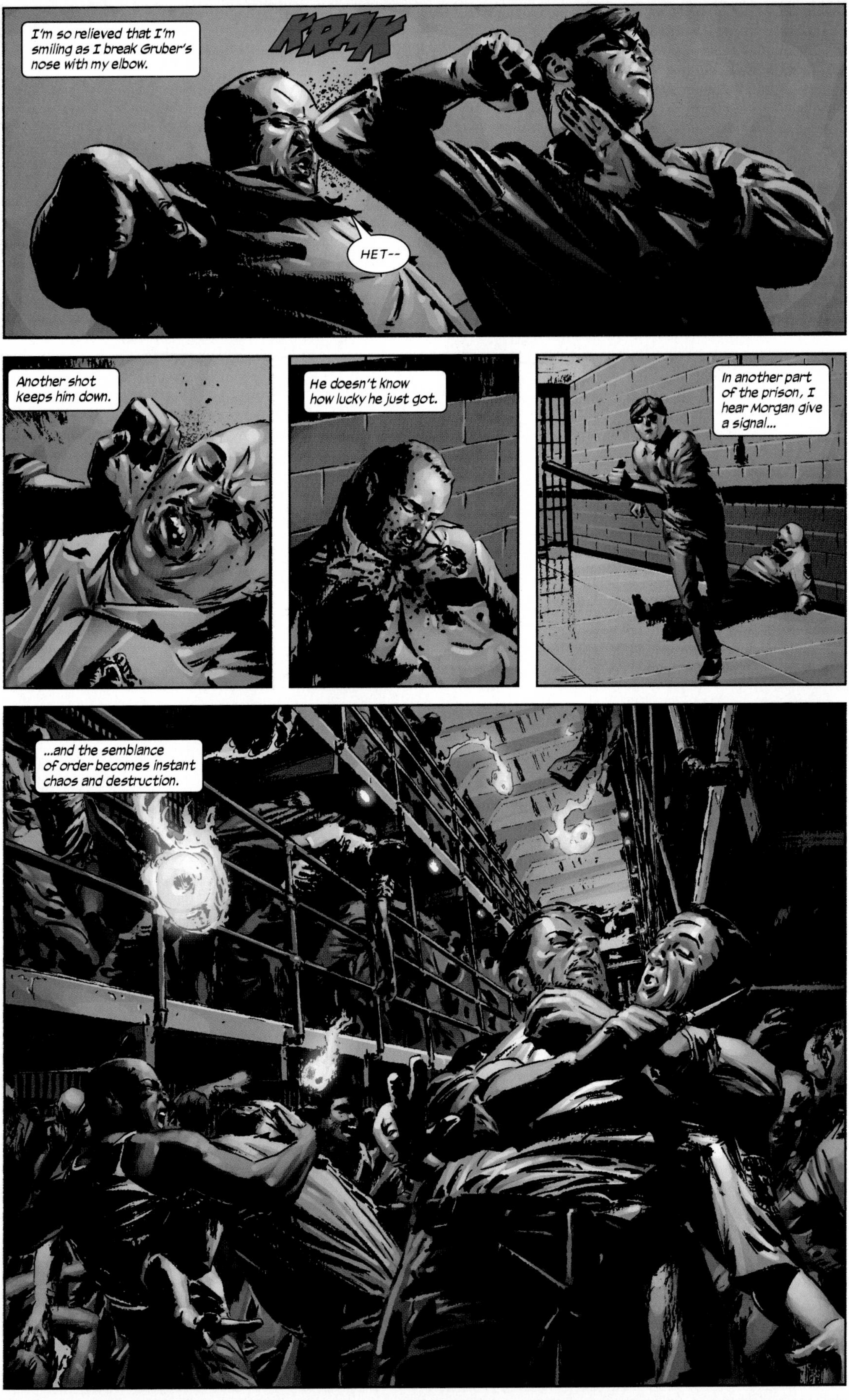
I'm so relieved that I'm smiling as I break Gruber's nose with my elbow.
KRAK
HET--
Another shot keeps him down.
He doesn't know how lucky he just got.
In another part of the prison, I hear Morgan give a signal...
...and the semblance of order becomes instant chaos and destruction.

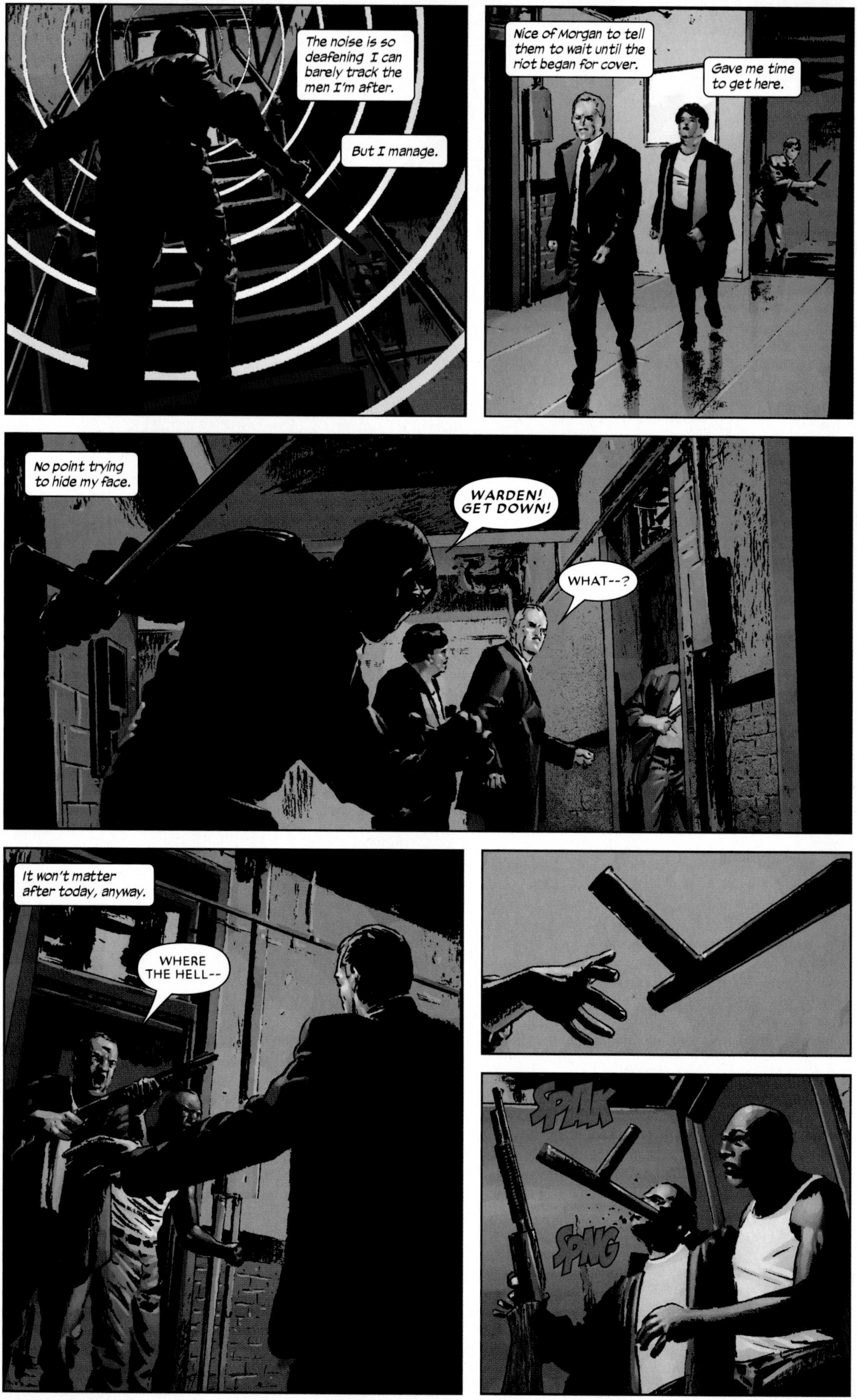
The noise is so deafening I can barely track the men I'm after.
But I manage.
Nice of Morgan to tell them to wait until the riot began for cover.
Gave me time to get here.
No point trying to hide my face.
WARDEN! GET DOWN!
WHAT--?
It won't matter after today, anyway.
WHERE THE HELL--
SPAK
SPANG

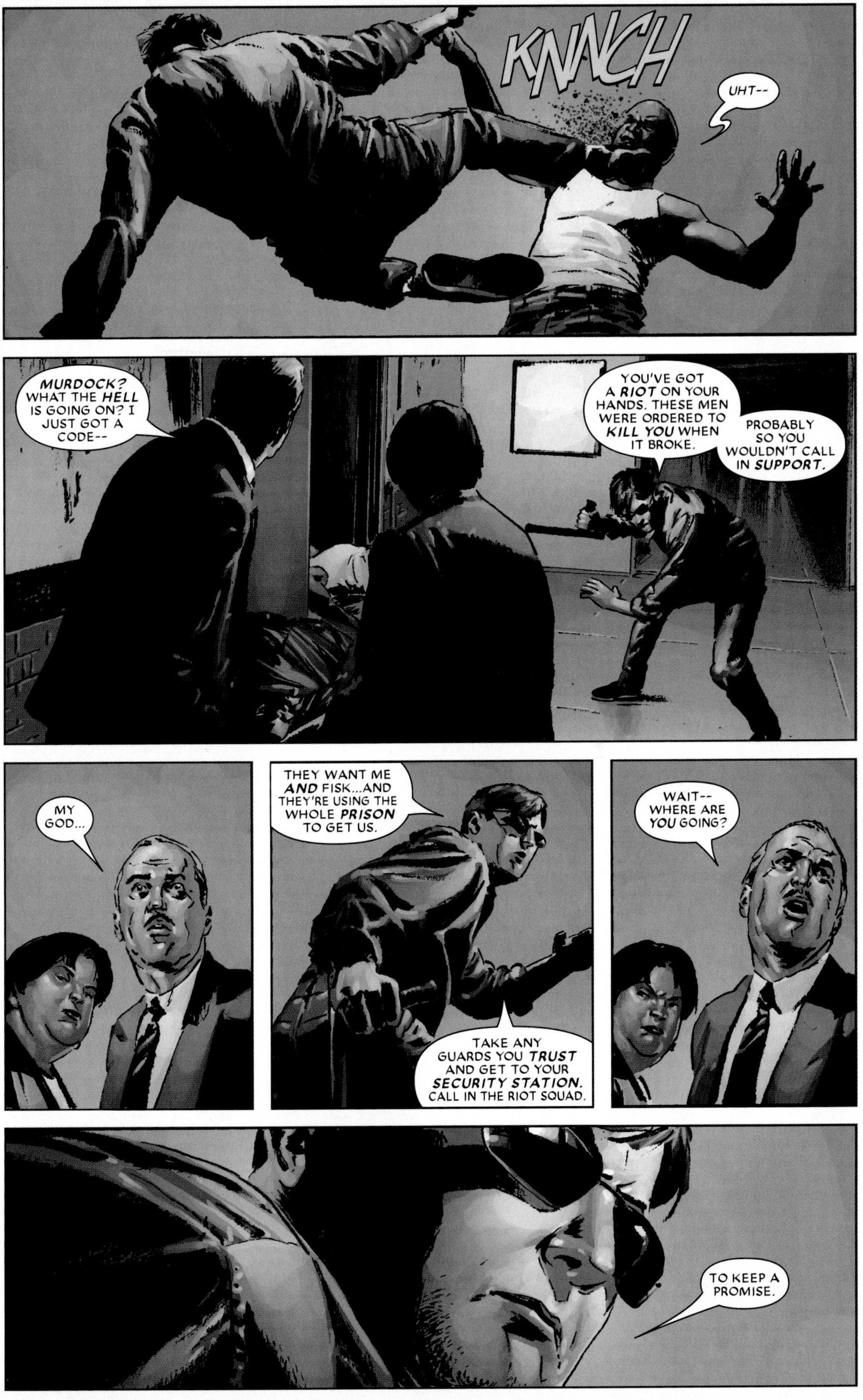
KNNCH
UHT--
MURDOCK? WHAT THE HELL IS GOING ON? I JUST GOT A CODE--
YOU'VE GOT A RIOT ON YOUR HANDS. THESE MEN WERE ORDERED TO KILL YOU WHEN IT BROKE.
PROBABLY SO YOU WOULDN'T CALL IN SUPPORT.
MY GOD...
THEY WANT ME AND FISK...AND THEY'RE USING THE WHOLE PRISON TO GET US.
TAKE ANY GUARDS YOU TRUST AND GET TO YOUR SECURITY STATION. CALL IN THE RIOT SQUAD.
WAIT-- WHERE ARE YOU GOING?
TO KEEP A PROMISE.

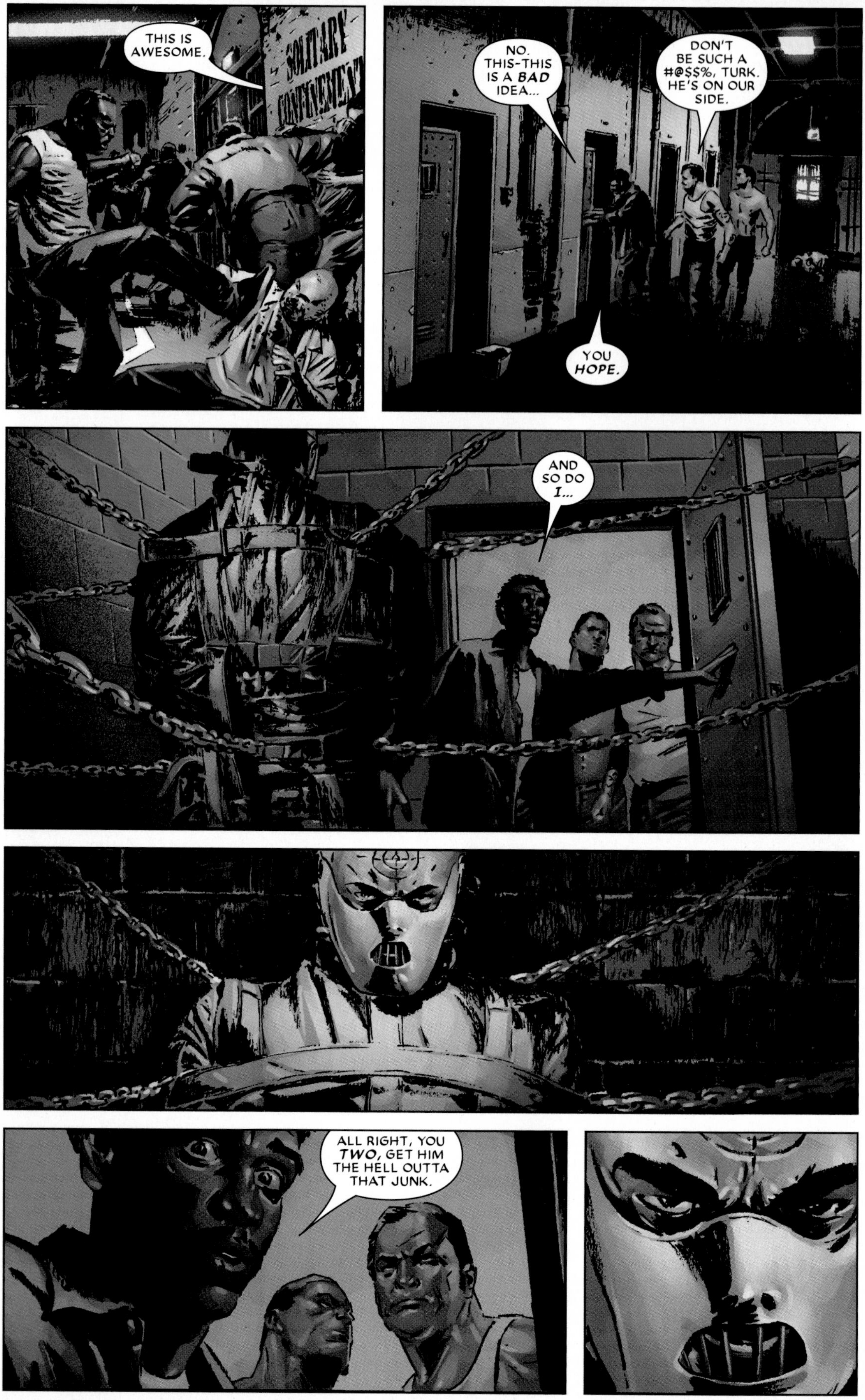

SOLITARY
THIS IS AWESOME.
NO. THIS-THIS IS A *BAD* IDEA...
DON'T BE SUCH A #@$$%, TURK. HE'S ON OUR SIDE.
YOU *HOPE.*
AND SO DO *I...*
ALL RIGHT, YOU *TWO,* GET HIM THE HELL OUTTA THAT JUNK.

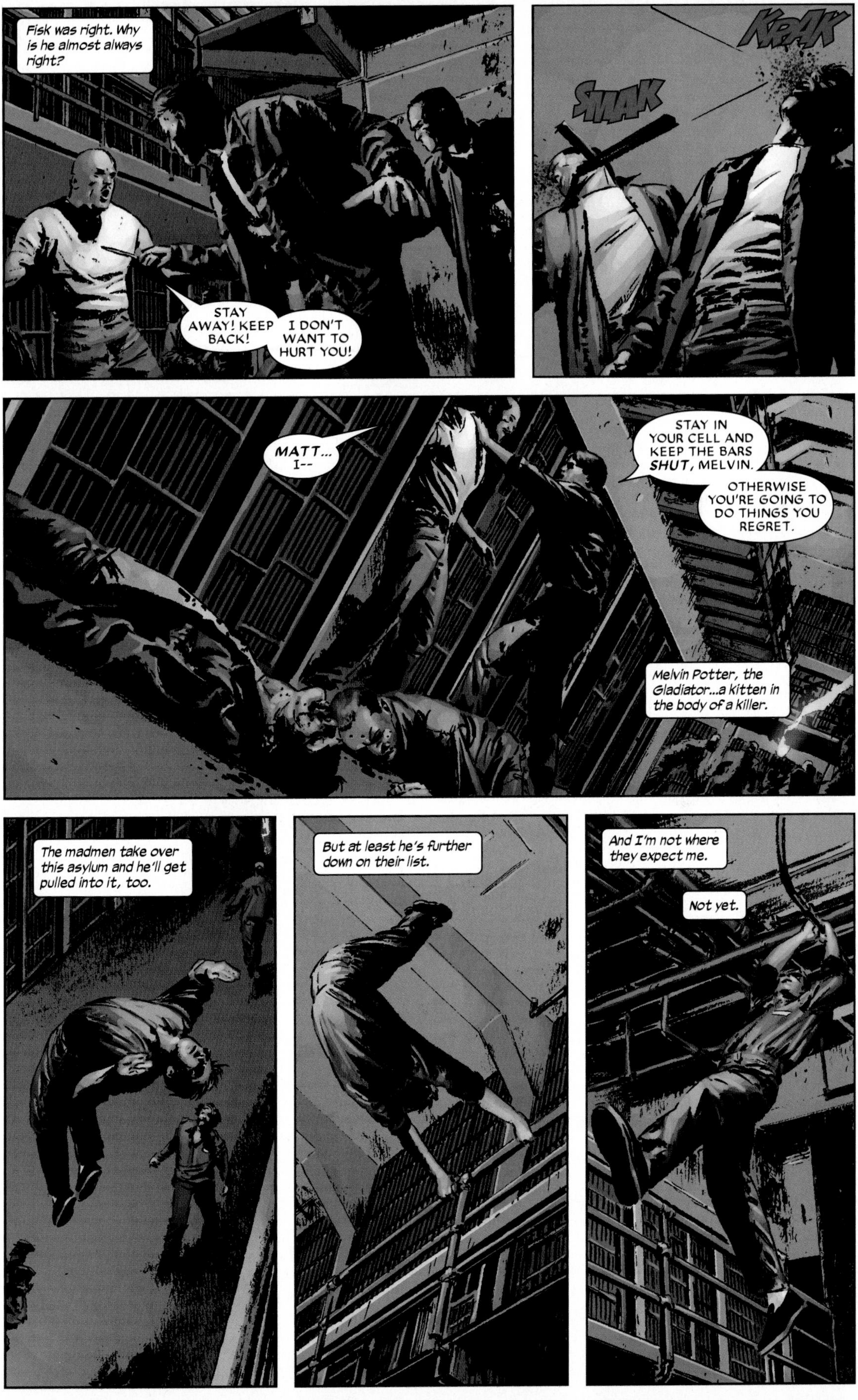
Fisk was right. Why is he almost always right?
STAY AWAY! KEEP BACK!
I DON'T WANT TO HURT YOU!
KRAK
SMAK
MATT... I--
STAY IN YOUR CELL AND KEEP THE BARS SHUT, MELVIN.
OTHERWISE YOU'RE GOING TO DO THINGS YOU REGRET.
Melvin Potter, the Gladiator...a kitten in the body of a killer.
The madmen take over this asylum and he'll get pulled into it, too.
But at least he's further down on their list.
And I'm not where they expect me.
Not yet.

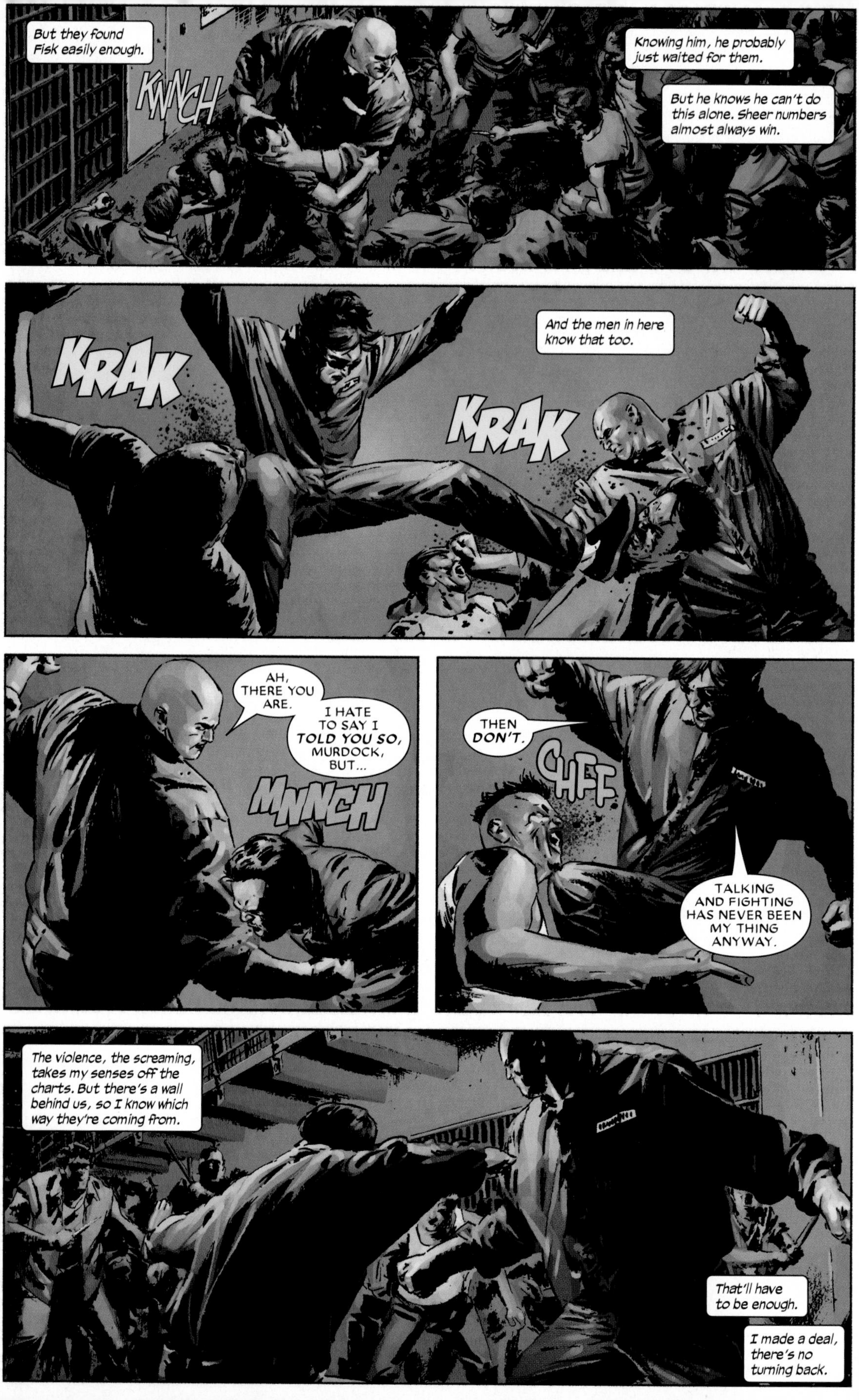

But they found Fisk easily enough.
KWNCH
Knowing him, he probably just waited for them.
But he knows he can't do this alone. Sheer numbers almost always win.
And the men in here know that too.
KRAK
KRAK
AH, THERE YOU ARE.
I HATE TO SAY I TOLD YOU SO, MURDOCK, BUT...
MNNCH
THEN DON'T.
CHFF
TALKING AND FIGHTING HAS NEVER BEEN MY THING ANYWAY.
The violence, the screaming, takes my senses off the charts. But there's a wall behind us, so I know which way they're coming from.
That'll have to be enough.
I made a deal, there's no turning back.

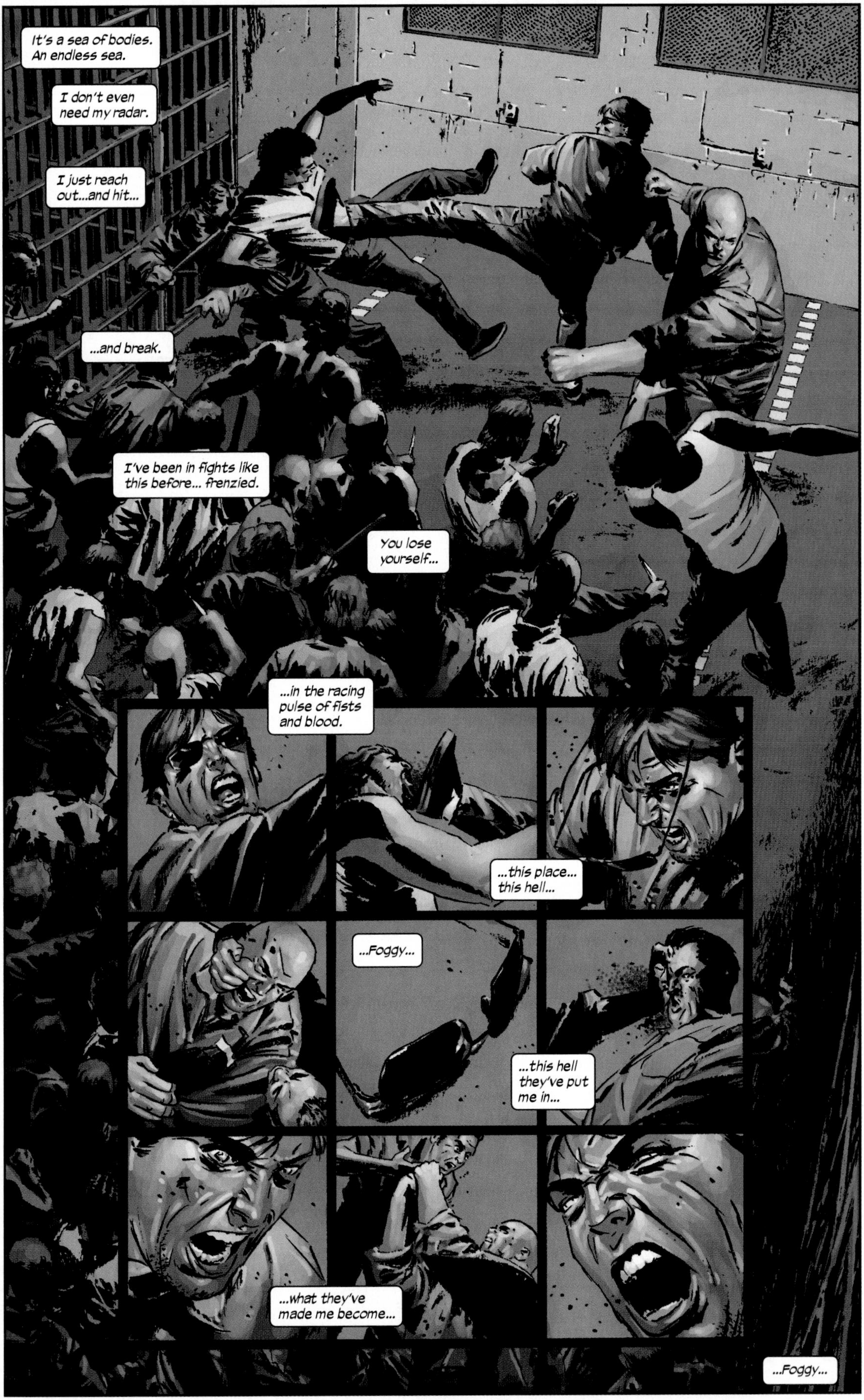
It's a sea of bodies. An endless sea.
I don't even need my radar.
I just reach out...and hit...
...and break.
I've been in fights like this before... frenzied.
You lose yourself...
...in the racing pulse of fists and blood.
...this place... this hell...
...Foggy...
...this hell they've put me in...
...what they've made me become...
...Foggy...

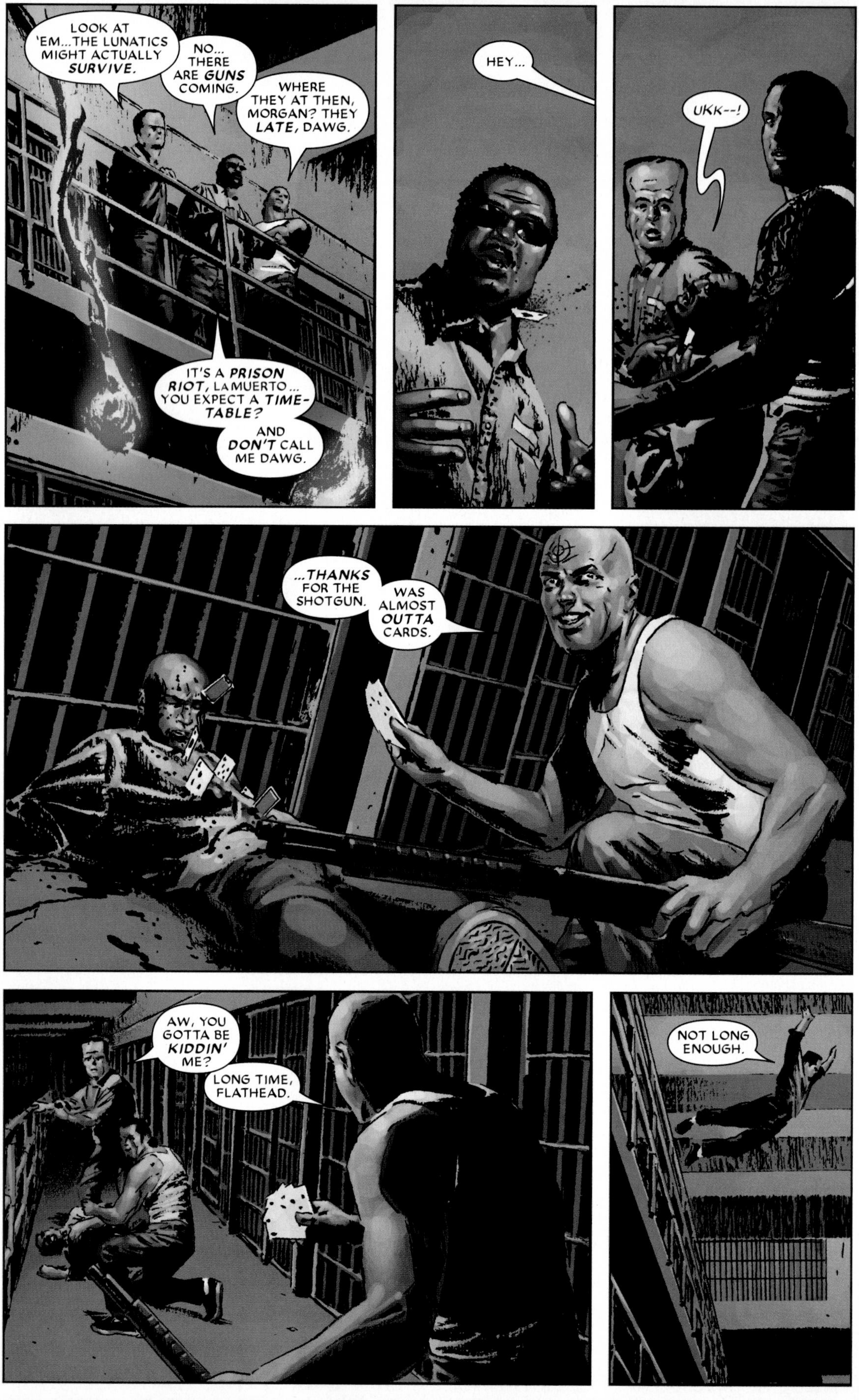
LOOK AT 'EM...THE LUNATICS MIGHT ACTUALLY SURVIVE.
NO... THERE ARE GUNS COMING.
WHERE THEY AT THEN, MORGAN? THEY LATE, DAWG.
IT'S A PRISON RIOT, LAMUERTO... YOU EXPECT A TIME-TABLE?
AND DON'T CALL ME DAWG.
HEY...
UKK--!
...THANKS FOR THE SHOTGUN.
WAS ALMOST OUTTA CARDS.
AW, YOU GOTTA BE KIDDIN' ME?
LONG TIME, FLATHEAD.
NOT LONG ENOUGH.

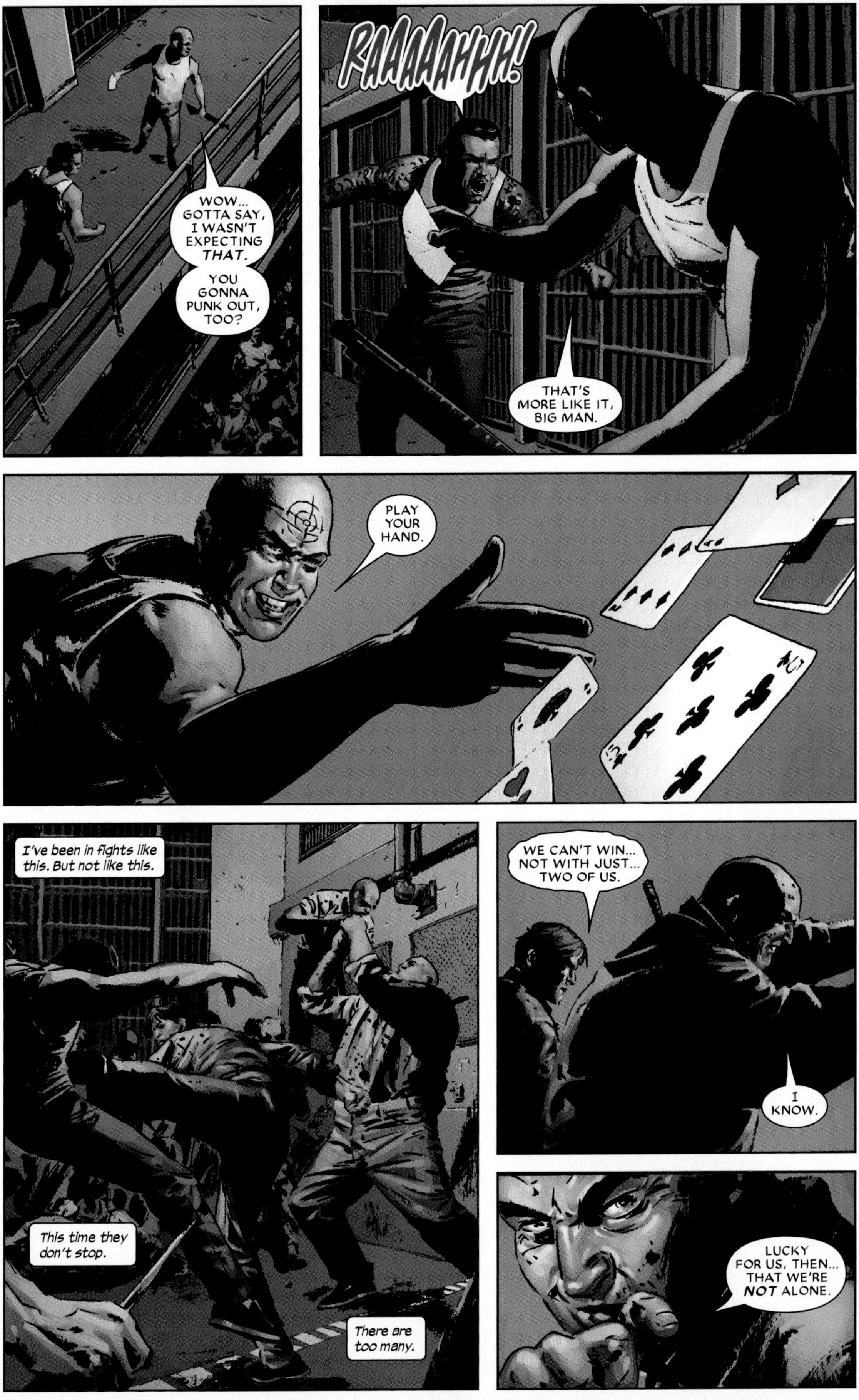
WOW... GOTTA SAY, I WASN'T EXPECTING *THAT*.
YOU GONNA PUNK OUT, TOO?
RAAAAAHHH!
THAT'S MORE LIKE IT, BIG MAN.
PLAY YOUR HAND.
I've been in fights like this. But not like this.
This time they don't stop.
There are too many.
WE CAN'T WIN... NOT WITH JUST... TWO OF US.
I KNOW.
LUCKY FOR US, THEN... THAT WE'RE ***NOT*** ALONE.

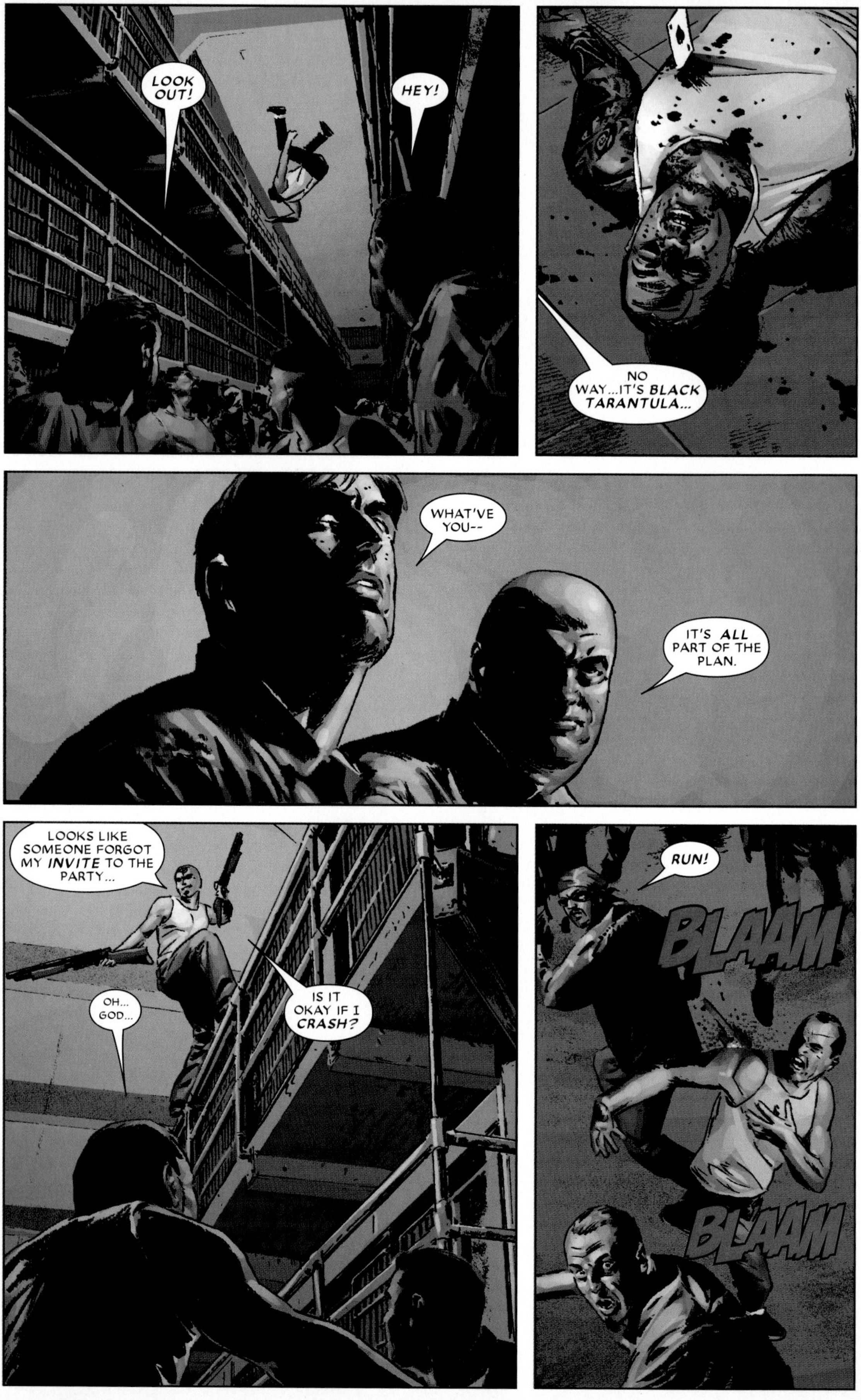
LOOK OUT!
HEY!
NO WAY...IT'S BLACK TARANTULA...
WHAT'VE YOU--
IT'S ALL PART OF THE PLAN.
LOOKS LIKE SOMEONE FORGOT MY INVITE TO THE PARTY...
IS IT OKAY IF I CRASH?
OH... GOD...
RUN!
BLAAM
BLAAM

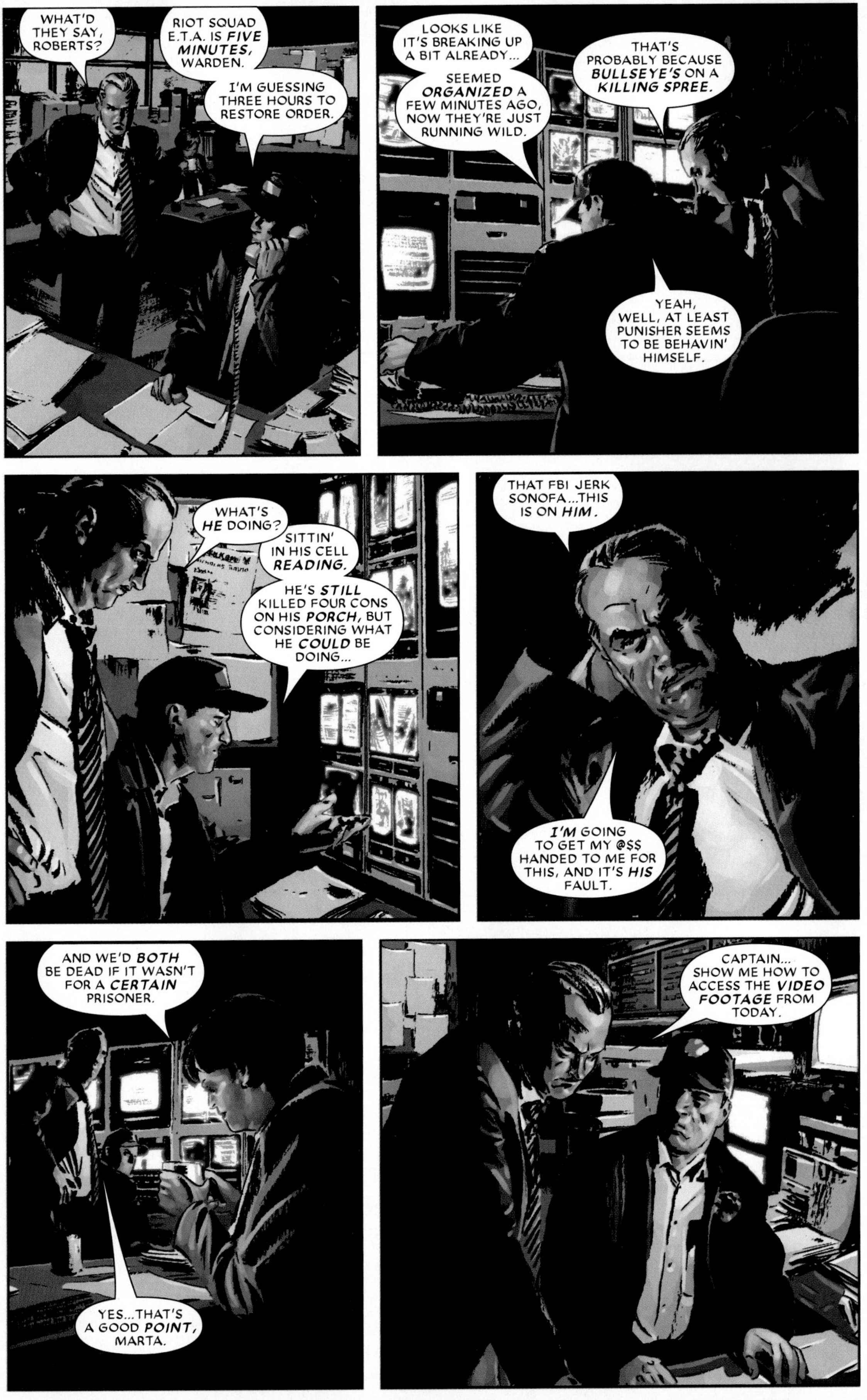
WHAT'D THEY SAY, ROBERTS?
RIOT SQUAD E.T.A. IS FIVE MINUTES, WARDEN.
I'M GUESSING THREE HOURS TO RESTORE ORDER.
LOOKS LIKE IT'S BREAKING UP A BIT ALREADY...
SEEMED ORGANIZED A FEW MINUTES AGO, NOW THEY'RE JUST RUNNING WILD.
THAT'S PROBABLY BECAUSE BULLSEYE'S ON A KILLING SPREE.
YEAH, WELL, AT LEAST PUNISHER SEEMS TO BE BEHAVIN' HIMSELF.
WHAT'S HE DOING?
SITTIN' IN HIS CELL READING.
HE'S STILL KILLED FOUR CONS ON HIS PORCH, BUT CONSIDERING WHAT HE COULD BE DOING...
THAT FBI JERK SONOFA...THIS IS ON HIM.
I'M GOING TO GET MY @$$ HANDED TO ME FOR THIS, AND IT'S HIS FAULT.
AND WE'D BOTH BE DEAD IF IT WASN'T FOR A CERTAIN PRISONER.
YES...THAT'S A GOOD POINT, MARTA.
CAPTAIN... SHOW ME HOW TO ACCESS THE VIDEO FOOTAGE FROM TODAY.

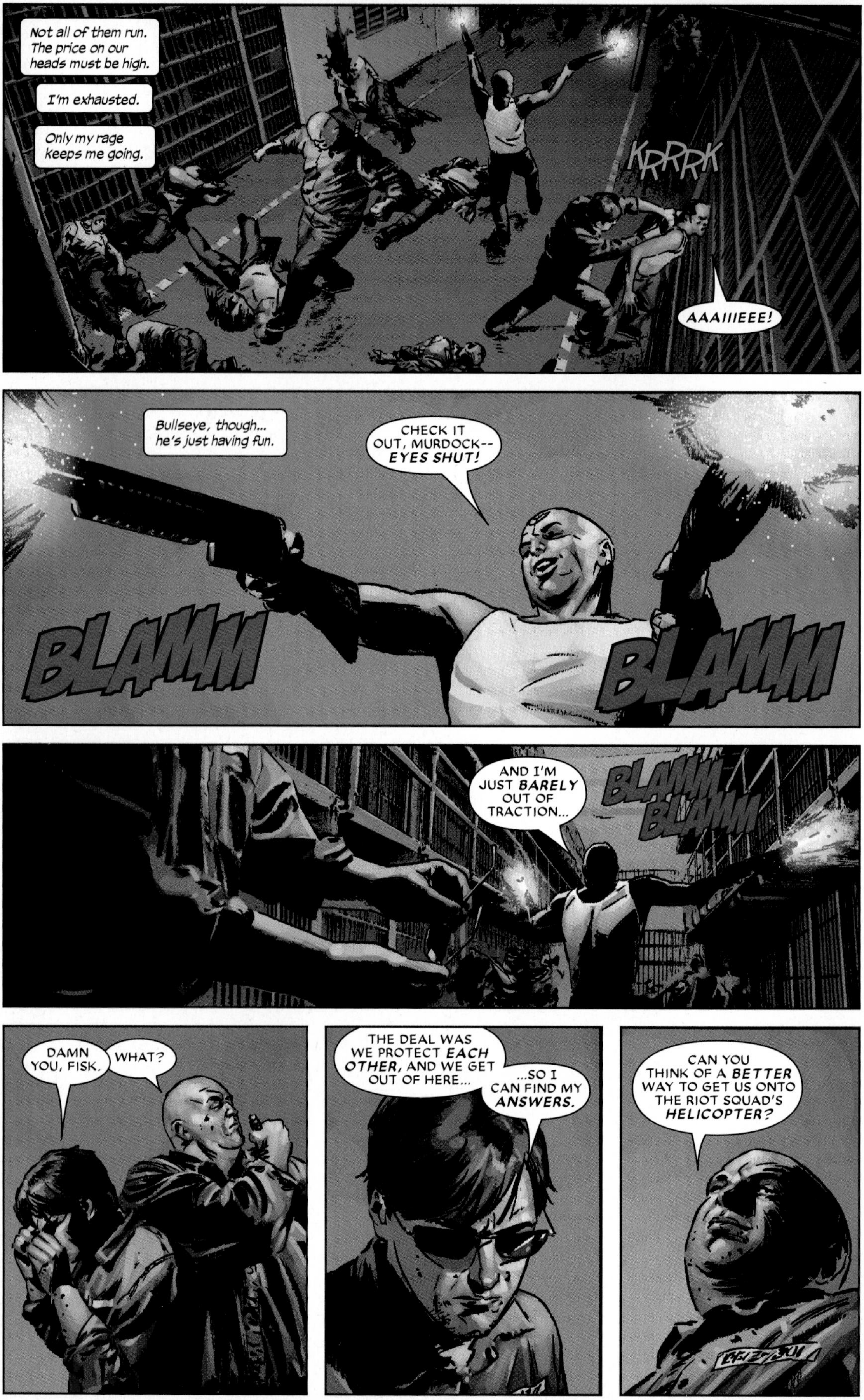

Not all of them run. The price on our heads must be high.
I'm exhausted.
Only my rage keeps me going.
KRRRK
AAAIIIEEE!
Bullseye, though... he's just having fun.
CHECK IT OUT, MURDOCK-- EYES SHUT!
BLAMM
BLAMM
AND I'M JUST BARELY OUT OF TRACTION...
BLAMM
BLAMM
DAMN YOU, FISK.
WHAT?
THE DEAL WAS WE PROTECT EACH OTHER, AND WE GET OUT OF HERE...
...SO I CAN FIND MY ANSWERS.
CAN YOU THINK OF A BETTER WAY TO GET US ONTO THE RIOT SQUAD'S HELICOPTER?

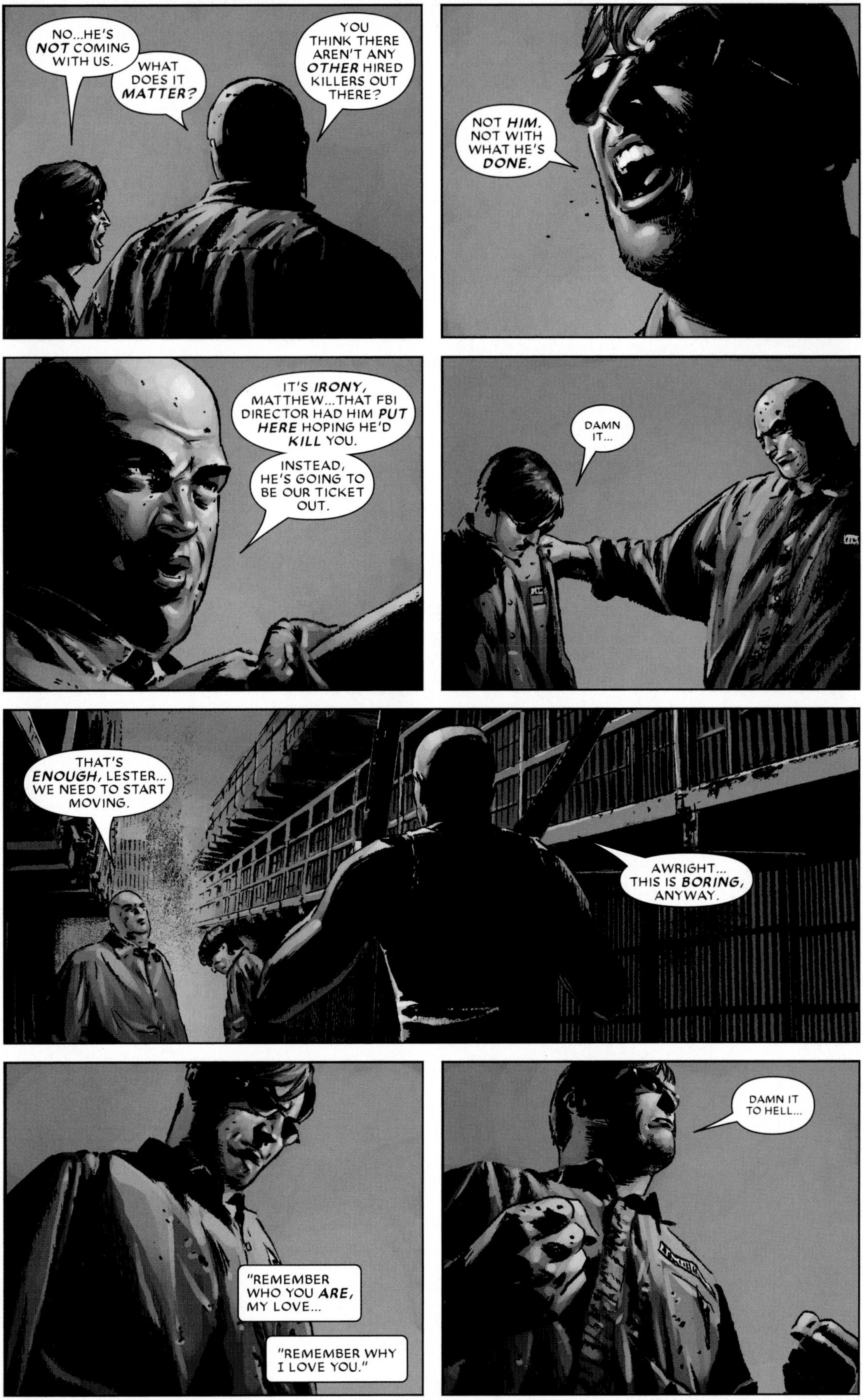
NO...HE'S NOT COMING WITH US.
WHAT DOES IT MATTER?
YOU THINK THERE AREN'T ANY OTHER HIRED KILLERS OUT THERE?
NOT HIM. NOT WITH WHAT HE'S DONE.
IT'S IRONY, MATTHEW...THAT FBI DIRECTOR HAD HIM PUT HERE HOPING HE'D KILL YOU.
INSTEAD, HE'S GOING TO BE OUR TICKET OUT.
DAMN IT...
THAT'S ENOUGH, LESTER... WE NEED TO START MOVING.
AWRIGHT... THIS IS BORING, ANYWAY.
"REMEMBER WHO YOU ARE, MY LOVE...
"REMEMBER WHY I LOVE YOU."
DAMN IT TO HELL...

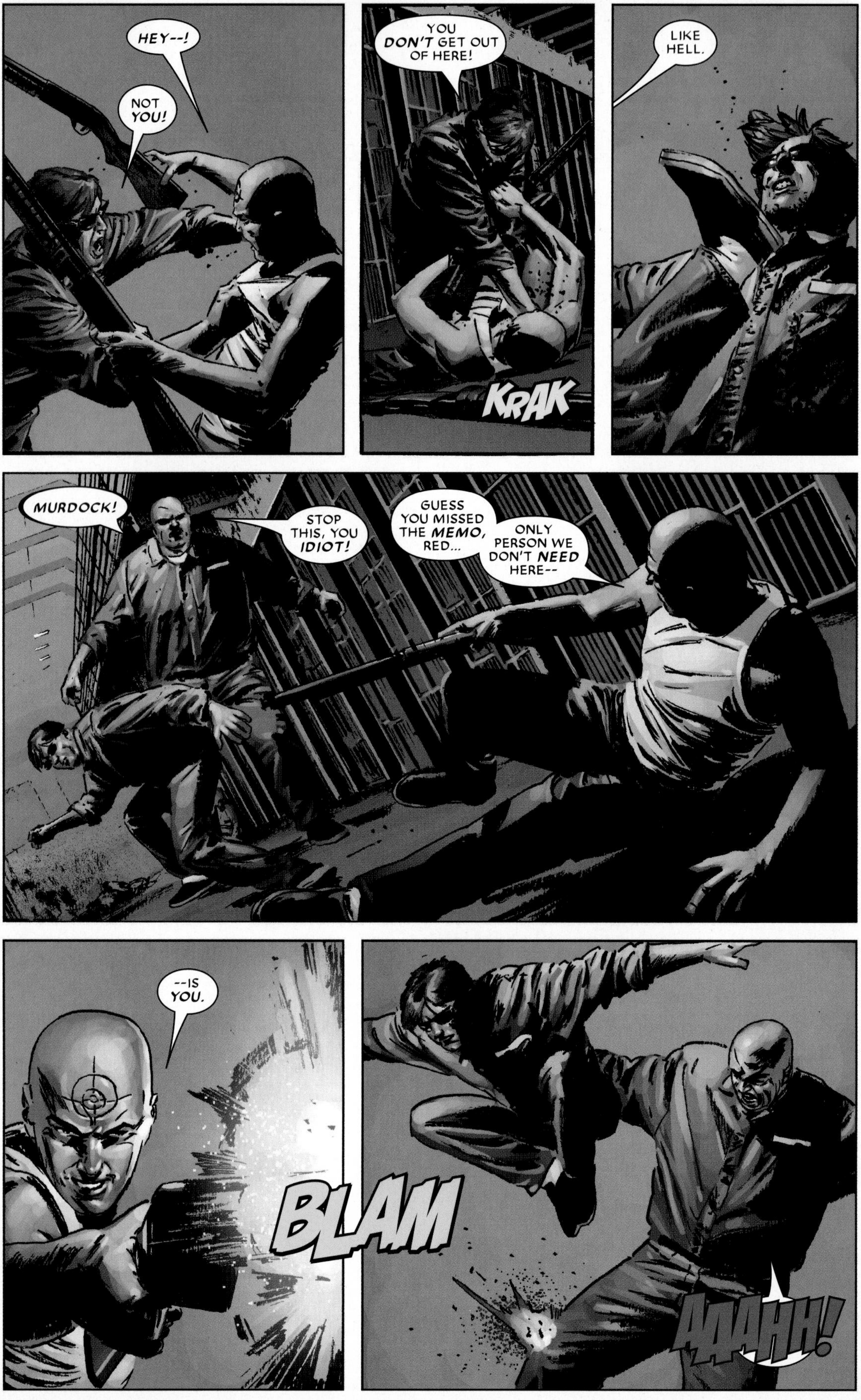
HEY--!
NOT YOU!
YOU DON'T GET OUT OF HERE!
KRAK
LIKE HELL.
MURDOCK!
STOP THIS, YOU IDIOT!
GUESS YOU MISSED THE MEMO, RED...
ONLY PERSON WE DON'T NEED HERE--
--IS YOU.
BLAM
AAAHH!

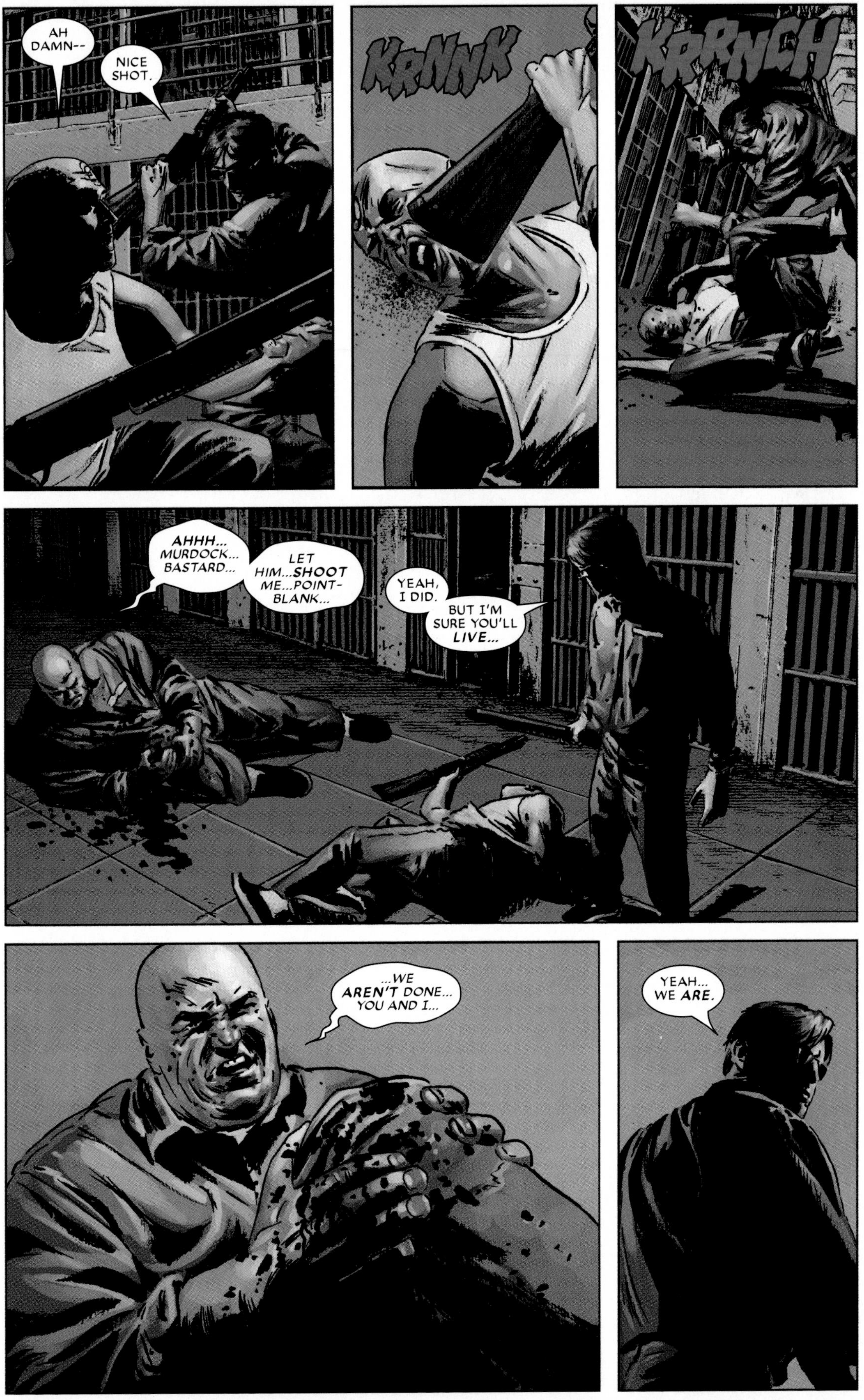
AH DAMN--
NICE SHOT.
KRNNK
KRRNCH
AHHH... MURDOCK... BASTARD...
LET HIM...SHOOT ME...POINT-BLANK...
YEAH, I DID.
BUT I'M SURE YOU'LL LIVE...
...WE AREN'T DONE... YOU AND I...
YEAH... WE ARE.

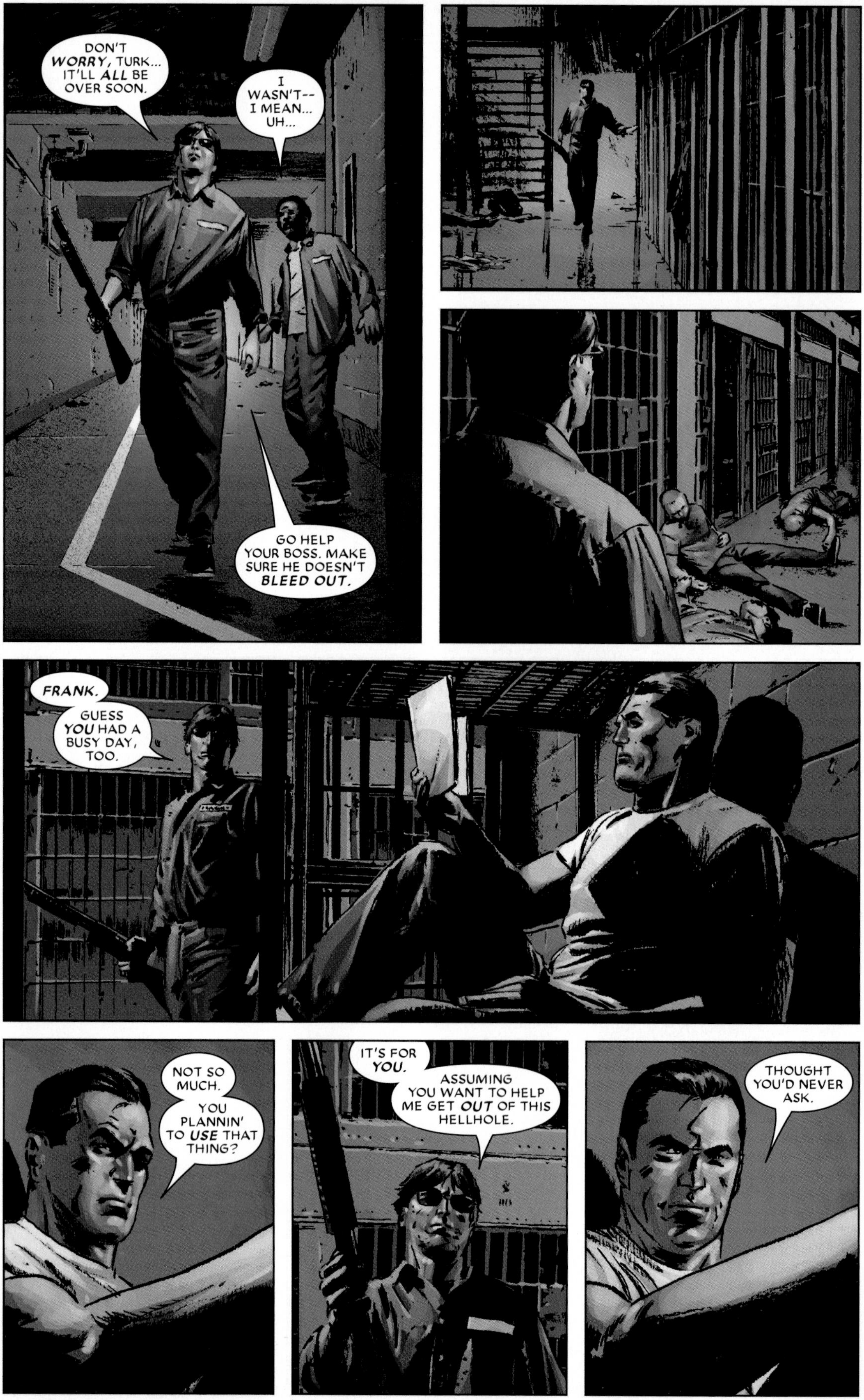
DON'T WORRY, TURK... IT'LL ALL BE OVER SOON.
I WASN'T-- I MEAN... UH...
GO HELP YOUR BOSS. MAKE SURE HE DOESN'T BLEED OUT.
FRANK.
GUESS YOU HAD A BUSY DAY, TOO.
NOT SO MUCH.
YOU PLANNIN' TO USE THAT THING?
IT'S FOR YOU.
ASSUMING YOU WANT TO HELP ME GET OUT OF THIS HELLHOLE.
THOUGHT YOU'D NEVER ASK.

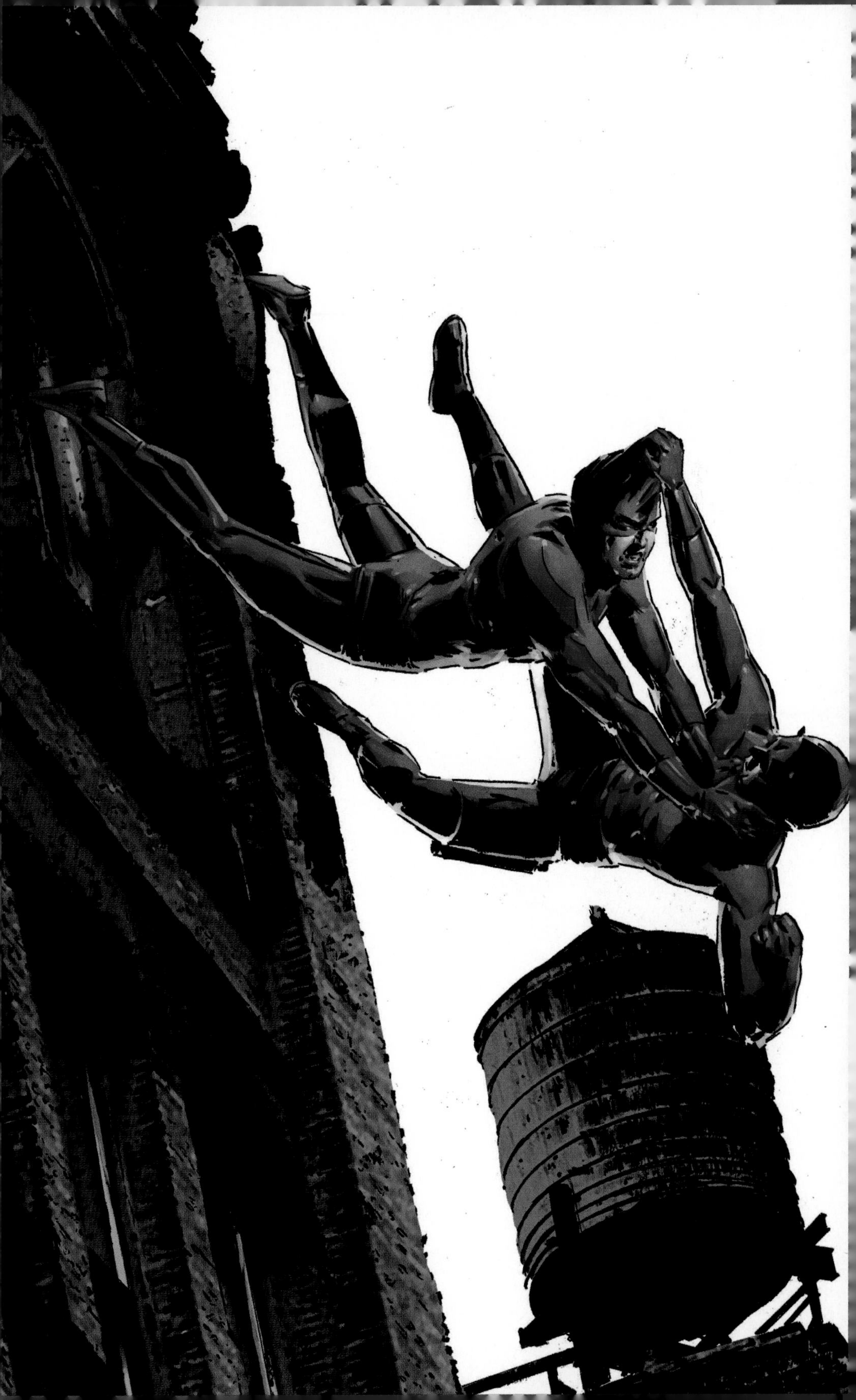

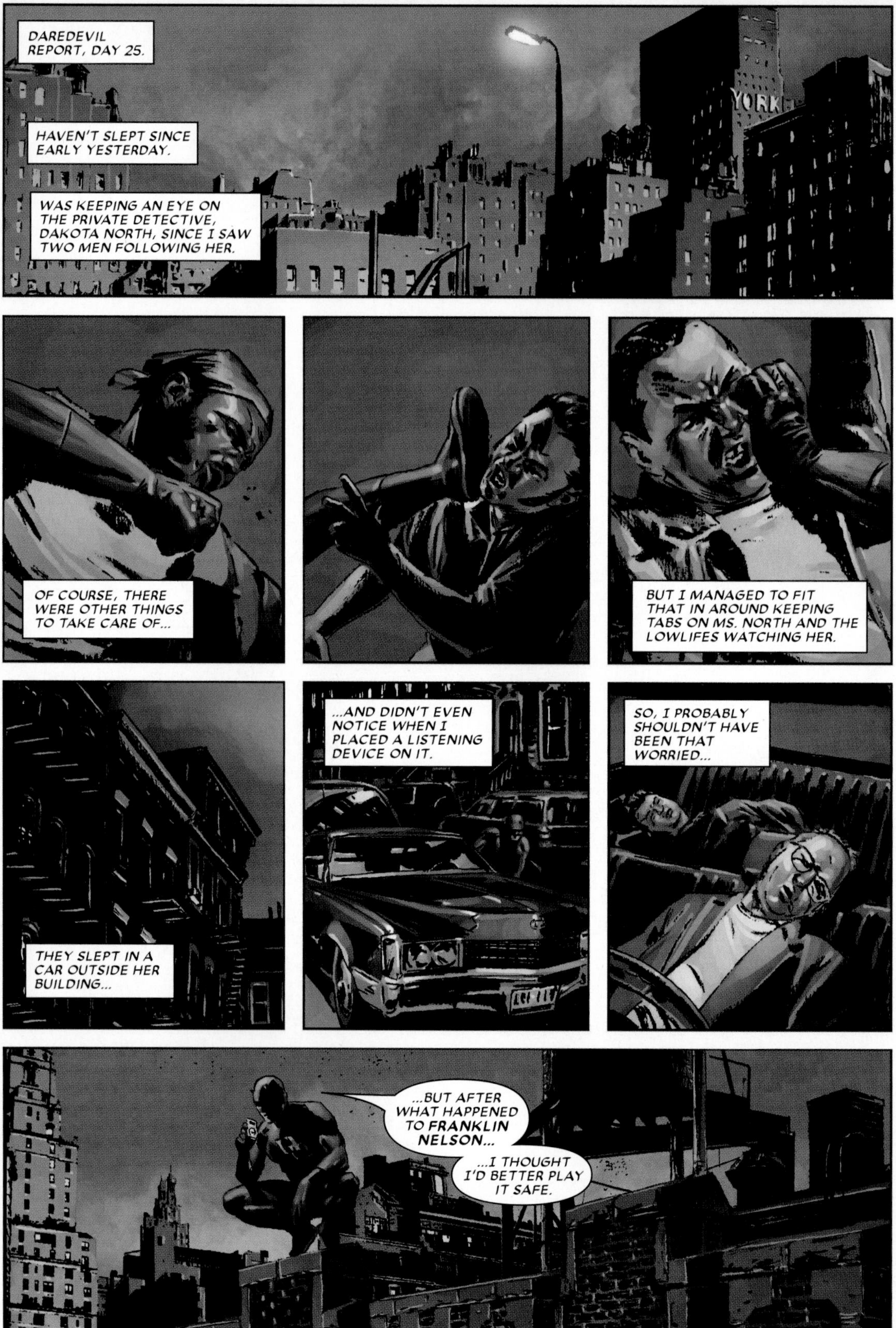
DAREDEVIL REPORT, DAY 25.
HAVEN'T SLEPT SINCE EARLY YESTERDAY.
WAS KEEPING AN EYE ON THE PRIVATE DETECTIVE, DAKOTA NORTH, SINCE I SAW TWO MEN FOLLOWING HER.
OF COURSE, THERE WERE OTHER THINGS TO TAKE CARE OF...
BUT I MANAGED TO FIT THAT IN AROUND KEEPING TABS ON MS. NORTH AND THE LOWLIFES WATCHING HER.
THEY SLEPT IN A CAR OUTSIDE HER BUILDING...
...AND DIDN'T EVEN NOTICE WHEN I PLACED A LISTENING DEVICE ON IT.
SO, I PROBABLY SHOULDN'T HAVE BEEN THAT WORRIED...
...BUT AFTER WHAT HAPPENED TO FRANKLIN NELSON...
...I THOUGHT I'D BETTER PLAY IT SAFE.

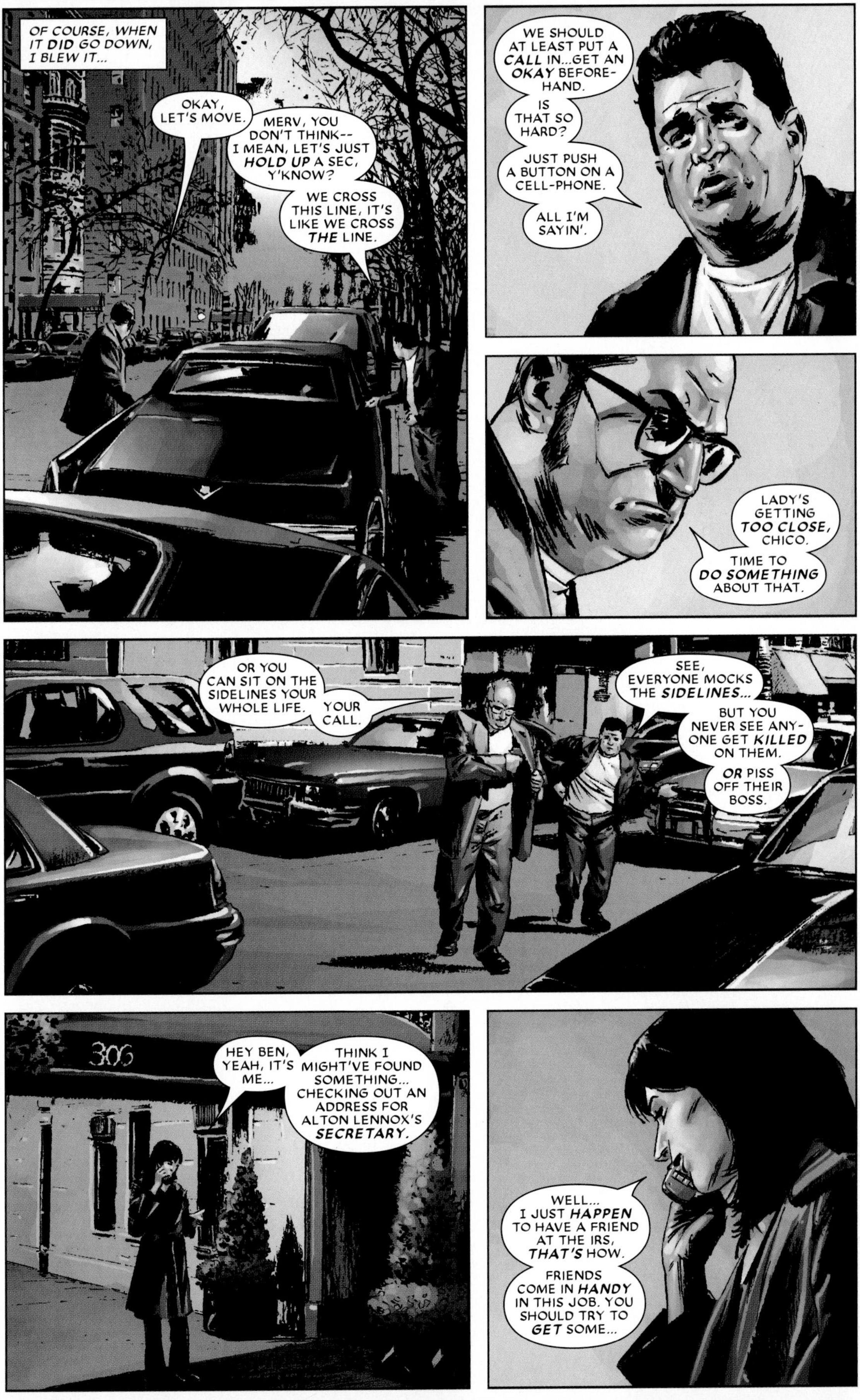
OF COURSE, WHEN IT DID GO DOWN, I BLEW IT...
OKAY, LET'S MOVE.
MERV, YOU DON'T THINK-- I MEAN, LET'S JUST HOLD UP A SEC, Y'KNOW?
WE CROSS THIS LINE, IT'S LIKE WE CROSS THE LINE.
WE SHOULD AT LEAST PUT A CALL IN...GET AN OKAY BEFORE-HAND.
IS THAT SO HARD?
JUST PUSH A BUTTON ON A CELL-PHONE.
ALL I'M SAYIN'.
LADY'S GETTING TOO CLOSE, CHICO.
TIME TO DO SOMETHING ABOUT THAT.
OR YOU CAN SIT ON THE SIDELINES YOUR WHOLE LIFE.
YOUR CALL.
SEE, EVERYONE MOCKS THE SIDELINES...
BUT YOU NEVER SEE ANY-ONE GET KILLED ON THEM.
OR PISS OFF THEIR BOSS.
306
HEY BEN, YEAH, IT'S ME...
THINK I MIGHT'VE FOUND SOMETHING... CHECKING OUT AN ADDRESS FOR ALTON LENNOX'S SECRETARY.
WELL... I JUST HAPPEN TO HAVE A FRIEND AT THE IRS, THAT'S HOW.
FRIENDS COME IN HANDY IN THIS JOB. YOU SHOULD TRY TO GET SOME...

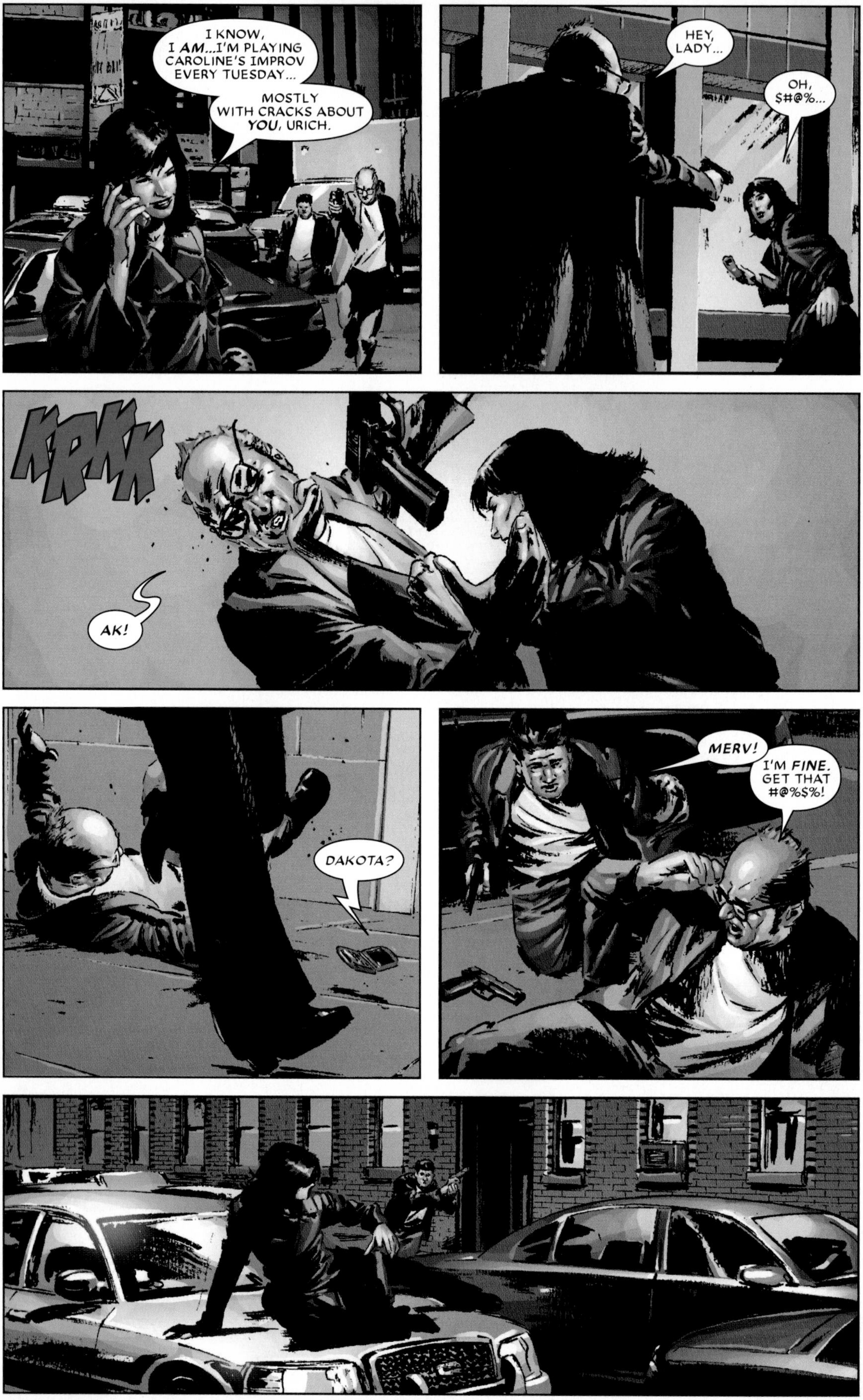

I KNOW, I AM...I'M PLAYING CAROLINE'S IMPROV EVERY TUESDAY...
MOSTLY WITH CRACKS ABOUT YOU, URICH.
HEY, LADY...
OH, $#@%...
KRKK
AK!
DAKOTA?
MERV!
I'M FINE. GET THAT #@%$%!

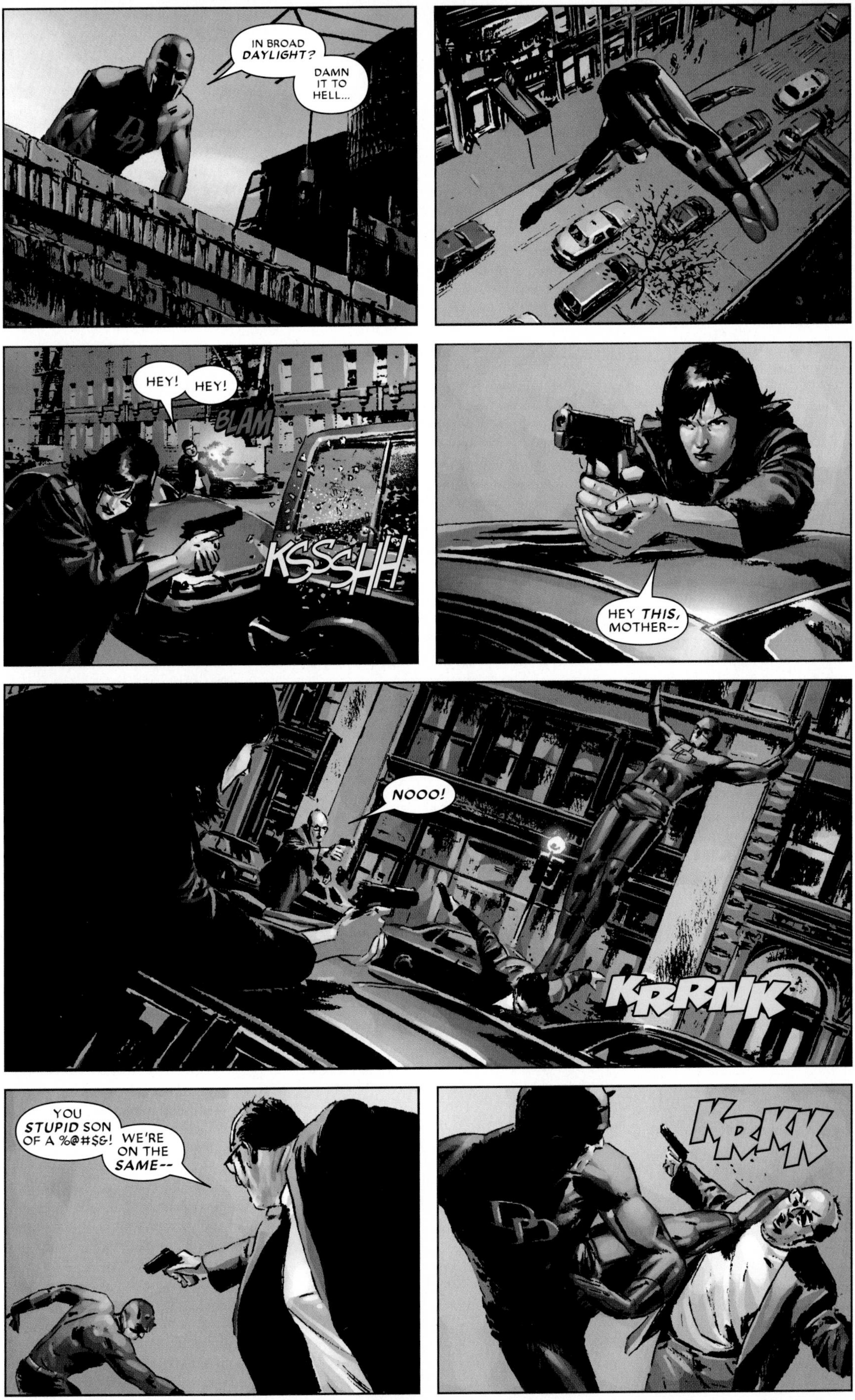

IN BROAD DAYLIGHT?
DAMN IT TO HELL...
HEY!
HEY!
BLAM
KSSSHH
HEY THIS, MOTHER--
NOOO!
KRRNK
YOU STUPID SON OF A %@#$&!
WE'RE ON THE SAME--
KRKK

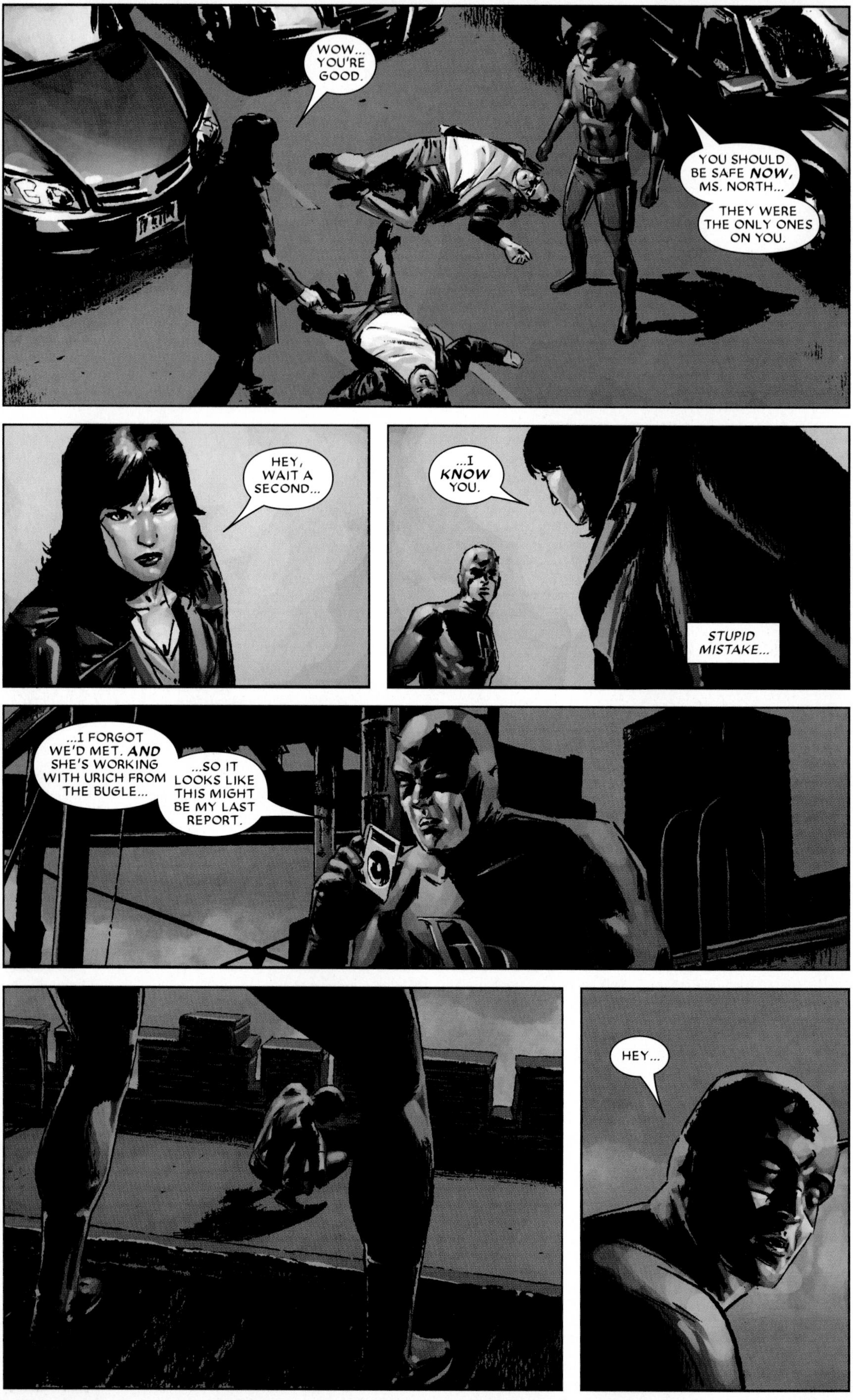
WOW... YOU'RE GOOD.
YOU SHOULD BE SAFE NOW, MS. NORTH...
THEY WERE THE ONLY ONES ON YOU.
HEY, WAIT A SECOND...
...I KNOW YOU.
STUPID MISTAKE...
...I FORGOT WE'D MET. AND SHE'S WORKING WITH URICH FROM THE BUGLE...
...SO IT LOOKS LIKE THIS MIGHT BE MY LAST REPORT.
HEY...

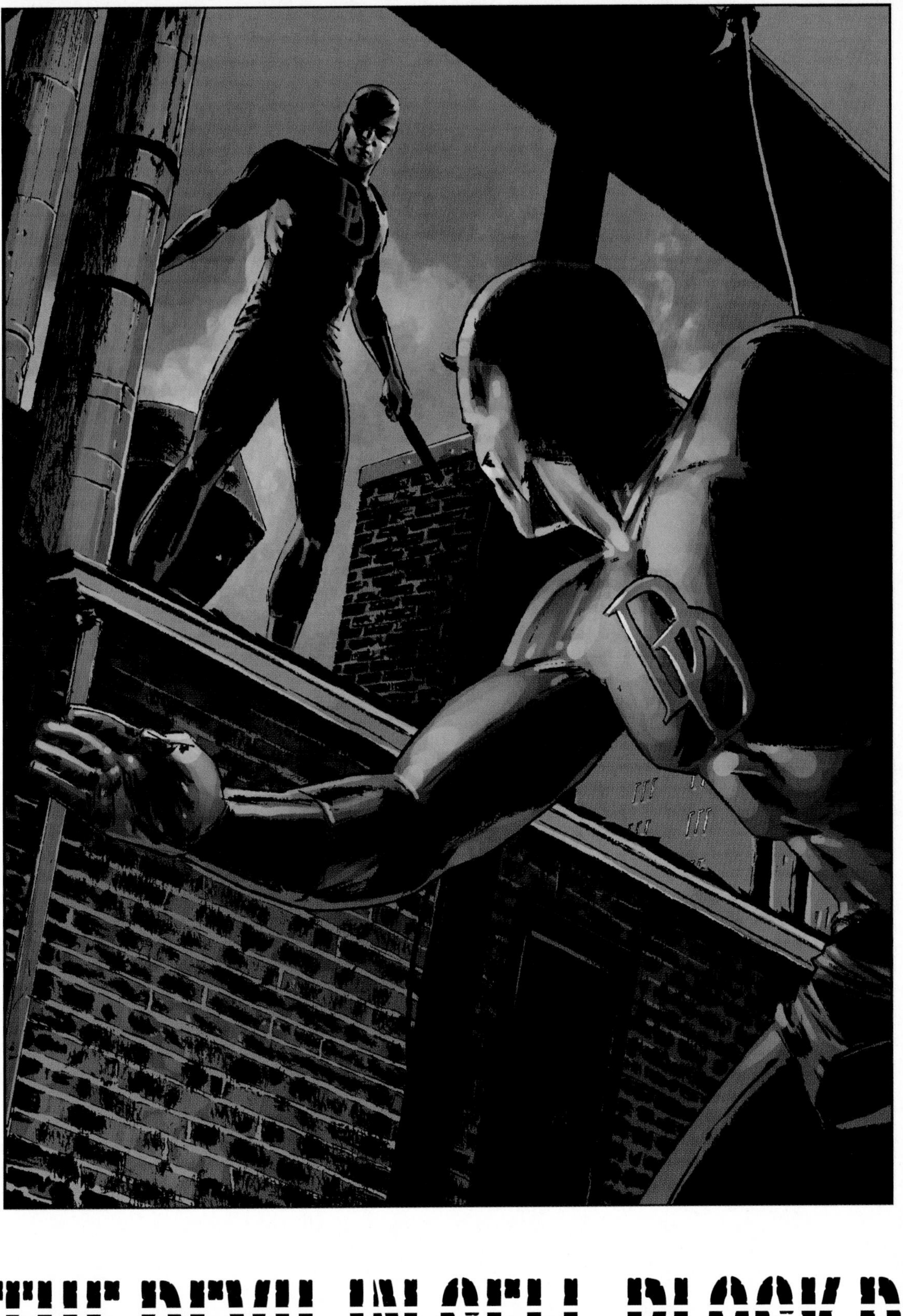

THE DEVIL IN CELL BLOCK D

FINALE

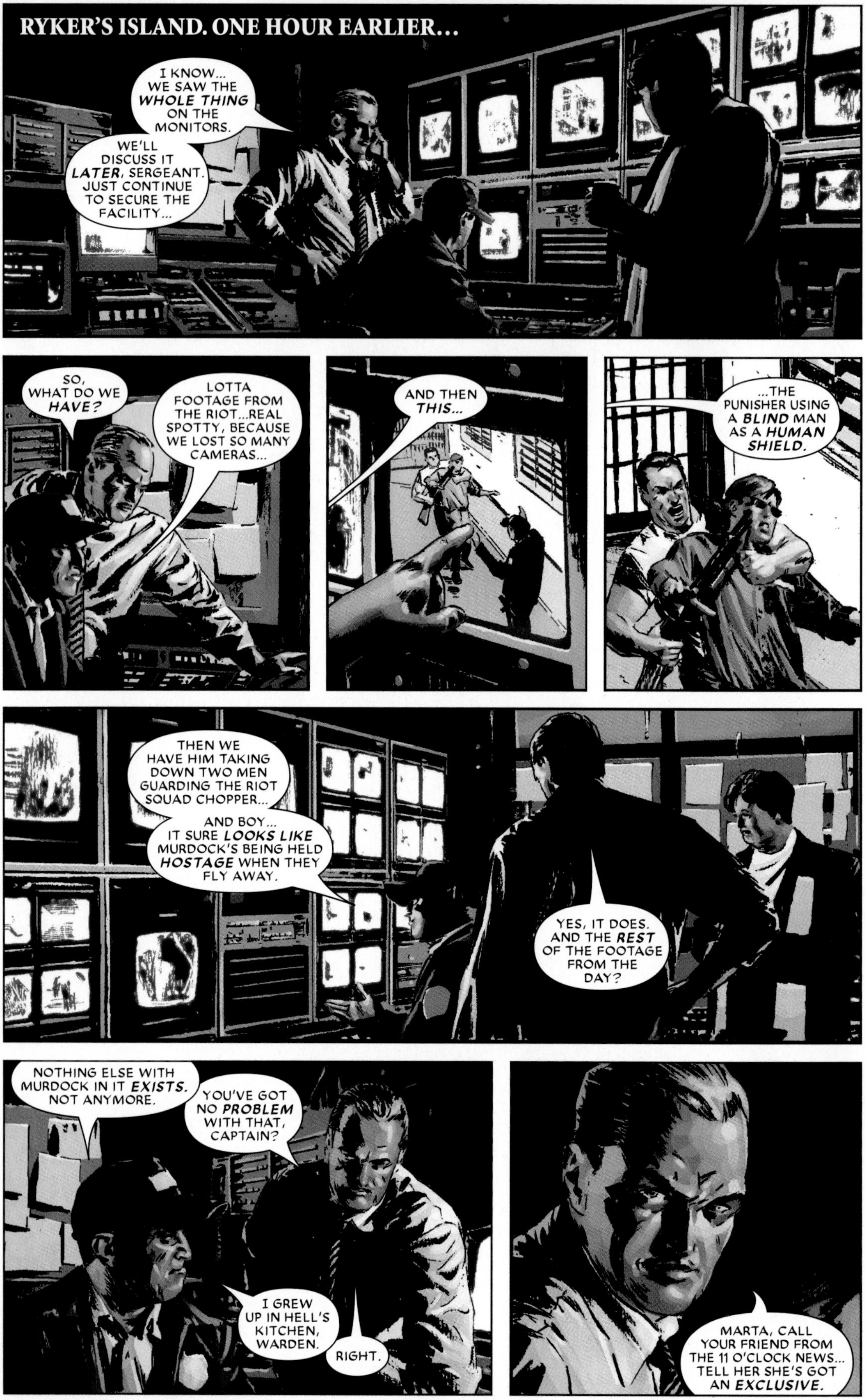
RYKER'S ISLAND. ONE HOUR EARLIER...
I KNOW... WE SAW THE WHOLE THING ON THE MONITORS.
WE'LL DISCUSS IT LATER, SERGEANT. JUST CONTINUE TO SECURE THE FACILITY...
SO, WHAT DO WE HAVE?
LOTTA FOOTAGE FROM THE RIOT...REAL SPOTTY, BECAUSE WE LOST SO MANY CAMERAS...
AND THEN THIS...
...THE PUNISHER USING A BLIND MAN AS A HUMAN SHIELD.
THEN WE HAVE HIM TAKING DOWN TWO MEN GUARDING THE RIOT SQUAD CHOPPER...
AND BOY... IT SURE LOOKS LIKE MURDOCK'S BEING HELD HOSTAGE WHEN THEY FLY AWAY.
YES, IT DOES. AND THE REST OF THE FOOTAGE FROM THE DAY?
NOTHING ELSE WITH MURDOCK IN IT EXISTS. NOT ANYMORE.
YOU'VE GOT NO PROBLEM WITH THAT, CAPTAIN?
I GREW UP IN HELL'S KITCHEN, WARDEN.
RIGHT.
MARTA, CALL YOUR FRIEND FROM THE 11 O'CLOCK NEWS... TELL HER SHE'S GOT AN EXCLUSIVE.

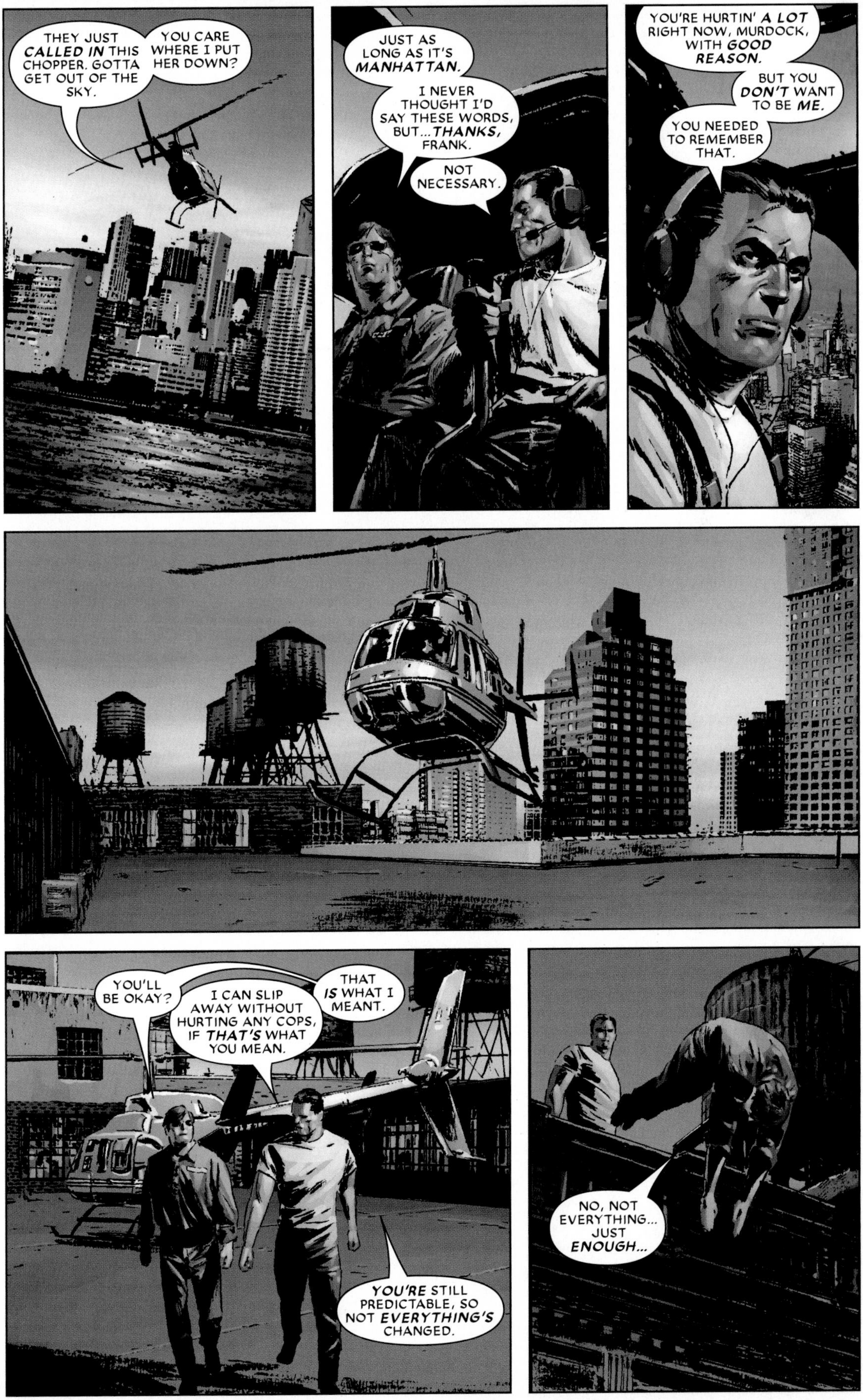
THEY JUST CALLED IN THIS CHOPPER. GOTTA GET OUT OF THE SKY.
YOU CARE WHERE I PUT HER DOWN?
JUST AS LONG AS IT'S MANHATTAN.
I NEVER THOUGHT I'D SAY THESE WORDS, BUT...THANKS, FRANK.
NOT NECESSARY.
YOU'RE HURTIN' A LOT RIGHT NOW, MURDOCK, WITH GOOD REASON.
BUT YOU DON'T WANT TO BE ME.
YOU NEEDED TO REMEMBER THAT.
YOU'LL BE OKAY?
I CAN SLIP AWAY WITHOUT HURTING ANY COPS, IF THAT'S WHAT YOU MEAN.
THAT IS WHAT I MEANT.
YOU'RE STILL PREDICTABLE, SO NOT EVERYTHING'S CHANGED.
NO, NOT EVERYTHING... JUST ENOUGH...

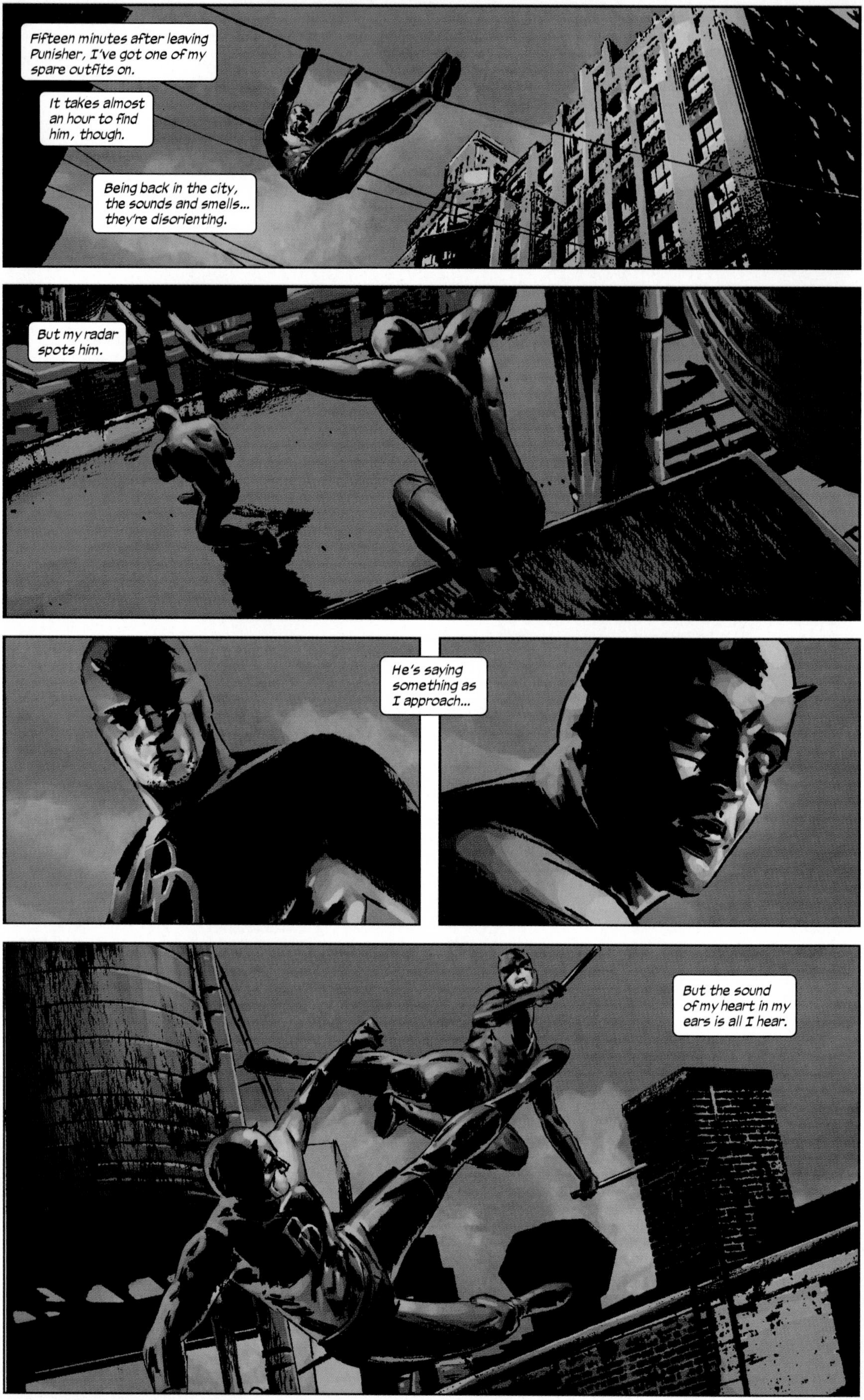
Fifteen minutes after leaving Punisher, I've got one of my spare outfits on.
It takes almost an hour to find him, though.
Being back in the city, the sounds and smells... they're disorienting.
But my radar spots him.
He's saying something as I approach...
But the sound of my heart in my ears is all I hear.

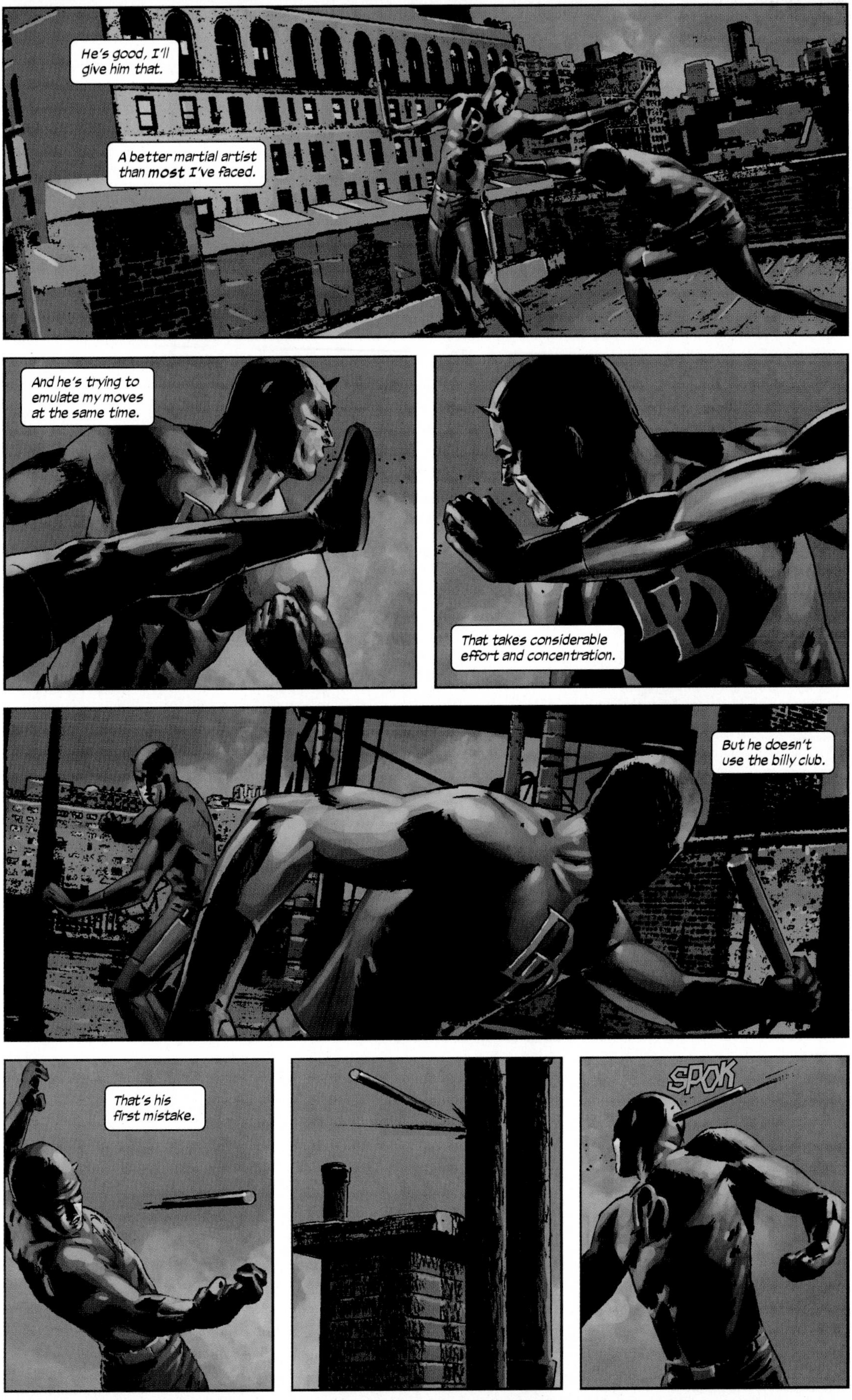
He's good, I'll give him that.
A better martial artist than **most** I've faced.
And he's trying to emulate my moves at the same time.
That takes considerable effort and concentration.
But he doesn't use the billy club.
That's his first mistake.
SPOK

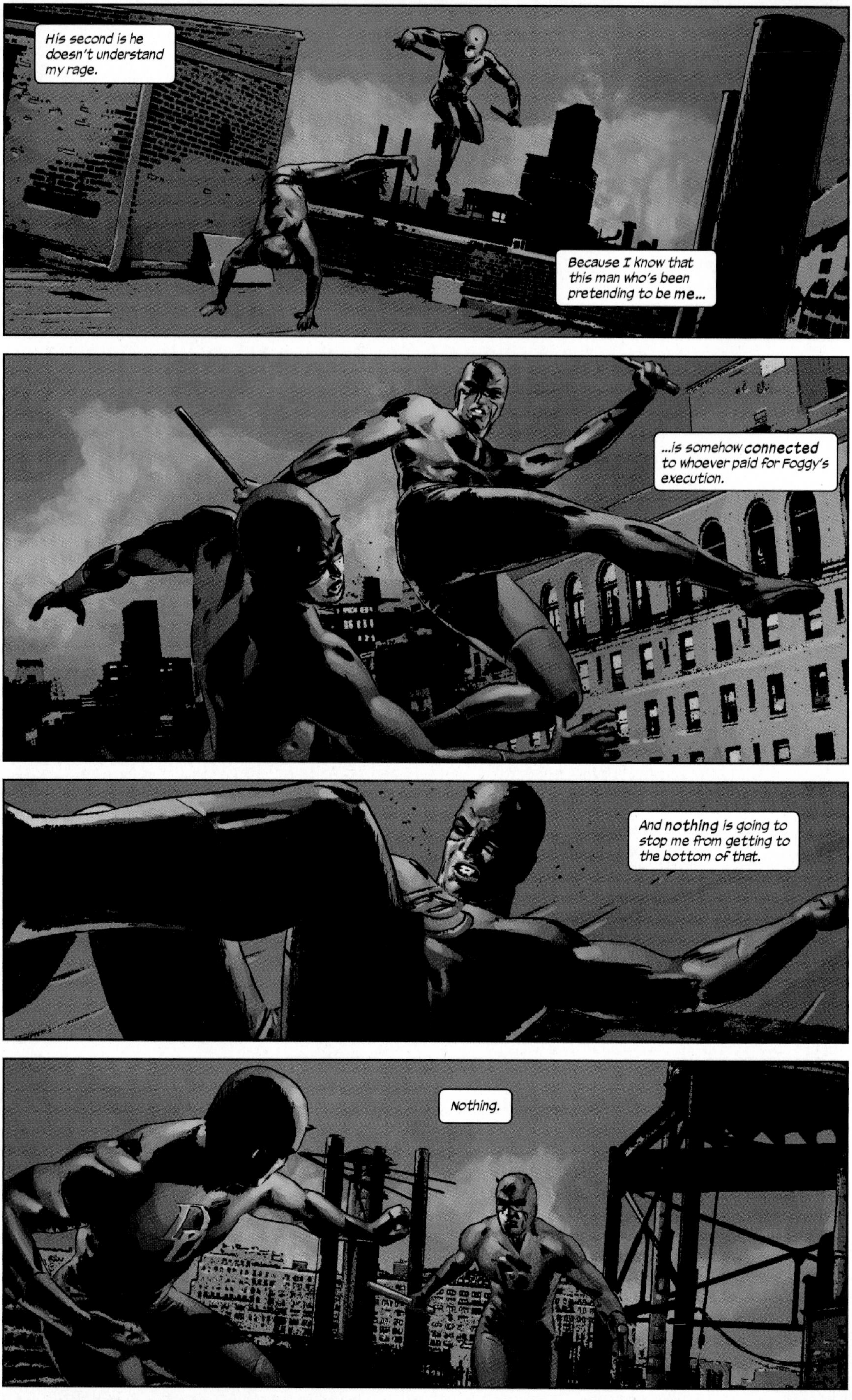
His second is he doesn't understand my rage.
Because I know that this man who's been pretending to be me...
...is somehow connected to whoever paid for Foggy's execution.
And nothing is going to stop me from getting to the bottom of that.
Nothing.

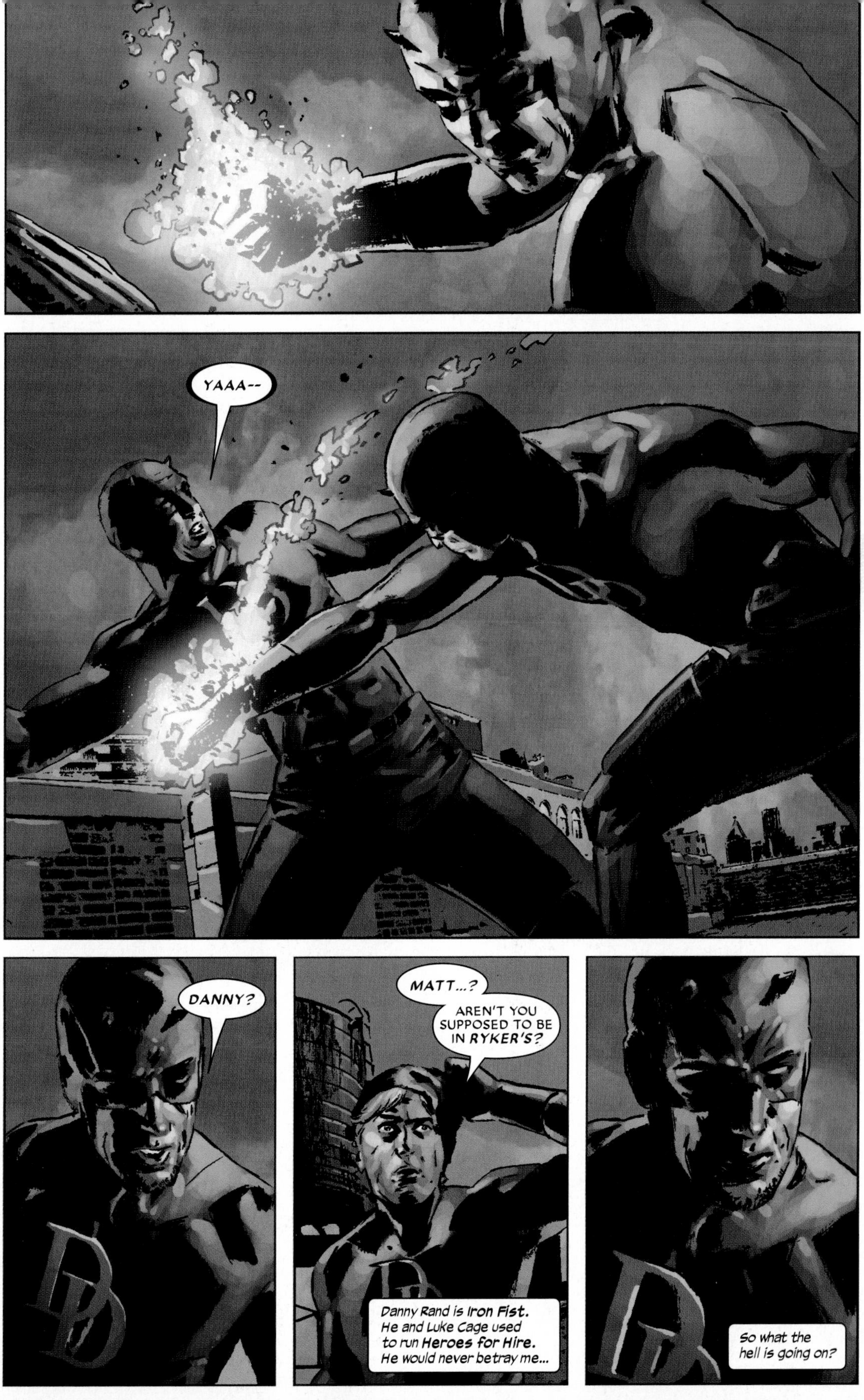
YAAA--
DANNY?
MATT...?
AREN'T YOU SUPPOSED TO BE IN RYKER'S?
Danny Rand is Iron Fist. He and Luke Cage used to run Heroes for Hire. He would never betray me...
So what the hell is going on?

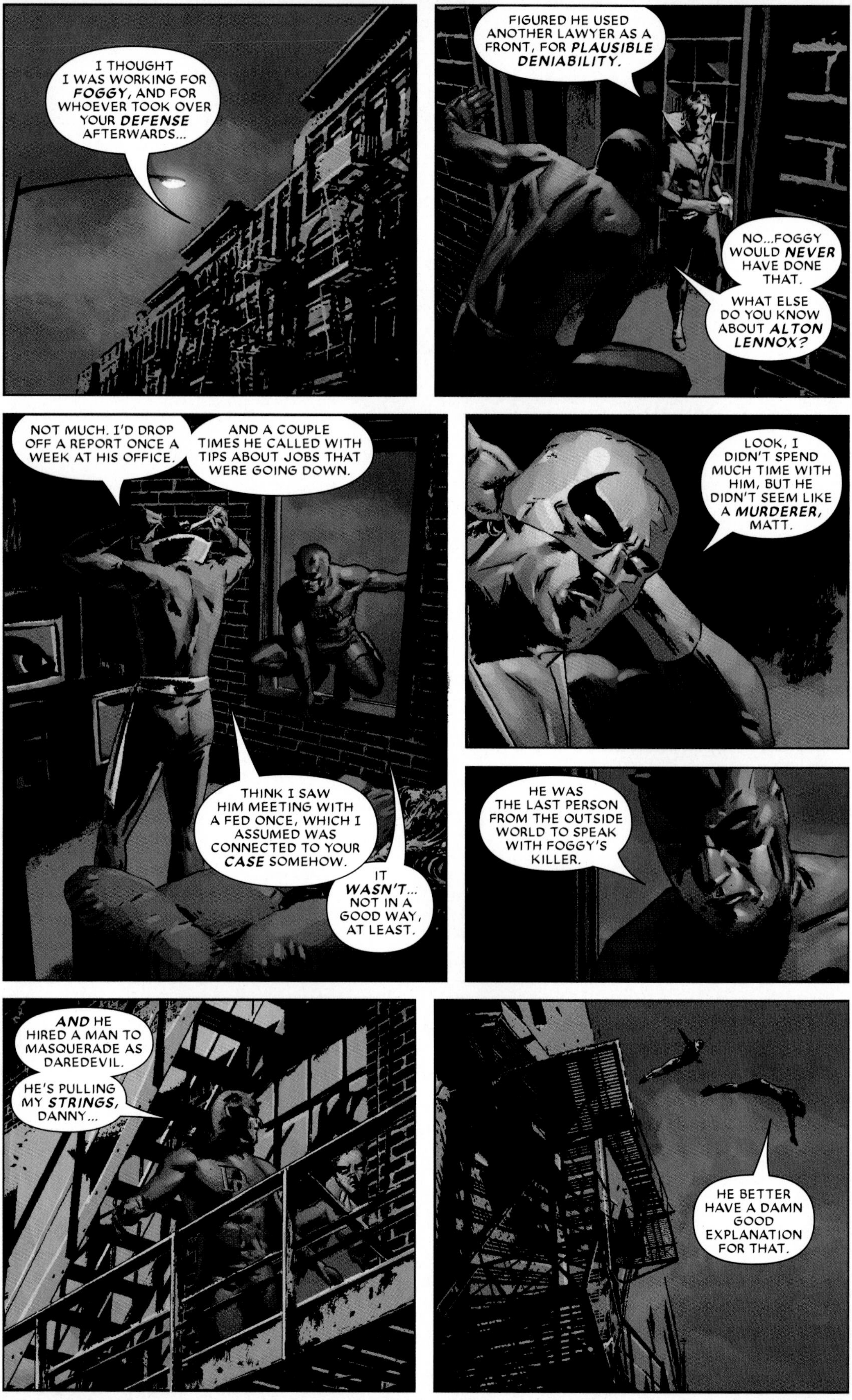
I THOUGHT I WAS WORKING FOR FOGGY, AND FOR WHOEVER TOOK OVER YOUR DEFENSE AFTERWARDS...
FIGURED HE USED ANOTHER LAWYER AS A FRONT, FOR PLAUSIBLE DENIABILITY.
NO...FOGGY WOULD NEVER HAVE DONE THAT.
WHAT ELSE DO YOU KNOW ABOUT ALTON LENNOX?
NOT MUCH. I'D DROP OFF A REPORT ONCE A WEEK AT HIS OFFICE.
AND A COUPLE TIMES HE CALLED WITH TIPS ABOUT JOBS THAT WERE GOING DOWN.
THINK I SAW HIM MEETING WITH A FED ONCE, WHICH I ASSUMED WAS CONNECTED TO YOUR CASE SOMEHOW.
IT WASN'T... NOT IN A GOOD WAY, AT LEAST.
LOOK, I DIDN'T SPEND MUCH TIME WITH HIM, BUT HE DIDN'T SEEM LIKE A MURDERER, MATT.
HE WAS THE LAST PERSON FROM THE OUTSIDE WORLD TO SPEAK WITH FOGGY'S KILLER.
AND HE HIRED A MAN TO MASQUERADE AS DAREDEVIL.
HE'S PULLING MY STRINGS, DANNY...
HE BETTER HAVE A DAMN GOOD EXPLANATION FOR THAT.

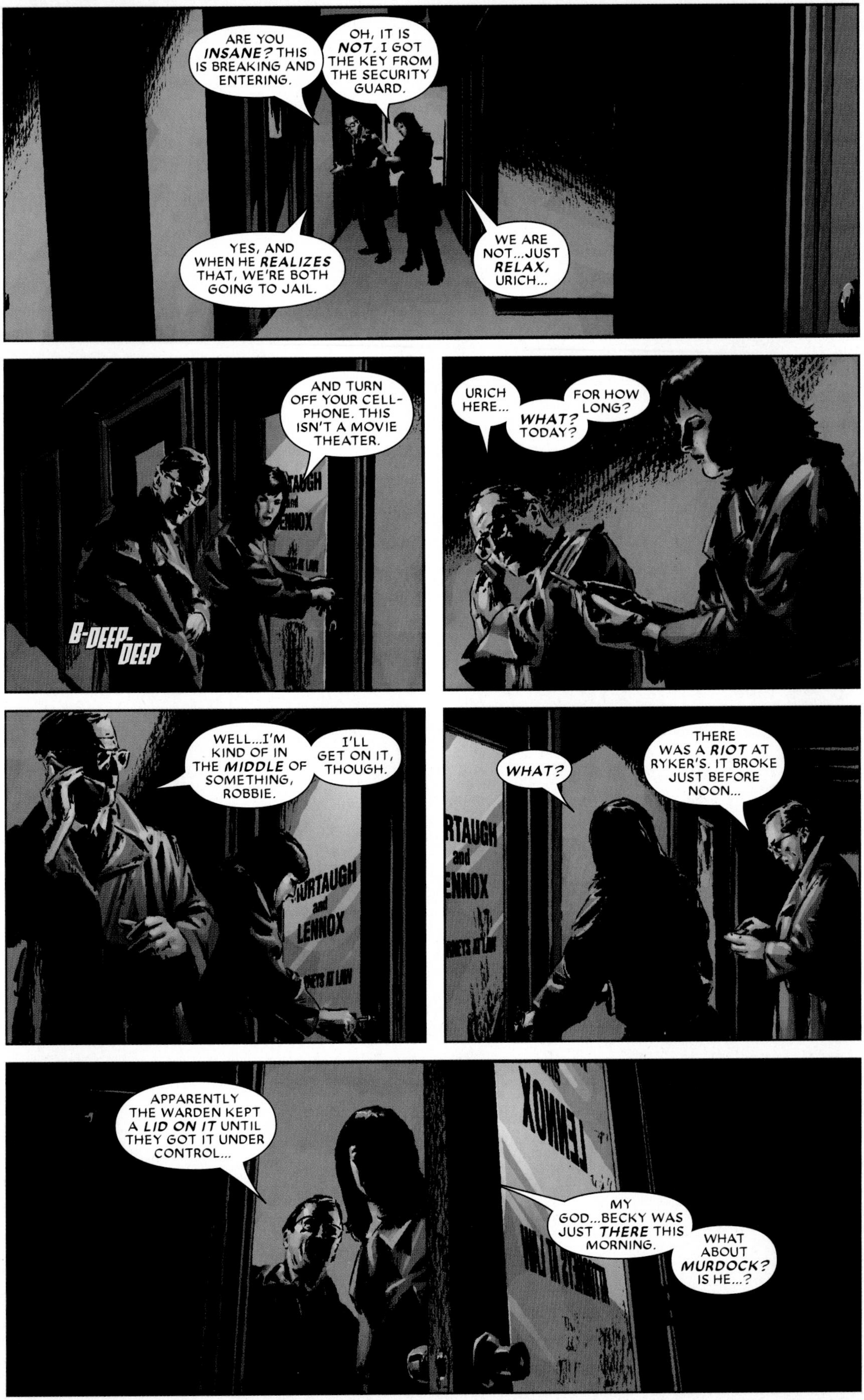
ARE YOU INSANE? THIS IS BREAKING AND ENTERING.
OH, IT IS NOT. I GOT THE KEY FROM THE SECURITY GUARD.
YES, AND WHEN HE REALIZES THAT, WE'RE BOTH GOING TO JAIL.
WE ARE NOT...JUST RELAX, URICH...
AND TURN OFF YOUR CELL-PHONE. THIS ISN'T A MOVIE THEATER.
B-DEEP-DEEP
URICH HERE...
WHAT? TODAY?
FOR HOW LONG?
WELL...I'M KIND OF IN THE MIDDLE OF SOMETHING, ROBBIE.
I'LL GET ON IT, THOUGH.
WHAT?
THERE WAS A RIOT AT RYKER'S. IT BROKE JUST BEFORE NOON...
APPARENTLY THE WARDEN KEPT A LID ON IT UNTIL THEY GOT IT UNDER CONTROL...
MY GOD...BECKY WAS JUST THERE THIS MORNING.
WHAT ABOUT MURDOCK? IS HE...?

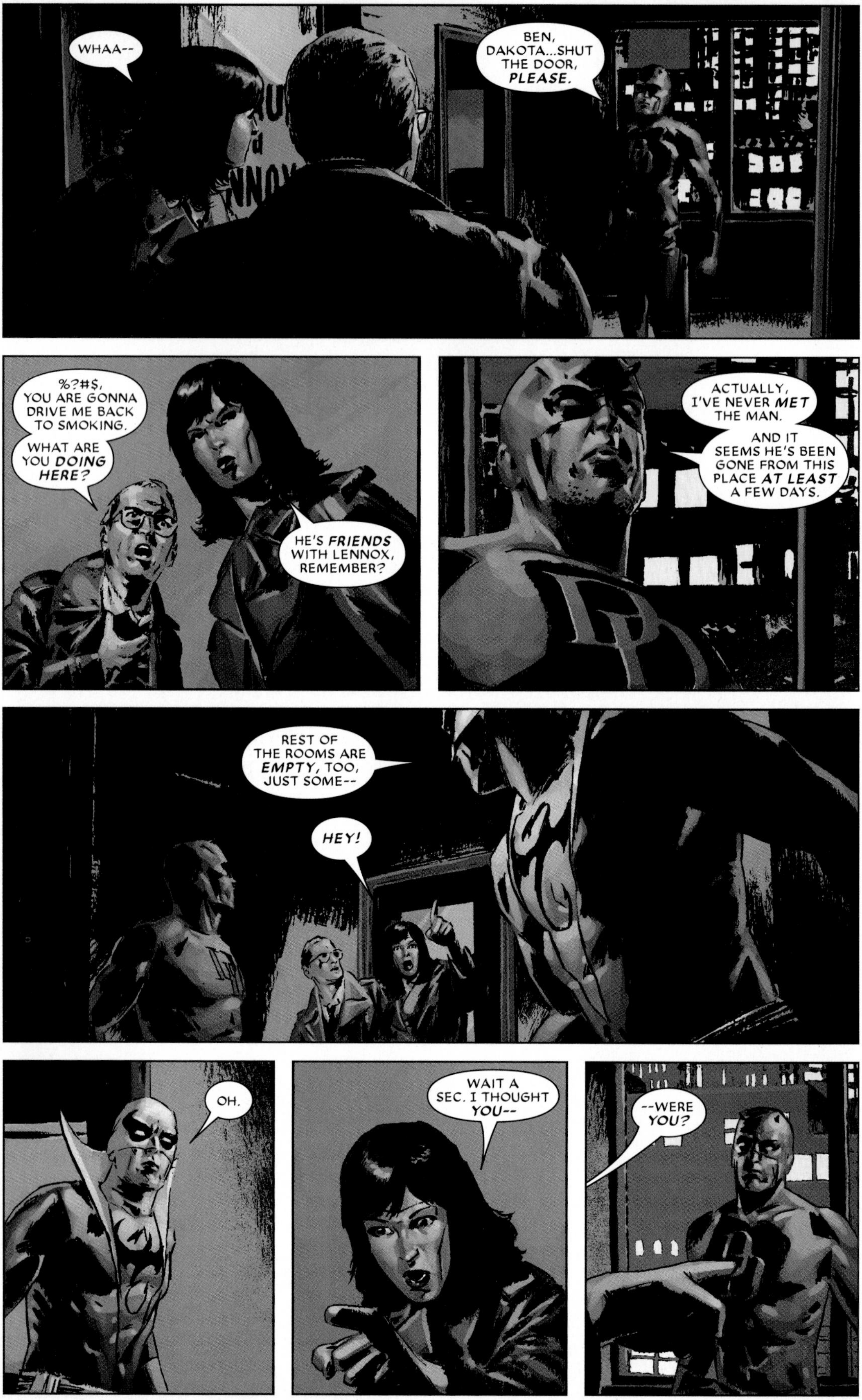

WHAA--
BEN, DAKOTA...SHUT THE DOOR, PLEASE.
%?#$, YOU ARE GONNA DRIVE ME BACK TO SMOKING.
WHAT ARE YOU DOING HERE?
HE'S FRIENDS WITH LENNOX, REMEMBER?
ACTUALLY, I'VE NEVER MET THE MAN.
AND IT SEEMS HE'S BEEN GONE FROM THIS PLACE AT LEAST A FEW DAYS.
REST OF THE ROOMS ARE EMPTY, TOO, JUST SOME--
HEY!
OH.
WAIT A SEC. I THOUGHT YOU--
--WERE YOU?

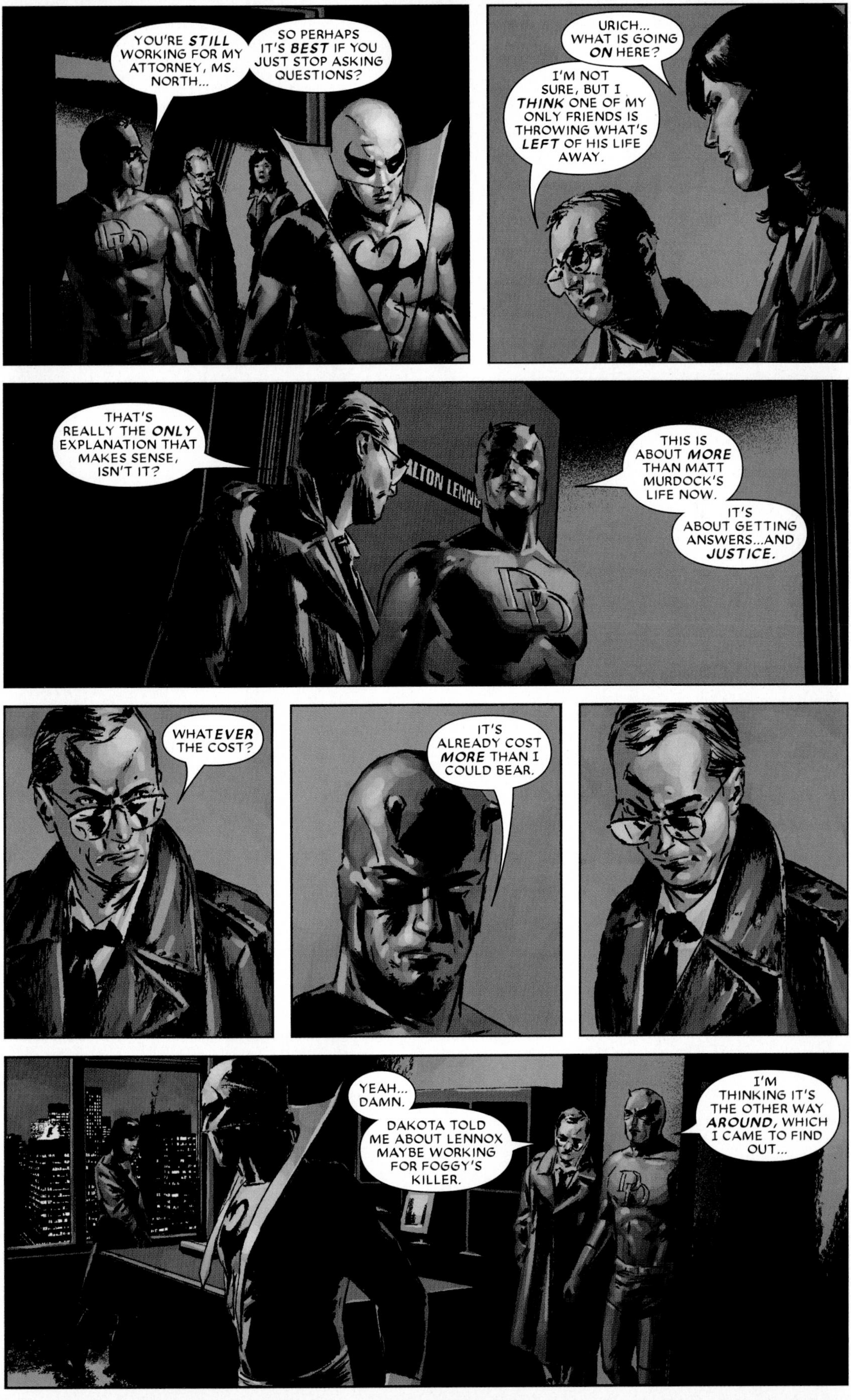
YOU'RE STILL WORKING FOR MY ATTORNEY, MS. NORTH...
SO PERHAPS IT'S BEST IF YOU JUST STOP ASKING QUESTIONS?
URICH... WHAT IS GOING ON HERE?
I'M NOT SURE, BUT I THINK ONE OF MY ONLY FRIENDS IS THROWING WHAT'S LEFT OF HIS LIFE AWAY.
THAT'S REALLY THE ONLY EXPLANATION THAT MAKES SENSE, ISN'T IT?
ALTON LENN
THIS IS ABOUT MORE THAN MATT MURDOCK'S LIFE NOW.
IT'S ABOUT GETTING ANSWERS...AND JUSTICE.
WHATEVER THE COST?
IT'S ALREADY COST MORE THAN I COULD BEAR.
YEAH... DAMN.
DAKOTA TOLD ME ABOUT LENNOX MAYBE WORKING FOR FOGGY'S KILLER.
I'M THINKING IT'S THE OTHER WAY AROUND, WHICH I CAME TO FIND OUT...

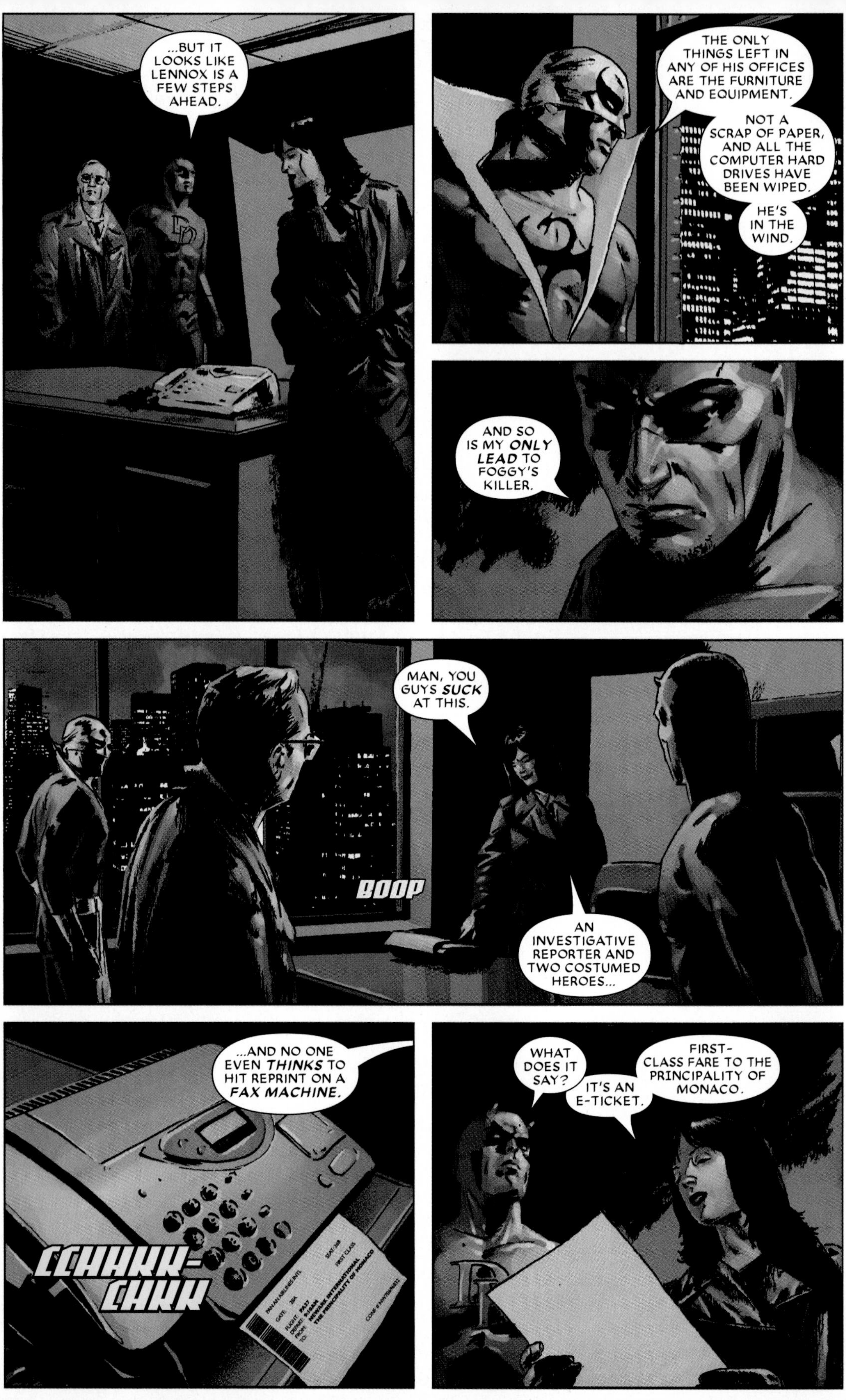
...BUT IT LOOKS LIKE LENNOX IS A FEW STEPS AHEAD.
THE ONLY THINGS LEFT IN ANY OF HIS OFFICES ARE THE FURNITURE AND EQUIPMENT.
NOT A SCRAP OF PAPER, AND ALL THE COMPUTER HARD DRIVES HAVE BEEN WIPED.
HE'S IN THE WIND.
AND SO IS MY *ONLY LEAD* TO FOGGY'S KILLER.
MAN, YOU GUYS *SUCK* AT THIS.
BOOP
AN INVESTIGATIVE REPORTER AND TWO COSTUMED HEROES...
...AND NO ONE EVEN *THINKS* TO HIT REPRINT ON A *FAX MACHINE.*
CCHKK-CHKK
WHAT DOES IT SAY?
IT'S AN E-TICKET.
FIRST-CLASS FARE TO THE PRINCIPALITY OF MONACO.

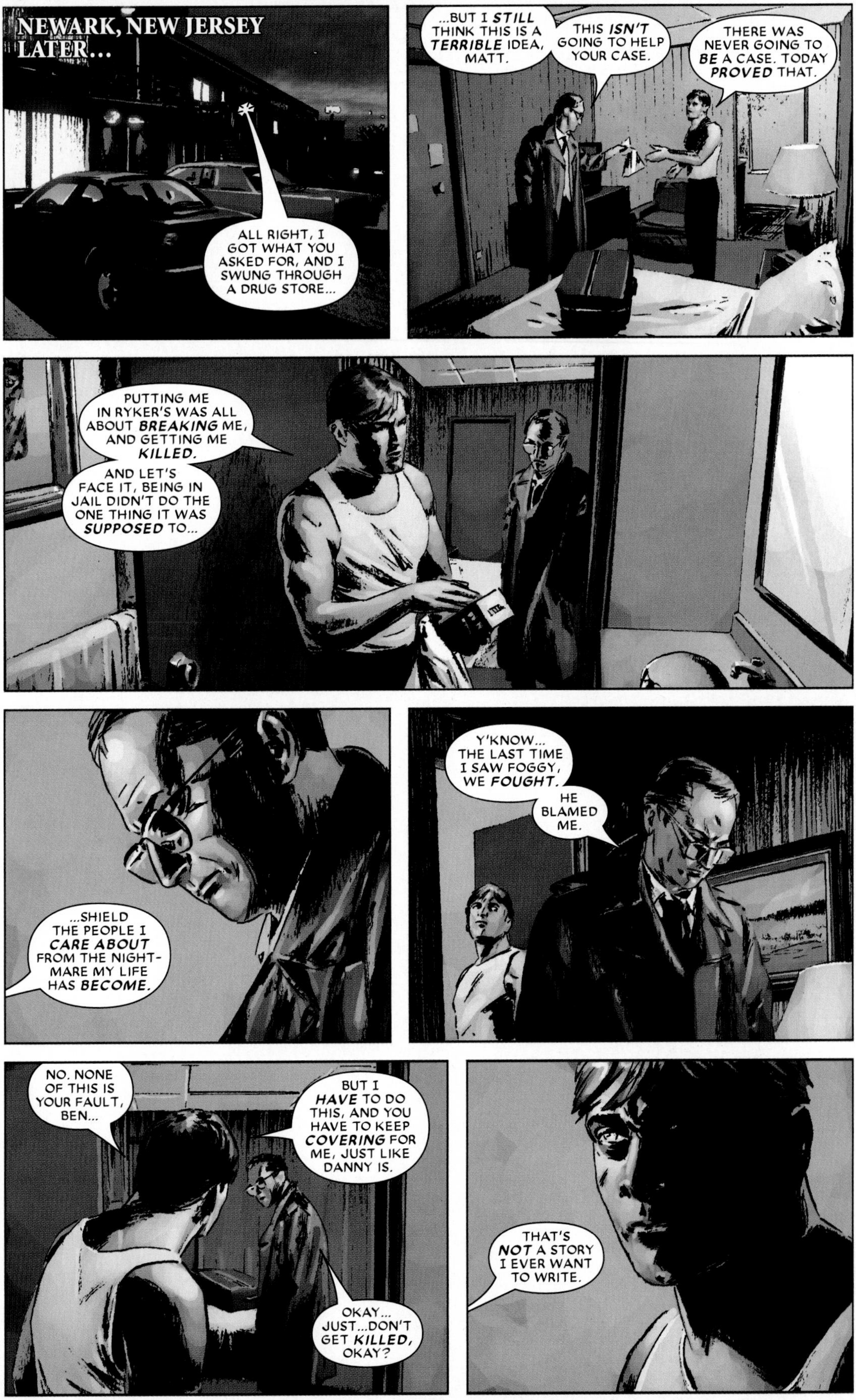
NEWARK, NEW JERSEY
LATER...
ALL RIGHT, I GOT WHAT YOU ASKED FOR, AND I SWUNG THROUGH A DRUG STORE...
...BUT I STILL THINK THIS IS A TERRIBLE IDEA, MATT.
THIS ISN'T GOING TO HELP YOUR CASE.
THERE WAS NEVER GOING TO BE A CASE. TODAY PROVED THAT.
PUTTING ME IN RYKER'S WAS ALL ABOUT BREAKING ME, AND GETTING ME KILLED.
AND LET'S FACE IT, BEING IN JAIL DIDN'T DO THE ONE THING IT WAS SUPPOSED TO...
...SHIELD THE PEOPLE I CARE ABOUT FROM THE NIGHT-MARE MY LIFE HAS BECOME.
Y'KNOW... THE LAST TIME I SAW FOGGY, WE FOUGHT.
HE BLAMED ME.
NO. NONE OF THIS IS YOUR FAULT, BEN...
BUT I HAVE TO DO THIS, AND YOU HAVE TO KEEP COVERING FOR ME, JUST LIKE DANNY IS.
OKAY... JUST...DON'T GET KILLED, OKAY?
THAT'S NOT A STORY I EVER WANT TO WRITE.

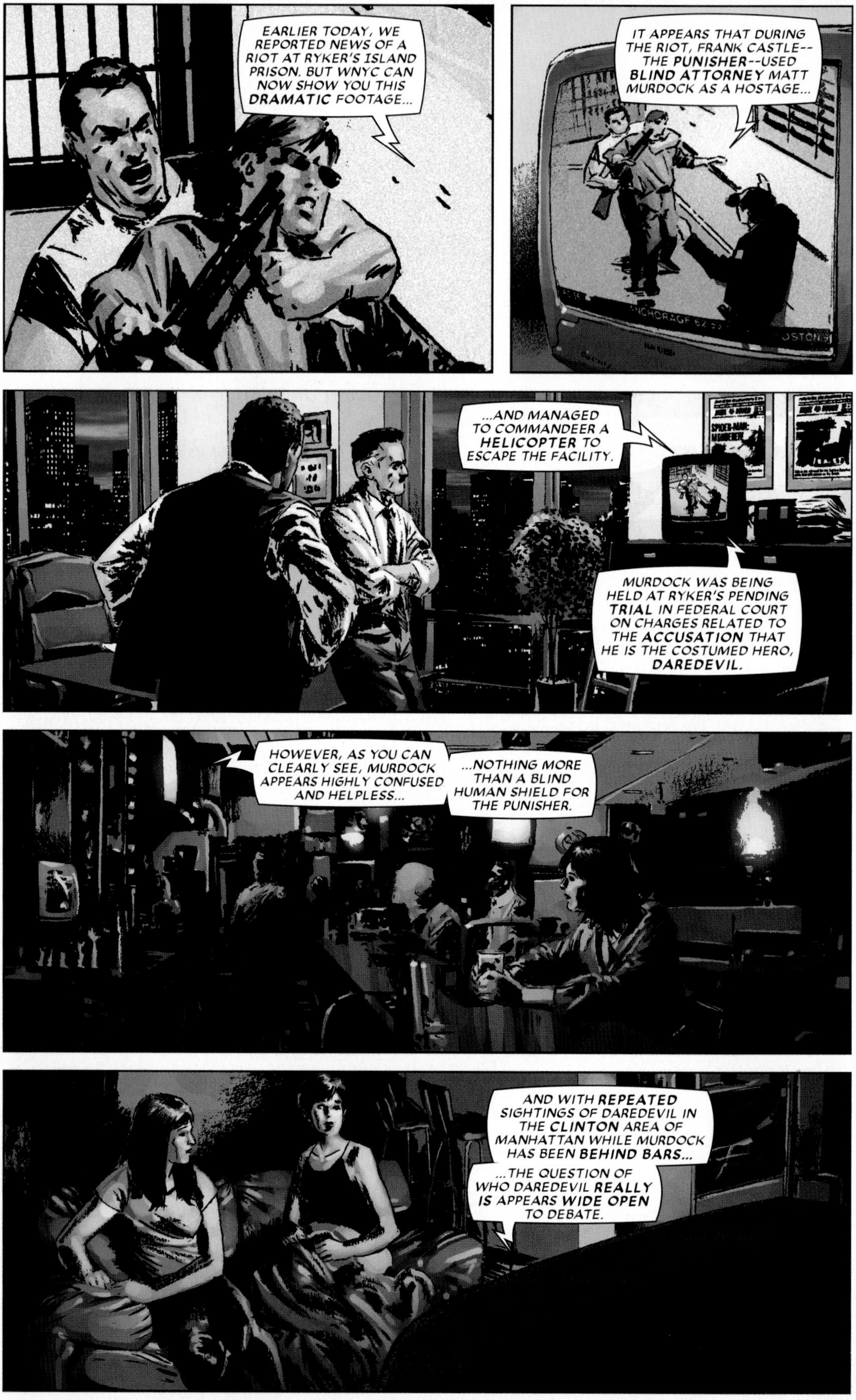
EARLIER TODAY, WE REPORTED NEWS OF A RIOT AT RYKER'S ISLAND PRISON. BUT WNYC CAN NOW SHOW YOU THIS DRAMATIC FOOTAGE...
IT APPEARS THAT DURING THE RIOT, FRANK CASTLE--THE PUNISHER--USED BLIND ATTORNEY MATT MURDOCK AS A HOSTAGE...
...AND MANAGED TO COMMANDEER A HELICOPTER TO ESCAPE THE FACILITY.
MURDOCK WAS BEING HELD AT RYKER'S PENDING TRIAL IN FEDERAL COURT ON CHARGES RELATED TO THE ACCUSATION THAT HE IS THE COSTUMED HERO, DAREDEVIL.
HOWEVER, AS YOU CAN CLEARLY SEE, MURDOCK APPEARS HIGHLY CONFUSED AND HELPLESS...
...NOTHING MORE THAN A BLIND HUMAN SHIELD FOR THE PUNISHER.
AND WITH REPEATED SIGHTINGS OF DAREDEVIL IN THE CLINTON AREA OF MANHATTAN WHILE MURDOCK HAS BEEN BEHIND BARS...
...THE QUESTION OF WHO DAREDEVIL REALLY IS APPEARS WIDE OPEN TO DEBATE.

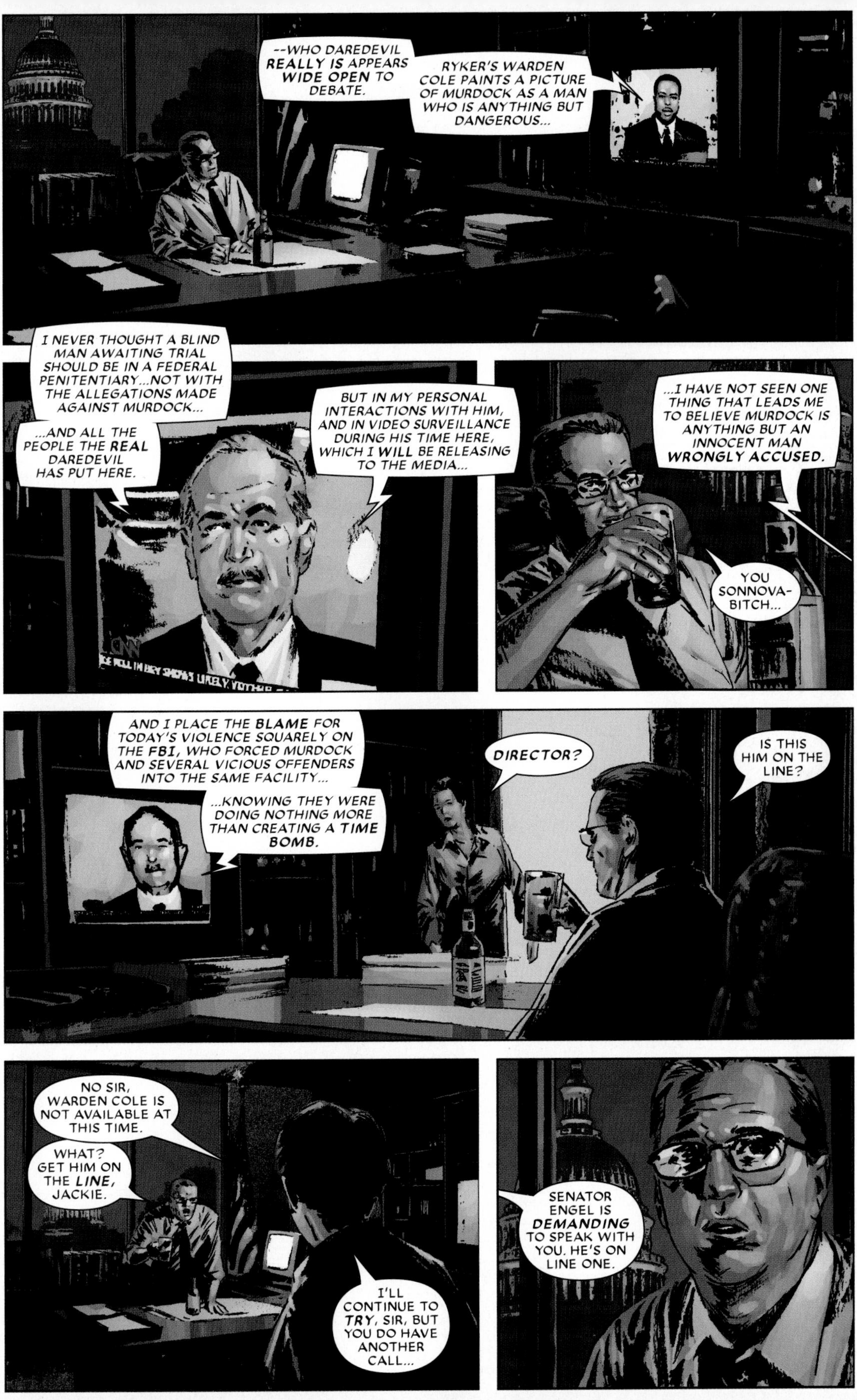
--WHO DAREDEVIL REALLY IS APPEARS WIDE OPEN TO DEBATE.
RYKER'S WARDEN COLE PAINTS A PICTURE OF MURDOCK AS A MAN WHO IS ANYTHING BUT DANGEROUS...
I NEVER THOUGHT A BLIND MAN AWAITING TRIAL SHOULD BE IN A FEDERAL PENITENTIARY...NOT WITH THE ALLEGATIONS MADE AGAINST MURDOCK...
...AND ALL THE PEOPLE THE REAL DAREDEVIL HAS PUT HERE.
BUT IN MY PERSONAL INTERACTIONS WITH HIM, AND IN VIDEO SURVEILLANCE DURING HIS TIME HERE, WHICH I WILL BE RELEASING TO THE MEDIA...
...I HAVE NOT SEEN ONE THING THAT LEADS ME TO BELIEVE MURDOCK IS ANYTHING BUT AN INNOCENT MAN WRONGLY ACCUSED.
YOU SONNOVA-BITCH...
AND I PLACE THE BLAME FOR TODAY'S VIOLENCE SQUARELY ON THE FBI, WHO FORCED MURDOCK AND SEVERAL VICIOUS OFFENDERS INTO THE SAME FACILITY...
...KNOWING THEY WERE DOING NOTHING MORE THAN CREATING A TIME BOMB.
DIRECTOR?
IS THIS HIM ON THE LINE?
NO SIR, WARDEN COLE IS NOT AVAILABLE AT THIS TIME.
WHAT? GET HIM ON THE LINE, JACKIE.
I'LL CONTINUE TO TRY, SIR, BUT YOU DO HAVE ANOTHER CALL...
SENATOR ENGEL IS DEMANDING TO SPEAK WITH YOU. HE'S ON LINE ONE.

"AT THIS TIME, THE WHERE-ABOUTS OF THE PUNISHER AND HIS *CAPTIVE*, BLIND ATTORNEY MATT MURDOCK ARE *UNKNOWN*..."

"...BUT POLICE ARE PURSUING *ALL LEADS*, AND HOPE FOR A SAFE RECOVERY OF THE HOSTAGE."

I got a lucky break, with Warden Cole covering for me...turning on the F.B.I. But I can't count on luck... not from this point on.

I'M AFRAID I'VE ONLY GOT FIRST CLASS LEFT ON THAT FLIGHT...DOES THAT WORK FOR YOU, MISTER...?

MURDOCK...

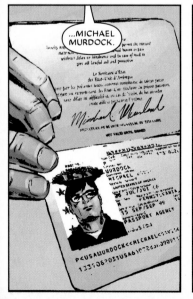

...MICHAEL MURDOCK.

AND THAT'LL BE FINE. WHEN DOES IT *LEAVE*?

They tried to kill me, and they failed.

They tried to break me, and maybe even succeeded a bit.

Whoever they are, they're going to regret that.

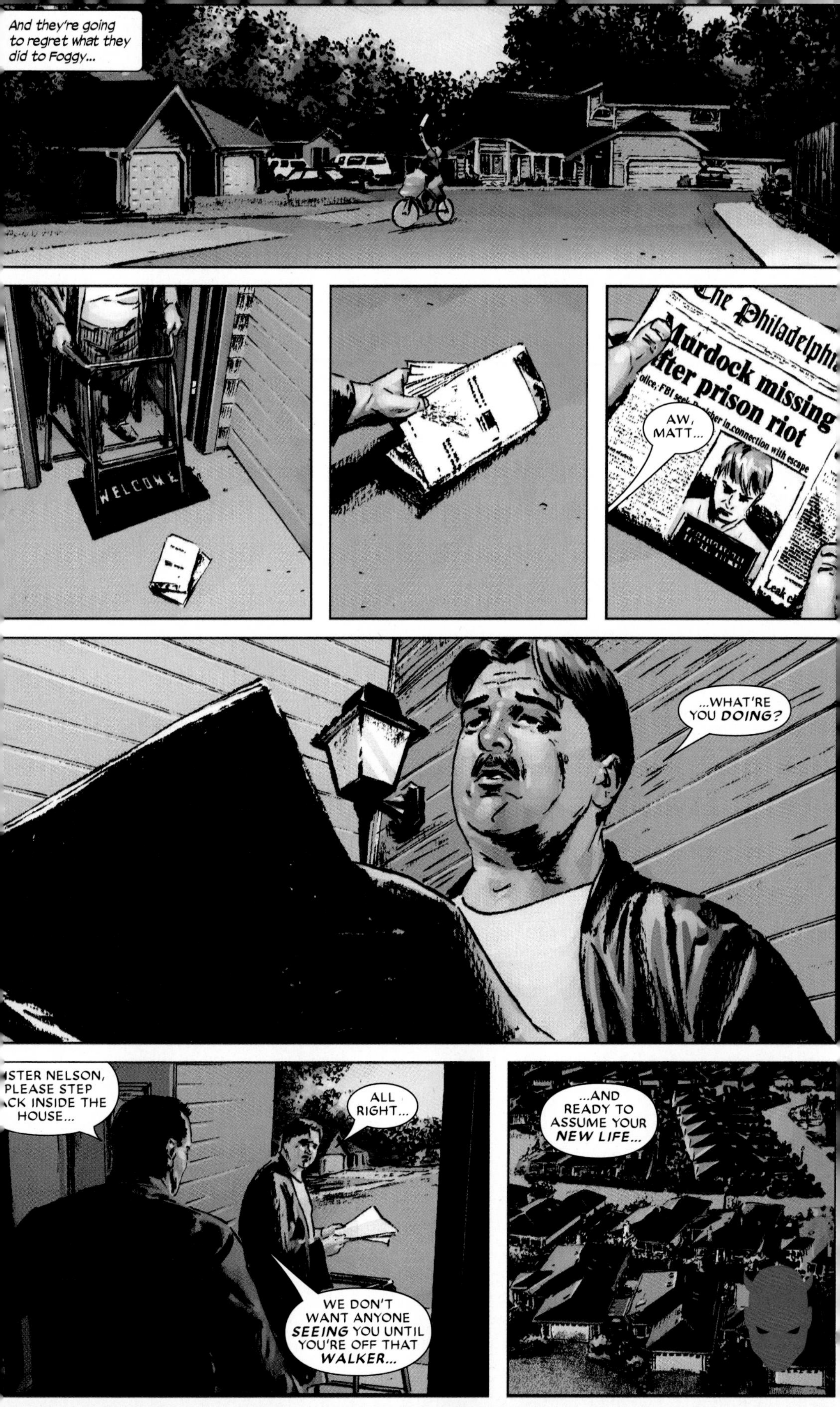

And they're going to regret what they did to Foggy...
WELCOME
Murdock missing
fter prison riot
AW, MATT...
...WHAT'RE YOU *DOING*?
ISTER NELSON, PLEASE STEP CK INSIDE THE HOUSE...
ALL RIGHT...
WE DON'T WANT ANYONE *SEEING* YOU UNTIL YOU'RE OFF THAT *WALKER*...
...AND READY TO ASSUME YOUR *NEW LIFE*...

82 variant cover by Steve McNiven

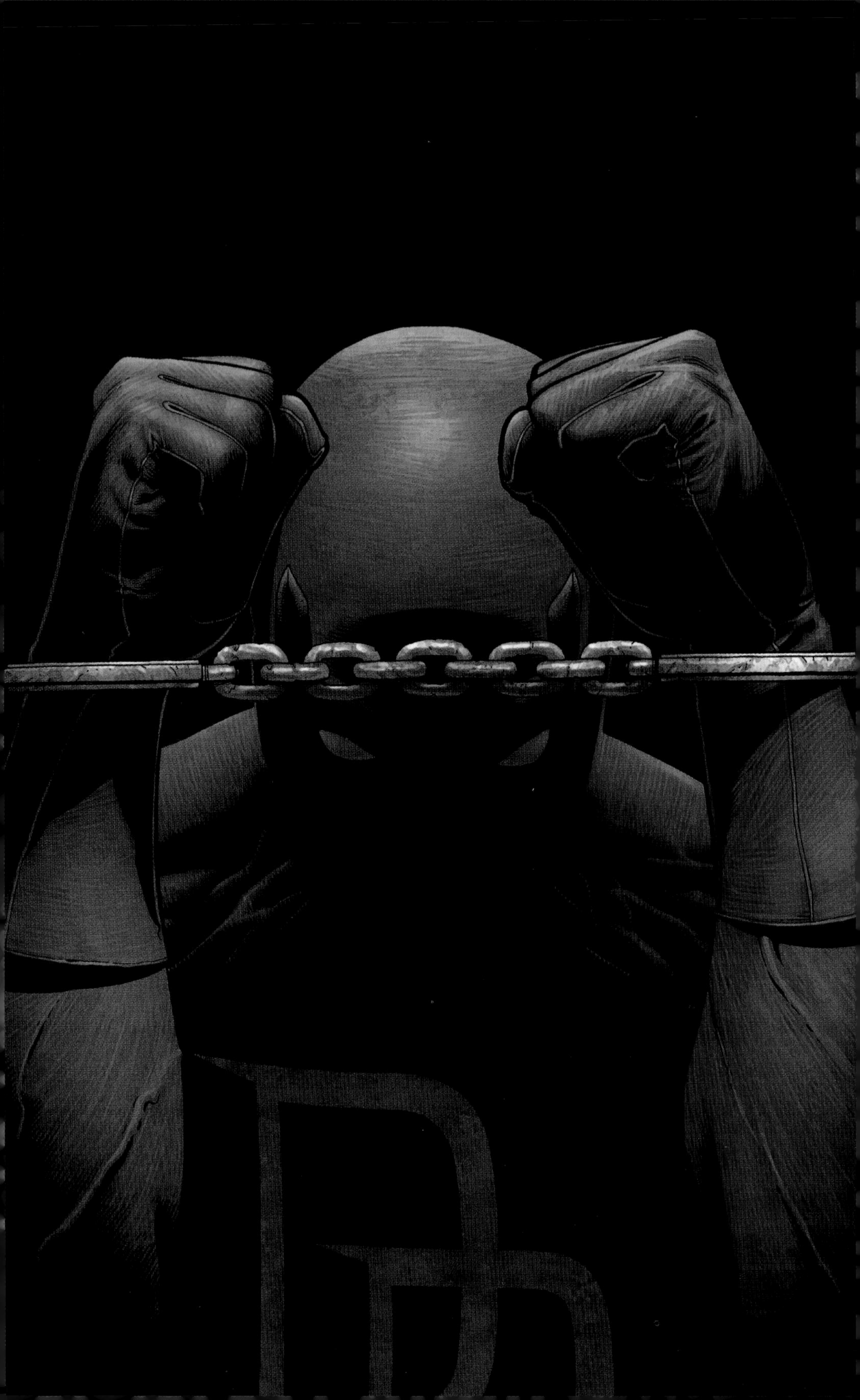
DD

MARVEL TEAM-UP:
MICHAEL LARK AND ED BRUBAKER

by John Rhett Thomas

Since Daredevil is the hot topic in Michael Lark's life right now, it seemed only natural to do a commentary track devoted to his first drawings of 'ol Hornhead. Our choice for discussion is the first five pages of Daredevil #82, the very pages that Michael and writer Ed Brubaker use to introduce themselves to readers and herald in a new era in Daredevil storytelling! It's high-octane DD action steeped in the nuances of noir and hardboiled superhero fiction.... and don't think Michael and Ed aren't enjoying every second!

In fact, Michael is enjoying his collaboration with Ed so much that he suggested it would be fun to invite his tag-team partner along for the commentary. Spotlight managed to keep these guys from laughing it up too much — a natural inclination of theirs, it seems — and get them focused on the matter at hand, which was explicating these fine pages of comic art for loyal Spotlight readers! And that's just what we did!

Plus, we're running these five pages in the finished black and white. Hey, the colors of Frank D'Armata really pop in the pages of Daredevil #82, but we thought it would be neat to show off Michael's penciled and inked pages for a nice change of pace.

SPOTLIGHT: Thanks for taking the time to get together and discuss these pages for Spotlight readers, guys!

ED: This is actually the first time Michael and I have ever spoken, actually.

MICHAEL: Until now, I had no idea what Ed sounded like.

ED: And I thought you lived in Argentina. (Laughter.)

SPOTLIGHT: Well, I'm footing the bill for this call, so let's make it quick, then!

ED: What issue of Marvel Spotlight are we doing this for?

SPOTLIGHT: This would be for the third Spotlight, featuring your buddy Michael and a fellow by the name of Joss Whedon.

ED: And who was in the second issue?

SPOTLIGHT: Warren Ellis and-

ED: (Interrupts.) Well, when am I gonna be in it!?!?

MICHAEL: They want people to buy it, Ed.

SPOTLIGHT: Marvel's kinda lukewarm on you, Ed. If we're headed for cancellation, we'll try and fit you in.

ED: Oh...thanks! (Laughter.)

SPOTLIGHT: Set the stage for us, Ed. What manner of story did you and Michael want to make sure would unfold to readers with these first five pages?

ED: I really wanted there to be a cool action sequence at the beginning. Even in my original pitch for the book, I made it clear that I wanted to have this big opening with a Daredevil-in-action sequence, and then Michael requested a double page spread. Because I never ever give him any — or if I do it's like a sliver across the top with like a hundred panels below it!

The following pages offer a commentary track between Marvel Spotlight, artist Michael Lark and writer Ed Brubaker. The commentary transcript appears alongside pages one through five of their premiere issue, Daredevil #82, which is the highly anticipated follow-up to the extremely popular run by Brian Michael Bendis and Alex Maleev.

Daredevil #82, page 1

SPOTLIGHT: This was an interesting way for you and Michael to put your stamp on your new title. We get a panel of our setting in Hell's Kitchen, and it's stretched across the page; then nine small panels indicating the kind of sordid deeds going on underneath. There's a lot of energy pent up in that first page just waiting to explode...

ED: Daredevil is one of the most experimental mainstream comics there is. You see more experimentation in Daredevil than you do on something like Batman, in general...unless Frank Miller is doing it. Because of that, I just went into it thinking we have a certain number of pages to get a story in. I wanted this story to feel really compact. And so that first page is a bunch of little images that act like flash card shots of close-ups before you get to that page turn. I wanted to get the implication of random cuts of violence from this one scene.

MICHAEL: I thought it was a really nice piece of storytelling. The crime that occurs that Daredevil must stop isn't really that important in the scheme of things, but it was important to set up the pacing so that when we do turn the page, it will have the desired effect.

You know, we're going to be seeing Daredevil really early. I think that when Brian and Alex did their first issue, we didn't see Daredevil until the last couple pages. But we're jumping in on page two and saying, "this is a Daredevil book!" As Axel Alonso (Daredevil editor) put it, we're pissing all over our territory.

I like the fact that there's a lot of beauty there before we turn the page, so it's almost as if you're seeing a whole scene before you get to that first big splash. As an artist, I really like that Ed allowed me to do something that wasn't just the traditional action-to-action storytelling that most American comics are. It was a really nice and different way to show things. A good way to kick off the book to also say, we're not gonna do things exactly the same as you're used to seeing in American comics. We're gonna experiment.

SPOTLIGHT: Being that you're both fans of crime noir conventions, the first page plays around with those iconographies: pistol in the grip of a hand, aiming at its target, playing cards splayed out across a table, window cracked, blinds open...

ED: Yeah, definitely...small time hood, robbing a mob poker game, getting away with $500.

MICHAEL: For me, it evoked the title sequence of the original Batman animated series by Bruce Timm. It's very much a title sequence. You could be using that as the title sequence for the Daredevil TV show.

ED: We'll do one of these every issue. (Laughter.) It's actually not a terrible idea...but we probably won't.

SPOTLIGHT: Michael, is that you in the last panel?? That dude looks like you!

MICHAEL: Oh...yeah! (Laughter.)

SPOTLIGHT: Ed, what do you think of Michael's two-page splash?

Daredevil #82, double-page splash pages 2 & 3